PEARSON CUSTOM
COMPUTER SCIENCE

CS 1114
Introduction to Software Desgin
Virginia Tech University

Pearson Learning Solutions

New York Boston San Francisco
London Toronto Sydney Tokyo Singapore Madrid
Mexico City Munich Paris Cape Town Hong Kong Montreal

Senior Vice President, Editorial and Marketing: Patrick F. Boles
Executive Marketing Manager: Nathan Wilbur
Senior Acquisition Editor: Debbie Coniglio
Development Editor: Annette Fantasia
Editorial Assistant: Jeanne Martin
Operations Manager: Eric M. Kenney
Production Manager: Jennifer Berry
Art Director: Renée Sartell
Cover Designer: Kristen Kiley

Cover Art: "Blend," courtesy of Getty Images/Jason Reed; "Binary Data Flowing," courtesy of iStockphoto/Andrey Solovyev; "Beech Forest," courtesy of iStockphoto; "Small Plant," courtesy of iStockphoto/Florea Marius Catalin; "Network," courtesy of iStockphoto/Andrey Prokhorov.

Printed in the United States of America.

Please visit our web site at *www.pearsoncustom.com*.

Attention Bookstores: For permission to return any unsold stock, contact us at *pe-uscustomreturns@pearson.com*.

Pearson Learning Solutions, 501 Boylston Street, Suite 900, Boston, MA 02116
A Pearson Education Company
www.pearsoned.com

PEARSON

ISBN 10: 0-558-90643-5
ISBN 13: 978-0-558-90643-6

Important Information Regarding Supplemental Materials for Your Book

Your custom book comes with additional student resources, designed to aid you, including source code, development environments, etc. These materials are available to you via the following website, searchable by author last name and title:

http://www.pearsonhighered.com/cs_custom

Before completing a project, it is sometimes necessary to download and open data files. These files provide the starting point for the project and the data with which to work. Check with your instructor for the best way to download these files, or use the following instructions.

Downloading Procedures for the Student Data Files in the Pearson Custom Publishing Program in Computer Science

1. From an open Web browser go to: http://www.pearsonhighered.com/cs_custom. Note: You may want to bookmark the appropriate page, as it contains links to additional products that you may be using in class.
2. Click on the appropriate title of your Computer Science text. This is where you will find all of the data files to complete the projects.
3. Because you have a Custom book, the chapter references in these data files may not match up with the chapter order in your book. This can be solved by browsing through the posted folders and matching the file name to the appropriate topic covered in your book.
4. When you find the file that you need, you may open it to view the file immediately, or you may save the file to a specific location on you hard drive. We recommend saving the files to your desktop to find them easily.

Any resources not found on http://www.pearsonhighered.com/cs_custom can be found at www.mycodemate.com.

MyCodeMate

MyCodeMate is a book-specific Web resource that provides tutorial help and evaluation of student programs. In addition to Student Data Files, your book may reference specific programs available through the www.mycodemate.com website. If your professor ordered an access card to accompany your book, you have access to the materials available through MyCodeMate. If you do not have an access card, you can purchase a subscription online at www.mycodemate.com.

The additional student resources through http://www.pearsonhighered.com/cs_custom and www.mycodemate.com are provided to assist you in learning and practicing the concepts covered in your Custom book. When these resources are mentioned in a chapter, please refer back to these instructions to access and download the correct content.

Contents

Introduction to the Internet and World Wide Web

Chapter Objectives

In this chapter, you will learn about ...

- The evolution of the Internet, Internet standards organizations, and the difference between the Internet, intranets, and extranets
- The beginning of the World Wide Web, ethical use of information on the Web, Web accessibility, and future Internet trends
- The client/server model, Internet protocols, networks, URLs and domain names, and markup languages

The Internet and the Web are parts of our daily lives. How did they begin? What networking protocols and programming languages work behind the scenes to display a Web page? This chapter provides an introduction to some of these topics and is a foundation for the information that Web developers need to know. Some material in this chapter may be a review from your life experience or earlier studies.

From Chapter 1 of *Web Development and Design Foundations with XHTML*, Fifth Edition. Terry Felke-Morris.

1 Evolution of the Internet

The **Internet**, the interconnected network of computer networks, seems to be everywhere today. It has become part of our lives. You can't watch television or listen to the radio without being urged to visit a Web site. Even newspapers have their place on the Net.

The Internet began as a network to connect computers at research facilities and universities. Messages in this network would travel to their destination by multiple routes or paths. This would allow the network to function even if parts of it were broken or destroyed. The message would be rerouted through a functioning portion of the network while traveling to its destination. This network was proposed to the Advanced Research Projects Agency (ARPA)—and the ARPAnet was born. Four computers (located at UCLA, Stanford Research Institute, University of California Santa Barbara, and the University of Utah) were connected by the end of 1969.

As time went on, other networks, such as the National Science Foundation's NSFnet, were created and connected with the ARPAnet. The communications protocol that enabled all this to happen is the Transmissions Control Protocol/Internet Protocol (TCP/IP), propsed by Vinton Cerf and Robert Kahn. Use of this interconnected network, or Internet, was originally limited to government, research, and educational purposes. Even with this restriction, by 1989 there were over 100,000 hosts on the Internet. The ban on commercial use was lifted in 1991, and by the end of 1992 there were over 1 million hosts connected. Hobbes' Internet Timeline reports that as of 2006, there were over 439 million host computers on the Internet. The growth of the Internet continues—Internet World Stats (http://www.internetworldstats.com/emarketing.htm) reported over 1.5 billion users on the Internet in early 2009.

If you are interested in the history of the Internet, visit either of the following links for more information.

- A brief history of the Internet written by the people who created it can be found at http://www.isoc.org/internet/history/brief.shtml.
- For a classic treatment of the Internet's history, visit Hobbes' Internet Timeline at http://www.zakon.org/robert/internet/timeline/.

FAQ

How can I tell whether a Web page is a reliable source of information?

There are many Web sites—but which ones are reliable sources of information? When visiting Web sites to find information it is important not to take everything at face value.

First, evaluate the credibility of the Web site itself. Does it have its own domain name, such as http://mywebsite.com, or is it a free Web site consisting of just a folder of files hosted on a free Web server? The URL of a site hosted on a free Web server usually includes part of the free Web server's name and might begin with something such as http://mysite.tripod.com or http://www.angelfire.com/foldername/mysite. Information obtained from a Web site that has its own domain name will usually (but not always) be more reliable than information obtained from a free Web site.

Evaluate the type of domain name—is it a nonprofit organization (.org), a business (.com or .biz), an educational institution (.edu)? Businesses may provide information in a way that gives them an advantage, so be careful. Nonprofit organizations or schools will sometimes treat a subject more objectively.

Another item to look at is the date the Web page was created or last updated. Although some information is timeless, very often a Web page that has not been updated for several years is outdated and not the best source of information.

2 Internet, Intranets, and Extranets

The Internet is an interconnected network of computer networks that is globally available. When an organization needs the communication capabilities of the Internet but doesn't want its information to be available to everyone, either an intranet or extranet is appropriate.

An **intranet** is a private network that is contained within an organization or business. Its purpose is to share organizational information and resources among coworkers. When an intranet connects to the outside Internet, usually a gateway or firewall protects the intranet from unauthorized access.

An **extranet** is a private network that securely shares part of an organization's information or operations with external partners such as suppliers, vendors, and customers. Extranets can be used to exchange data, share information exclusively with business partners, and collaborate with other organizations. Privacy and security are important issues in extranet use. Digital certificates, encryption of messages, and virtual private networks (VPNs) are some technologies used to provide privacy and security for an extranet.

The Evolution of the World Wide Web

Recall that the original Internet—the ARPAnet—began with four hosts. The number of host computers connected to the Internet grew each year. However, the communication was text-based and the information stored on computers connected to the Internet was not easy to obtain. Initially, the use of the Internet was limited to academics, researchers, students, and government employees. Even with these restrictions there were over 300,000 hosts in 1990.

Why did the Internet grow from 300,000 hosts in 1990 to over 109 million in just over a decade? In the early 1990s, the convergence of three events occurred to cause explosive growth of the Internet.

In 1991, the NSFnet removed the restriction on commercial use of the Internet, setting the stage for future electronic commerce. Businesses were now welcome on the Internet. However, while businesses were no longer banned, the Internet was still text-based and not easy to use. The next developments solved this issue.

While working at CERN, a research facility in Switzerland, Tim Berners-Lee envisioned a means of communication for scientists where they could easily "hyperlink" to another research paper or article and immediately view it. Berners-Lee created the **World Wide Web** to fulfill this need and in 1991 he posted the code in a newsgroup. This version of the World Wide Web used **Hypertext Transfer Protocol** (**HTTP**) to communicate between the client computer and the Web server, used **Hypertext Markup Language** (**HTML**) to format the documents, and was text-based.

In 1993, the first graphics-based Web browser, Mosaic, became available. Marc Andreessen and graduate students working at the National Center for Supercomputing Applications (NCSA) at the University of Illinois Urbana-Champaign developed Mosaic. Some individuals in this group later created another well-known Web browser—Netscape Navigator.

The combination of commercial use, HTTP, and a graphical user interface made the information on the Internet much easier to access. The World Wide Web—the graphical user interface to the information stored on computers connected to the Internet—had arrived!

3 Standards and Coordination

You are probably aware that no single person or group runs the entire Internet. Each separate network is managed individually. However, there are a number of groups that develop standards and guidelines. These groups are a driving force in the growth and evolution of the Internet.

The **Internet Society**, http://www.isoc.org, is a professional organization that provides leadership in issues related to the future of the Internet. The Internet Society is the organizational home for the groups responsible for Internet infrastructure standards, including the **Internet Engineering Task Force (IETF)** and the **Internet Architecture Board (IAB)**.

You can think of the IETF as the protocol engineering and development arm of the Internet. It is the principal body engaged in the development of new Internet standard specifications. The IETF is an open international community of network designers, operators, vendors, and researchers concerned with the evolution of Internet architecture and the smooth operation of the Internet. The actual technical work of the IETF is completed in its working groups. These working groups are organized into areas by topic, such as security and routing.

The IAB is a committee of the IETF and provides guidance and broad direction to the IETF. As a function of this purpose, the IAB is responsible for the publication of the **Request for Comments (RFC)** document series.

An RFC is a formal document from the IETF that is drafted by a committee and subsequently reviewed by interested parties. RFCs are available for online review at http://www.ietf.org/rfc.html. Some RFCs are informational in nature, while others are meant to become Internet standards. In the latter case, the final version of the RFC becomes a new standard. Future changes to the standard must be made through subsequent RFCs.

The **Internet Corporation for Assigned Numbers and Names (ICANN)**, http://www.icann.org, was created in 1998 and is a nonprofit organization. Its main function is to coordinate the assignment of Internet domain names, IP address numbers, protocol parameters, and protocol port numbers. Prior to 1998, the **Internet Assigned Numbers Authority (IANA)** coordinated these functions. IANA still performs certain functions under the guidance of ICANN and maintains a Web site at http://www.iana.org.

4 Standards and the World Wide Web Consortium

As with the Internet in general, no one person or group runs the World Wide Web. However, the **World Wide Web Consortium (W3C)**, http://www.w3.org, takes a proactive role in developing recommendations and prototype technologies related to the Web. Four major areas that the W3C addresses are Web architecture, user interface, technology and society, and the **Web Accessibility Initiative (WAI)**. In an effort to standardize Web technologies, the W3C produces specifications called recommendations.

The W3C Recommendations are created in working groups with input from many major corporations involved in building Web technologies. These recommendations are not rules; they are guidelines. Major software companies that build Web browsers, such as Microsoft and Netscape, do not always follow the W3C Recommendations. This makes life difficult for Web developers because not all browsers will display a Web page in exactly the same way.

The good news is that there is a convergence toward the W3C Recommendations in new versions of major browsers. There are even organized groups such as The Web Standards Project, http://webstandards.org, whose mission is to promote W3C Recommendations (often called Web standards) not only to the creators of browsers but also to Web developers and designers.

Accessibility and the Web

Focus on Accessibility

The Web Accessibility Initiative (WAI), http://www.w3.org/WAI/, is a major area of work by the W3C. Since the Web has become an integral part of daily life, there is a need for all individuals to be able to access it. According to Tim Berners-Lee at http://www.w3.org/WAI/, "The power of the Web is in its universality. Access by everyone regardless of disability is an essential aspect."

The Web can present barriers to individuals with visual, auditory, physical, and neurological disabilities. The WAI has developed recommendations for Web content developers, Web authoring tool developers, Web browser developers, and developers of other user agents to facilitate use of the Web by those with special needs. See the WAI's Web Content Accessibility Guidelines (WCAG) at http://www.w3.org/WAI/WCAG20/quickref/ for a list of these recommendations.

The Americans with Disabilities Act (ADA) of 1990 is a Federal civil rights law that prohibits discrimination against people with disabilities. The ADA requires that business, federal, and state services are accessible to individuals with disabilities. A 1996 Department of Justice ruling, http://www.usdoj.gov/crt/foia/cltr204.txt, indicated that ADA accessibility requirements apply to Internet resources.

Section 508 of the Federal Rehabilitation Act was amended in 1998 to require that U.S. government agencies give individuals with disabilities access to information technology that is comparable to the access available to others. This law requires developers creating information technology (including Web pages) for use by the federal government to provide for **accessibility**. The Federal IT Accessibility Initiative, http://www.section508.gov, provides accessibility requirement resources for information technology developers. In recent years, state governments have also begun to encourage and promote Web accessibility. The Illinois Information Technology Accessibility Act (IITAA) guidelines, http://www.dhs.state.il.us/IITAA/IITAAWebImplementationGuidelines.html, are an example of this trend.

Forward-thinking Web developers design with accessibility in mind. Providing access for visitors with visual, auditory, and other challenges should be an integral part of Web design rather than an afterthought.

A person with visual difficulties may not be able to use graphical navigation buttons and may use a screen reader device to provide an audible description of the Web page. By making a few simple changes, such as providing text descriptions for the images and perhaps providing a text navigation area at the bottom of the page, Web developers can make the page accessible. Often, providing for accessibility increases the usability of the Web site for all visitors. For example, text in high contrast to the background is easier for everyone to read.

Ethical Use of Information on the Web

Focus on Ethics

This wonderful technology called the World Wide Web provides us with information, graphics, and music—all virtually free (after you pay your Internet service provider, of course). Let's consider the following issues relating to the ethical use of this information:

- Is it acceptable to copy someone's graphic to use on your own Web site?
- Is it acceptable to copy someone's Web site design to use on your own site or on a client's site?
- Is it acceptable to copy an essay that appears on a Web page and use it or parts of it as your own writing?
- Is it acceptable to insult someone on your Web site or link to their site in a derogatory manner?

The answer to all these questions is no. Using someone's graphic without permission is the same as stealing it. In fact, if you link to it you are actually using up some of their bandwidth and may be costing them money. Copying the Web site design of another person or company is also a form of stealing. The Web site http://pirated-sites.com presents a somewhat quirky look at this issue. Any text or graphic on a Web site is automatically copyrighted in the United States whether or not a copyright symbol appears on the site. Insulting a person or company on your Web site or linking to them in a derogatory manner could be considered a form of defamation.

Issues like these, related to intellectual property, copyright, and freedom of speech are regularly discussed and decided in courts of law. Good Web etiquette requires that you ask permission before using others' work, give credit for what you use ("fair use" in the U.S. copyright law), and exercise your freedom of speech in a manner that is not harmful to others. The **World Intellectual Property Organization (WIPO)**, http://wipo.int, is dedicated to protecting intellectual property rights internationally.

What if you'd like to retain ownership but make it easy for others to use or adapt your work? Creative Commons, http://creativecommons.org, is a nonprofit organization that provides free services that allow authors and artists to register a type of a copyright license called a Creative Commons license. There are several licenses to choose from—depending on the rights you wish to grant. The Creative Commons license informs others exactly what they can and cannot do with your creative work. See http://meyerweb.com/eric/tools/color-blend for a Web page licensed under a Creative Commons Attribution-ShareAlike 1.0 License with "Some Rights Reserved."

CHECKPOINT 1

1. Describe the difference between the Internet and an intranet.
2. Explain three events that contributed to the commercialization and exponential growth of the Internet.
3. Describe the difference between the Internet and the Web.

5 Network Overview

A **network** consists of two or more computers connected for the purpose of communicating and sharing resources. Common components of a network are shown in Figure 1 and include the following:

- Server computer(s)
- Client workstation computer(s)
- Shared devices such as printers
- Networking devices (router and switch) and the media that connect them

Figure 1
Common components of a network

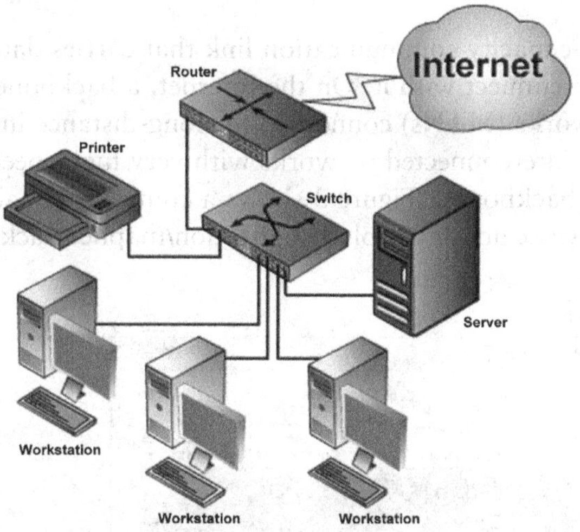

The **clients** are the computer workstations used by individuals, such as a PC on a desk. The **server** receives requests from client computers for resources such as files. Computers used as servers are usually kept in a protected, secure area and are only accessed by network administrators. Networking devices such as hubs and switches provide network connections for computers, and routers direct information from one network to another. The **media** connecting the clients, servers, peripherals, and networking devices may consist of copper cables, fiber optic cables, or wireless technologies.

Networks vary in scale. A **Local Area Network (LAN)** is usually confined to a single building or group of connected buildings. Your school computer lab may use a LAN. If you work in an office, you probably use a computer connected to a LAN. Recently, many people have begun to set up LANs in their homes to share resources among computers. A **Metropolitan Area Network (MAN)** connects users with computer resources in a geographical area. It also can be used to connect two or more LANs. A **Wide Area Network (WAN)** is geographically dispersed and usually uses some form of public or commercial communications network. For example, an organization with offices on both the East and West Coasts of the United States probably uses a WAN to provide a link between the LANs at each of the offices. See Figure 2 for a diagram of this connectivity.

Figure 2
WAN connecting two LANs

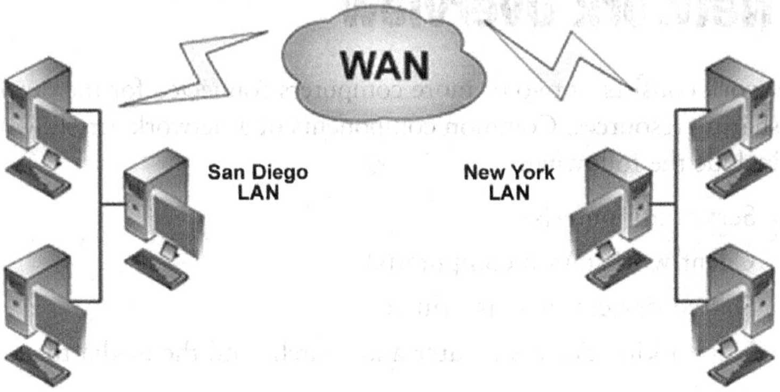

A **backbone** is a high-capacity communication link that carries data gathered from smaller links that interconnect with it. On the Internet, a backbone is a set of paths that local or regional networks (MANs) connect to for long-distance interconnection. The Internet is a group of interconnected networks with very high-speed connectivity provided by the Internet backbones. Figure 3 shows a commercial backbone network map generated by http://www.caida.org/tools/visualization/mapnet/Backbones.

Figure 3
A commercial backbone network

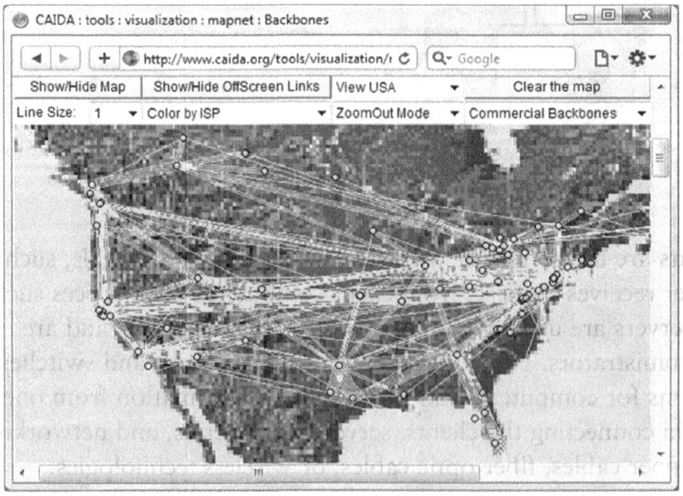

6 The Client/Server Model

The term **client/server** dates from the last millennium (the 1980s) and refers to personal computers joined by a network. Client/server can also describe a relationship between two computer programs—the client and the server. The client requests some type of service (such as a file or database access) from the server. The server fulfills the request and transmits the results to the client over a network. While both the client and the server programs can reside on the same computer, typically they run on different computers. It is common for a server to handle requests from multiple clients.

The Internet is a great example of client/server architecture at work. Consider the following scenario: An individual is at a computer using a Web browser client to access the Internet. The individual uses the Web browser to visit a Web site, let's say http://www.yahoo.com. The server is the Web server program running on the computer with an IP address that corresponds to yahoo.com. It is contacted, locates the Web page and related resources that were requested, and responds by sending them to the individual.

In short, here's how to distinguish between Web clients and Web servers:

Web Client

- Connected to the Internet when needed
- Usually runs Web browser (client) software such as Internet Explorer or Netscape
- Uses HTTP
- Requests Web pages from a server
- Receives Web pages and files from a server

Web Server

- Continually connected to the Internet
- Runs Web server software (such as Apache or Internet Information Server)
- Uses HTTP
- Receives a request for the Web page
- Responds to the request and transmits the status code, Web page, and associated files

When clients and servers exchange files, they often need to indicate the type of file that is being transferred; this is done through the use of a MIME type. **Multi-Purpose Internet Mail Extensions (MIME)** are rules that allow multimedia documents to be exchanged among many different computer systems. MIME was initially intended to extend the original Internet e-mail protocol, but it is also used by HTTP. MIME provides for the exchange of seven different media types on the Internet: audio, video, image, application, message, multipart, and text. MIME also uses subtypes to further describe the data. The MIME type of a Web page is text/html. MIME types of gif and jpeg images are image/gif and image/jpeg respectively.

A Web server determines the MIME type of a file before it is transmitted to the Web browser. The MIME type is sent along with the document. The Web browser uses the MIME type to determine how to display the document.

How does information get transferred from the Web server to the Web browser? Clients (such as Web browsers) and servers (such as a Web server) exchange information through the use of communication protocols such as HTTP, TCP, and IP.

7 Internet Protocols

Protocols are rules that describe how clients and servers communicate with each other over a network. There is no single protocol that makes the Internet and Web work—a number of protocols with specific functions are needed.

File Transfer Protocol (FTP)

File Transfer Protocol (FTP) is a set of rules that allow files to be exchanged between computers on the Internet. Unlike HTTP, which is used by Web browsers to request Web pages and their associated files in order to display a Web page, FTP is used simply to move files from one computer to another. Web developers commonly use FTP to transfer Web page files from their computers to Web servers. FTP is also commonly used to download programs and files from other servers to individual computers.

E-mail Protocols

Most of us take e-mail for granted, but there are two servers involved in its smooth functioning—an incoming mail server and an outgoing mail server. When you send e-mail to others, **Simple Mail Transfer Protocol (SMTP)** is used. When you receive e-mail, **Post Office Protocol** (POP; currently **POP3**) and **Internet Message Access Protocol (IMAP)** can be used.

Hypertext Transfer Protocol (HTTP)

HTTP is a set of rules for exchanging files such as text, graphic images, sound, video, and other multimedia files on the Web. Web browsers and Web servers usually use this protocol. When the user of a Web browser requests a file by typing a Web site address or clicking a hyperlink, the browser builds an HTTP request and sends it to the server. The Web server in the destination machine receives the request, does any necessary processing, and responds with the requested file and any associated media files.

Transmission Control Protocol/Internet Protocol (TCP/IP)

Transmission Control Protocol/Internet Protocol (TCP/IP) has been adopted as the official communication protocol of the Internet. TCP and IP have different functions that work together to ensure reliable communication over the Internet.

TCP. The purpose of TCP is to ensure the integrity of network communication. TCP starts by breaking files and messages into individual units called **packets**. These packets (see Figure 4) contain information such as the destination, source, sequence number, and checksum values used to verify the integrity of the data.

Figure 4
TCP packet

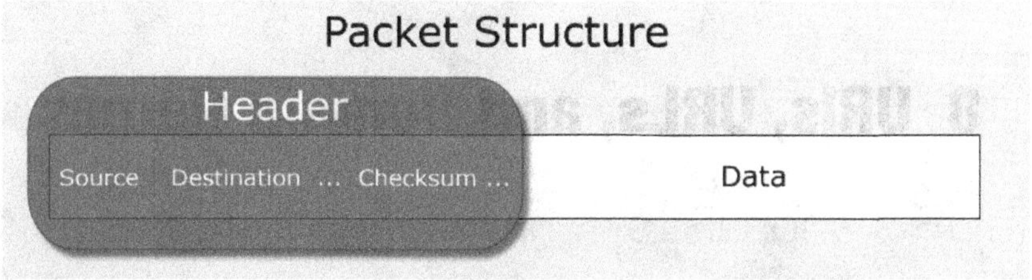

TCP is used together with IP to transmit files efficiently over the Internet. IP takes over after TCP creates the packets, using IP addressing to send each packet over the Internet using the best path at the particular time. When the destination address is reached, TCP verifies the integrity of each packet using the checksum, requests a resend if a packet is damaged, and reassembles the file or message from the multiple packets.

IP. Working in harmony with TCP, IP is a set of rules that controls how data is sent between computers on the Internet. IP routes a packet to the correct destination address. Once sent, the packet gets successively forwarded to the next closest router (a hardware device designed to move network traffic) until it reaches its destination.

Each device connected to the Internet has a unique numeric **IP address**. These addresses consist of a set of four groups of numbers, called octets. The current version of IP, IPv4, uses 32-bit (binary digit) addressing. This results in a decimal number in the format of xxx.xxx.xxx.xxx, where each xxx is a value from 0 to 255. The IP address may correspond to a domain name. The **Domain Name System (DNS)** associates these IP addresses with the text-based URLs and domain names you type into a Web browser address box (more on this later). For example, at the time this was written the IP address of Google was 74.125.95.104.

You can enter this number in the address text box in a Web browser (as shown in Figure 5), press Enter, and the Google home page will display. Of course, it's much

Figure 5
Entering an IP address in a Web browser

easier to type "google.com," which is why domain names such as google.com were created in the first place!

Since long strings of numbers are difficult for humans to remember, the Domain Name System was introduced as a way to associate text-based names with numeric IP addresses.

8 URIs, URLs, and Domain Names

URIs and URLs

A Uniform Resource Identifier (URI) identifies a resource on the Internet. A **Uniform Resource Locator (URL)** is a type of URI which represents the network location of a resource such as a Web page, a graphic file, or an MP3 file. The URL consists of the protocol, the domain name, and the hierarchical location of the file on the Web server.

The URL http://www.webdevfoundations.net, shown in Figure 6, denotes the use of HTTP protocol and the Web server named www at the domain name of webdevfoundations.net. In this case, the root file (usually index.html or index.htm) will be displayed.

Figure 6
Parts of a URL

If the URL was of the form http://www.webdevfoundations.net/chapter1/links.html, as shown in Figure 7, it would denote the use of HTTP protocol and a Web server named www at the domain name of webdevfoundations.net. The resource to be displayed is the Web page named links.html in the chapter1 folder.

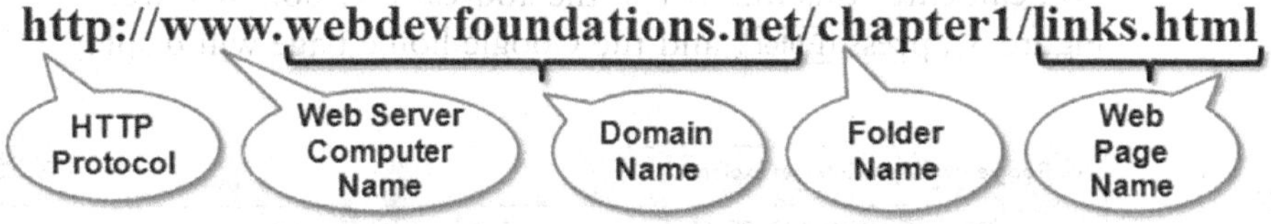

Figure 7
URL describing a file within a folder

FAQ

What is a Universal Resource Locator?

Officially, URL stands for Uniform Resource Locator; but originally, Tim Berners-Lee (the inventor of the Web) envisioned a Universal Resource Locator. That is why some texts or Web pages refer to the URL in that manner. Read Tim Berners-Lee's book *Weaving the Web* for an interesting view of the creation of the Web.

Figure 8 shows a URL used to display files available for FTP download in the format of ftp://ftp.microsoft.com. This denotes the use of the FTP protocol, the server named ftp, and the domain name of microsoft.com.

Figure 8
URL using FTP

Domain Names

A **domain name** locates an organization or other entity on the Internet. The purpose of the Domain Name System (DNS) is to divide the Internet into logical groups and understandable names by identifying the exact address and type of the organization. The DNS associates the text-based domain names with the unique numeric IP address assigned to a device.

Let's consider the domain name www.yahoo.com. The .com is the top-level domain name. The portion yahoo.com is the domain name that is registered to Yahoo! and is considered a second-level domain name. The www is the name of the Web server (sometimes called **Web host server**) at the yahoo.com domain. Taken all together, www.yahoo.com is considered to be a **Fully-Qualified Domain Name (FQDN)**.

Top-Level Domain Names (TLDs). A **top-level domain** (TLD) identifies the right-most part of the domain name. A TLD is either a generic top-level domain, such as com for commercial, or a country code top-level domain, such as fr for France. ICANN administers the generic top-level domains shown in Table 1.

Table 1 Top-level domains

Generic TLD	Used By
.aero	Air-transport industry
.asia	Pan-Asia and Asia Pacific community
.biz	Businesses
.cat	Catalan linguistic and cultural community
.com	Commercial entities
.coop	Cooperative
.edu	Restricted to accredited degree-granting institutions of higher education
.gov	Restricted to government use
.info	Unrestricted use
.int	International organization (rarely used)
.jobs	Human resource management community
.mil	Restricted to military use
.mobi	Corresponds to a .com Web site—the .mobi site is designed for easy access by mobile devices
.museum	Museums
.name	Individuals
.net	Entities associated with network support of the Internet, usually Internet service providers or telecommunication companies
.org	Nonprofit entities
.pro	Accountants, physicians, and lawyers
.tel	Contact information for individuals and businesses
.travel	Travel industry

The .com, .org, and .net TLD designations are currently used on the honor system, which means that an individual who owns a shoe store (not related to networking) can register shoes.net.

Country Code Top-Level Domain Names. Two-character country codes have also been assigned as top-level domain names. These were originally intended to be meaningful and relate the domain name country code to the geographical location of the individual or organization that registered the name. In practice, it is fairly easy to obtain a domain name with a country code TLD that is not local to the registrant. See http://register.com and many other domain name registration companies for examples. Table 2 lists some popular country codes used on the Web.

Table 2 Country codes

Country Code TLD	Country
.au	Australia
.de	Germany
.in	India
.jp	Japan
.nl	The Netherlands
.us	United States
.eu	European Union (a group of countries rather than a single country)

The IANA Web site at http://www.iana.org/cctld/cctld-whois.htm has a complete list. Domain names with country codes are often used for municipalities, schools, and community colleges in the United States. The domain name www.harper.cc.il.us denotes the United States, Illinois, community college, Harper, and the Web server named www as the site for William Rainey Harper College in Illinois.

The DNS associates domain names with IP addresses. The following happens each time a new URL is typed into a Web browser:

1. The DNS is accessed.
2. The corresponding IP address is obtained and returned to the Web browser.
3. The Web browser sends an HTTP request to the destination computer with the corresponding IP address.
4. The HTTP request is received by the Web server.
5. The necessary files are located and sent by HTTP responses to the Web browser.
6. The Web browser renders and displays the Web page and associated files.

The next time you wonder why it's taking so long to display a Web page, think about all of the processing that goes on behind the scenes.

9 Markup Languages

Markup languages consist of sets of directions that tell the browser software (and other user agents such as mobile phones) how to display and manage a Web document. These directions are usually called tags and perform functions such as displaying graphics, formatting text, and referencing hyperlinks.

Standard Generalized Markup Language (SGML)

Standard Generalized Markup Language (SGML) is a standard for specifying a markup language or tag set. SGML in itself is not a document language, but a description of how to specify one and create a document type definition (DTD). When Tim Berners-Lee created HTML, he used SGML to create the specification.

Hypertext Markup Language (HTML)

HTML is the set of markup symbols or codes placed in a file intended for display on a Web browser. The Web browser renders the code in the HTML file and displays the Web page document and associated files. The W3C (http://www.w3.org) sets the standards for HTML. Although the most recent version of HTML is called **XHTML** 1.1, this text uses XHTML 1.0 because it is less strict and is well-supported by popular browsers.

Extensible Markup Language (XML)

XML was developed by the W3C as a flexible method to create common information formats and share the format and the information on the Web. It is a text-based syntax designed to describe, deliver, and exchange structured information. It is not intended to replace HTML, but to extend the power of HTML by separating data from presentation. Using XML, developers can create whatever tags they need to describe their information.

Extensible Hypertext Markup Language (XHTML)

XHTML was developed by the W3C to reformulate HTML 4.01 as an application of XML. It combines the formatting strengths of HTML 4.01 *and* the data structure and extensibility strengths of XML.

The primary advantages of XHTML include the ability to extend the language by creating new tags and the promise of increased platform interoperability as mobile devices are used more frequently to access the Web.

HTML 5—The Next Version of (X)HTML

As this was written, the W3C's HTML Working Group (HTML WG) was busy creating a draft recommendation for HTML 5—which is intended to be the next version of HTML 4 and will replace XHTML. HTML 5, currently in draft status, incorporates features of both HTML and XHTML, adds new elements, and is intended to be backward compatible. Check the blog on the Web site, http://webdevfoundations.net, for new developments.

CHECKPOINT 2

1. Describe the components of the client/server model as applied to the Internet.
2. Identify two protocols used on the Internet to convey information that use the Internet but do not use the Web.
3. Explain the similarities and differences between a URL and a domain name.

10 Internet and Web Trends

E-commerce, the buying and selling of goods on the Internet, is already an important part of the Web. According to a recent study by Jupiter Research (http://www.jupitermedia.com/corporate/releases/06.02.06-newjupresearch.html), revenue generated by e-commerce will continue to grow. By 2012, over $183 billion in online retail sales are projected by eMarketer (http://www.emarketer.com/Article.aspx?R=1006813). With over 1.5 billion people online worldwide (http://www.internetworldstats.com/emarketing.htm), that's quite a few potential shoppers!

As wireless Web access becomes more commonplace, e-commerce and Internet access not only will be regularly done from stationary computers but also from mobile devices—Palm Pilots, netbooks, smartphones, and devices we haven't even imagined yet.

How do we keep track of all the devices (wireless and otherwise) that are connected to the Internet? You are already aware that each device on the Internet is assigned a unique number called an IP address. Currently, IPv4 is being used. Theoretically, this allows for at most 4 billion possible IP addresses (although many potential addresses are reserved for special uses). With the proliferation of mobile devices, even this many addresses may not be enough. **IP Version 6 (IPv6)** will provide a huge increase in the number of possible addresses and many technological advances.

FAQ

What is IPv6?

IPv6, Internet Protocol Version 6, is the most recent version of the Internet Protocol. IPv6 was designed as an evolutionary set of improvements to the current IPv4 and is backwardly compatible with it. Service providers and Internet users can update to IPv6 independently without having to coordinate with each other.

IPv6 provides for more Internet addresses because the IP address is lengthened from 32 bits to 128 bits. This means that there are potentially 2^{128} unique IP addresses possible, or 340,282,366,920,938,463,463,347,607,431,768,211,456. (Now there will be enough IP addresses for everyone's PC, notebook, cell phone, pager, PDA, automobile, toaster, and so on!)

The development of the Internet2 is another effort in advancing Internet technology. The Internet2 consortium comprises more than one hundred U.S. universities in partnership with industry and government. Their mission is to develop and deploy advanced network applications and technologies, focusing on applications related to learning and research such as telemedicine, digital libraries, and virtual laboratories. Visit the Internet2 Web site at http://www.internet2.edu for information on this initiative.

Another technology to be aware of is web services. A **web service** is a self-describing, self-contained application that provides some business functionality through an Internet connection. For example, an organization could create a Web service to facilitate information exchange with its partners or vendors. The Universal Discovery,

Description, and Integration (UDDI) standard, http://uddi.xml.org, is backed by a number of technology companies, including IBM, Microsoft, and Sun Microsystems. Essentially, UDDI provides a method of describing a service, invoking a service, and locating available services. Microsoft's .NET platform supports Web services. Microsoft and IBM jointly developed Web Services Description Language (WSDL) to facilitate the use of Web services.

While the Web service initiative is driven by large corporations, the trend of keeping a Web log, or blog, has been driven by individuals as a forum for personal expression. A **blog** is a journal that is available on the Web—it's a frequently updated page with a chronological list of ideas and links. Blog topics range from political journals to technical information to personal diaries. Blogs can focus on one subject or range across a diverse group of topics—it's up to the person, called a blogger, who creates and maintains the blog. Bloggers usually update their blogs daily with easy-to-use software designed to allow people with little or no technical background to update and maintain the blog. The PEW Internet & American Life Project (http://www.pewinternet.org) reports that 42 percent of American adults read blogs daily and about 12 percent of American adults keep a blog. Many blogs are hosted at blog communities such as http://blogspot.com, http://wordpress.com, or http://www.xanga.com. Others are hosted at individual Web sites, such as the blog kept by the CSS expert Eric Meyer at http://meyerweb.com. Businesses have noted the value of blogs as communication and customer relationship tools. Companies such as IBM, http://www.ibm.com/developerworks/blogs/, and Adobe, http://feeds.adobe.com, utilize blogs in this manner.

A **wiki** is a Web site that can be updated immediately at any time by visitors using a simple form on a Web page. Some wikis are intended for a small group of people, such as the members of an organization. The most powerful wiki is Wikipedia, http://wikipedia.org, an online encyclopedia, which can be updated by anyone at any-time. This is a form of social software in action—visitors sharing their collective knowl-edge to create a resource freely used by all. While there have been isolated incidents of practical jokes and occasionally inaccurate information posted at Wikipedia, the infor-mation and resource links are a good starting point when exploring a topic.

Blogs and wikis provide Web visitors new methods to utilize and interact with Web sites and other people—referred to as **social computing** or **social networking.** A trendy activity these days is participating in a social networking site such as Facebook (http://facebook.com), MySpace (http://myspace.com), or LinkedIn (http://linkedin.com). The PEW Internet & American Life Project reported that in a recent three year period, the use of a social networking site by American adults increased from 8% to 35%. The popularity of these sites seems to keep growing—Facebook welcomed its 200 millionth active user in 2009! While LinkedIn was created with professional and business networking in mind, businesses have also found it useful to create Facebook and MySpace site to promote their products and services.

Twitter (http://twitter.com) is a social networking site for **microblogging,** or frequently communicating with a brief messages (140 characters or less) called a **tweet.** Twitter users (called twitterers) tweet to update a network of friends and followers with daily activities and observations. The PEW Internet & American Life Project reported over 11% of American adults used a microblogging service such as Twitter in 2008. The research firm eMarketer (http://www.emarketer.com/Article.aspx?R=1007059) predicted that there would be over 18 million Twitter users by 2010. However, Twitter is not limited to personal use only. The business world has also discovered the marketing reach that Twitter can provide. Business Week reported that Dell's use of Twitter resulted in $500,000 of new orders within a 12-month period.

Really Simple Syndication or Rich Site Summary (RSS) is used to create newsfeeds from blog postings and other Web sites. The RSS feeds contain a summary of new items posted to the site. The URL to the RSS feed is usually indicated by the letters XML or RSS in white text within an orange rectangle. A **newsreader** is needed to access the information. Some browsers, such as Firefox, Safari, and Internet Explorer (version 7 or later) can display RSS feeds. Commercial and shareware newsreader applications are also available. The newsreader will poll the feed URL at intervals and display the new headlines when requested. RSS provides Web site developers with a method to push new content to interested parties and (hopefully) generate return visits to the site.

Podcasts are audio files on the Web—they may take the format of an audio blog, radio show, or interview. Podcasts are typically delivered by an RSS feed but can also be made available by recording an MP3 file and providing a link on a Web page. These files can be saved to your computer or to an MP3 player (such as an iPod) for later listening. Forrester Research (http://forrester.com/Research/Document/Excerpt/0,7211,36428,00.html) predicts that by 2010 more than 12 million households will access podcasts.

Flickr (http://www.flickr.com/) and del.icio.us (http://del.icio.us/) are two social software sites that provide information-sharing opportunities. Flickr, a photo sharing site, calls itself the "best way to store, search, sort, and share your photos." Acquired by Yahoo!, del.icio.us is a collection of favorite sites—allowing registered users to post lists of favorites, share their favorites with others, and discover new sites. Web sites such as Wikipedia, Flickr, Twitter, and del.icio.us are examples of what is called **Web 2.0**. While a consensus on the definition of Web 2.0 still needs to be reached, think of it as the next step in the transition of the Web from isolated static Web sites to a platform that utilizes technology to provide rich interfaces and social networking opportunities. Visit http://www.go2web20.net and use the search engine to find Web 2.0 sites. Read Tim O'Reilly's informative Web 2.0 essay at http://oreillynet.com/pub/a/oreilly/tim/news/2005/09/30/what-is-web-20.html for more information on this developing topic.

The single future trend that you can expect to remain the same is the trend of constant change. Internet- and Web-related technologies are in a constant state of development and improvement. If constant change and the need to learn something new excites you, Web development is a fascinating field.

FAQ

What is the next big thing on the Web?

The Web is changing by the minute. Check this text's companion Web site at http://webdevfoundations.net for a blog that will help you stay current about Web trends.

CHAPTER SUMMARY

This chapter provided a brief overview of Internet, Web, and introductory networking concepts. Much of this information may be familiar to you. Visit http://www.webdevfoundations.net for the links listed in this chapter and for updated information.

Key Terms

accessibility
backbone
blog
client/server
clients
domain name
Domain Name System (DNS)
extranet
File Transfer Protocol (FTP)
Fully-Qualified Domain Name (FQDN)
Hypertext Markup Language (HTML)
Hypertext Transfer Protocol (HTTP)
Internet
Internet Architecture Board (IAB)
Internet Assigned Numbers Authority (IANA)
Internet Corporation for Assigned Numbers and Names (ICANN)
Internet Engineering Task Force (IETF)
Internet Message Access Protocol (IMAP)
Internet Society
intranet
IP
IP address
IP Version 6 (IPv6)
Local Area Network (LAN)
markup languages
media
microblogging
Metropolitan Area Network (MAN)
Multi-Purpose Internet Mail Extensions (MIME)
network
newsreader
packets
podcasts
Post Office Protocol (POP3)
protocols
Really Simple Syndication or Rich Site Summary (RSS)
Request for Comments (RFC)
server
Simple Mail Transfer Protocol (SMTP)
social computing
social networking
Standard Generalized Markup Language (SGML)
TCP
Top-level domain (TLD)
Transmission Control Protocol/Internet Protocol (TCP/IP)
tweet
Uniform Resource Indicator (URI)
Uniform Resource Locator (URL)
Web 2.0
Web Accessibility Initiative (WAI)
Web host server
Web service
Wide Area Network (WAN)
wiki
World Intellectual Property Organization (WIPO)
World Wide Web
World Wide Web Consortium (W3C)
XHTML
XML

Review Questions

Multiple Choice

1. Of the following organizations, which one coordinates applications for new TLDs?
   a. Assigned Numbers Authority (IANA)
   b. Engineering Task Force (IETF)
   c. Corporation for Assigned Numbers and Names (ICANN)
   d. World Wide Web Consortium (W3C)

2. Which of the following is a network that covers a small area, such as a group of buildings or campus?
   a. LAN
   b. WAN
   c. Internet
   d. WWW

3. Which of the markup languages listed below is intended to extend the power of HTML by separating data from presentation?

   a. XML
   b. XHTML
   c. HTML 5
   d. SGML

4. What is a unique text-based Internet address corresponding to a computer's unique numeric IP address called?

   a. IP address
   b. domain name
   c. URL
   d. user name

5. Which of the organizations listed below take a proactive role in developing recommendations and prototype technologies related to the Web?

   a. World Wide Web Consortium (W3C)
   b. Web Professional Standards Organization (WPO)
   c. Internet Engineering Task Force (IETF)
   d. Internet Corporation for Assigned Numbers and Names (ICANN)

True or False

6. ____ Markup languages contain sets of directions that tell the browser software how to display and manage a Web document.

7. ____ The World Wide Web was developed to allow companies to conduct e-commerce over the Internet.

8. ____ A URL is one type of URI.

9. ____ A domain name that ends in .net indicates that the Web site is for a networking company.

Fill in the Blank

10. ___________ combines the formatting strengths of HTML 4.0 and the data structure and extensibility strengths of XML.

11. A standard language used for specifying a markup language or tag set is ___________.

12. ___________ is the set of markup symbols or codes placed in a file intended for display on a Web browser.

13. The World Wide Web was developed by an individual working at ___________.

14. Frequently communicating by posting brief messages at a social networking site is called ___________.

15. The purpose of ___________ is to ensure the integrity of the communication.

Hands-On Exercise

1. Create a blog to document your learning experiences as you study Web development. Visit one of the many sites that offer free blogs, such as http://blogspot.com, http://www.wordpress.com, or http://www.xanga.com. Follow their instructions to establish your own blog. Your blog could be a place to note Web sites that you find useful or interesting. You might report on sites that contain useful Web design resources. You might describe sites that have interesting features, such as compelling graphics or easy to use navigation. Write a few sentences about the site that you find intriguing. After you begin to develop your own sites, you could include the URLs and reasons for your design decisions. Share this blog with your fellow students and friends. Display your page in a browser and print the page. Hand in the printout to your instructor.

Web Research

1. The World Wide Web Consortium creates standards for the Web. Visit its site at http://www.w3c.org and then answer the following questions:
   a. How did the W3C get started?
   b. Who can join the W3C? What does it cost to join?
   c. The W3C home page lists a number of technologies. Choose one that interests you, click its link, and read the associated pages. List three facts or issues you discover.
2. The Internet Society takes an active leadership role in issues related to the Internet. Visit its site at http://www.isoc.org and answer the following questions:
   a. Why was the Internet Society created?
   b. Determine the local chapter closest to you. Visit its Web site. List the Web site URL and an activity or service that the chapter provides.
   c. How can you join the Internet Society? What does it cost to join? Would you recommend that a beginning Web developer join the Internet Society? Why or why not?
3. The World Organization of Webmasters (WOW) is a professional association dedicated to the support of individuals and organizations that create and manage Web sites. Visit its site at http://www.joinwow.org and answer the following questions:
   a. How can you join WOW? What does it cost to join?
   b. List one of the events that WOW participates in. Would you like to attend this event? Why or why not?
   c. List three ways that WOW can help you in your future career as a Web developer.

Focus on Web Design

1. Visit a Web site referenced in this chapter that interests you. Print the home page or one other pertinent page from the site. Write a one-page summary and your reaction to the site. Address the following topics:
   a. What is the purpose of the site?
   b. Who is the intended audience?
   c. Do you think that the site reaches its intended audience? Why or why not?
   d. Is the site useful to you? Why or why not?
   e. List one interesting fact or issue that this site addresses.
   f. Would you encourage others to visit this site?
   g. How could this site be improved?

Answers

Checkpoint 1

1. The Internet is a public, globally connected network of computer networks. An intranet uses the same protocols as the Internet, but it is a private network used to share organizational information and resources among coworkers.
2. The commercialization and exponential growth of the Internet that occurred in the early 1990s was due largely to three main events: the removal of the restriction of commercial use on NSFnet, the development of the World Wide Web by Tim Berners-Lee at CERN, and the development of a graphical browser (called Mosaic) at the NCSA. These events combined to provide the commercial incentive and an easy way to share and access information in a way that had never been experienced.
3. The Internet is a global, interconnected network of computer networks— a maze of phone lines, cable lines, and satellites that connect computers around the world. Information is stored in many formats on computers connected to the Internet. The World Wide Web, or Web, is a graphical user interface to some of the information stored on computers connected to the Internet—the computers that use HTTP to provide information in Web page format. The Web provides access to a portion of the information available on the Internet.

Checkpoint 2

1. An example of a Web client is a computer running a browser software application such as Internet Explorer. The computer is typically connected to the Internet only when needed. The Web browser software uses HTTP to request Web pages and related resources from a Web server. A Web server is a computer that is continually connected to the Internet and that runs some type of Web server software application. It uses the HTTP protocol to receive requests for Web pages and related resources. It responds to these requests and sends the resources.
2. There are several protocols discussed in this chapter that use the Internet but do not use the Web. E-mail messages are transmitted using the Internet. SMTP (Simple Mail Transfer Protocol) is used to send e-mail messages. POP (Post Office Protocol) and IMAP (Internet Message Access Protocol) can be used to receive e-mail messages. FTP (File Transfer Protocol) can be used to exchange files (send and receive) with a computer connected to the Internet.
3. A URL (Uniform Resource Locator) represents the address of a resource that is available on the Internet. A URL consists of a protocol, a domain name, and the hierarchical location of the file or resource. An example of a URL is http://www.webdevfoundations.net/chapter1/index.htm. A domain name locates an organization or other entity on the Internet and is associated with a unique numeric IP address. A domain name is part of a URL.

Review Questions

1. c
2. a
3. a
4. b
5. a
6. True
7. False
8. True
9. False
10. XHTML
11. SGML
12. HTML
13. CERN
14. microblogging
15. TCP

XHTML Basics

Chapter Objectives

In this chapter, you will learn about ...

- The development of HTML
- The transition from HTML to XHTML
- XHTML syntax, elements, and document type definitions
- The anatomy of a Web page
- Formatting the body of a Web page
- Formatting the text on a Web page
- Physical and logical style elements
- Special characters
- Using the anchor element to link from page to page
- Creating absolute, relative, and e-mail links

This chapter introduces Hypertext Markup Language (HTML), the language used to create Web pages, and eXtensible Hypertext Markup Language (XHTML), the most recent standardized version of HTML. The chapter begins with an introduction to the syntax of XHTML, continues with the anatomy of a Web page, and introduces block-level and inline formatting and demonstrates hyperlinks as sample pages are created. You will learn more if you work along with the sample pages in the text. Coding XHTML is a skill and every skill improves with practice.

1 What Is HTML?

The World Wide Web is composed of files containing **Hypertext Markup Language (HTML)** and other markup languages that describe Web pages. HTML was developed using Standard Generalized Markup Language (SGML). SGML prescribes a standard format for embedding descriptive markup within a document and for describing the structure of a document. SGML is not in itself a document language, but rather a description of how to specify one and create a **document type definition (DTD)**.

The W3C, http://w3c.org, sets the standards for HTML and its related languages. HTML (like the Web itself) is in a constant state of change.

HTML is the set of markup symbols or codes placed in a file intended for display on a Web browser page. These markup symbols and codes identify structural elements such as paragraphs, headings, and lists. HTML can also be used to place media (such as graphics, video, and audio) on a Web page and describe fill-in forms. The browser interprets the markup code and renders the page. HTML permits the platform-independent display of information across a network. That is, no matter what type of computer a Web page was created on, any browser running on any operating system can display the page.

Each individual markup code is referred to as an **element** or **tag**. Each tag has a purpose. Tags are enclosed in angle brackets, the < and > symbols. Most tags come in pairs: an opening tag and a closing tag. These tags act as containers and are sometimes referred to as container tags. For example, the text that is between the `<title>` and `</title>` tags on a Web page would display in the title bar on the browser window.

Some tags are used alone and are not part of a pair. For example, a tag that displays a horizontal line on a Web page, `<hr />`, is a stand-alone or self-contained tag and does not have a closing tag. You will become familiar with these as you use them. Most tags can be modified with **attributes** that further describe their purpose.

2 Why XHTML and Not HTML?

The most recent standardized version of HTML used today is actually **eXtensible HyperText Markup Language (XHTML)**. XHTML uses the tags and attributes of HTML 4 along with the syntax of XML. HTML was originally developed to provide access to electronic documents via a Web browser. Web browsers that evolved along with HTML were written to forgive coding errors, ignore syntax errors, and allow "sloppy" HTML code. Web browsers contain many program instructions that are designed to ignore mistakes such as missing ending tags and to guess how the developer meant the page to display. This is not a problem for a personal computer, which has relatively large processing power. However, this could be an issue for electronic devices with fewer resources, such as a personal digital assistant (PDA) or mobile phone.

Also, as new versions of Web browsers were developed and competed for market share, they often created their own proprietary extensions to HTML—tags that were not part of the standard and supported by one browser only. This created a lot of nonstandard HTML pages, and browsers are coded to accept this and ignore tags they don't recognize. However, this extra processing is not efficient, especially for devices with limited resources.

Finally, HTML is a structural language—it was originally intended to mark up printed documents for online viewing. It describes the structure of the document instead of the contents or information contained in the document. The Web has changed from a medium used to display electronic versions of paper documents to a medium that provides diverse information for a variety of devices. HTML does not fit this need. How will a table 600 pixels wide be displayed on a mobile phone? With the expansion of the Web to include devices other than personal computers, the need for a descriptive rather than structural language became evident and XHTML was created.

The purpose of XHTML was to provide a foundation for device-independent Web access. XHTML was developed by the W3C to be the reformulation of HTML as an application of XML. Tim Berners-Lee, the W3C director and inventor of the Web, stated in a press release (http://www.w3.org/2000/01/xhtml-pressrelease), "XHTML 1.0 connects the present Web to the future Web. It provides the bridge to page and site authors for entering the structured data, XML world, while still being able to maintain operability with user agents that support HTML 4." XHTML combines the formatting strengths of HTML and the data structure and extensibility strengths of XML. Since XHTML was designed using XML, let's take a quick look at XML.

XML (eXtensible Markup Language) is the W3C standard method for creating new markup languages that will support the display of nontraditional content such as mathematical notation, as well as support newer display devices such as PDAs and mobile phones. XML can fulfill these diverse needs because it is an extensible language—it is designed to allow the definition of new tags or markup. The syntax of XML is very exacting so that the portable devices will not have to waste processing power guessing how the document should display, but will be able to display information efficiently. XHTML, which combines the language of HTML with the syntax of XML, is a markup language that should adapt to future needs. An XML document must be well formed. A **well-formed document** is a document that adheres to the syntax rules of the language. The XHTML examples in the text will guide you in creating well-formed Web pages using XHTML.

3 Document Type Definition

Because multiple versions and types of HTML and XHTML exist, the W3C recommends identifying the type of markup language used in a Web page document. The three types of XHTML 1.0, **XHTML 1.0 Transitional, XHTML 1.0 Strict**, and **XHTML 1.0 Frameset**, are defined in Table 1.

Table 1 XHTML document types

Document Type Definition	Description
XHTML 1.0 Transitional	The least strict specification for XHTML 1.0; allows the use of Cascading Style Sheets and traditional formatting instructions such as fonts; used for most of the coding in this book
XHTML 1.0 Strict	Requires the exclusive use of Cascading Style Sheets; not used in this book
XHTML 1.0 Frameset	Required for pages using XHTML framesets; not used in this book

The version and type of XHTML is listed in the Document Type Definition (DTD) tag (commonly called the **DOCTYPE**). The DTD identifies the version and type of XHTML contained in your document. Browsers and HTML code validators can use the information in the DTD when processing the Web page. The DTD tag is placed at the top of a Web page document, even before the **<html>** tag. The DTD for XHTML 1.0 Transitional is as follows:

```
<!DOCTYPE html PUBLIC "-//W3C//DTD XHTML 1.0 Transitional//EN"
  "http://www.w3.org/TR/xhtml1/DTD/xhtml1-transitional.dtd">
```

You will place the DTD as the second line in each Web page document you create. Are you ready to create your first Web page?

4 Your First Web Page

After the DTD, each Web page begins with an opening `<html>` tag and ends with a closing `</html>` tag. These tags indicate that the text between them is HTML formatted. It tells the browser how to interpret the document.

```
<!DOCTYPE html PUBLIC "-//W3C//DTD XHTML 1.0 Transitional//EN"
  "http://www.w3.org/TR/xhtml1/DTD/xhtml1-transitional.dtd">
<html> an opening tag
... page information goes here
</html> a closing tag
```

There are two sections on a Web page: the **head** and the **body**. The head section, sometimes called the **header**, contains information that describes the Web page document. Tags that are located in the head section include the title of the Web page, meta tags that describe the document (such as the character encoding used and information that may be accessed by search engines), and references to scripts and styles. Many of these do not show directly on the Web page. The head section begins with the **<head>** tag and ends with the `</head>` tag. You'll always code at least two other tags in the head section: a <title> tag and a <meta /> tag.

The first tag in the head section, the **`<title>` tag,** contains the text that will appear in the title bar of the browser window. This text is called the **title** of the Web Page and is accessed when Web pages are bookmarked and printed. The title should be descriptive. If the Web page is for a business or organization, the title should include the name of the organization or business.

The **meta tag** is used to describe a characteristic of a Web page, such as the character encoding. **Character encoding** is the internal representation of letters, numbers, and symbols in a file such as a Web page or other file that is stored on a computer and may be transmitted over the Internet. There are many different character encoding sets. However, it is common practice to use a character encoding set that is widely supported, such as utf-8, which is a form of Unicode. The meta tag shown below indicates that the content of the document is a Web page that uses utf-8 character encoding.

```
<meta http-equiv="Content-Type" content="text/html; charset=utf-8"/>
```

The body section contains text and elements that do show directly on the Web page. The purpose of the body section is to describe the contents of the Web page. You will spend most of your time coding XHTML in the body of a Web page. If you type text in the body section, it will appear directly on the page.

The body section begins with the **<body>** tag and ends with the </body> tag.

The following code sample describes the anatomy of a Web page: a header section followed by a body section.

```
<!DOCTYPE html PUBLIC "-//W3C//DTD XHTML 1.0 Transitional//EN"
  "http://www.w3.org/TR/xhtml1/DTD/xhtml1-transitional.dtd">
<html>
<head>
... header information goes here
</head>
<body>
... body information goes here
</body>
</html>
```

Notice that the XHTML tags are lowercase. This conforms to XML syntax. Notice also that the DTD statement does not follow this syntax. The DTD statement indicates the markup language being used and has its own formatting—mixed case.

In XHTML, the `<html>` tag also needs to describe the **XML namespace (xmlns)**, which is the location of the documentation for the elements being used. This additional information is added to the `<html>` tag in the form of an attribute. The `xmlns` attribute points to the URL of the XHTML namespace used in the document, the standard http://www.w3.org/1999/xhtml. The optional `lang` and `xml:lang` attributes specify the spoken language of the document. For example, lang="en" xml:lang="en" indicate the English language. Search engines and screen readers may access these attributes.

FAQ

What are Web page editors?

No special software is needed to create an XHTML document—all you need is a text editor. Notepad is a text editor that is included with Microsoft Windows. TextEdit is distributed with the Mac OS X operating system. BBEdit is another popular editing program for Mac users. An alternative to using a simple text editor or word processor is to use a commercial Web authoring tool, such as Microsoft Expression Web or Adobe Dreamweaver. There are also many free or shareware editors available, including PageBreeze and Emacs. Regardless of the tool you use, having a solid foundation in XHTML will be useful. The examples in this text use Notepad.

The final version of the basic anatomy of a Web page follows. Note that with the exception of the specific page title, the first eight lines will usually be the same on every Web page that you create.

```
<!DOCTYPE html PUBLIC "-//W3C//DTD XHTML 1.0 Transitional//EN"
  "http://www.w3.org/TR/xhtml1/DTD/xhtml1-transitional.dtd">
<html xmlns="http://www.w3.org/1999/xhtml" lang="en" xml:lang="en">
```

```
<head>
<title>Page Title Goes Here</title>
<meta http-equiv="Content-Type" content="text/html; charset=utf-8"/>
</head>
<body>
... body information goes here
</body>
</html>
```

FAQ What if I'm using a Mac?

No worries! Use the Mac's built-in TextEdit application—but first you'll need to set some preferences. Launch TextEdit and select Preferences.

- Set the new document format to plain text.
- Set the saving option to *not* save documents with a .txt extension.
- Set the rich text processing preference to: Ignore rich text commands in HTML files.

See http://support.apple.com/kb/TA20406 for more configuration information. Now you're ready to edit Web pages with TextEdit! As you follow along with the book, just launch TextEdit when you are directed to use Notepad.

HANDS-ON PRACTICE 1

Launch Notepad or another text editor and type in the following XHTML:

```
<!DOCTYPE html PUBLIC "-//W3C//DTD XHTML 1.0 Transitional//EN"
  "http://www.w3.org/TR/xhtml1/DTD/xhtml1-transitional.dtd">
<html xmlns="http://www.w3.org/1999/xhtml" lang="en" xml:lang="en">
<head>
<title>My First Web Page</title>
<meta http-equiv="Content-Type" content="text/html; charset=utf-8"/>
</head>
<body>
Hello World
</body>
</html>
```

Notice that the first lines in the file contain the DTD. The XHTML code begins with an opening `<html>` tag and ends with a closing `</html>` tag. The purpose of these tags is to indicate that the content between the tags makes up a Web page. The head section is delimited by `<head>` and `</head>` tags and contains a pair of title tags with the words "My First Web Page" in between along with a `<meta />` tag to indicate the character encoding. The meta tag is used alone—it is not used as a pair of opening and closing tags. It is considered to be a stand-alone or self-contained tag. Because you are using XHTML (which follows XML syntax), the meta tag is coded with an ending />, which indicates a self-contained tag. The body section is delimited by `<body>` and `</body>`

tags. The words "Hello World" are typed on a line between the body tags. See Figure 1 for a screenshot of the code as it would appear in Notepad. You have just created the source code for a Web document.

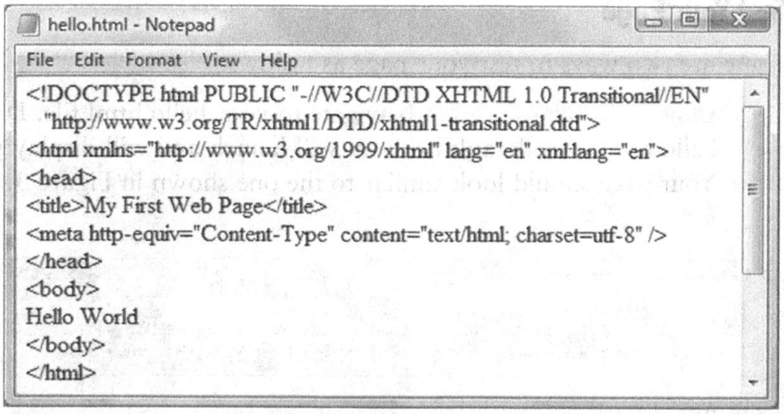

Figure 1
Source code of hello.html

FAQ

Do I have to start each tag on its own line?

No. A browser can display a page even if all the tags follow each other on one line with no spaces. Humans, however, find it easier to write and read XHTML if line breaks and indentation (more on this later) are used.

Save Your File

You will save your file with the name of hello.html. Web pages use either an .htm or .html file extension. Select File from the menu bar, and then select Save As. The Save As dialog box appears. Using Figure 2 as an example, type the file name.

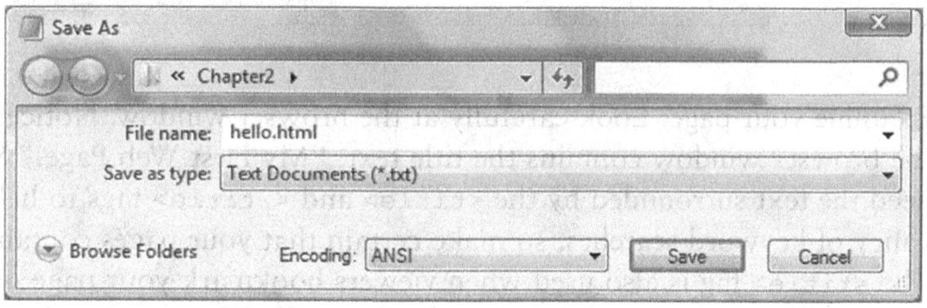

Figure 2
The Save As dialog box

FAQ

Why does my file have a .txt file extension?

In some older versions of Windows, Notepad will automatically append a .txt file extension. If this happens, type the name of the file within quotes, "hello.html", and save your file again.

Click the Save button after you type the file name. Sample solutions for the Hands-On Practice exercises are available in the student files. If you would like, compare your work with the solution (Chapter2/hello.html) before you test your page.

Test Your Page

There are two ways to test your page as follows:

1. **Launch Windows Explorer.** Navigate to your hello.html file. Double-click hello.html. The default browser will launch and will display your hello.html page. Your page should look similar to the one shown in Figure 3.

Figure 3
Web page displayed by Internet Explorer

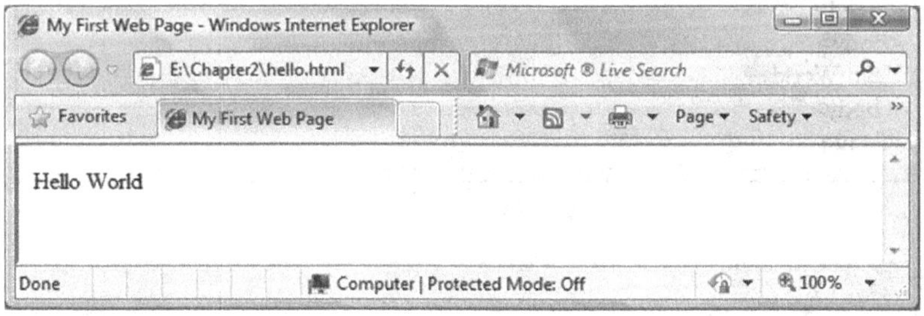

2. **Launch a Browser.** (If you are using Internet Explorer 8, select Tools, Menu Bar.) Select File, Open, Browse, My Computer, and then select your drive. Double-click hello.html and click OK. If you used Internet Explorer, your page should look similar to the one shown in Figure 3. A display of the page using Firefox is shown in Figure 4.

Figure 4
Web page displayed by Firefox

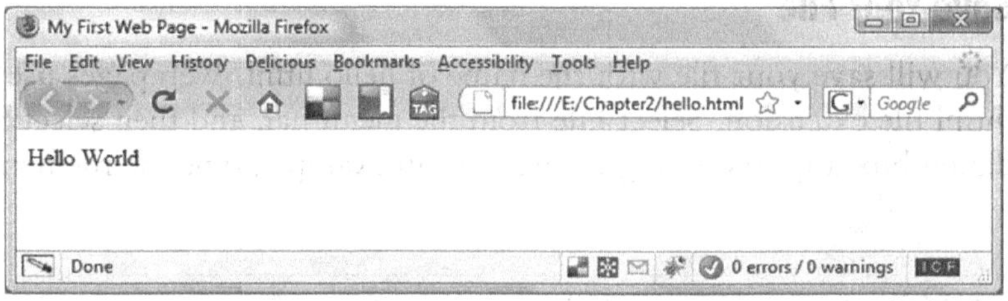

Examine your page. Look carefully at the browser window. Notice how the title bar of the browser window contains the title text, "My First Web Page." Some search engines need the text surrounded by the `<title>` and `</title>` tags to help determine relevancy of keyword searches, so make certain that your pages contain descriptive titles. The `<title>` tag is also used when viewers bookmark your page or add it to their Favorites. An engaging and descriptive page title may entice a visitor to revisit your page. If your Web page is for a company or an organization, it's a good idea to include the name of the company or organization in the title.

You might be thinking "Hmmm ... white background, black text, no images, can't we make the page look more interesting?" Sure we can. That's what you'll begin to learn in the next section.

CHECKPOINT 1

1. Describe the origin, purpose, and features of HTML.
2. Explain why you would use XHTML instead of HTML.
3. Describe the purpose of the header and body sections of a Web page.

5 XHTML—Body and Text Basics

Have you noticed the wide variety of page designs on Web sites? Whether a Web page contains mostly text, uses blocks of color, displays images, employs animation, or is interactive, the foundation of the page is the <body> tag.

The Body Element

The purpose of the <body> element is to contain the text and XHTML elements that will display in the browser window. As you noticed when you created your first Web page, any text that you type in the body section of a Web page document will be displayed by the browser in the actual Web page. Often, this text is organized by structural elements that indicate important headings, text paragraphs, and lists. These structural elements are **block-level elements**—they control blocks of text such as headings, paragraphs, and lists. Tags that affect individual sections of text are called **inline-level elements.** Web development is a skill—the more you practice, the better you get. Why not try each example as you read?

The Heading Element

Headings are block-level elements that are organized into levels h1 through h6. The size of the text is largest for **<h1>** and smallest for **<h6>**. Depending on the font being used, text contained in <h5> and <h6> tags may be displayed smaller than the default text size.

HANDS-ON PRACTICE 2

Launch Notepad or another text editor and type in the following XHTML:

```
<!DOCTYPE html PUBLIC "-//W3C//DTD XHTML 1.0 Transitional//EN"
  "http://www.w3.org/TR/xhtml1/DTD/xhtml1-transitional.dtd">
<html xmlns="http://www.w3.org/1999/xhtml" lang="en" xml:lang="en">
<head>
<title>Sample Heading Tags</title>
<meta http-equiv="Content-Type" content="text/html; charset=utf-8"/>
</head>
```

```
<body>
  <h1>Heading Level 1</h1>
  <h2>Heading Level 2</h2>
  <h3>Heading Level 3</h3>
  <h4>Heading Level 4</h4>
  <h5>Heading Level 5</h5>
  <h6>Heading Level 6</h6>
</body>
</html>
```

Save the file as heading.html. Launch a browser such as Internet Explorer or Firefox to test your page. It should look similar to the page shown in Figure 5. You can compare your work with the solution found in the student files (Chapter2/heading.html).

Notice that each heading in Figure 5 is on its own line and that there is a blank line between headings. The heading tag is a container tag. Notice how there are always corresponding opening <h#> and closing </h#> tags. It's a good idea to use headings to emphasize important topics or sections on a Web page.

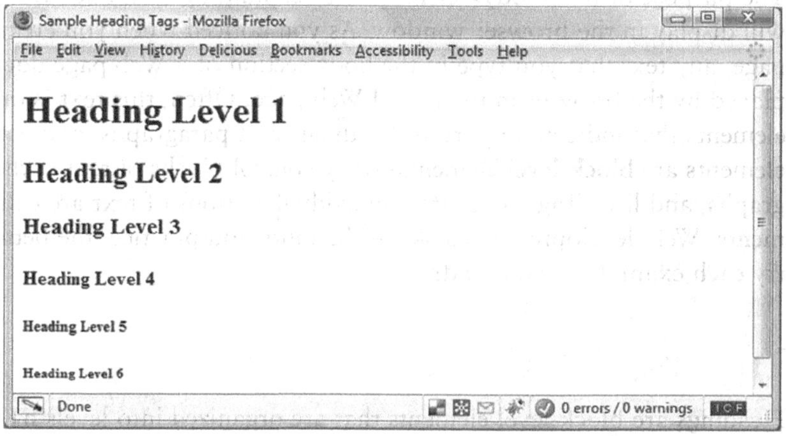

Figure 5 Sample heading.html

Accessibility and Headings

Focus on Accessibility

WWW

Heading tags can help to make your pages more accessible and usable. To indicate areas within a page hierarchically, code heading tags numerically as appropriate (h1, h2, h3, and so on) and include page content in block-level elements such as paragraphs and lists. Visually challenged visitors who are using a screen reader can configure the software to display a list of the headings used on a page to focus on the topics that interest them. Your well-organized page will be more usable for every visitor to your site, including those who are visually challenged.

The Paragraph Element

Paragraph elements are block-level elements used to group sentences and sections of text together. Text that is contained by **<p>** and </p> tags will have a blank line above and below it.

HANDS-ON PRACTICE 3

Open your heading.html file in a text editor. Use the following sample code and add a paragraph of text to your page below the line with the <h1> tags and above the line with the <h2> tags. Save your page as heading2.html.

```
<!DOCTYPE html PUBLIC "-//W3C//DTD XHTML 1.0 Transitional//EN"
  "http://www.w3.org/TR/xhtml1/DTD/xhtml1-transitional.dtd"
<html xmlns="http://www.w3.org/1999/xhtml" lang="en" xml:lang="en">
<head>
<title>Sample Heading Tags</title>
<meta http-equiv="Content-Type" content="text/html; charset=utf-8"/>
</head>
<body>
  <h1>Heading Level 1</h1>
  <p>This is a sample paragraph about HTML and XHTML. XHTML is the
newest version of HTML. XHTML uses the tags and attributes of HTML
along with the syntax of XML.</p>
  <h2>Heading Level 2</h2>
  <h3>Heading Level 3</h3>
  <h4>Heading Level 4</h4>
  <h5>Heading Level 5</h5>
  <h6>Heading Level 6</h6>
</body>
</html>
```

Launch a browser to test your page. It should look similar to the page shown in Figure 6 and to the solution in the student files (Chapter2/heading2.html).

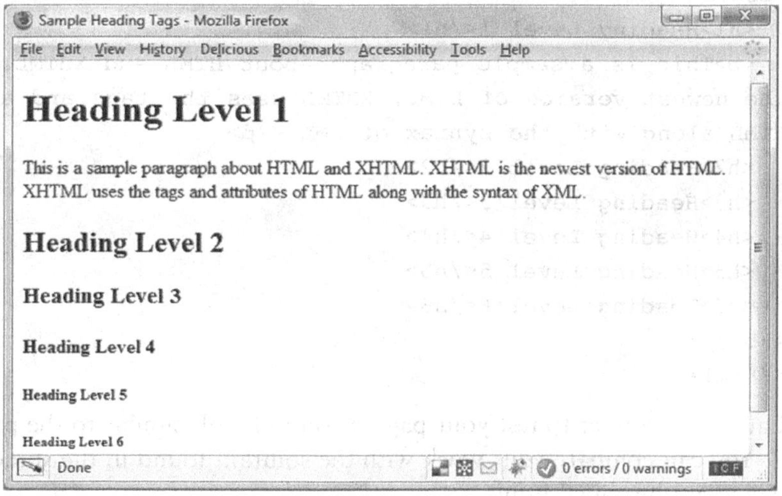

Figure 6 Web page using headings and a paragraph

Notice how the text wraps automatically as you resize your browser window. If you wanted to have the second sentence in the paragraph begin on its own line, you would need to add a line break.

The Line Break Element

The line break tag, **
**, is used to force a new line when the text on the Web page document is displayed by a browser. The line break tag is used alone—it is not used as a pair of opening and closing tags. It is considered to be a stand-alone or self-contained tag. If you were using HTML syntax, the line break tag would be coded as <br>. Because you are using XHTML (which follows XML syntax), the line break tag is coded as
 (the ending /> indicates a self-contained tag).

HANDS-ON PRACTICE 4

Open your heading2.html file in Notepad. Place your cursor after the first sentence in the paragraph (after "This is a sample paragraph about HTML and XHTML."). Press the Enter key. Save your page. Test your page in a browser and notice that even though your source code showed the "This is a sample paragraph about HTML and XHTML." sentence on its own line, the browser did not render it that way. A <br /> tag is needed to configure the browser. Open the heading2.html file in Notepad and add a <br /> tag after the first sentence in the paragraph. Save your page as heading3.html. Your source code should look similar to the following:

```
<!DOCTYPE html PUBLIC "-//W3C//DTD XHTML 1.0 Transitional//EN"
  "http://www.w3.org/TR/xhtml1/DTD/xhtml1-transitional.dtd">
<html xmlns="http://www.w3.org/1999/xhtml" lang="en" xml:lang="en">
<head>
<title>Sample Heading Tags</title>
<meta http-equiv="Content-Type" content="text/html; charset=utf-8"/>
</head>
<body>
  <h1>Heading Level 1</h1>
  <p>This is a sample paragraph about HTML and XHTML.<br /> XHTML is
the newest version of HTML. XHTML uses the tags and attributes of
HTML along with the syntax of XML.</p>
  <h2>Heading Level 2</h2>
  <h3>Heading Level 3</h3>
  <h4>Heading Level 4</h4>
  <h5>Heading Level 5</h5>
  <h6>Heading Level 6</h6>
</body>
</html>
```

Launch a browser to test your page. It should look similar to the page shown in Figure 7. You can compare your work with the solution found in the student files (Chapter2/heading3.html).

As you tested your Web pages, you may have noticed that the headings and text begin near the left margin. This is called **left alignment** and is the default alignment for Web pages. There are times when you want a paragraph or heading to be centered or right-aligned (justified). The `align` attribute can be used for this. The purpose of an **attribute** is to modify the properties of an XHTML element. In this case, the align attribute modifies the element's horizontal alignment (left, center, or right) on a Web page. To center an element on a Web page use the attribute `align="center"`. To right-justify an element on a Web page, use `align="right"`. The default alignment is left. The `align` attribute can be used with a number of block level elements, including the paragraph (`<p>`) and heading (`<h1>` through `<h6>`) tags.

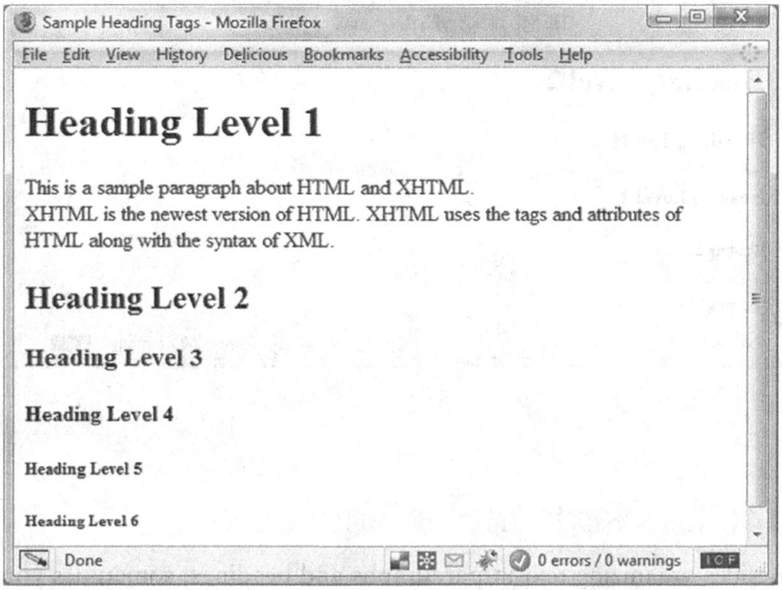

Figure 7
A `<br />` tag creates the line break after the first sentence

FAQ

Why does my Web page still look the same?

Often, students make changes to a Web page but get frustrated because their browser shows an older version of the page. The following troubleshooting tips are helpful when you know you modified your Web page but the changes do not show up in the browser:

1. Make sure you save your page after you make the changes.
2. Verify the location that you are saving your page to—the hard drive, a particular folder.
3. Verify the location that your browser is requesting the page from—the hard drive, a particular folder.
4. Be sure to click the Refresh or Reload button in your browser.

Open your heading3.html file in Notepad. Modify the heading to be centered. Change the `<h1>` tag to `<h1 align="center">` but do not change the closing `</h1>` tag. Also modify the paragraph to be centered on the Web page. Change the `<p>` tag to `<p align="center">`, but do not change the closing `</p>` tag. Save your page as heading4.html and test it in a browser. Your page should look similar to the page shown in Figure 8. You can compare your work with the solution found in the student files (Chapter2/heading4.html).

Legacy Alert. You will find many Web pages that use the `align` attributes to center block-level elements such as paragraphs and headings. Be aware that the `align` attribute is supported in XHTML 1.0 Transitional but is deprecated.

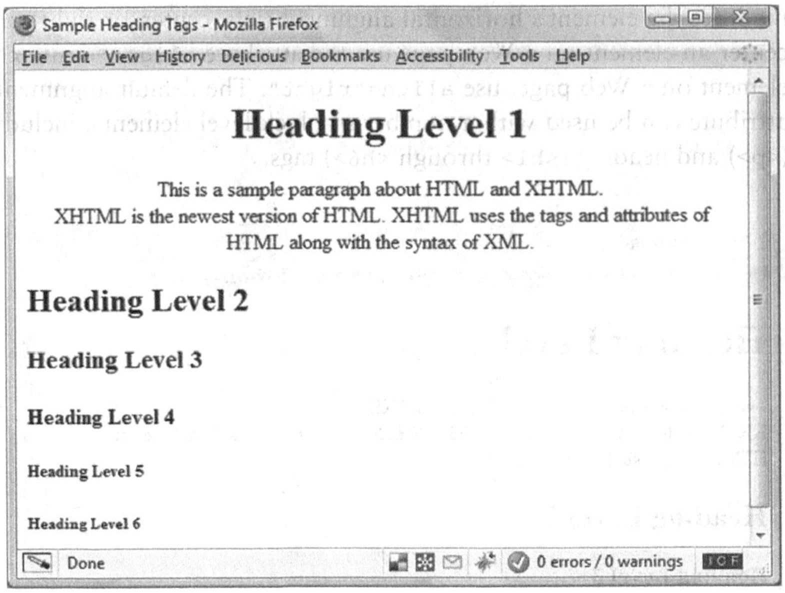

Figure 8 Using the `align` attribute to center the first heading and paragraph

The Blockquote Element

Besides organizing text in paragraphs and headings, sometimes you need to add a quotation to a web page. The **<blockquote>** tag is intended to be used to display a block of quoted text in a special way—indented from both the left and right margins. A block of indented text begins with a **<blockquote>** tag and ends with a </blockquote> tag.

HANDS-ON PRACTICE 5

Launch Notepad or another text editor and type in the following XHTML:

```
<!DOCTYPE html PUBLIC "-//W3C//DTD XHTML 1.0 Transitional//EN"
  "http://www.w3.org/TR/xhtml1/DTD/xhtml1-transitional.dtd">
<html xmlns="http://www.w3.org/1999/xhtml" lang="en" xml:lang="en">
<head>
<title>Blockquote Example</title>
<meta http-equiv="Content-Type" content="text/html; charset=utf-8"/>
</head>
<body>
  <h1>Power of the Web</h1>
<p>According to Tim Berners-Lee at
http://www.w3.org/WAI/:</p>
   <blockquote>
     The power of the Web is in its universality. Access by everyone
regardless of disability is an essential aspect.
   </blockquote>
</body>
</html>
```

Save your file as blockquote.html. Launch a browser and test your file. Your page should look similar to the page shown in Figure 9 and the solution in the student files (Chapter2/blockquote.html). Notice how the text that was entered between `<blockquote>` tags is indented.

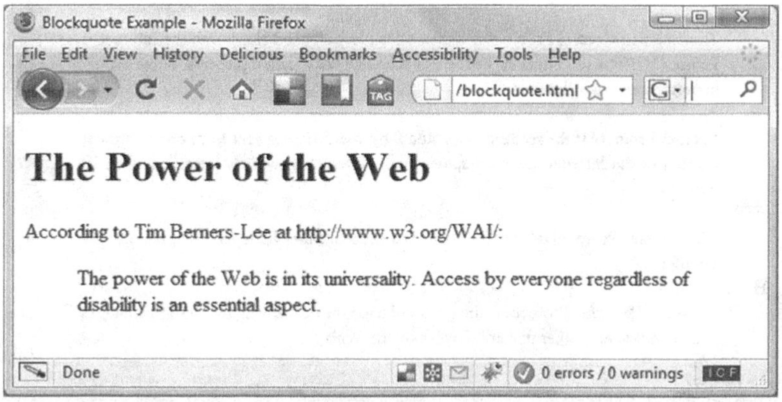

Figure 9
Sample blockquote.html

6 XHTML—List Basics

Lists are used on Web pages to organize information. When writing for the Web, remember that headings and bulleted lists make your pages clear and easy to read. XHTML can be used to create three types of lists: **definition lists, ordered lists,** and **unordered lists.**

Definition Lists

Definition lists help to organize terms and their definitions. The terms stand out and their definitions can be as long as needed to convey your message.

Definition lists are also handy for organizing Frequently Asked Questions (FAQs) and their answers. The questions and answers are offset with indentation. Each defined term begins on its own line at the margin. Each definition begins on its own line and is indented. See Figure 10 for an example of a Web page that uses a definition list.

Any type of information that consists of a number of corresponding terms and longer descriptions is well suited to being organized in a definition list.

Definition lists begin with the **`<dl>`** tag and end with the `</dl>` tag. Each defined term in the list begins with the **`<dt>`** tag and ends with the `</dt>` tag. Each term definition (data definition) begins with the **`<dd>`** tag and ends with the `</dd>` tag. A definition list is created in the following Hands-On Practice.

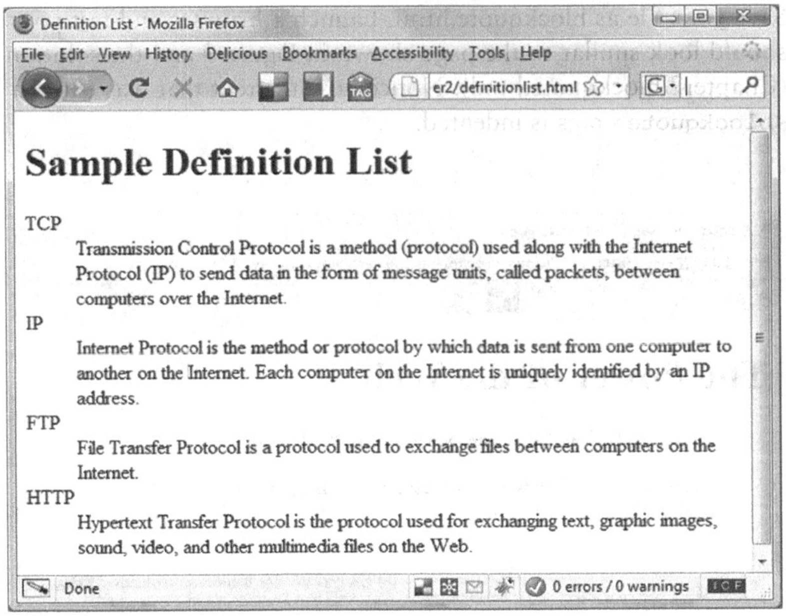

Figure 10
Sample definitionlist.html

HANDS-ON PRACTICE 6

Open a new file in Notepad. Use the following sample code to create a definition list.

```
<!DOCTYPE html PUBLIC "-//W3C//DTD XHTML 1.0 Transitional//EN"
  "http://www.w3.org/TR/xhtml1/DTD/xhtml1-transitional.dtd">
<html xmlns="http://www.w3.org/1999/xhtml" lang="en" xml:lang="en">
<head>
<title>Definition List</title>
<meta http-equiv="Content-Type" content="text/html; charset=utf-8"/>
</head>
<body>
  <h1>Sample Definition List</h1>
    <dl>
      <dt>TCP</dt>
        <dd>Transmission Control Protocol is a method (protocol) used
along with the Internet Protocol (IP) to send data in the form of
message units, called packets, between computers over the
Internet.</dd>
      <dt>IP</dt>
        <dd>Internet Protocol is the method or protocol by which data
is sent from one computer to another on the Internet. Each computer
on the Internet is uniquely identified by an IP address.</dd>
      <dt>FTP</dt>
```

```
        <dd>File Transfer Protocol is a protocol used to exchange
files between computers on the Internet.</dd>
      <dt>HTTP</dt>
        <dd>Hypertext Transfer Protocol is the protocol used for
exchanging text, graphic images, sound, video, and other multimedia
files on the Web.</dd>
    </dl>
</body>
</html>
```

Save your file as definitionlist.html and test it in a browser. Your page should look similar to the one shown in Figure 10 and to the solution in the student files (Chapter2/definitionlist.html). Don't worry if the word wrap is a little different—the important formatting is that each `<dt>` term should be on its own line and the corresponding `<dd>` definition should be indented under it. Try resizing your browser window and notice how the word wrap on the definition text changes.

Ordered Lists

Ordered lists use a numbering or lettering system to organize the information contained in the list. An ordered list can be organized by the use of numerals (the default), uppercase letters, lowercase letters, uppercase Roman numerals, and lowercase Roman numerals. See Figure 11 for a sample ordered list.

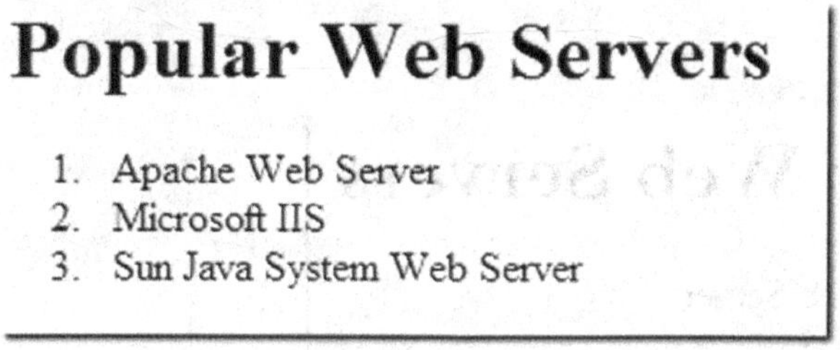

Figure 11
Sample ordered list

Ordered lists begin with an **`<ol>`** tag and end with an `</ol>` tag. Each list item begins with an **`<li>`** tag and ends with an `</li>` tag. The `type` attribute can be used to change the symbol used for ordering the list. For example, to create an ordered list organized by uppercase letters, use `<ol type="A">`. Table 2 documents the `type` attribute and its values for ordered lists.

Table 2 `type` attributes for ordered lists

Attribute	Value	Symbol
`type`	1	Numerals (the default)
	A	Uppercase letters
	a	Lowercase letters
	I	Roman numerals
	i	Lowercase Roman numerals

FAQ

Why is the XHTML code in the Hands-On Practice examples indented?

It doesn't matter to the browser if XHTML code is indented, but humans find it easier to read and maintain code when it is logically indented. Review the definition list created in Hands-On Practice 6. Notice how each tag level (`<dl>`, `<dt>`, and `<dd>`) is indented two spaces. This makes it easier for you or another Web developer to understand the source code in the future. There is no "rule" as to how many spaces to indent, although your instructor or the organization you work for may have a standard. Consistent indentation helps to create more easily maintainable Web pages.

The XHTML code to create the ordered list shown in Figure 11 follows:

```
<h1>Popular Web Servers</h1>
<ol>
  <li>Apache Web Server</li>
  <li>Microsoft IIS</li>
  <li>Sun Java System Web Server</li>
</ol>
```

Unordered Lists

Unordered lists show a bullet before each entry in the list. This bullet can be one of several types: disc (the default), square, and circle. See Figure 12 for a sample unordered list.

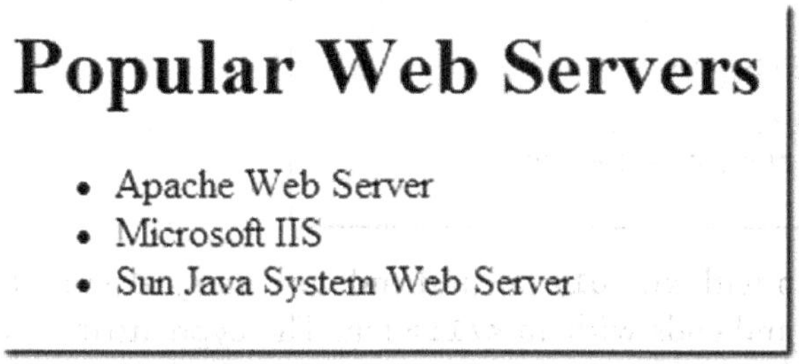

Figure 12
Sample unordered list

Unordered lists begin with an `<ul>` tag and end with an `</ul>` tag. Each list item begins with an `<li>` tag and ends with an `</li>` tag. The `type` attribute can be used to change the type of bullet. For example, to create an unordered list organized with square bullets, use `<ul type="square">`. Table 3 documents the `type` attribute and its values for unordered lists.

Table 3 `type` attributes for unordered lists

Attribute	Value
`type`	`disc` (the default)
	`square`
	`circle`

The XHTML code to create the unordered list shown in Figure 12 follows:

```
<h1>Popular Web Servers</h1>
<ul>
  <li>Apache Web Server</li>
  <li>Microsoft IIS</li>
  <li>Sun Java System Web Server</li>
</ul>
```

Legacy Alert. You will find many Web pages that use the type attribute to configure the numbering system of ordered lists and the bullet style of unordered lists. Be aware that the type attribute is supported in XHTML 1.0 Transitional but is deprecated.

HANDS-ON PRACTICE 7

In this Hands-On Practice you will use heading tags and lists on the same page. Launch Notepad or another text editor and type in the following XHTML:

```
<!DOCTYPE html PUBLIC "-//W3C//DTD XHTML 1.0 Transitional//EN"
  "http://www.w3.org/TR/xhtml1/DTD/xhtml1-transitional.dtd">
<html xmlns="http://www.w3.org/1999/xhtml" lang="en" xml:lang="en">
<head>
<title>Headings and Lists</title>
<meta http-equiv="Content-Type" content="text/html; charset=utf-8"/>
</head>
<body>
  <h1>Web Servers and Web Browsers</h1>
    <h2>Popular Web Servers</h2>
      <ol>
        <li>Apache Web Server</li>
        <li>Microsoft IIS</li>
        <li>Sun Java System Web Server</li>
      </ol>
    <h2>Popular Web Browsers</h2>
      <ul>
        <li>Internet Explorer</li>
        <li>Firefox</li>
        <li>Opera</li>
      </ul>
</body>
</html>
```

Save your file as heading5.html. Launch a browser and test your page. It should look similar to the page shown in Figure 13. You can compare your work with the solution in the student files (Chapter2/heading5.html).

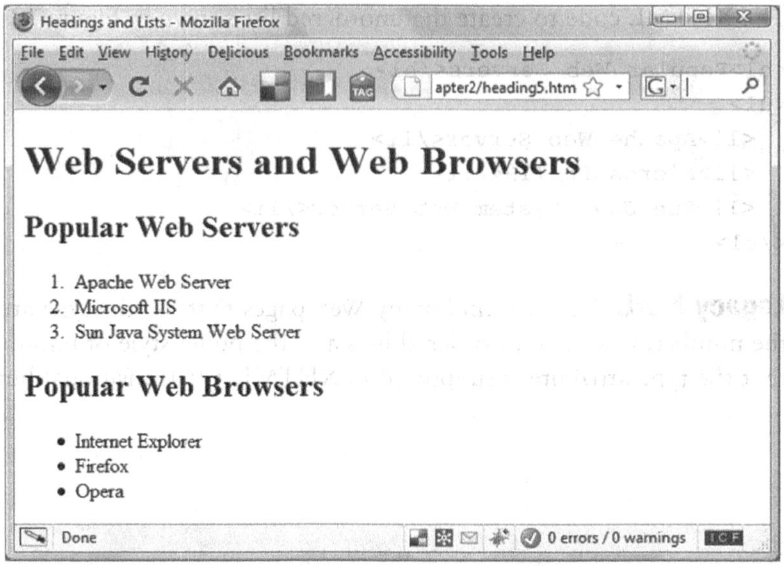

Figure 13 Web page using an ordered and unordered list

Take a few minutes to experiment with the `type` attribute. Configure the unordered list to use square bullets. Configure the ordered list to use uppercase letters instead of numerals. Save your page as heading6.html. Test your page in a browser. It should look similar to the page shown in Figure 14 and the solution in the student files (Chapter2/heading6.html).

Figure 14 Using the `type` attribute with unordered and ordered lists

CHECKPOINT 2

1. Describe the features of a heading element and how it configures the text.
2. Describe the difference between ordered lists and unordered lists.
3. Describe the purpose of the blockquote element.

7 XHTML—Text Formatting

Text can be formatted in various ways using **logical style elements, physical style elements**, and **special characters**. These are considered to be inline-level elements because they can apply to either a section of text or a single character of text. This is not the only method for formatting text; Cascading Style Sheets is commonly used for this purpose.

FAQ

What about the font tag?

The **<font>** tag allows you to configure the typeface, color, and size of the text between the <font> and </font> container tags. However, the <font> tag is deprecated. A **deprecated** XHTML element or attribute is still supported by XHTML 1.0 Transitional and currently popular browsers, but may not be supported in the future. The W3C recommends using Cascading Style Sheets to format text instead of using the <font> tag. If you'd like more information about the <font> tag, see Appendix A, XHTML Reference.

XHTML Logical Style Elements

Logical style elements, sometimes called phrase elements, indicate the logical style used to display the text between the container tags. It is up to each browser to interpret that style. For example, the **<strong>** element indicates that the text associated with it be displayed in a "strong" manner in relation to normal text on the page. Usually, but not always, the browser (or other user agent) will display <strong> text in bold. A screen reader, such as Jaws or Window-Eyes, might interpret <strong> text to indicate that the text should be more strongly spoken. With more and more devices used to access the Web, the use of logical style elements instead of physical style elements (whenever possible) is preferred. Both are still used on the Web.

Note that all logical style elements are container tags—an opening and a closing tag should be used. For example, if you wanted the phone number in the following line to have a strong logical style

```
Call for a free quote for your Web development needs: 888.555.5555
```

the XHTML would look like

```
<p>Call for a free quote for your Web development needs:
<strong>888.555.5555</strong></p>
```

Notice that the <strong> opening and closing tags are contained within the paragraph tags (<p> and </p>). This XHTML code is nested properly, follows XML syntax, and is considered to be well formed. An example of improper nesting follows:

```
<p>Call for a free quote for your Web development needs:
<strong>888.555.5555</p></strong>
```

When improperly nested, the <p> and <strong> tag pairs overlap each other instead of being nested within each other. Improperly nested code will not pass XHTML validation testing (see section 9) and may cause display issues. Appendix D, Comparison of HTML and XHTML, contains a list of the key syntax rules of XML.

Table 4 lists logical style tags and examples of their use.

Table 4 Logical style elements

Element	Example	Usage
<strong>	**strong** text	Causes text to be emphasized or to stand out from surrounding text; usually displayed in bold
<em>	*emphasized* text	Causes text to be emphasized in relation to other text; usually displayed in italics
<cite>	*cite* text	Identifies a citation or reference; usually displayed in italics
<code>	code text	Identifies program code samples; usually a fixed-space font
<dfn>	*dfn* text	Identifies a definition of a word or term; usually displayed in italics
<kbd>	kbd text	Identifies user text to be typed; usually a fixed-space font
<samp>	samp text	Shows program sample output; usually a fixed-space font
<var>	*var* text	Identifies and displays a variable or program output; usually displayed in italics

FAQ

Why do the displays look so similar?

As you look at Table 4, you may notice that some tags, such as <cite> and <dfn>, result in the same type of display (italics) as the <em> tag in today's browsers. These tags are logically describing the text as a citation or definition, but the physical display is usually italics in both cases. Cascading Style Sheets are a better way to format elements than logical style tags. However, logical style tags are preferred over physical style tags. If you find this a little confusing and think that there are too many tags with similar purposes, you are correct. Please keep in mind that Cascading Style Sheets is the preferred method to format text—not physical style and logical style elements. However, we introduce physical style and logical style elements in this chapter because they are still used on the Web.

XHTML—Physical Style Elements

Physical style elements are sometimes called font style elements because they provide specific font instructions for the browser. This type of tag is still commonly used and generated by some Web authoring tools. Be aware that logical style elements and Cascading Style Sheets provide for a wider range of Web access. Physical style elements are included in this book because many existing Web pages use them. Table 5 lists physical style tags and examples of their use.

Table 5 Physical style elements

Element	Example	Usage
<b>	**bold** text	Displays text as bold
<i>	*emphasized* text	Displays text in italics
<big>	big text	Displays text larger than normal size
<small>	small text	Displays text smaller than normal size
<sub>	$_{\text{sub}}$text	Displays small text below the baseline
<sup>	^{sup}text	Displays small text above the baseline
<strike>	~~strike~~ text	Displays text with a line through it (deprecated)
<u>	u text	Displays text underlined; avoid using this because underlined text can be confused with hyperlinks (deprecated)
<tt>	teletype text	Displays text in teletype or fixed-space font

You may have noticed that the <strong> logical style tag usually has the same effect as the <b> physical style tag. Also, the **<em>** logical style tag usually has the same effect as the <i> physical style tag. In order to create XHTML that describes logical styles instead of font instructions for browsers, use <strong> instead of <b> and use <em> instead of <i>. As you continue to study Web development, you will learn about Cascading Style Sheets and their use in text formatting.

Special XHTML Characters

In order to use special characters such as quotation marks, greater than (>), lesser than (<), and the copyright symbol (©) in your Web document, you need to use special characters, sometimes called entity characters. For example, if you wanted to include a copyright line on your page as follows:

```
© Copyright 2008 My Company. All rights reserved.
```

You would use the special character **`©`** to display the copyright symbol. The XHTML would look as follows:

```
<p>&copy; Copyright 2008 My Company. All rights reserved.</p>
```

Another useful special character is **` `**, which stands for nonbreaking space. You may have noticed that Web browsers treat multiple spaces as a single space. If you need a small number of spaces in your text, you may use ` ` multiple times to indicate multiple blank spaces. This is acceptable if you simply need to tweak the position of an element a little. If you find that your Web pages contain many ` ` special characters in a row, you should use a different method to align elements, such as a table or Cascading Style Sheets.

See Table 6 for a description of special characters and their codes.

Table 6 Common special characters

Character	Entity Name	Code
"	Quotation mark	`"`
©	Copyright symbol	`©`
&	Ampersand	`&`
Empty space	Nonbreaking space	` `
—	Em dash	`—`
|	Vertical Bar	`|`

HANDS-ON PRACTICE 8

Figure 15 shows the Web page you will create. Launch Notepad and open one of the Web page files that you have already created, such as blockquote.html from Hands-On Practice 5. Modify the title of the Web page by changing the text between the `<title>` and `</title>` tags to Web Design Steps. Since our Web Design Steps page will be quite different from the previous page you created, delete the code between the `<body>` and `</body>` tags. Save the file as design.html.

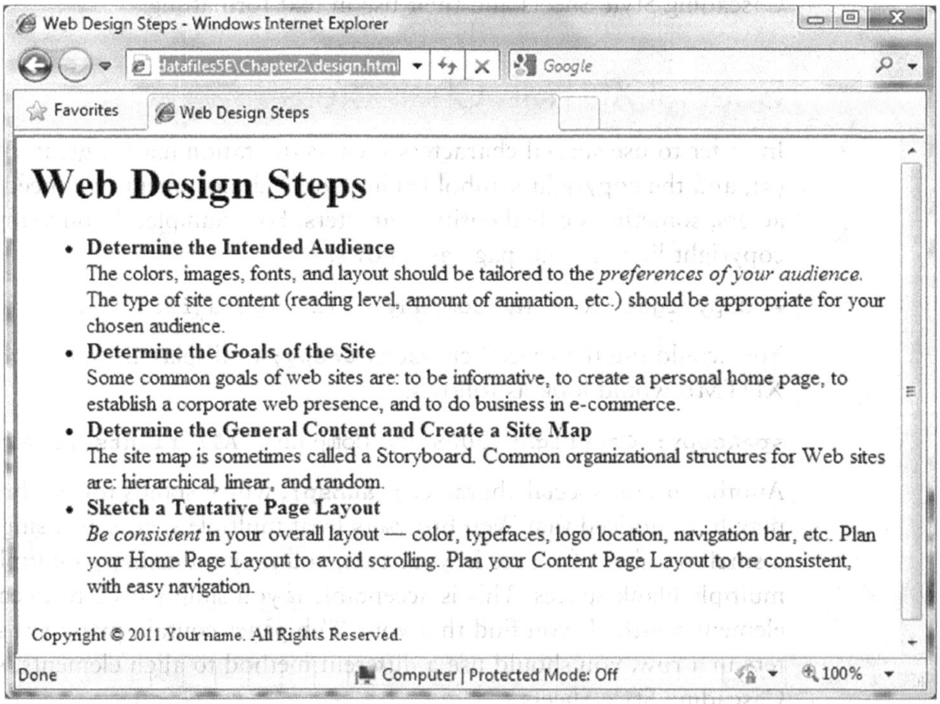

Figure 15
Sample design.html

The sample page shown in Figure 15 contains a heading, an unordered list, and copyright information.

Configure the heading Web Design Steps as a level 1 heading (`<h1>`) as follows:

```
<h1>Web Design Steps</h1>
```

Now create the unordered list. The first line of each bulleted item is the title of the Web design step. In the sample, each step title should be strong, or stand out from the rest of the text. The code for the beginning of the unordered list follows:

```
<ul>
  <li><strong>Determine the Intended Audience</strong><br />
  The colors, images, fonts, and layout should be tailored to the
<em>preferences of your audience.</em> The type of site content
(reading level, amount of animation, etc.) should be appropriate for
your chosen audience.</li>
```

Edit your design.html file and code the entire ordered list. Remember to code the closing `</ul>` tag at the end of the list. Don't worry if your text wraps a little differently—your screen resolution or browser window size may be different.

Finally, configure the copyright information. This should be smaller than the rest of the text. Use the special character, `©`, for the copyright symbol. The code for the copyright line follows:

```
<p><small>Copyright &copy; 2008 Your name. All Rights Reserved.
</small></p>
```

How did you do? Compare your work to the sample in the student files (Chapter2/design.html).

8 XHTML—Hyperlinks

The Anchor Element

The **anchor element** can be used to specify a hyperlink reference (`href`) to a Web page you want to display. Each **hyperlink** begins with an `<a>` tag and ends with an `</a>` tag. The opening and closing anchor tags surround the text to click to perform the hyperlink.

You have probably seen many links on the Web but may have never thought about how they are created. To create an **absolute link** to a Web site such as Yahoo!, you would create a hyperlink with the URL for Yahoo! for the value of the **`href` attribute** as follows:

```
<a href="http://yahoo.com">Yahoo!</a>
```

"Yahoo!", the text contained between the anchor tags, is displayed in the browser window. By default, this text is underlined and blue. Figure 16 shows an example of a hyperlink to the Yahoo! Web site in a browser.

Figure 16
A hyperlink to the Yahoo! Web site

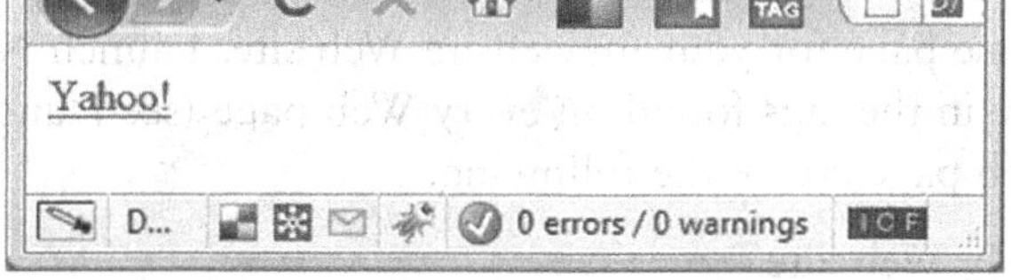

Absolute and Relative Links

The link to Yahoo! you just created is an absolute link. Notice that the XHTML code for the link indicates the protocol being used, http://, and continues with the domain name, yahoo.com. This indicates the absolute location of the Web resource. Use absolute links when you are creating links to other Web sites.

When you need to link to Web pages within your site, use a **relative link**. This link does not begin with http://. It only contains the file name or file name and folder of the Web page you want to display. The link location is relative to the page currently being displayed. For example, if you had a home page called index.html and wanted to link to a page with your resumé (called resume.html) located in the same folder as index.html, the XHTML for the relative link would be as follows:

```
<a href="resume.html">My Resume</a>
```

HANDS-ON PRACTICE 9

The best way to learn XHTML is by writing it. Let's experiment with the anchor tag and create a sample Web site to use to practice creating hyperlinks.

First, create a new folder called mywebsite.

- **Windows XP Users.** Launch Windows Explorer by selecting Start, Programs, Windows Explorer with your pointing (mouse) cursor. Click your drive to select it. Select File, New, Folder.
- **Windows Vista Users.** Launch the Computer folder by selecting Start, Computer with your pointing (mouse) cursor. Click your drive to select it. Select Organize, New Folder.
- **Mac Users.** Look in the Dashboard for the Finder icon and click on it with your pointing (mouse) cursor. Select the Documents folder. Select File, New Folder.

Name your folder mywebsite. This site is an example of a personal Web site. It will contain a home page called index.html and two content pages called resume.html and favorites.html. A sample site map that was created using Adobe Dreamweaver (see Figure 17) shows the architecture of the site—a home page (index.html) with major links to two pages (resume.html and favorites.html).

Figure 17
Site map

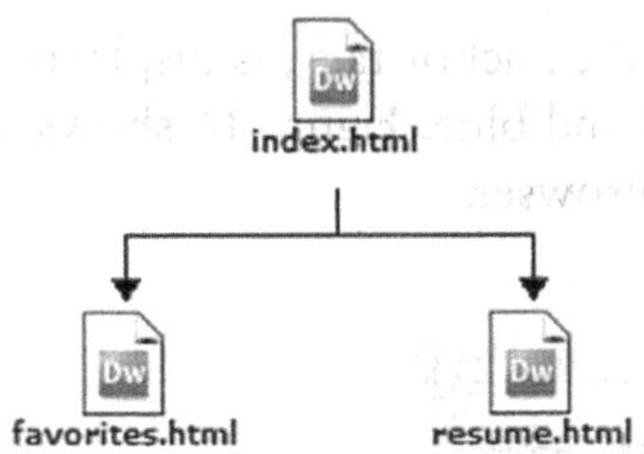

Now create the home page for your mywebsite Web site. Launch Notepad or another text editor and type in the tags found on every Web page (see Hands-On Practice 1). In the body of the Web page create the following:

- A heading: My Web Site
- An absolute link to Yahoo!

- An absolute link to the Web site of your school
- A relative link to resume.html
- A relative link to favorites.html

Save your page as index.html in the mywebsite folder. Display your page in a browser. It should look similar to the page shown in Figure 18. Compare your work to the sample in the student files (Chapter2/2.9/index.html).

Figure 18 Sample index.html displayed in the Apple Safari browser

Test your page by clicking each link. When you click the absolute links to Yahoo! and your school you should see those pages displayed if you are connected to the Internet. The relative links should not work yet—let's create those pages next.

Create the resume.html page. Launch Notepad or another text editor and type in the tags found on every Web page (see Hands-On Practice 1). In the body of the Web page place the following:

- A heading of Resumé
- Some text that describes your job objective
- A navigation bar that contains a relative link to the Home page (index.html), and a relative link to the Favorites page (favorites.html)

FAQ

What if my absolute links don't work?

Check the following:

- Are you currently connected to the Internet?
- Are you certain that you spelled the URLs of the Web sites correctly?
- Did you begin with http://?
- When you place your mouse over a link, the URL will display in the status bar in the lower edge of the browser window. Verify that this is the correct URL.
- *Hint*: When you are about to put an absolute link in a Web page, display the Web site in a browser, then copy and paste the URL. Don't rely on typing the URL accurately.

See Figure 19 for a sample Resumé page. Save your Resumé page as resume.html in your mywebsite folder.

Figure 19
Sample resume.html

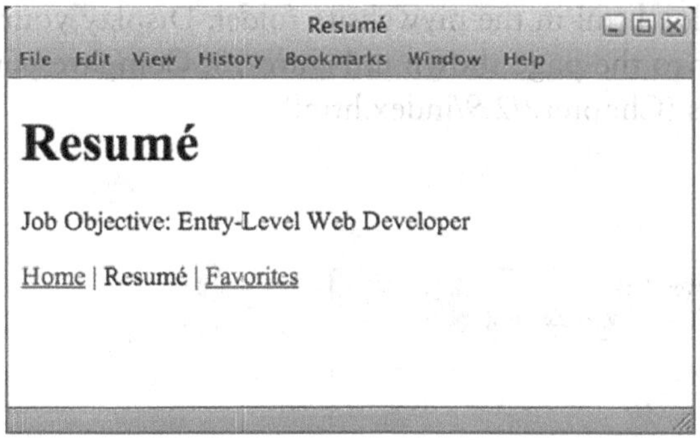

Test your index.html page again. This time when you click the Resumé link, your new page should display. Use the Home link on your resume.html page to redisplay your home page.

Create the favorites.html page. Launch Notepad or another text editor and type in the tags found on every Web page (see Hands-On Practice 1). In the body of the Web page place the following:

- A heading: Favorite Sites
- An unordered list that contains the following categories:
  Hobbies
  XHTML
  JavaScript
  Professional Groups
- A navigation bar that contains a relative link to the Home page (index.html) and a relative link to the Resumé page (resume.html)

See Figure 20 for a sample Favorites page. Save your page as favorites.html in your mywebsite folder.

Figure 20
Sample favorites.html

Test your index.html page again and try the links between the Home page, Resumé page, and Favorites pages. Don't worry if the links don't work perfectly the first time. If you have problems, carefully examine the source code of the pages and verify the existence of the files using Windows Explorer.

FAQ

What if my relative links don't work?

Check the following:

- Did you save your index.html and resume.html pages in your mywebsite folder?
- Did you save the files with the names as requested? Use Windows Explorer or My Computer to verify the actual names of the files you saved.
- Did you type the file names correctly in the link's `href` property? Check for typographical errors.
- When you place your mouse over a link, the file name of a relative link will display in the status bar in the lower edge of the browser window. Verify that this is the correct file name.
- On many operating systems such as UNIX or Linux, the use of uppercase and lowercase in file names matters—make sure that the file name and the reference to it are in the same case. It's a good practice to always use lowercase for file names used on the Web.
- *Hint*: Tiny details such as spelling file names correctly and consistently are very important in Web development.

E-Mail Links

The anchor tag can also be used to create e-mail links. An **e-mail link** will automatically launch the default mail program configured for the browser. It is similar to an external hyperlink with the following two exceptions:

- It uses mailto: instead of http://.
- It launches the default e-mail application for the visitor's browser with your e-mail address as the recipient.

For example, to create an e-mail link to the e-mail address help@terrymorris.net, code the following:

```
<a href="mailto:help@terrymorris.net">help@terrymorris.net</a>
```

It is good practice to place the e-mail address both on the Web page and within the anchor tag. Not everyone has an e-mail program configured with his or her browser. By placing the e-mail address in both places, you increase usability for all your visitors.

HANDS-ON PRACTICE 10

Open the home page of your mywebsite Web site and add an e-mail link to the bottom of the page. Save and test it in a browser. The page should look similar to the page shown in Figure 21. Compare your work with the sample in the student files (Chapter2/2.10/index.html).

Figure 21
E-mail link added to index.html

This section provided a quick introduction to the anchor element. You should now be able to code different types of text hyperlinks: e-mail links, links relative to a Web page, and absolute links to other Web sites. As you continue to study, you will learn to use images as hyperlinks, to code links internal to a Web page, and to target specific windows.

Accessibility and Links

Focus on Accessibility

Visually challenged visitors who are using a screen reader can configure the software to display a list of the hyperlinks in the document. In addition, some popular browsers, such as Opera (visit http://www.opera.com for free download information), provide this feature as a convenience for all users. However, a list of links is only useful if the text describing each link is actually helpful and descriptive. For example, on your college Web site a "Search the course schedule" link would be more useful than a link that simply says "More information." Keep this in mind as you are coding hyperlinks in your Web pages.

FAQ

Can you share some tips on using links?

- Make your link names descriptive and brief to minimize possible confusion.
- Avoid using the phrase "Click here for" in your links. In the beginning of the Web, this phrase was needed because clicking links was a new experience for Web users. Now that the Web is a daily part of our lives, this phrase seems slightly redundant and almost archaic.
- Try not to bury links in large blocks of text—use bullets or definition lists. It is more difficult to read Web pages than printed pages.
- Be careful when linking to external Web sites. The Web is dynamic and it's possible that the external site may change the name of the page or even delete the page. If this happens, your link will be broken.

CHECKPOINT 3

1. Provide a reason for using logical style tags rather than physical style tags.
2. Describe the purpose of special characters.
3. Describe when to use an absolute link. Is the http protocol used in the **`href`** value?
4. Describe when to use a relative link. Is the http protocol used in the **`href`** value?

9 XHTML Validation

The W3C has a free Markup Validation Service available at http://validator.w3.org/ that will validate your XHTML code and check it for syntax errors. **XHTML validation** provides students with quick self-assessment—you can prove that your code uses correct syntax. In the working world, XHTML validation serves as a quality assurance tool. Invalid code may cause browsers to render the pages slower than otherwise.

HANDS-ON PRACTICE 11

In this Hands-On Practice you will use the W3C Markup Validation Service to validate a Web page. This example uses the design.html page completed in Hands-On Practice 8 (student files Chapter2/design.html). Locate design.html and open it in Notepad. We will add an error to the design.html page. Delete the first closing </li> tag. This modification should generate several error messages. The first error message will be a direct result of the incorrect syntax.

Next, attempt to validate the design.html file. Launch a browser and visit the W3C Markup Validation Service file upload page at http://validator.w3.org/#validate_by_upload. Click the Browse button and select the Chapter2/design.html file from your computer. Select More Options. Verify that the check boxes next to Show Source and Verbose Output are checked, as shown in Figure 22. Click the Check button to upload the file to the W3C site.

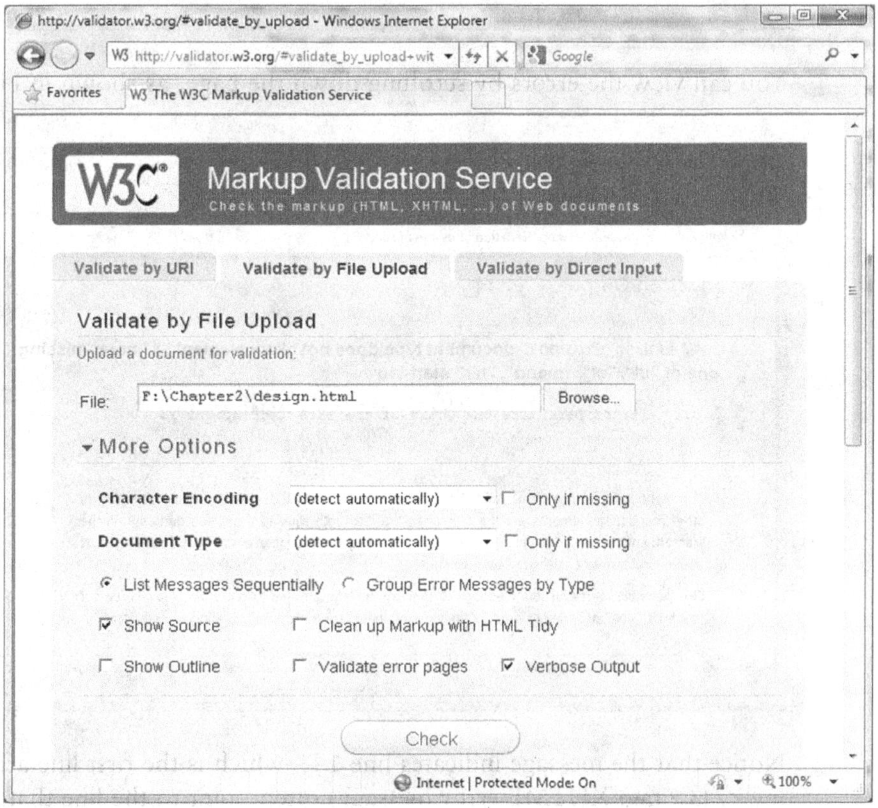

Figure 22
Validate your page

Your display should be similar to that shown in Figure 23. Notice the “Errors found while checking this document” message.

Figure 23
The validation results indicate errors

You can view the errors by scrolling down the page, as shown in Figure 24.

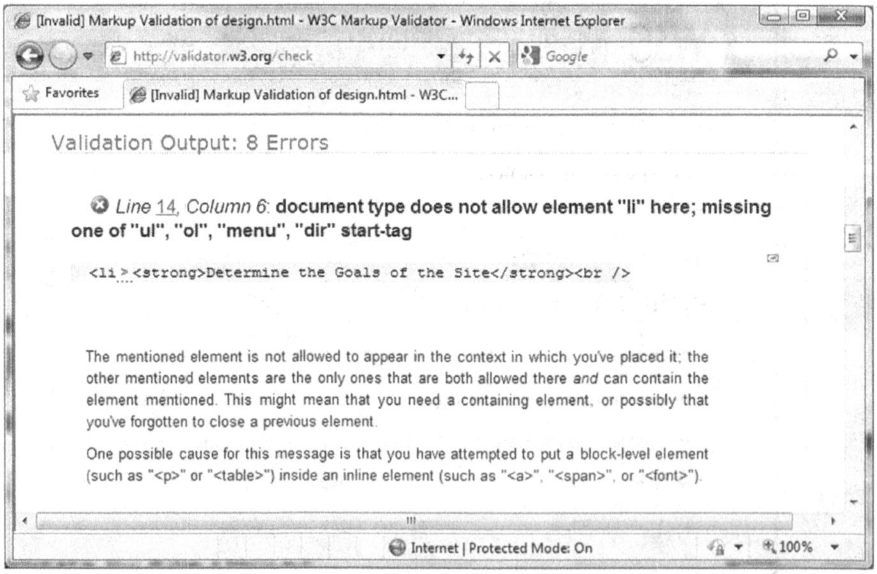

Figure 24
The error indicates line 14

Notice that the message indicates line 14—which is the first line after the missing closing `</li>` tag. XHTML error messages often point to the line that follows the error.

The text of the message 'document type does not allow element "li" here; missing one of "ul", "ol", "menu", "dir" start-tag' lets you know that something is wrong. It's up to you to figure out what it is. A good place to start is to check your container tags and make sure they are in pairs. In this case, that is the problem. You can scroll down to view the other errors. However, since multiple error messages are often displayed after a single error occurs, it's a good idea to fix one item at a time and then revalidate.

Edit the design.html file in Notepad and add the missing `</li>` tag. Save the file. Launch a browser and visit http://validator.w3.org/#validate_by_upload. Select your file, select More Options, and verify the Show Source and Verbose Output check boxes are checked. Click the Revalidate button to begin the validation.

Your display should be similar to that shown in Figure 25. Notice the "This document was successfully checked as XHTML 1.0 Transitional!" message. This means your page passed the validation test. Congratulations, your design.html page is a valid XHTML page! It's a good practice to validate your Web pages. However, when validating code use common sense. Since Web browsers still do not completely follow W3C recommendations, there will be situations, such as when adding multimedia to a Web page, when XHTML code configured to work reliably across a variety of browsers and platforms will not pass XHTML validation.

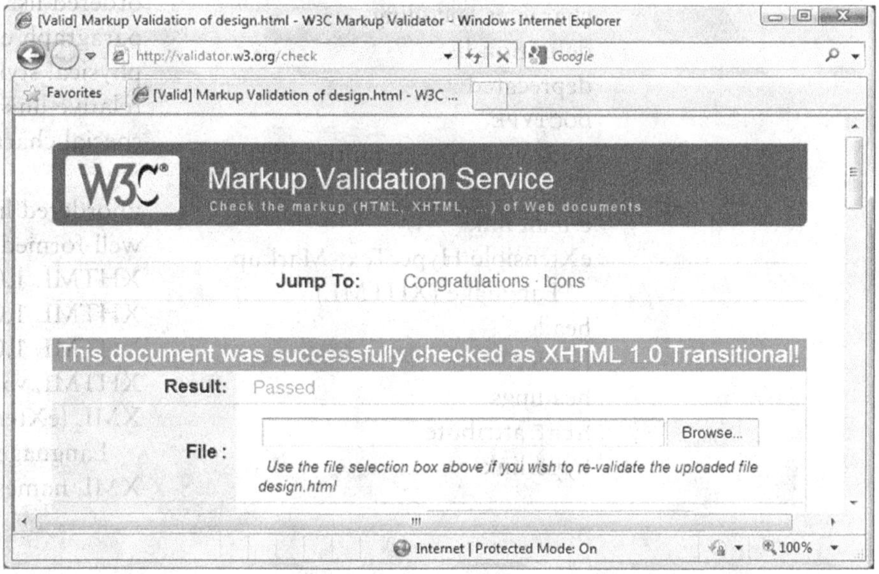

Figure 25
The page has passed the validation test

CHAPTER SUMMARY

This chapter provided an introduction to XHTML. It began with an introduction to HTML, discussed the transition to XHTML, continued with the anatomy of a Web page, introduced inline- and block-level formatting, and demonstrated coding anchor elements to link Web pages. If you worked along with the samples in the chapter, you should be ready to create some Web pages on your own. The Hands-On Exercises and Web Case Studies that follow will provide some practice.

Visit http://www.webdevfoundations.net for the links listed in this chapter and for updated information.

Key Terms

©

<a>
<blockquote>
<body>

<dd>
<dl>
<dt>
<em>
<font>
<h1>
<h6>
<head>
<html>
<li>
<meta />
<ol>
<p>
<strong>
<title>
<ul>
absolute link
anchor element
attribute
block-level element
body
character encoding
definition list
deprecated
DOCTYPE
document type definition (DTD)
element
e-mail link
eXtensible HyperText Markup Language (XHTML)
head
header
headings
href attribute
hyperlink
Hypertext Markup Language (HTML)
inline-level element
left alignment
logical style element
ordered list
paragraph element
physical style element
relative link
special characters
tag
unordered list
well-formed document
XHTML 1.0 Frameset
XHTML 1.0 Strict
XHTML 1.0 Transitional
XHTML validation
XML (eXtensible Markup Language)
XML namespace (xmlns)

Review Questions

Multiple Choice

1. Which tag pair contains text that is indented from both the left and right margins?
   a. <ul> </ul>
   b. <blockquote> </blockquote>
   c. <p> </p>
   d. <strong> </strong>

2. Which tag pair is used to create the largest heading?
   a. <h1> </h1>
   b. <h9> </h9>
   c. <h type="largest"> </h>
   d. <h6> </h6>

3. Which tag configures the next text or element to display on a new line?
   a. `<new line />`
   b. `<nl />`
   c. `<br />`
   d. `<line />`

4. Which tag is used to link Web pages to each other?
   a. `<link>` tag
   b. `<hyperlink>` tag
   c. `<a>` tag
   d. `<body>` tag

5. What is the default alignment for headings and paragraphs?
   a. `center`
   b. `left`
   c. `right`
   d. wherever you type them in the source code

6. Which type of XHTML list will automatically number the items for you?
   a. numbered list
   b. ordered list
   c. unordered list
   d. definition list

7. Which of the following is a reason why the text contained by the title tag should be descriptive and include the business or organization name?
   a. The title is saved by default when a visitor bookmarks a web page.
   b. The title may be printed when a visitor prints a web page.
   c. The title may be listed in search engine results.
   d. All of the above are reasons why the text contained by the title tag should be descriptive and include the business or organization name.

8. When do you need to use a fully qualified URL in a hyperlink?
   a. always
   b. when linking to a Web page file on the same site
   c. when linking to a Web page file on an external site
   d. never

9. Which tag pair contains the items in an ordered or unordered list?
   a. `<item> </item>`
   b. `<li> </li>`
   c. `<dd> </dd>`
   d. all of the above

10. What does an e-mail link do?
    a. automatically sends you an e-mail message with the visitor's e-mail address as the reply-to field
    b. launches the default e-mail application for the visitor's browser with your e-mail address as the recipient
    c. displays your e-mail address so that the visitor can send you a message later
    d. links to your mail server

Fill in the Blank

11. The `<meta/>` tag can be used to ____________________.

12. ____________________ can be used to display characters such as the copyright symbol.

13. The ____________________ is the preferred element to use when you need to emphasize text.

14. The ____________________ is used to place a nonbreaking space on a Web page.

Short Answer

15. Explain why it is good practice to place the e-mail address on the Web page and within the anchor tag when creating an e-mail link.

Apply Your Knowledge

1. **Predict the Result.** Draw and write a brief description of the Web page that will be created with the following XHTML code:

```
<!DOCTYPE html PUBLIC "-//W3C//DTD XHTML 1.0 Transitional//EN"
  "http://www.w3.org/TR/xhtml1/DTD/xhtml1-transitional.dtd">
```

```
<html xmlns="http://www.w3.org/1999/xhtml" lang="en" xml:lang="en">
<head>
<title>Predict the Result</title>
<meta http-equiv="Content-Type" content="text/html; charset=utf-8"/>
</head>
<body>
  <h1><em>Favorite Sites</em></h1>
  <ol>
    <li><a href="http://myspace.com">My Space</a></li>
    <li><a href="http://google.com">Google</a></li>
  </ol>
  <p><small>Copyright &copy; 2011 Your name here</small></p>
</body>
</html>
```

2. **Fill in the Missing Code.** This Web page should display a heading and a definition list, but some XHTML tags, indicated by <_> are missing. Fill in the missing code.

```
<!DOCTYPE html PUBLIC "-//W3C//DTD XHTML 1.0 Transitional//EN"
  "http://www.w3.org/TR/xhtml1/DTD/xhtml1-transitional.dtd">
<html xmlns="http://www.w3.org/1999/xhtml" lang="en" xml:lang="en">
<head>
<title>Door County Wild Flowers</title>
<meta http-equiv="Content-Type" content="text/html; charset=utf-8"/>
</head>
<body>
  <_>Door County Wild Flowers<_>
  <dl>
    <dt>Trillium<_>
      <_>This white flower blooms from April through June in
wooded areas.<_>
      <_>Lady Slipper<_>
      <_>This yellow orchid blooms in June in wooded areas.</dd>
    <_>
</body>
</html>
```

3. **Find the Error.** Why won't this page display in a browser?

```
<!DOCTYPE html PUBLIC "-//W3C//DTD XHTML 1.0 Transitional//EN"
  "http://www.w3.org/TR/xhtml1/DTD/xhtml1-transitional.dtd">
<html xmlns="http://www.w3.org/1999/xhtml" lang="en" xml:lang="en">
<head>
<title>Find the Error<title>
<meta http-equiv="Content-Type" content="text/html; charset=utf-8"/>
</head>
<body>
  <h1>Why don't I display?</h1>
</body>
</html>
```

Hands-On Exercises

1. Write the XHTML to display your name in the largest size heading element.
2. Write the XHTML to create an absolute link to a Web site whose domain name is google.com.
3. Write the XHTML for an unordered list to display the days of the week.
4. Write the XHTML for an ordered list that uses uppercase letters to order the item. This ordered list will display the following terms: HTML, XML, and XHTML.
5. Think of a favorite quote by someone you admire. Write the XHTML code to display the person's name in a heading and the quote in a blockquote.
6. Modify the following code snippet to use logical style tags instead of physical style tags.

```
<p>A diagram of the organization of a web site is called a
<b>site map</b> or <b>storyboard</b>. <i>Creating the <b>site
map</b> is one of the initial steps in developing a web
site.</i></p>
```

7. Modify the blockquote.html Web page you created in Hands-On Practice 5. Configure the URL http://www.w3.org/WAI/ as a hyperlink. Save the file as blockquote2.html. Open your file in Notepad and print the source code for the page. Display your page in a browser and print the page. Hand in both printouts to your instructor.
8. Create a Web page that uses a definition list to display three network protocols (see Chapter 1) and their descriptions. Include a hyperlink to a Web site that provides information about the protocols. Add an appropriate heading to the page. Save the page as network.html. Open your file in Notepad and print the source code for the page. Display your page in a browser and print the page. Hand in both printouts to your instructor.
9. Create a Web page about your favorite musical group. Include the name of the group, the individuals in the group, a hyperlink to the group's Web site, your favorite three (or fewer if the group is new) CD releases, and a brief review of each CD.
   - Use an unordered list to organize the names of the individuals.
   - Use a definition list for the names of the CDs and your reviews.

   Save the page as band.html. Open your file in Notepad and print the source code for the page. Display your page in a browser and print the page. Hand in both printouts to your instructor.
10. Create a Web page about your favorite recipe. Use an unordered list for the ingredients and an ordered list to describe the steps needed to prepare the food. Include a hyperlink to a Web site that offers free recipes. Save the page as recipe.html. Open your file in Notepad and print the source code for the page. Display your page in a browser and print the page. Hand in both printouts to your instructor.

Web Research

1. There are many HTML and XHTML tutorials on the Web. Use your favorite search engine to discover them. Choose two that are helpful. For each, print out the home page or other pertinent page and create a Web page that contains the answers to the following questions:

   a. What is the URL of the Web site?

   b. Is the tutorial geared toward the beginner level, intermediate level, or both levels?

   c. Would you recommend this site to others? Why or why not?

   d. List one or two concepts that you learned from this tutorial.

   Open your file in Notepad and print the source code for the page. (*Hint*: Select File, Print.) Display your page in a browser and print the page. Hand in both printouts to your instructor.

Focus on Web Design

1. You are learning the syntax of XHTML. However, coding alone does not make a Web page—design is very important. Surf the Web and find two Web pages—one that is appealing to you and one that is unappealing to you. Print each page. Create a Web page that answers the following questions for each of your examples.

   a. What is the URL of the Web site?

   b. Is the page appealing or unappealing? List three reasons for your answer.

   c. If the page is unappealing, what would you do to improve it?

   Open your file in Notepad and print the source code for the page. Display your page in a browser and print the page. Hand in both printouts to your instructor.

WEB SITE CASE STUDY

This chapter introduces several Web site scenarios, presents site maps or storyboards, and directs you to create two pages for each site.

JavaJam Coffee House

Julio Perez is the owner of the JavaJam Coffee House, a gourmet coffee shop that serves snacks, coffee, tea, and soft drinks. Local folk music performances and poetry readings are held a few nights during the week. The customers of JavaJam are mainly college students and young professionals. Julio would like a Web presence for his shop that will display his services and provide a calendar for the performances. He would like a home page, menu page, music performance schedule page, and job opportunities page.

A site map for the JavaJam Coffee House Web site is shown in Figure 26.

The site map describes the architecture of the Web site, a Home page with three main content pages: Menu, Music, and Jobs.

Figure 26
JavaJam site map

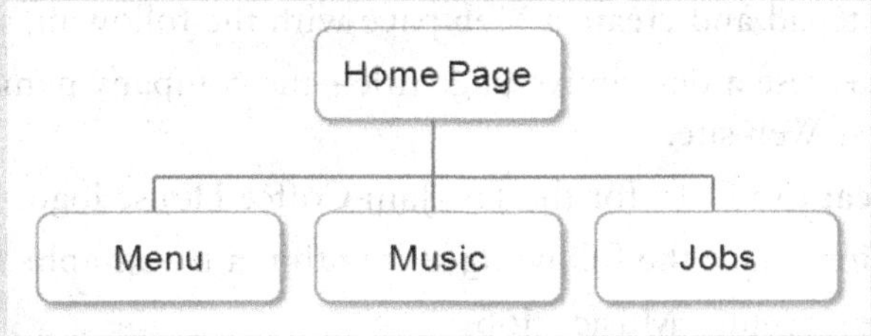

Figure 27 displays a sample layout for the pages. It contains a site logo, a navigation area, a content area, and a footer area for copyright information.

Figure 27
JavaJam page layout

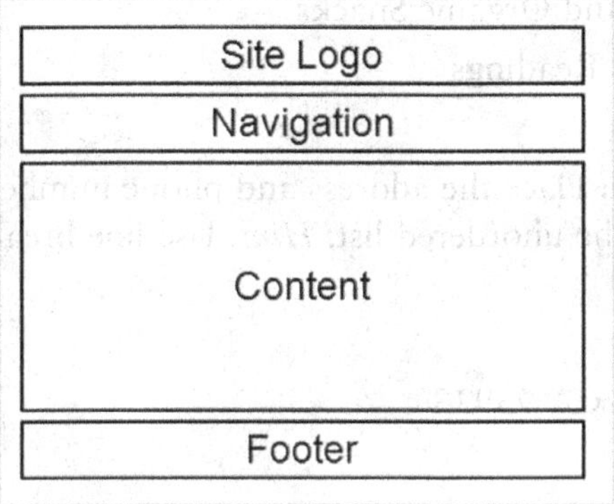

You have two tasks in this case study:

1. Create the Home page: index.html.
2. Create the Menu page: menu.html.

Hands-On Practice Case

Create a folder called javajam to contain your JavaJam Web site files.

1. **The Home Page.** You will use Notepad to create the Home page for the JavaJam Coffee House Web site. The Home page is shown in Figure 28.

Figure 28
JavaJam index.html

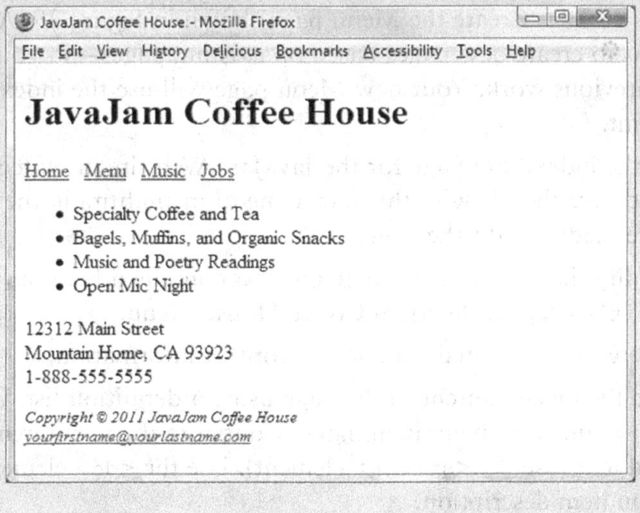

Launch Notepad and create a Web page with the following specifications:

- **Web page:** Use a descriptive page title—the company name is a good choice for a business Web site.
- **Logo area:** Use `<h1>` for the JavaJam Coffee House logo.
- **Navigation:** Place the following text within a paragraph:

  Home   Menu   Music   Jobs

  Code anchor tags so that Home links to index.html, Menu links to menu.html, Music links to music.html, and Jobs links to jobs.html.
- **Content:** Place the following content in an unordered list:

  Specialty Coffee and Tea

  Bagels, Muffins, and Organic Snacks

  Music and Poetry Readings

  Open Mic Night
- **Contact information:** Place the address and phone number information within a paragraph below the unordered list. *Hint*: Use line break tags to help you configure this area.

  12312 Main Street

  Mountain Home, CA 93923

  1-888-555-5555
- **Footer:** Place the following information in a small text size (use the `<small>` physical style element) and emphasized font style (use the `<em>` logical style element):

  Copyright © 2011 JavaJam Coffee House

  Place your name in an e-mail link on the line under the copyright information.

The page in Figure 28 may seem a little sparse, but don't worry, as you gain experience and learn to use more advanced techniques, your pages will look more professional. White space (blank space) on the page can be added with `<br />` tags where needed. Your page does not need to look exactly the same as the sample. Your goal at this point should be to practice and get comfortable using XHTML.

Save your page in the javajam folder and name it index.html.

2. **The Menu Page.** Create the Menu page shown in Figure 29. A productivity technique is to create new pages based on existing pages—so you can benefit from your previous work. Your new Menu page will use the index.html page as a starting point.

   Open the index.html page for the JavaJam Web site in Notepad. Select File, Save As, and save the file with the new name of menu.html in the javajam folder. Now you are ready to edit the page.

   - Modify the page title. Change the text contained between the `<title>` and `</title>` tags to JavaJam Coffee House Menu.
   - Delete the unordered list and the contact information.
   - Add the menu content to the page using a definition list. Use the `<dt>` element to contain each menu item name. Configure the menu item name to display in bold text (use the `<strong>` element). Use the `<dd>` element to contain the menu item description.

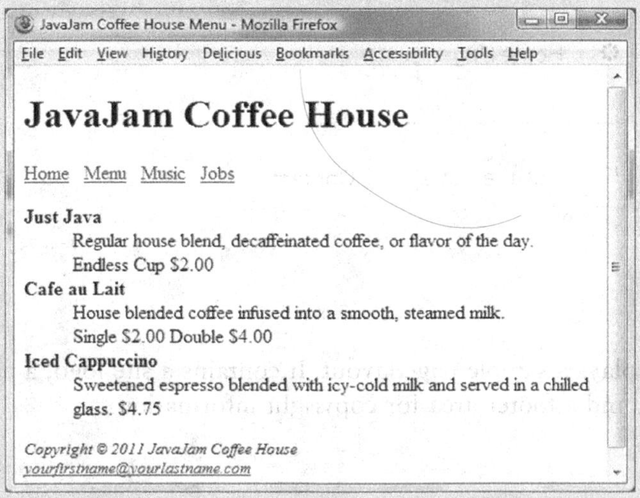

Figure 29
JavaJam menu.html

- The menu items names and descriptions are as follows:

  Just Java
  Regular house blend, decaffeinated coffee, or flavor of the day.
  Endless Cup $2.00

  Cafe au Lait
  House blended coffee infused into a smooth, steamed milk.
  Single $2.00 Double $4.00

  Iced Cappuccino
  Sweetened espresso blended with icy-cold milk and served in a chilled glass.
  $4.75

Save your page and test it in a browser. Test the hyperlink from the menu.html page to index.html. Test the hyperlink from the index.html page to menu.html. If your links do not work, review your work with close attention to these details:

- Verify that you have saved the pages with the correct names in the correct folder.
- Verify your spelling of the page names in the anchor tags.
- After you make changes, test again.

Fish Creek Animal Hospital

Magda Patel is a veterinarian and owner of the Fish Creek Animal Hospital. Her customers are local pet owners who range in age from children to senior citizens. Magda would like a Web site to provide information to her current and potential customers. She has requested a home page, a services page, an ask the vet page, and a contact page.

A site map for the Fish Creek Animal Hospital Web site is shown in Figure 30.

The site map describes the architecture of the Web site, a Home page with three main content pages: Services, Ask the Vet, and Contact.

Figure 30
Fish Creek site map

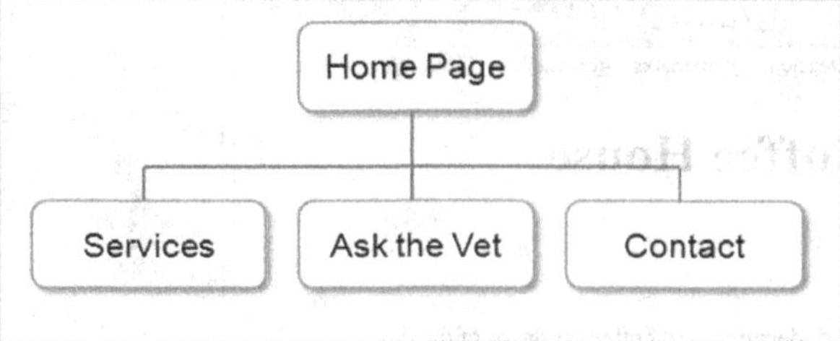

Figure 31 displays a sample page layout. It contains a site logo, a navigation area, a content area, and a footer area for copyright information.

Figure 31
Fish Creek page layout

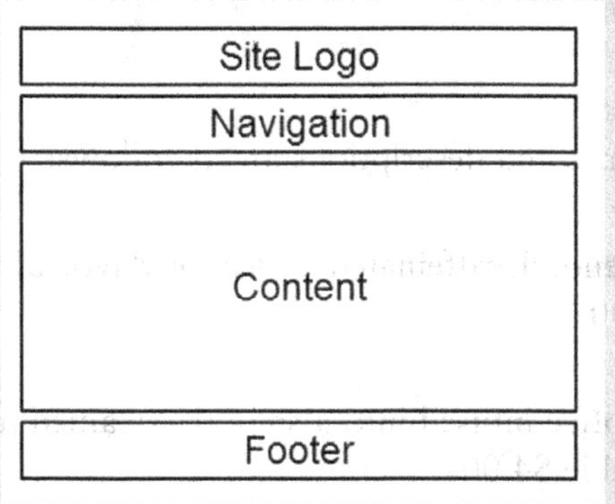

You have two tasks in this case study:

1. Create the Home page: index.html.
2. Create the Services page: services.html.

Hands-On Practice Case

Create a folder called fishcreek to contain your Fish Creek Web site files.

1. **The Home Page.** You will use Notepad to create the Home page for the Fish Creek Animal Hospital Web site. The Home page is shown in Figure 32.

   Launch Notepad and create a Web page with the following specifications:

   - **Web page:** Use a descriptive page title—the company name is a good choice for a business Web site.
   - **Logo area:** Use `<h1>` for the Fish Creek Animal Hospital logo.
   - **Navigation:** Place the following text using the `<strong>` logical style element within a paragraph:

     Home Services Ask the Vet Contact

     Code anchor tags so that Home links to index.html, Services links to services.html, Ask the Vet links to askvet.html, and Contact links to contact.html.

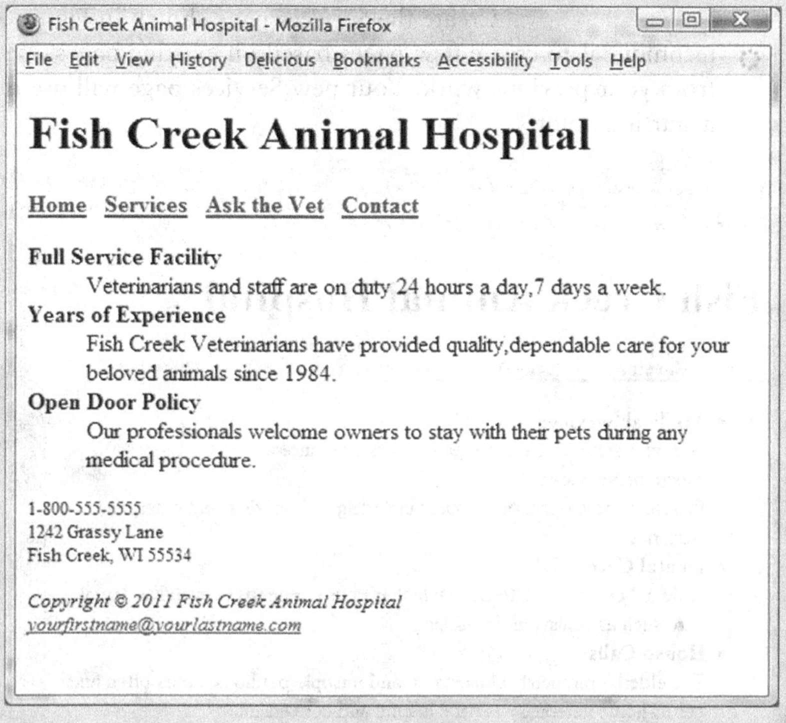

Figure 32 Fish Creek index.html

- **Content:** Place the following content in a definition list:

  Full Service Facility

  Veterinarians and staff are on duty 24 hours a day, 7 days a week.

  Years of Experience

  Fish Creek Veterinarians have provided quality, dependable care for your beloved animals since 1984.

  Open Door Policy

  Our professionals welcome owners to stay with their pets during any medical procedure.

- **Contact information:** Place the address and phone number information within a paragraph below the definition list. *Hints*: Use line break tags to help you configure this area. The text size is configured with the `<small>` physical style element.

  1-800-555-5555
  1242 Grassy Lane
  Fish Creek, WI 55534

- **Footer:** Place the following information in a small text size (use the `<small>` physical style element) and emphasized font style (use the `<em>` logical style element):

  Copyright © 2011 Fish Creek Animal Hospital

  Place your name under the copyright information.

The page in Figure 32 may seem a little sparse, but don't worry, as you gain experience and learn to use more advanced techniques, your pages will look more professional. White space (blank space) on the page can be added with `<br />` tags where needed. Your page does not need to look exactly the same as the sample. Your goal at this point should be to practice and get comfortable using XHTML.

Save your page in the fishcreek folder and name it index.html.

2. **The Services Page.** Create the Services page shown in Figure 33. A productivity technique is to create new pages based on existing pages—so you can benefit from your previous work. Your new Services page will use the index.html page as a starting point.

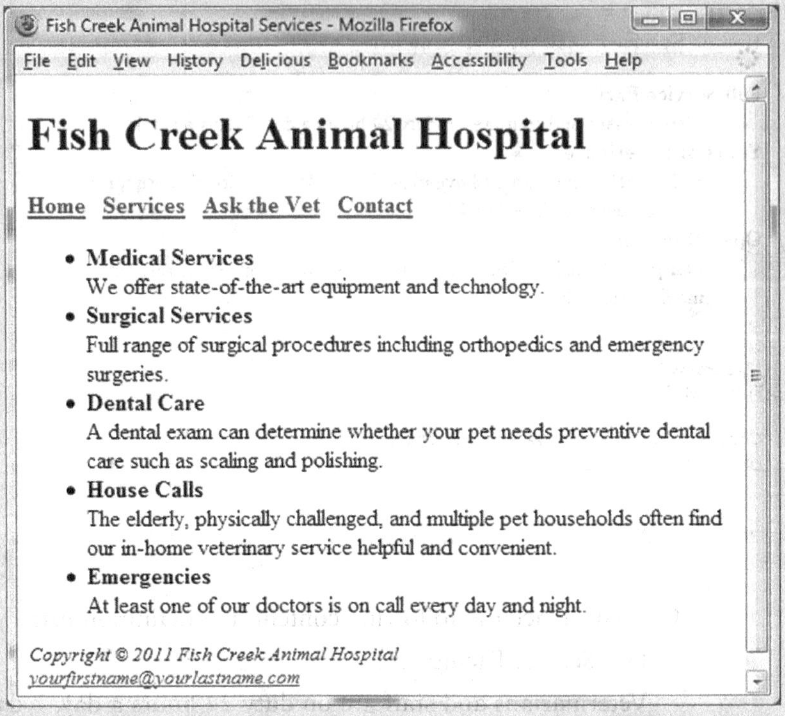

Figure 33
Fish Creek services.html

Open the index.html page for the Fish Creek Web site in Notepad. Select File, Save As, and save the file with the new name of services.html in the fishcreek folder. Now you are ready to edit the page.

- Modify the page title. Change the text contained between the `<title>` and `</title>` tags to Fish Creek Animal Hospital Services.
- Delete the definition list and the contact information.
- Add the services content to the page using an unordered list. Configure the name of each services category to be bold (use the `<strong>` logical style element). Code line breaks after each category name.
- The service categories and descriptions are as follows:

  Medical Services
  We offer state-of-the-art equipment and technology.

  Surgical Services
  Full range of surgical procedures including orthopedics and emergency surgeries.

  Dental Care
  A dental exam can determine whether your pet needs preventive dental care such as scaling and polishing.

  House Calls
  The elderly, physically challenged, and multiple pet households often find our in-home veterinary service helpful and convenient.

  Emergencies
  At least one of our doctors is on call every day and night.

Save your page and test it in a browser. Test the hyperlink from the services.html page to index.html. Test the hyperlink from the index.html page to services.html. If your links do not work, review your work with close attention to these details:

- Verify that you have saved the pages with the correct names in the correct folder.
- Verify your spelling of the page names in the anchor tags.
- After you make changes, test again.

Pasha the Painter

Pasha Poduslawa is an independent home painter and decorator. He would like to have a Web site to advertise his business. His clients are mainly homeowners in the middle-class suburbs of a large city. They range in age from thirties to fifties. Pasha would like a site that contains a home page, a services page, an estimates page, and a testimonial page.

A site map for the Pasha the Painter Web site is shown in Figure 34.

Figure 34
Pasha the Painter site map

The site map describes the architecture of the Web site, a Home page with three main content pages: Services, Testimonials, and Estimates.

Figure 35 displays a sample page layout. It contains a site logo, a navigation area, a content area, and a footer area for copyright information.

You have two tasks in this case study:

1. Create the Home page: index.html.
2. Create the Services page: services.html.

Figure 35
Pasha the Painter page layout

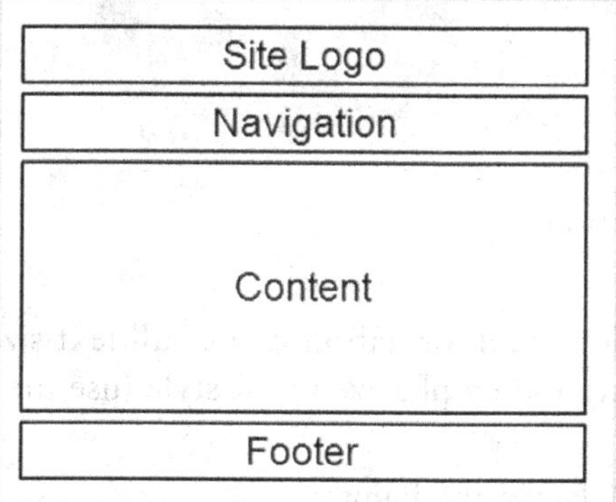

Hands-On Practice Case

Create a folder called painter to contain your Pasha the Painter Web site files.

1. **The Home Page.** You will use Notepad to create the Home page for the Pasha the Painter Web site. The Home page is shown in Figure 36.

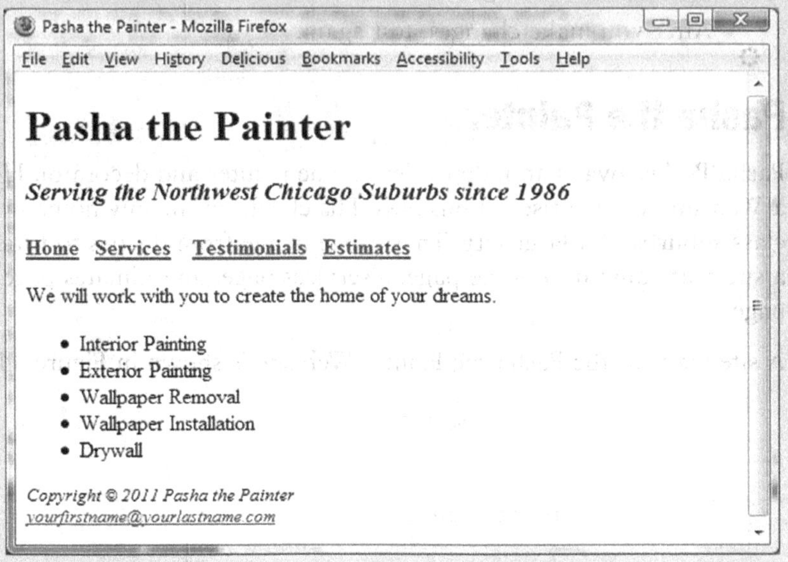

Figure 36
Pasha the Painter index.html

Launch Notepad and create a Web page with the following specifications:

- **Web page:** Use a descriptive page title—the company name is a good choice for a business Web site.
- **Logo area:** Use `<h1>` for the Pasha the Painter logo. The motto should be contained within an `<h3>` element. Emphasize (display in italics) the motto: Serving the Northwest Chicago Suburbs since 1986.
- **Navigation:** Place the following text using the `<strong>` logical style element within a paragraph:

  Home Services Testimonials Estimates

  Code anchor tags so that Home links to index.html, Services links to services.html, Testimonials links to testimonials.html, and Estimates links to estimates.html.
- **Content:** Place this sentence in a paragraph: We will work with you to create the home of your dreams.

  Place the following content in an unordered list:

  Interior Painting
  Exterior Painting
  Wallpaper Removal
  Wallpaper Installation
  Drywall
- **Footer:** Place the following information in a small text size (use the `<small>` physical style element) and emphasized font style (use the `<em>` logical style element):

  Copyright © 2011 Pasha the Painter

  Place your name in an e-mail link on the line under the copyright information.

The page in Figure 36 may seem a little sparse, but don't worry, as you gain experience and learn to use more advanced techniques, your pages will look more professional. White space (blank space) on the page can be added with `<br />` tags where needed. Your page does not need to look exactly the same as the sample. Your goal at this point should be to practice and get comfortable using XHTML.

Save your page in the painter folder and name it index.html.

2. **The Services Page.** Create the Services page shown in Figure 37. A productivity technique is to create new pages based on existing pages—so you can benefit from your previous work. Your new Services page will use the index.html page as a starting point.

Figure 37
Pasha the Painter services.html

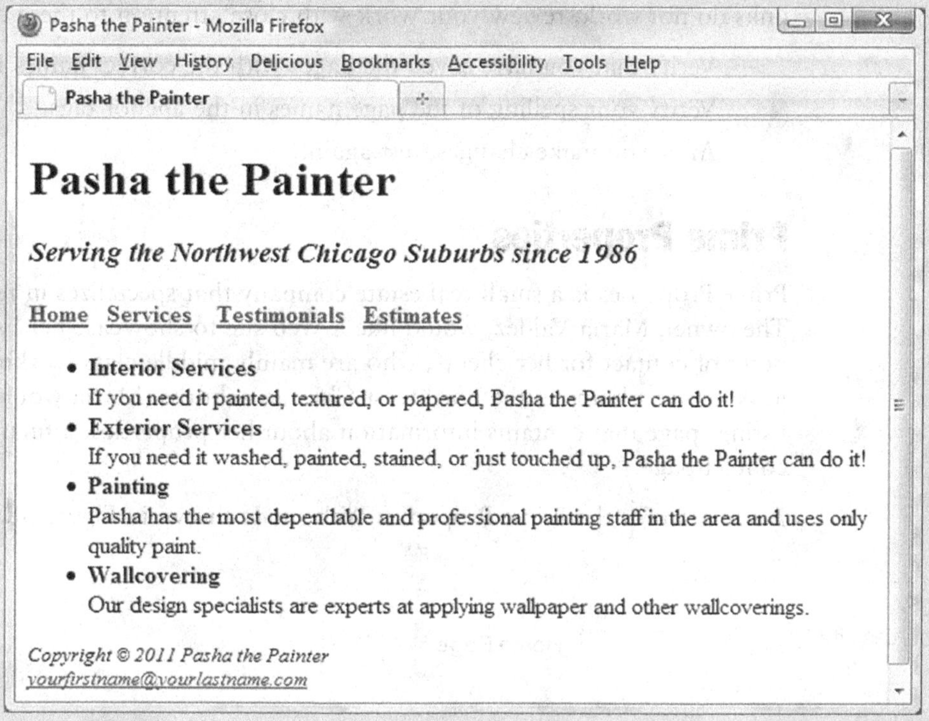

Open the index.html page for the Pasha the Painter Web site in Notepad. Select File, Save As, and save the file with the new name of services.html in the painter folder. Now you are ready to edit the page.

- Modify the page title. Change the text contained between the `<title>` and `</title>` tags to Pasha the Painter Services.
- Delete the content paragraph and unordered list.
- Add the services content to the page using an unordered list. Configure the name of each services category to be bold (use the `<strong>` logical style element). Code line breaks after each category name.

- The service categories and descriptions are as follows:

  Interior Services
  If you need it painted, textured, or papered, Pasha the Painter can do it!

  Exterior Services
  If you need it washed, painted, stained, or just touched up, Pasha the Painter can do it!

  Painting
  Pasha has the most dependable and professional painting staff in the area and uses only quality paint.

  Wallcovering
  Our design specialists are experts at applying wallpaper and other wallcoverings

Save your page and test it in a browser. Test the hyperlink from the services.html page to index.html. Test the hyperlink from the index.html page to services.html. If your links do not work, review your work with close attention to these details:

- Verify that you have saved the pages with the correct names in the correct folder.
- Verify your spelling of the page names in the anchor tags.
- After you make changes, test again.

Prime Properties

Prime Properties is a small real estate company that specializes in residential properties. The owner, Maria Valdez, would like a Web site to showcase her listings and provide a point of contact for her clients, who are mainly middle-class working adults who are looking for a home in the northwest Chicago suburbs. Maria would like a home page, a listings page that contains information about her properties, a financing page, and a contact page.

A site map for the Prime Properties Web site is shown in Figure 38.

Figure 38
Prime Properties site map

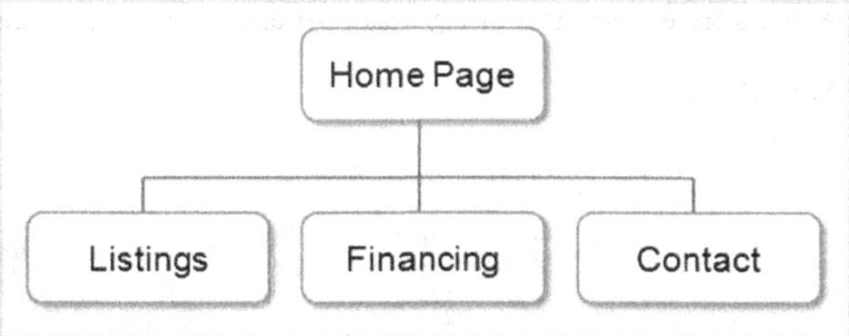

The site map describes the architecture of the Web site, a Home page with three main content pages: Listings, Financing, and Contact.

Figure 39 displays a sample page layout. It contains a site logo, a navigation area, a content area, and a footer area for copyright information.

You have two tasks in this case study:

1. Create the Home page: index.html.
2. Create the Financing page: financing.html.

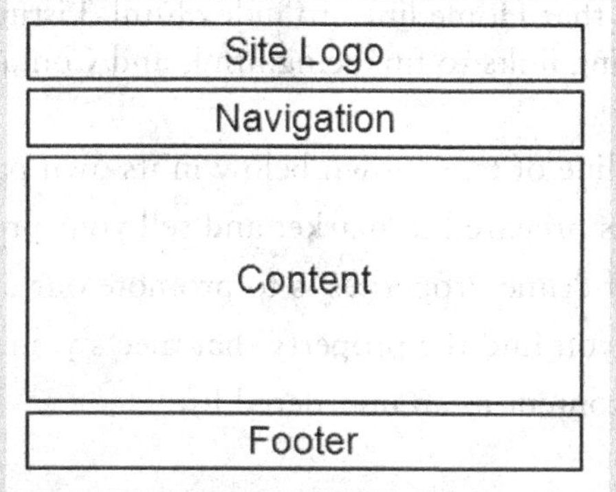

Figure 39
Prime Properties page layout

Hands-On Practice Case

Create a folder called prime to contain your Prime Properties Web page files.

1. **The Home Page.** You will use Notepad to create the Home page for the Prime Properties Web site. The Home page is shown in Figure 40.

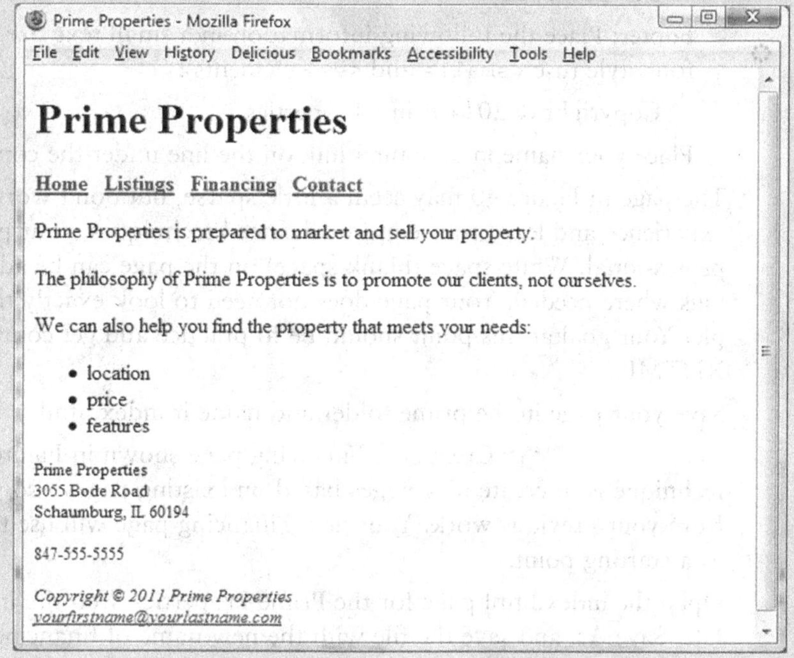

Figure 40
Prime Properties index.html

Launch Notepad and create a Web page with the following specifications:

- **Web page:** Use a descriptive page title—the company name is a good choice for a business Web site.
- **Logo area:** Use <h1> for the Prime Properties logo.
- **Navigation:** Configure the following text to display in bold font (use the <strong> logical style element) within a paragraph:

  Home Listings Financing Contact

Code anchor tags so that Home links to index.html, Listings links to listings.html, Financing links to financing.html, and Contact links to contact.html.

- **Content:** Place each line of text shown below in its own paragraph.

  Prime Properties is prepared to market and sell your property.

  The philosophy of Prime Properties is to promote our clients, not ourselves.

  We can also help you find the property that meets your needs:

  Place the following content in an unordered list:

  location

  price

  features

- **Contact information:** The address and phone information should display in small text (use the `<small>` physical style element).

  Prime Properties
  3055 Bode Road
  Schaumburg, IL 60194
  847-555-5555

- **Footer:** Place the following information in a small text size and emphasized font style (use `<small>` and `<em>` elements):

  Copyright © 2011 Prime Properties

  Place your name in an e-mail link on the line under the copyright information.

The page in Figure 40 may seem a little sparse, but don't worry, as you gain experience and learn to use more advanced techniques, your pages will look more professional. White space (blank space) on the page can be added with `<br />` tags where needed. Your page does not need to look exactly the same as the sample. Your goal at this point should be to practice and get comfortable using XHTML.

Save your page in the prime folder and name it index.html.

2. **The Financing Page.** Create the Financing page shown in Figure 41. A productivity technique is to create new pages based on existing pages—so you can benefit from your previous work. Your new Financing page will use the index.html page as a starting point.

Open the index.html page for the Prime Properties Web site in Notepad. Select File, Save As, and save the file with the new name of financing.html in the prime folder. Now you are ready to edit the page.

- Modify the page title. Change the text contained between the `<title>` and `</title>` tags to Prime Properties :: Financing.
- Delete the content paragraphs, unordered list, and contact information.
- Add the financing content to the page.

  First, configure the following text in an `<h2>` element: Financing.

  Next, place the following sentence in a paragraph:

  We work with many area mortgage and finance companies.

  Finally, configure the following phrase with an `<h3>` element:

  Mortgage FAQs

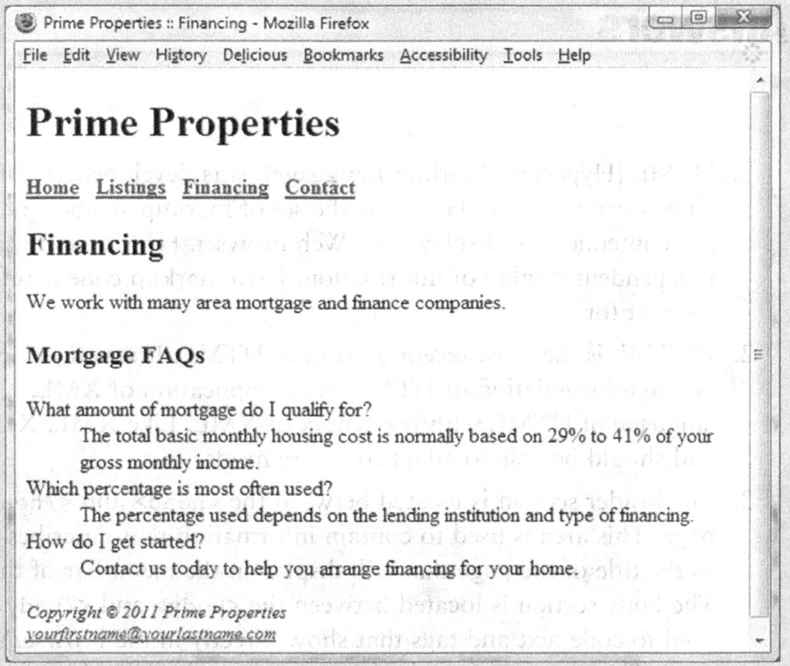

Figure 41
Prime Properties financing.html

Use a definition list to configure the FAQs. Use <dt> elements for the questions and <dd> elements for the answers. The FAQ questions and answers are as follows:

What amount of mortgage do I qualify for?

The total basic monthly housing cost is normally based on 29% to 41% of your gross monthly income.

Which percentage is most often used?

The percentage used depends on the lending institution and type of financing.

How do I get started?

Contact us today to help you arrange financing for your home.

Save your page and test it in a browser. Test the hyperlink from the financing.html page to index.html. Test the hyperlink from the index.html page to financing.html. If your links do not work, review your work with close attention to these details:

- Verify that you have saved the pages with the correct names in the correct folder.
- Verify your spelling of the page names in the anchor tags.
- After you make changes, test again.

Answers

Checkpoint 1

1. HTML (Hypertext Markup Language), was developed by Tim Berners-Lee at CERN using SGML. HTML is the set of markup symbols or codes placed in a file intended for display on a Web browser. HTML configures a platform-independent display of information. Each markup code is referred to as an element (or tag).
2. XHTML is the most recent version of HTML. It was developed by the W3C to be the reformulation of HTML as an application of XML. XHTML combines the language of HTML with the syntax of XML. Like XML, XHTML is extensible and should be able to adapt to future needs.
3. The header section is located between the `<head>` and `</head>` tags on a Web page. This area is used to contain information that describes the Web page, such as the title of the page that will display in the menu bar of the browser window. The body section is located between the `<body>` and `</body>` tags. This area is used to code text and tags that show directly in the browser's display of the Web page. The purpose of the body section is to describe the contents of the Web page.

Checkpoint 2

1. The heading tag is used to display headings and subheadings of documents. The size of the heading is configured with the particular heading level used—ranging from 1 to 6. `<h1>` is the largest heading. `<h6>` is the smallest heading. Text contained between heading tags will be displayed using a bold font and will have a line break above and below.
2. Information on a Web page can be organized using ordered lists and unordered lists. Unordered lists display a small symbol or bullet in front of each item. Use the `<ul>` tag to configure an unordered list. Ordered lists by default display a sequence of numbers in front of each item. Use the `<ol>` tag to configure an ordered list. Configure individual items in both ordered and unordered lists using the `<li>` tag.
3. The purpose of the `blockquote` tag is to indent a section of text on a Web page. A line break is placed before and after the text. The text is indented from both the left and right margins.

Checkpoint 3

1. Physical file tags such as `<b>` describe font instructions rather than general styles for the presentation of information. The Web is accessed by many applications other than regular browsers. For example, a screen reader may interpret `<strong>` to indicate that the text should be spoken stronger than normal.
2. Special characters are used to display items such as quotation marks, greater than (>), less than (<), and the copyright symbol © on a Web page. These special characters, sometimes called entity characters, are interpreted by the browser when the page is rendered.

3. Use an absolute link to display a Web page document from a Web site other than your own. The http protocol is used in the `href` value. Example:

   `<a href="http://www.google.com">Google</a>`

4. Use a relative link to display a Web page document from your Web site. The http protocol is not used in the `href` value.

   Example: `<a href="contact.htm">Contact Us</a>`

Review Questions

1. b
2. a
3. c
4. c
5. b
6. b
7. d
8. c
9. b
10. b
11. describe a characteristic of a Web page, such as the character encoding.
12. special characters
13. `<em>`
14. ` `
15. Not everyone has an e-mail program configured with their browser. By placing the e-mail address in both places, you increase usability for all your visitors.

Configuring Color and Text with CSS

Chapter Objectives

In this chapter, you will learn how to ...

- Describe the evolution of style sheets from print media to the Web
- List advantages of using Cascading Style Sheets
- Use color on Web pages
- Create style sheets that configure common color and text properties
- Apply inline styles
- Use embedded style sheets
- Use external style sheets
- Create CSS `class` and `id` selectors
- Validate CSS

Once you have been introduced to XHTML, you are ready to explore **Cascading Style Sheets (CSS)**. CSS is not new—it was first proposed as a standard by the W3C in 1996. However, browsers and other user agents have only supported this technology consistently for the past several years. Now that there is fairly steady support, Web developers have begun to use CSS to separate the presentation style of a Web page from the information on the Web page itself. CSS is used to configure text, color, and page layout.

This chapter introduces you to the use of CSS on the Web as you explore configuring color and text.

1 Overview of Cascading Style Sheets

For years, style sheets have been used in desktop publishing to apply typographical styles and spacing instructions to printed media. CSS provides this functionality (and much more) for Web developers. It allows Web developers to apply typographic styles (typeface, font size, and so on) and page layout instructions to a Web page. The CSS Zen Garden, http://www.csszengarden.com, exemplifies the power and flexibility of CSS. Visit this site for an example of CSS in action. Notice how the content looks dramatically different depending on the design (CSS style rules) you select. Although the designs on CSS Zen Garden are created by CSS masters, at some point these designers were just like you—starting out with CSS basics.

CSS is a flexible, cross-platform, standards-based language developed by the W3C. Its description of CSS can be found at http://www.w3.org/Style/. Be aware that CSS, even though it has been in use for many years, is still considered an emerging technology and the two most popular browsers do not support it in exactly the same way. There are CSS reference pages at http://reference.sitepoint.com/css and http://www.westciv.com/style_master/academy/browser_support that list the way styles are supported by various browsers and platforms. This chapter concentrates on those aspects of CSS that are well supported by popular browsers.

Advantages of Cascading Style Sheets

There are several advantages to using CSS:

- **Typography and page layout can be better controlled.** These features include font size, line spacing, letter spacing, indents, margins, and element positioning.
- **Style is separate from structure.** The format of the text and colors used on the page can be configured and stored separately from the body section of the Web page document.
- **Styles can be stored.** You can store styles in a separate document and associate them with the Web page. When the styles are modified, the XHTML remains intact. This means that if your client decides to change the background color from red to white you only need to change one file that contains the styles, instead of each Web page document.
- **Documents are potentially smaller.** The formatting is separate from the document; therefore, the actual documents should be smaller.
- **Site maintenance is easier.** Again, if the styles need to be changed it's possible to complete the modifications by changing the style sheet only.

Do you see that there might be advantages to using CSS? You may be wondering if there are any disadvantages to using CSS. In fact, there is one large disadvantage—CSS technology is not yet uniformly supported by browsers. This disadvantage will be less of an issue in the future as browsers comply with standards.

Types of Cascading Style Sheets

There are four methods used to incorporate CSS technology in a Web site: inline, embedded, external, and imported.

- **Inline styles** are coded in the body of the Web page as an attribute of an XHTML tag. The style only applies to the specific element that contains it as an attribute.
- **Embedded styles** are defined in the header of a Web page. These style instructions apply to the entire Web page document.
- **External styles** are coded in a separate text file. This text file is associated with the Web page by using a `<link />` element in the header section.
- **Imported styles** are similar to external styles in that they can connect styles coded in a separate text file with a Web page document. An external style sheet can be imported into embedded styles or into another external style sheet by using the @import directive. This chapter concentrates on the other three uses of CSS.

Introduction to CSS Syntax

Style sheets are composed of rules that describe the styling to be applied. Each **rule** contains a **selector** and a **declaration**. The selector can be an XHTML element, a class name (that you create yourself), or an id name (that you create yourself). This example concentrates on applying styles to XHTML elements. The declaration is the **property** you are setting (such as color or typeface) and the value you are assigning to it.

For example, the CSS rule shown in Figure 1 would set the color of the text used on a Web page to blue. The selector is the XHTML body tag and the declaration sets the **`color` property** to the value of blue.

Figure 1
Using CSS to set the text color to blue

If you wanted the background color of the Web page to be yellow, the CSS rule could be expanded as follows:

```
body { color: blue; background-color: yellow; }
```

This could also be written using hexadecimal color values as follows:

```
body { color: #0000FF; background-color: #FFFF00; }
```

Notice that both the `background-color` and text `color` properties were configured in the previous example. To avoid surprising results caused by default browser colors, the W3C recommends that the **`background-color` property** is set when the text color is configured.

Have you ever wondered why some text-based links are not underlined? This can be accomplished with a style applied to the anchor tag. The following style rule selects the anchor tag (denoted by a) and sets the **`text-decoration` property** (the underline) to none:

```
a { text-decoration: none }
```

You might be asking yourself how you would know what properties and values are allowed to be used. This chapter introduces you to some of the CSS properties commonly used to configure color and text. Table 1 presents a summary of the CSS properties used in this chapter. In the next sections, we'll take a look at how color is used on Web pages and we'll explore how to use CSS to configure color.

Table 1 CSS properties used in this chapter

Property	Description	Values
`background-color`	Background color on the Web page	Any valid color
`color`	Text color	Any valid color
`font-family`	Name of a font or font family	Any valid font or a font family such as `serif`, `sans-serif`, `fantasy`, `monospace`, or `cursive`
`font-size`	The size of the text font	This varies; a numeric value with `pt` (standard font point sizes), `px` (pixels), the unit `em` (which corresponds to the width of the uppercase M of the current font); numeric percentage; the text values `xx-small`, `x-small,small`, `medium`, `large`, `x-large`, and `xx-large` are also valid
`font-style`	The style of the font	`normal`, `italic`, `oblique`
`font-weight`	The "boldness" or weight of the font	This varies; the text values `normal`, `bold`, `bolder`, and `lighter`; the numeric values `100`, `200`, `300`, `400`, `500`, `600`, `700`, `800`, and `900`
`line-height`	The spacing allowed for the line of text	It is most common to use a percentage for this value; for example, a value of 200% would be double-spaced
`margin`	Shorthand notation to configure the margin surrounding an element	A numeric value (`px` or `em`); for example, `body { margin: 10px}` will set the page margins in the document to 10 pixels. When eliminating the margin, do not use the px or em unit, for example, body {margin:0}
`margin-left`	Configures the space in the left margin of the element	A numeric value (`px` or `em`), `auto`, or 0
`margin-right`	Configures the space in the right margin of the element	A numeric value (`px` or `em`), `auto`, or 0
`text-align`	The alignment of text	`center`, `justify`, `left`, `right`
`text-decoration`	Determines whether text is underlined; this style is most often applied to hyperlinks	The value `none` will cause a hyperlink not to be underlined in a browser that normally processes in this manner
`width`	The width of an element	A numeric value (`px` or `em`), numeric percentage, or `auto` (default)

2 Using Color on Web Pages

Monitors display color as a combination of different intensities of red, green, and blue, also known as **RGB color**. RGB intensity values are numerical from 0 to 255. Each

RGB color will have three values, one each for red, green, and blue. These are always listed in that order (red, green, blue) and specify the numerical value of each color used. For example, the RGB values for red are (255,0,0)—all red, no green and no blue. The RGB values for blue are (0,0,255)—no red, no green, and all blue. These colors can also be specified using hexadecimal values.

Hexadecimal is the name for the Base 16 numbering system, which uses the characters 0, 1, 2, 3, 4, 5, 6, 7, 8, 9, A, B, C, D, E, and F to specify numeric values. When a hexadecimal value is used to specify RGB color, the numeric value pairs range from 00 to FF (0 to 255 in Base 10). The hexadecimal value contains three numeric value pairs written sequentially as one number. Each pair is associated with the amount of red, green, and blue displayed. Using this notation, the color red would be specified as `#FF0000` and the color blue as `#0000FF`. The `#` symbol signifies that the value is in hexadecimal. You can use either uppercase or lowercase letters in **hexadecimal color values**–`#FF0000` and `#ff0000` both configure the color red.

Don't worry—you won't need to do calculations to work with Web colors. Just become familiar with the numbering scheme. See Figure 2 for an excerpt from the color chart at http://webdevfoundations.net/color.

Figure 2
Partial color chart

#FFFFFF	#FFFFCC	#FFFF99	#FFFF66	#FFFF33	#FFFF00
#FFCCFF	#FFCCCC	#FFCC99	#FFCC66	#FFCC33	#FFCC00
#FF99FF	#FF99CC	#FF9999	#FF9966	#FF9933	#FF9900
#FF66FF	#FF66CC	#FF6699	#FF6666	#FF6633	#FF6600
#FF33FF	#FF33CC	#FF3399	#FF3366	#FF3333	#FF3300
#FF00FF	#FF00CC	#FF0099	#FF0066	#FF0033	#FF0000

Go to the end of the chapter for a full color version of this figure

Take a few moments to examine the color chart. You will observe a display of colors and their associated hexadecimal RGB values in hexadecimal. You may notice that there is a pattern to the hexadecimal numbers (pairs of 00, 33, 66, 99, CC, or FF). This pattern signifies a color on the **Web Safe Color Palette** (more on this later). As you examine the color chart further, you will see a list of colors using color names. Some Web developers find it easier to use the color names. However, the names are not uniformly supported by all versions of all browsers, so the W3C recommends using numeric color values instead of color names.

Web Color Palette

A Web developer usually has no way of knowing what type of computer or browser the Web site visitors will be using. The various operating systems and browsers display colors differently, and sometimes not at all. The Web Safe Color Palette, also known as the Web Color Palette, is a collection of 216 colors that display the same on both the Windows and Mac OS platforms. It is easy to tell if a color is on the Web Color Palette when you consider the individual hexadecimal RGB value pairs. The values of 00, 33, 66, 99, CC, and FF are the only values for hexadecimal RGB value pairs on the Web Color Palette. Take another look at the color chart at http://webdevfoundations.net/color and note that all the colors listed by RGB follow this numbering scheme—they comprise the Web Color Palette. See Figure 3 (shown also in the color insert section) for

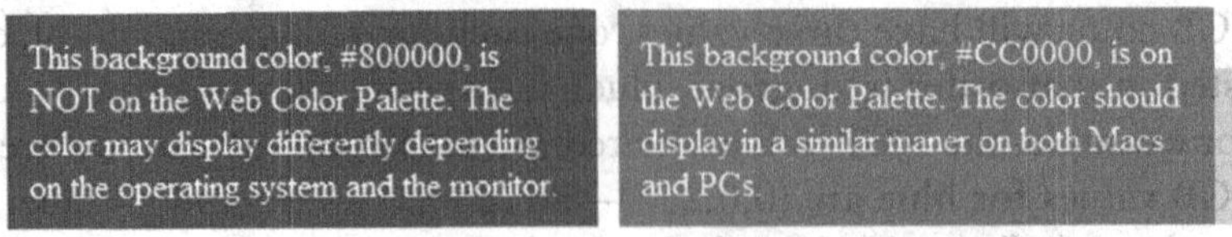

Figure 3 Web safe colors display predictably

Go to the end of the chapter for a full color version of this figure

a comparison of a Web Safe Color, `#CC0000`, and a non-Web safe color, `#880000`. Both are a shade of red; however, the Web safe color will display predictably across Windows and Mac OS platforms and the other color will not. Using Web safe colors has become less important now that most monitors display billions of colors. The Web Color Palette is rather limited and it is common for today's Web designers to choose colors creatively rather than select them from the Web Color Palette.

Making Color Choices

You may be wondering how to select colors to display on Web pages. One easy way to choose colors is to use a monochromatic color scheme—all shades or tints of the same color. Try the Color Blender at http://meyerweb.com/eric/tools/color-blend to select colors for a monochromatic color scheme. Another way to create a color scheme is to base it on a photograph or image. Visit http://www.colr.org to generate a color scheme based on an image from the Web or one that you upload. If you have a favorite color and would like to create a color scheme around it, visit one of the following sites that suggest color schemes:

- http://colorsontheweb.com/colorwizard.asp
- http://kuler.Adobe.com
- http://www.leestreet.com/QuickColor.swf
- http://colorschemedesigner.com/
- http://www.colorjack.com/articles/color_formulas.html

Accessibility and Color

Focus on Accessibility

While using color can help you create a compelling Web page, keep in mind that not all your visitors will see or be able to distinguish between colors. Some visitors will use a screen reader and will not experience your colors, so your information must be clearly conveyed even if colors cannot be viewed. Other visitors may be challenged with color vision deficiency (color blindness) and will not see the colors as you intended. According to Vischeck (http://www.vischeck.com/vischeck/) about 1 out of 20 people experience some type of color deficiency. To increase Web page accessibility, choose background and text colors with a high amount of contrast. The choice of colors is important—avoid using red, green, brown, gray, or purple next to each other. White, black, and shades of blue and yellow are easier for individuals with color vision deficiencies to differentiate. Visit http://www.vischeck.com/vischeck/vischeckURL.php to simulate how a person with a color deficiency experiences the colors on a Web page.

3 Configuring Color with Inline CSS

Now that you are aware of how color on Web pages is specified and where to get ideas for color schemes on Web pages, let's start configuring color with inline styles. **Inline styles** are coded as attributes on XHTML tags.

The Style Attribute

The **`style` attribute** is used with the value of the style rule declaration you need to set. Recall that a declaration consists of a property and a value. Each property is separated from its value with a colon (:). The following code will set the text color of an `<h1>` tag to a shade of red:

```
<h1 style="color:#cc0000">This is displayed as a red heading</h1>
```

If there is more than one property, they are separated by a semicolon (;). The following code configures the heading with a red text color and a gray background color.

```
<h1 style="color:#cc0000;background-color:#cccccc">This is displayed
as a red heading on a gray background</h1>
```

The following code example uses an inline style to set the background color to `green` and text color to `white`:

```
<p style="background-color:green;color:white">This paragraph is using
an inline style.</p>
```

FAQ: Are there different ways to configure colors using CSS?

CSS syntax allows you to configure colors in a number of ways, including hexadecimal color values, color names, and decimal color values. For example, Table 2 shows the syntax for setting the color of text in a paragraph to red.

The examples in this text use either hexadecimal color value or color name to configure colors using CSS. The color chart on this text's companion Web site at http://webdevfoundations.net/color provides examples of the color created by hexadecimal values in the Web Color Palette.

Table 2 Syntax for setting the color of text in a paragraph to red

CSS Syntax	Color Type
`p { color: red }`	Color name
`p { color: #FF0000 }`	Hexadecimal color value
`p { color: #F00 }`	Shorthand hexadecimal (one character for each hexadecimal pair)
`p { color: rgb(255,0,0) }`	Decimal color value (RGB triplet)

HANDS-ON PRACTICE 1

By now you are aware that the best way to learn new coding technologies is to practice them. In this Hands-On Practice you will configure a paragraph using inline styles. The styles will specify a green background with white text. A sample is shown in Figure 4.

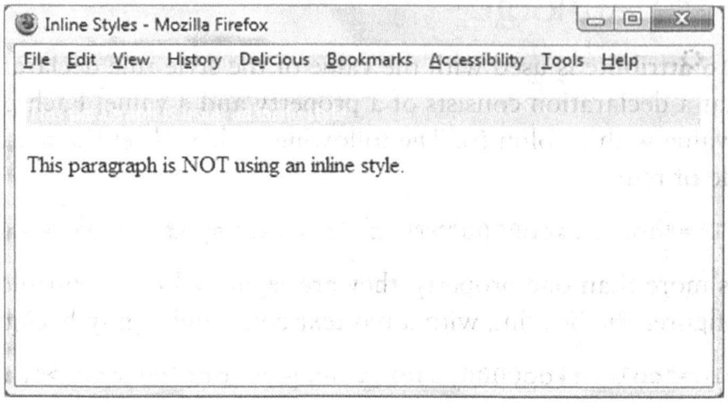

Figure 4
Web page using inline styles

Launch Notepad and type in the following XHTML:

```
<!DOCTYPE html PUBLIC "-//W3C//DTD XHTML 1.0 Transitional//EN"
  "http://www.w3.org/TR/xhtml1/DTD/xhtml1-transitional.dtd">
<html xmlns="http://www.w3.org/1999/xhtml" lang="en" xml:lang="en">
<head>
<title>Inline Styles</title>
<meta http-equiv="Content-Type" content="text/html; charset=utf-8"/>
</head>
<body>
<p style="background-color:#00FF00;color:#FFFFFF">This paragraph is
using an inline style.</p>
<p>This paragraph is NOT using an inline style.</p>
</body>
</html>
```

Save your file as inline.html. Test your page in a browser and compare it with Figure 4. The student files contain a sample solution at Chapter3/inline.html. Note that the paragraph that used a style has the green background and white text. The paragraph that does not use a style is displayed using default browser settings.

4 Configuring Color with Embedded Styles

In the previous Hands-On Practice you added inline styles for one of the paragraphs. You needed to code a style attribute on the paragraph element. But what if you needed to configure the styles for ten or twenty paragraphs instead of just one. Using inline styles, you might be doing a lot of repetitive coding! While inline styles apply to one XHTML element, embedded styles apply to an entire Web page.

The Style Element

Embedded styles are placed within a **<style> element** located in the header section of a Web page. The opening `<style>` tag begins the embedded style rules and the closing `</style>` tag ends the area containing embedded style rules. When using the `<style>` tag, you do not need the `style` attribute. However, the `<style>` tag does use a **`type` attribute** that should have the value of `"text/css"`.

Figure 5
Web page using embedded styles

The following code is an example of a Web page (shown in Figure 5) that uses embedded styles to set the text color and background color of the page.

```
<!DOCTYPE html PUBLIC "-//W3C//DTD XHTML 1.0 Transitional//EN"
  "http://www.w3.org/TR/xhtml1/DTD/xhtml1-transitional.dtd">
<html xmlns="http://www.w3.org/1999/xhtml" lang="en" xml:lang="en">
<head>
<title>Embedded Styles</title>
<meta http-equiv="Content-Type" content="text/html; charset=utf-8" />
<style type="text/css">
body { background-color: #CCFFFF;
       color: #000033;
}
</style>
</head>
<body>
   <h1>Embedded Styles</h1>
   <p>This page uses embedded styles.</p>
</body>
</html>
```

Notice the way the style rules were coded with each rule on its own line. The formatting is not required for the styles to work, but it makes the styles more readable and easier to maintain than one long row of text. The styles are in effect for the entire Web page document because they were applied to the `<body>` tag using the `body` selector.

HANDS-ON PRACTICE 2

Now let's see a working example. Launch Notepad and open the starter.html file from the Chapter3 folder in the student files.

Save your page as embedded.html and test it in a browser. Your page should look similar to the one shown in Figure 6.

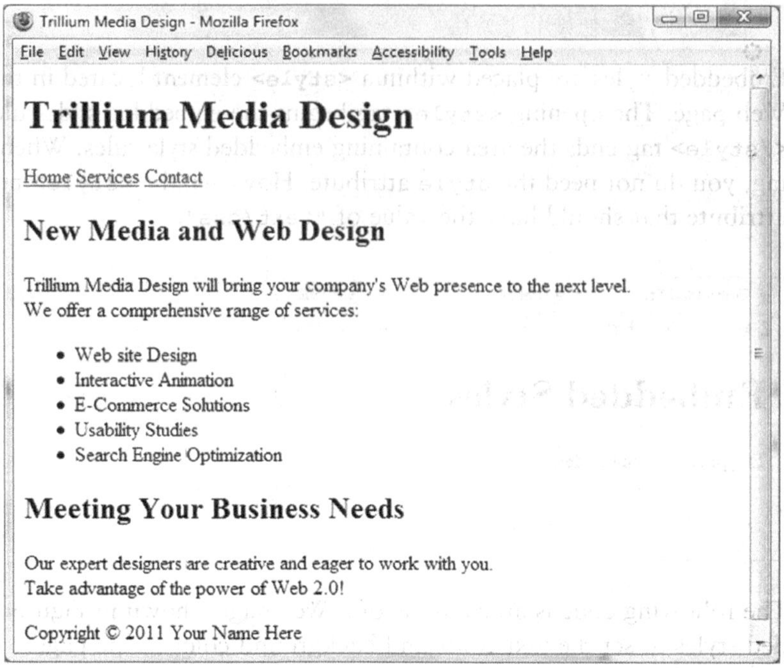

Figure 6
The Web page without any styles

Open the file in Notepad and view the source code. Notice that the XHTML code uses the `<h1>`, `<h2>`, `<p>`, `<ul>`, and `<li>` elements. In this Hands-On Practice you'll code embedded styles to configure selected background and text colors. You'll use the `body` selector to configure the default background color (`#E6E6FA`) and default text color (`#191970`) for the entire page. You'll also use the `h1` and `h2` selectors to configure different background and text colors for the heading areas.

Edit the embedded.html page in Notepad and add the following code below `<title>` element in the head section of the Web page.

```
<style type="text/css">
body {  background-color: #E6E6FA;
        color: #191970;
}
h1 {  background-color: #191970;
      color: #E6E6FA;
}
h2 {  background-color: #AEAED4;
      color: #191970;
}
</style>
```

Save and test your file in a browser. Figure 7 (shown also in the color insert section) displays the Web page along with color swatches. The monochromatic color scheme was chosen using the Color Blender at http://meyerweb.com/eric/tools/color-blend. Notice how the repetition of a limited number of colors adds interest and unifies the design of the Web page.

View the source code for embedded.html and review the CSS and XHTML code. Note that all the styles were located in a single place on the Web page. Since embedded styles are coded in a specific location, they are easier to maintain over time than inline styles. Also notice that you only needed to code the styles for the `h2` selector once (in the head

Figure 7 embedded.html with styles applied

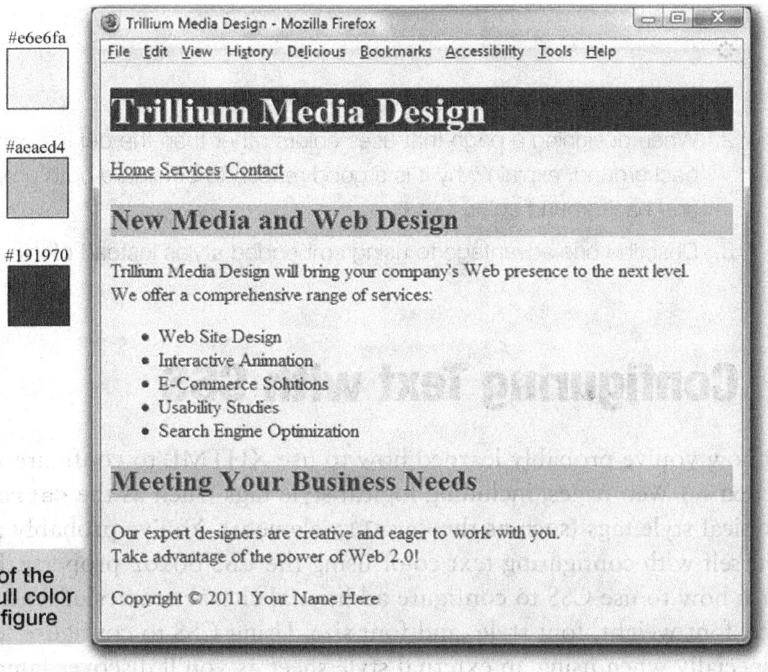

Go to the end of the chapter for a full color version of this figure

section) and *both* of the `<h2>` XHTML elements applied the `h2` style. This is more efficient than coding the same inline style on each `<h2>` element.

FAQ My CSS doesn't work, what can I do?

Coding CSS is a detail-oriented process. There are several common errors that can cause the browser not to apply CSS correctly to a Web page. With a careful review of your code and the following tips, you should get your CSS working:

- Verify that you are using the **:** and **;** symbols in the right spots—they are easy to confuse. The **:** should separate the properties from their values, the **;** should be placed between each ***property*:*value*** configuration.
- Check that you are not using = signs instead of **:** between each property and its value.
- Verify that the **{** and **}** symbols are properly placed around the style rules for each selector.
- Check the syntax of your selectors, their properties, and property values for correct usage.
- If part of your CSS works, and part doesn't—read through the CSS and check to determine the first rule that is not applied. Often the error is in the rule above the rule that is not applied.
- Use a program to check your CSS code. The W3C has a free CSS code validator at http://jigsaw.w3.org/css-validator. The W3C's CSS validator can help you find syntax errors. See Section 9 for an overview of how to use this tool to validate your CSS.

CHECKPOINT 1

1. List three reasons to use CSS on a Web page.
2. When designing a page that uses colors other than the default colors for text and background, explain why it is a good reason to configure both properties: text color and background color.
3. Describe one advantage to using embedded styles instead of inline styles.

5 Configuring Text with CSS

By now you've probably learned how to use XHTML to configure some characteristics of text on Web pages, including logical style tags (such as the `<strong>` element) and physical style tags (such as the `<small>` element). You've probably also familiarized yourself with configuring text color using the CSS `color` property. In this section you'll learn how to use CSS to configure additional characteristics of text, including font typeface, font weight, font style, and font size. Using CSS to configure text is more flexible (especially when using an external style sheet as you'll discover later in the chapter) than using XHTML elements and is the method preferred by today's Web developers.

CSS and Fonts

Let's take a closer look at the CSS properties useful for configuring fonts: `font-weight`, `font-style`, `font-size`, and `font-family`.

The **`font-weight` property** configures the boldness of the text. You can use either numeric values (`100`, `200`, `300`, `400`, `500`, `600`, `700`, `800`, and `900`) or text values (including `normal` (default), `bold`, `bolder`, and `lighter`). Configuring the CSS rule `font-weight:bold` has a similar effect as the `<strong>` or `<b>` XHTML element.

The **`font-style` property** typically is used to configure text displayed in italics (the same visual effect as an `<i>` or `<em>` XHTML element). The `font-style` property values are `normal` (default), `italic`, and `oblique`.

The **`font-size` property** sets the size of the font. There are a wide variety of text and numeric values. Text values for `font-size` include `xx-small`, `x-small`, `small`, `medium` (default), `large`, `x-large`, and `xx-large`. Valid numeric values include units of `px` (**pixels**), `pt` (standard font **point** sizes), percentage values, and `em`. Figure 8 demonstrates examples of text with various `font-size` configurations displayed in the Firefox

Figure 8
A sampling of CSS font-size values

Text Values	Em Units	Px Units	Pt Units	Percentage
xx-small	.5 em	10 px	6 pt	50%
x-small	.60 em	11 px	8 pt	60%
small	.75 em	13 px	10 pt	75%
medium	1 em	16 px	12 pt	100%
x-large	1.5 em	24 px	18 pt	150%
xx-large	2 em	28 px	24 pt	200%

browser on a monitor set to 1440×900 screen resolution. Compare font sizes on your own computer— launch a browser and view chapter3/fonts.html in the student files.

Be aware that the text values and the `pt` (**point**) unit size are browser dependent. For example, text configured with the CSS rule `font-size: 12pt` may look different when various browsers are used to display Web pages. The `px` (pixel) unit is monitor resolution dependent and looks different depending on the screen resolution used. The **em unit** is a relative font unit that has its roots in the print industry. Recall that printers used to set type manually with blocks of characters. An em unit is the width of a square block of type (typically the uppercase M) for a particular font and type size. On Web pages an em unit corresponds to the width of the font and size used in the parent element (typically the body element). With this in mind, the size of an em unit is relative to the font typeface and default size. Percentage values work in a similar manner to em units. For example, font-size: 100% and font-size: 1em should render the same in a browser.

Focus on Accessibility

With all these available choices, what's the best way to configure font-sizes? The W3C recommends the use of em units or percentages in their specification for CSS2 at http://www.w3.org/TR/REC-CSS2/fonts.html. So, usually the best choice is either em units or percentages. In addition, modern browsers such as Firefox, Opera, Google Chrome, and Internet Explorer 8 allow visitors to increase (or "zoom") the text size on the page easily even if nonrelative units, such as `px`, are used to configure font size. Expect to see more browser support of page customization and zoom features in the future. For certain graphic-dependent designs that require "pixel-perfect" rendering, `px` units might be more appropriate than `em` units or percentages—it's up to you to choose. As you work through the Hands-On Practice and Case Study exercises in this chapter, you'll gain experience using a variety of font-size configurations. In all cases, it is crucial to test your Web pages in a variety of client platforms (including browser and monitor resolution). This testing is part of the Web design and development process. Statistics available at http://thecounter.com indicate that at the time this was written Internet Explorer at 1028×768 resolution is most commonly used, although use of the Firefox browser continues to grow.

The **`font-family` property** configures font typefaces. A Web browser displays text using the fonts that have been installed on the user's computer. For example, the CSS rule `font-family: Arial` causes the browser to display text using Arial instead of the default browser font. Table 3 shows font family categories and some common font typefaces. See http://www.ampsoft.net/webdesign-l/WindowsMacFonts.html for a list of "Web-safe" fonts.

Table 3 Common fonts

Font-family Category	Font Typeface
serif	Times New Roman, Georgia, Times
sans-serif	Arial, Verdana, Geneva
monospace	Courier New, Lucida Console
cursive	Brush Script M7, Comic Sans MS
fantasy	Jokerman, Curlz MT

When a font is specified that is not installed on the Web visitor's computer, the default font is substituted. Times New Roman is the default font displayed by most Web browsers. You can list multiple fonts and categories for the value of the font face attribute. The browser will attempt to use the fonts in the order listed. When processing a CSS rule such as `font-family: Arial, Verdana, sans-serif`, the browser will use Arial if it is installed. If Arial is not installed, the browser will use Verdana if it is installed. If neither Arial nor Verdana are installed, the browser will use any sans-serif font installed on the computer. Finally, if no sans-serif fonts are installed on the computer, the default font face will be used.

Now that you are familiar with font configuration using CSS, we'll quickly explore three other CSS properties that modify the appearance of text: `text-align`, `text-decoration`, and `line-height`.

As you already know, the default alignment of text on a Web page is at the left margin, called left alignment. The **`text-align` property** is used to specify the alignment of text. Values for the `text-align` property are `left` (default), `right`, and `center`.

Have you ever seen a hyperlink on a Web page that was not underlined? This is typically configured with the **`text-decoration` property** (`text-decoration: none`). See Table 1 for additional values that are less commonly used with the `text-decoration` property.

The **`line-height` property** modifies the default height of a line of text. For example, code `line-height: 200%` to configure text to appear double-spaced.

HANDS-ON PRACTICE 3

Now that you've got a collection of new CSS properties for font and text configuration, let's try them out and modify the embedded.html page. Launch Notepad and open embedded.html. You'll code additional CSS style rules to configure the text on the page. When complete, your Web page will look similar to the one shown in Figure 9.

Figure 9
CSS configures the text on the Web page

Set Default Font Properties for the Page

As you have already seen, CSS rules applied to the `body` selector apply to the entire page. Modify the CSS for the `body` selector to display most text using a sans-serif font. The new font typeface style rule will apply to the entire Web page unless more specific styles rules are applied to a selector (such as `h1` or `p`), a class, or an id (more on classes and ids later).

```
body {  background-color: #E6E6FA;
        color: #191970;
        font-family: Arial, Verdana, sans-serif;
}
```

Save your page as embedded1.html and test it in a browser. Your page should look similar to the one shown in Figure 10. Notice that just a single line of CSS changed the font typeface of all the text on the page!

Figure 10
Text is displayed using a sans-serif font

Configure the `h1` Selector

You will configure the `line-height` and `font-family` CSS properties. Set the `line-height` property to 200%—this will add a bit of empty space above and below the heading text. (Other CSS properties, such as the margin, border, and padding are more commonly used to configure space surrounding an element.) Next, modify the `h1` selector to use a serif font. When a font name contains spaces, type quotes as indicated in the code below. While it is generally recognized that blocks of text using sans-serif fonts are easier to read, it is common to use a serif font to configure page or section headings.

```
h1 {  background-color: #191970;
      color: #E6E6FA;
      line-height: 200%;
      font-family: Georgia, "Times New Roman", serif;
}
```

Save and test your page in a browser. If you notice that the Trillium Media Design text seems to crowd the left margin, add a ` ` nonbreaking space special character in the body of the Web page after the opening <h1> tag.

Configure the `h2` Selector

Configure the CSS rule to use the same font typeface as the `h1` selector.

```
h2 { background-color: #AEAED4;
     color: #191970;
     font-family: Georgia, "Times New Roman", serif;
}
```

Add a New Paragraph Element Selector

Configure text in paragraphs to display just slightly smaller than the default text size. Use the `font-size` property set to `.90em`.

```
p { font-size: .90em; }
```

Configure the Unordered List

Configure the text displayed in the unordered list to be bold.

```
ul { font-weight: bold; }
```

Save your page as embedded2.html and test it in a browser. Your page should look similar to the one shown in Figure 9. The student files contain a sample solution at Chapter3/embedded2.html. CSS is quite powerful—just a few lines of code significantly changed the appearance of the Web page. You may be wondering if even more customization is possible. For example, what if you did not want all the paragraphs to display in exactly the same way? While you could add inline styles to the Web page code, that's usually not the most efficient technique. The next section introduces the CSS `class` and `id` selectors, which are widely utilized to configure specific page elements.

FAQ

Is there a quick way to apply the same styles to more than one XHTML tag or more than one class?

Yes, you can apply the same style rules to multiple selectors (such as XHTML elements, `classes`, or `ids`) by listing the selectors in front of the rule. The code sample below shows the `font-size` of `1em` being applied to both the paragraph and line item elements.

```
p, li { font-size: 1em; }
```

6 The `Class` and `Id` Selectors

The `Class` Selector

There are times when you'd like to apply a CSS rule to a certain class of elements on a Web page and not necessarily tie the style to a particular XHTML tag. This is when you use the **class selector**. For example, perhaps you would prefer if the paragraph containing the navigation area information in embedded2.html was displayed with large, bold text. When setting a style for a class, configure the class name as the selector. Place a dot or period (.) in front of the class name in the style sheet. The following code configures a class called nav in a style sheet.

```
.nav { font-weight: bold;
       font-size: 1.25em;
}
```

The styles set in the nav class can be applied to any XHTML element you wish. You do this by using the **class attribute**, such as `class="nav"`. Do not write the dot in front of the class value in the XHTML tag where the class is being applied. The following code will apply the nav class styles to a <p> element:

```
<p class="nav">This paragraph will be displayed using the styles in
the nav class.</p>
```

FAQ

Why is the class called nav?

You can choose almost any name you wish for a CSS class. However, CSS class names are more flexible and easier to maintain over time if they are descriptive of the structure rather than of specific formatting. For example, a class name of `largeBold` would no longer be meaningful if the design was changed to display the area differently; but a structural class name such as `nav`, `logo`, `footer`, `content`, or `subheading` is meaningful regardless of how the area is configured. Here are more hints for class names:

- Use short but descriptive names.
- Avoid class names that are the same as XHTML element names—they could be confusing to anyone working on the page.
- Both letters and numbers may be used.
- Avoid spaces in class names.
- Class names are not case sensitive, but consistency will make page maintenance easier.

A final tip about CSS classes is to be wary of "classitis"— that is, creating a brand new class each time you need to configure text a bit differently. Decide ahead of time how you will configure page areas, code your classes, and apply them. The result will be a more cohesive and better organized Web page.

The `Id` Selector

Use an **id selector** instead of a `class` selector if you plan to identify and apply a CSS rule uniquely to a single area on a Web page. For example, perhaps you would prefer if the paragraph containing the copyright information in the page footer area of embedded2.html was displayed with small italics text. While a `class` selector could be used, an `id` selector is more appropriate if your page layout contains a single footer area. For example, you can create a style for an `id` named `footer` to configure the footer area to use small, italicized text. When setting a style for an `id`, place a hash mark (`#`) in front of the `id` name in the style sheet. The following code will configure an `id` called `footer` in a style sheet:

```
#footer {  font-size: .75em;
           font-style: italic;
}
```

The styles set in the `footer id` can be applied to any XHTML element you wish by using the **id attribute**, `id="footer"`. Do not write the `#` in front of the `id` value in the XHTML tag.

The following code will apply the `footer id` styles to a `<p>` tag:

```
<p id="footer">This paragraph will be displayed using styles
configured in the footer id.</p>
```

Using CSS with an `id` selector is similar to using CSS with a `class` selector. It's common practice to use an `id` selector to refer to a *single* XHTML element and a `class` selector to refer to multiple XHTML elements.

HANDS-ON PRACTICE 4

In this Hands-On Practice you will modify the CSS and the XHTML in the Trillium Technologies page—configuring the navigation and page footer areas. Launch Notepad and open embedded2.html.

Configure the Navigation Area

The navigation links would be more prominent if they displayed in a larger and bolder font. Create a class named nav, which sets the `font-size` and `font-weight` properties. The code follows:

```
.nav { font-weight: bold;
       font-size: 1.25em;
}
```

Modify the opening paragraph tag of the navigation area. Add a `class` attribute that associates the paragraph with the nav class as follows:

```
<p class="nav"><a href="index.html">Home</a>
<a href="services.html">Services</a>
<a href="contact.html">Contact</a></p>
```

Configure the Footer Area

Create an `id` named `footer`, which sets the `font-size` and `font-style` properties.

```
#footer { font-size: .75em;
          font-style: italic;
}
```

Modify the opening paragraph tag of the `footer` area. Add an `id` attribute that associates the paragraph with the `id` class.

```
<p id="footer">Copyright &copy; 2011 Your Name Here</p>
```

Figure 11 Using classes and ids

Save your file embedded3.html and test it in a browser. Your page should look similar to the image shown in Figure 11. The student files contain a sample solution at Chapter3/embedded3.html. Notice how the class and id styles are applied.

7 The Div and Span XHTML Elements

The **<div>** and **<span>** XHTML elements are used along with CSS to format page areas. The block-level <div> element configures a section or division on a Web page with a line break above and below. Use the <div> tag when you need to format a section that is separated from the rest of the Web page by line breaks. The <div> element is also useful to define a section that contains block-level elements, such as <p>, <blockquote>, <ul>, <ol>, and even other <div> elements within it.

In contrast, the <span> element defines a section on a Web page that is *not* physically separated from other areas by line breaks. Use the <span> tag if you need to format an area that is contained within another, such as within a <p>, <blockquote>, <li>, or <div> element.

HANDS-ON PRACTICE 5

You will experiment with the <div> and <span> elements in this Hands-On Practice. First, you will place the navigation area within a <div> element. Next, you will configure a new class to format the company name when displayed within the text on the page and use the <span> element to apply this class. Open the embedded3.html file in Notepad. Your Web page will look similar to the one shown in Figure 12 after the changes are complete.

Figure 12
This Web page uses <div> and <span> elements

Configure the Navigation Area

View the source code of embedded3.html and notice that the hyperlinks (anchor elements) in the navigation area are contained within a paragraph element. While this is valid XHTML, it isn't the best choice *semantically* since the navigation is a list of hyperlinks and not a true paragraph of text. Replace the <p> tags with <div> tags as follows:

```
<div class="nav"><a href="index.html">Home</a>
<a href="services.html">Services</a>
<a href="contact.html">Contact</a></div>
```

Save your file as embedded4.html and test in a browser. You'll notice that the navigation area does not look any different— however, "under the hood" the code is better semantically.

Configure the Company Name

View Figure 12 and notice that the company name, Trillium Technologies, is displayed in bold and serif font within the first paragraph. You'll code both CSS and XHTML to accomplish this. First, create a new CSS rule that configures a class called `companyname` as bold, serif font, and 1.25em in size. The code follows:

```
.companyname {  font-weight: bold;
                font-family: Georgia, "Times New Roman", serif;
                font-size: 1.25em;
}
```

Next, modify the beginning of the first paragraph of XHTML to use the <span> element to apply the class as follows:

```
<p><span class="companyname">Trillium Media Design</span> will bring
```

Save your file and test in a browser. Your page should look similar to the one shown in Figure 12. The student files contain a sample solution at Chapter3/embedded4.html.

8 Using External Style Sheets

External style sheets are contained in a text file separate from the XHTML documents. The `<link />` element is a self-contained tag used in the header section of an XHTML document to associate the style sheet with the Web page. This allows multiple Web pages to link to the same external style sheet file. The external style sheet text file is saved with the file extension .css and contains style rules only—it does not contain any XHTML tags.

The advantage of this technique is that styles are configured in a single file. This means that when styles need to be modified only one file needs to be changed, instead of multiple Web pages. On large sites this can save a Web developer much time and increase productivity. Let's get some practice with this useful technique.

HANDS-ON PRACTICE 6

Launch Notepad and type in the style rules to set the `background-color` of a page to blue and the text to white. Save it as color.css. The code is as follows:

```
body {  background-color: #0000FF;
        color: #FFFFFF;
}
```

Figure 13 shows the external color.css style sheet displayed in Notepad. Notice that there is no XHTML in this file. `<style>` tags are not coded within an external style sheet. Only CSS rules (selectors, properties, and values) are coded in an external style sheet.

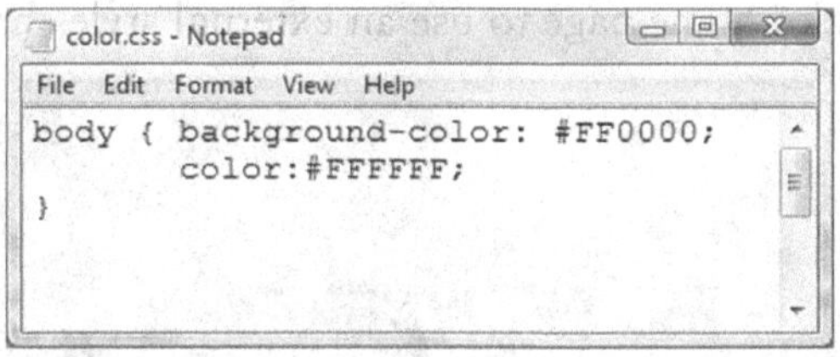

Figure 13 The external style sheet `color.css`

Next, associate that style to a Web page using the `<link />` element in the header section of the page. Three attributes are used with the `<link />` element to associate a Web page with an external style sheet: `rel`, `href`, and `type`. The value of the **`rel` attribute** is `stylesheet`. The value of the `href` attribute is the name of the style sheet file. The value of the `type` attribute is `text/css`, which is the MIME type for a style sheet. The XHTML code to link color.css to a Web page is as follows:

```
<link rel="stylesheet" href="color.css" type="text/css" />
```

Ready to try it out? Launch Notepad and type in the following XHTML:

```
<!DOCTYPE html PUBLIC "-//W3C//DTD XHTML 1.0 Transitional//EN"
  "http://www.w3.org/TR/xhtml1/DTD/xhtml1-transitional.dtd">
```

```
<html xmlns="http://www.w3.org/1999/xhtml" lang="en" xml:lang="en">
<head>
<title>External Styles</title>
<meta http-equiv="Content-Type" content="text/html; charset=utf-8"/>
<link rel="stylesheet" href="color.css" type="text/css" />
</head>
<body>
  <p>This web page uses an external style sheet.</p>
</body>
</html>
```

Save the file as external.html in the same folder as color.css. Test your page in a browser. Your file should look similar to Figure 14.

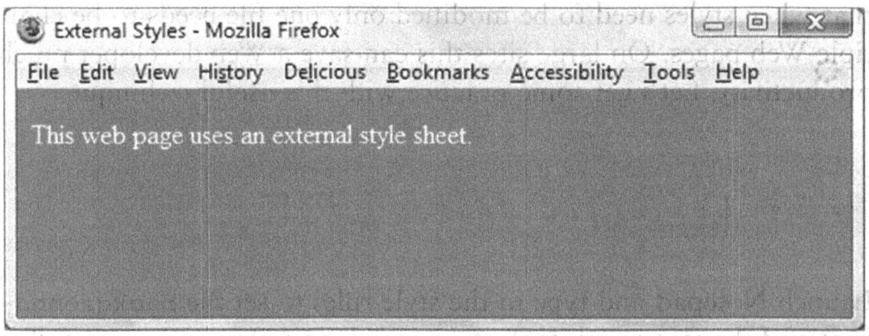

Figure 14
This page is associated with an external style sheet

The color.css style sheet can be associated with any number of Web pages. If you ever need to change the style of formatting, you only need to change a single file (color.css) instead of multiple files (all the Web pages). As mentioned earlier, this technique can boost productivity on a large site.

This is a simple example, but the advantage of having only a single file to update is significant for both small and large Web sites. In the next Hands-On Practice you'll modify the Trillium Technologies home page to use an external style sheet.

HANDS-ON PRACTICE 7

In this Hands-On Practice you continue to gain experience using external style sheets as you create the external style sheet file named trillium.css, modify the Trillium Technologies home page to use external styles instead of embedded styles, and associate a second Web page with the trillium.css style sheet.

A version of the Trillium home page is in the student files. Open the embedded4.html file in a browser. The display should be the same as the Web page shown in Figure 12 from Hands-On Practice 5.

Now that you've seen what you're working with let's begin. Launch Notepad and save the file as index.html in a folder called trillium. You are ready to convert the embedded

CSS to external CSS. Select the CSS rules (all the lines of code between, but not including, the opening and closing `<style>` tags). Use Edit, Copy or press the Ctrl+C keys to copy the CSS code to the clipboard. You will place the CSS in a new file. Launch Notepad, paste the CSS style rules (use Edit, Paste or press the Ctrl+V keys), and save the file as trillium.css. See Figure 15 for a screenshot of the new trillium.css file in Notepad. Notice that there are no XHTML elements in trillium.css— not even the `<style>` element. The file contains CSS rules only.

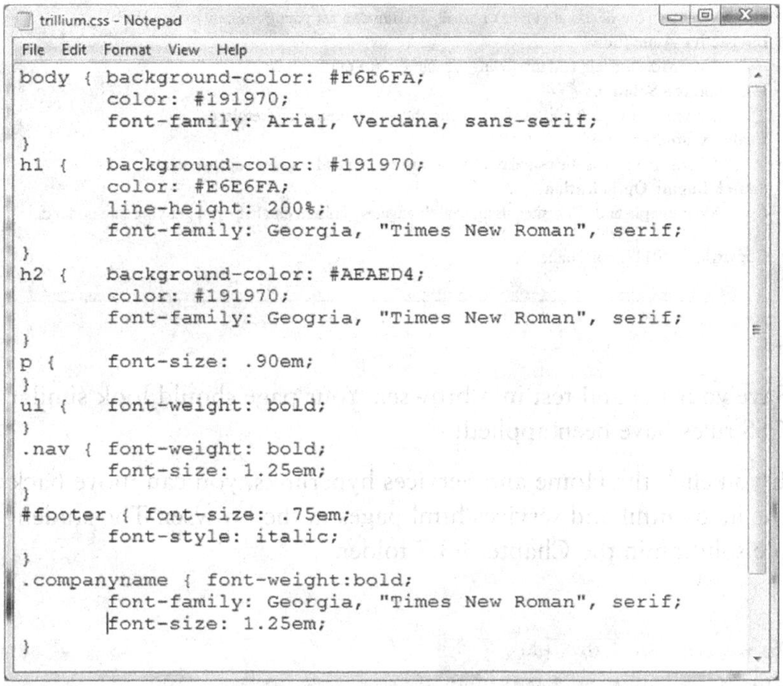


```
body { background-color: #E6E6FA;
       color: #191970;
       font-family: Arial, Verdana, sans-serif;
}
h1 {   background-color: #191970;
       color: #E6E6FA;
       line-height: 200%;
       font-family: Georgia, "Times New Roman", serif;
}
h2 {   background-color: #AEAED4;
       color: #191970;
       font-family: Geogria, "Times New Roman", serif;
}
p {    font-size: .90em;
}
ul {   font-weight: bold;
}
.nav { font-weight: bold;
       font-size: 1.25em;
}
#footer { font-size: .75em;
       font-style: italic;
}
.companyname { font-weight:bold;
       font-family: Georgia, "Times New Roman", serif;
       font-size: 1.25em;
}
```

Figure 15
The external style sheet named trillium.css

Next, edit the index.html file in Notepad. Delete the CSS code you just copied. Delete the closing `</style>` tag. Replace the opening `<style>` tag with a `<link>` element to associate the style sheet named `trillium.css`. The `<link>` element code follows:

```
<link href="trillium.css" rel="stylesheet" type="text/css" />
```

Save the file and test in a browser. Your Web page should look just like the one shown in Figure 12. Although it looks the same, the difference is in the code—the page now uses external instead of embedded CSS.

Now, for the fun part—you'll associate a second page with the style sheet. The student files contain a services.html page for Trillium at Chapter3/services.html. When you display this page in a browser it should look similar to the one shown in Figure 16. Notice that although the structure of the page is similar to the home page, the styling of the text and colors are absent.

Launch Notepad to edit the services.html file. If you view the XHTML code you'll notice that this page is ready for our trillium.css styles—for example, the `nav` class and `footer` id have been coded as attributes in the corresponding navigation and page footer areas. All that's left for you to do is to code an XHTML `<link>` element to associate the services.html Web page with the trillium.css external style sheet. Place the following code in the header section above the closing `</head>` tag:

```
<link href="trillium.css" rel="stylesheet" type="text/css" />
```

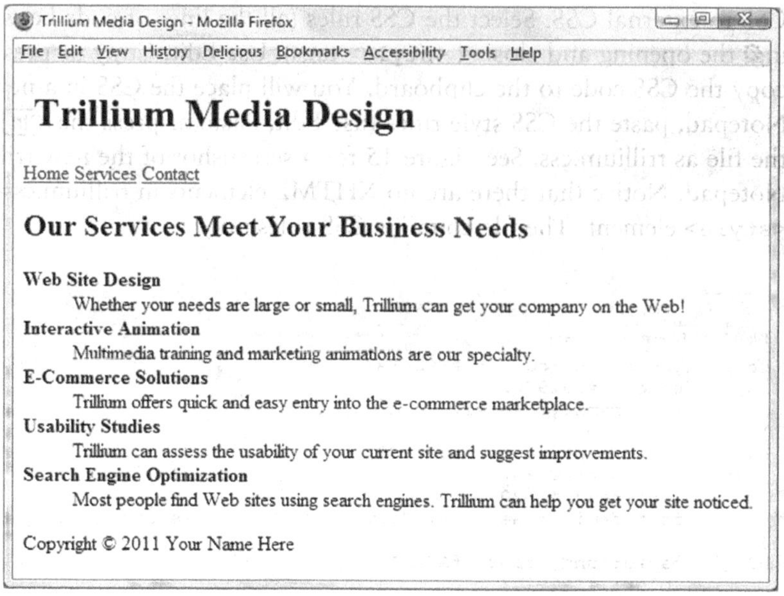

Figure 16 The services.html page is not associated with a style sheet

Save your file and test in a browser. Your page should look similar to Figure 17—the CSS rules have been applied!

If you click the Home and Services hyperlinks, you can move back and forth between the index.html and services.html pages in the browser. The student files contain a sample solution in the Chapter3/3.7 folder.

Figure 17 The services.html page has been associated with trillium.css

Notice that when using an external style sheet, if the use of color or fonts on the page ever needs to be changed, modifications only need to be made to the external style sheet. Think about how this can improve productivity on a site with many pages. Instead of modifying hundreds of pages to make a color or font change, only a single file—the CSS external style sheet— needs to be updated. Becoming comfortable with CSS and other technologies such as Extensible Style Sheet Language (XSL) will be important as you develop your skills and increase your technical expertise.

CHECKPOINT 2

1. Describe a reason to use embedded styles. Explain where embedded styles are placed on a Web page.
2. Describe a reason to use external styles. Explain where external styles are placed and how Web pages indicate they are using external styles.
3. Write the code to configure a Web page to associate with an external style sheet called `mystyles.css`.

FAQ

When designing a new Web page or Web site, how do I begin to work with CSS?

The following guidelines can be helpful when configuring a page using CSS:

- Review the design of the page—check if common fonts are used. Define global properties (the default for the entire page) for characteristics such as fonts and colors attached to the `body` selector.
- Identify typical elements used for organization in the page (such as `<h1>`, `<h3>`, and so on) and declare style rules for these if different from default.
- Identify various page areas such as logo, navigation, footer, and so on—and list any special configurations needed for these areas. You may decide to configure classes or ids in your CSS to configure these areas.
- Create one prototype page that contains most of the elements you plan to use and test. Revise your CSS as needed.
- Plan and test. These are important activities when designing a Web site.

9 Centering XHTML Elements with CSS

Recall that by default, XHTML elements are left-aligned— they begin at the left margin. You can use the XHTML `align="center"` attribute to center text on a Web page. While this is valid, it is more efficient to configure the alignment using CSS. The CSS `text-align` property configures the alignment of text. The CSS code sample below configures an `<h1>` XHTML element to have centered text.

```
h1 { text-align:center;
}
```

While it can be quite effective to center the text displayed in Web page headings, be careful about centering text in paragraphs. According to WebAIM (http://www.webaim.org/techniques/textlayout), studies have shown that centered text is more difficult to read than left-aligned text.

Center the Page Content

A popular page layout design that is easy to accomplish with just a few lines of CSS is to center the entire content of a Web page within a browser window. The Web page shown in Figure 18 uses this type of page layout.

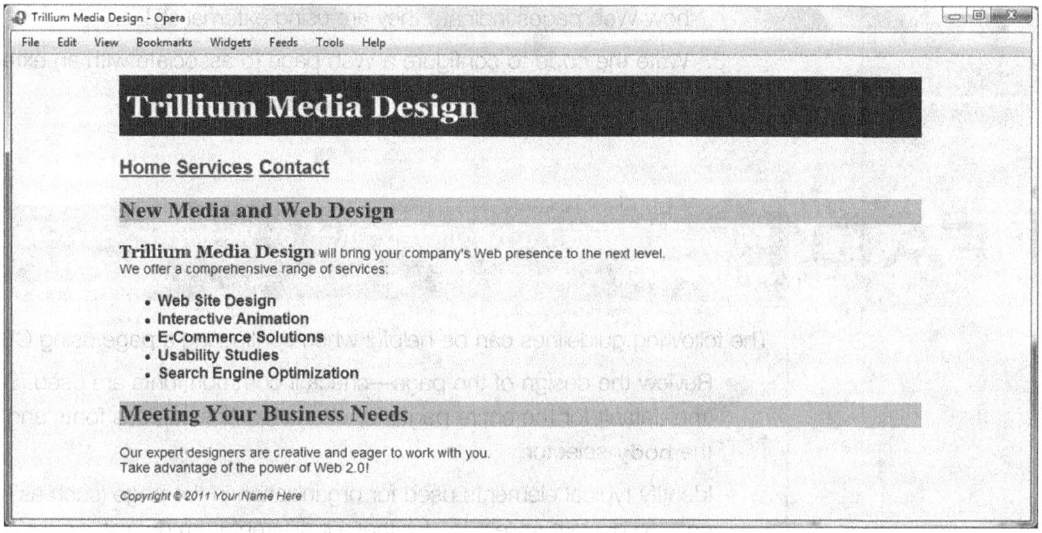

Figure 18
The Web page content is centered in the browser window

Compare the left and right margins of Figure 18 to the Web page displayed in Figure 12. It's easy to configure this centered layout. Create a `<div>` to contain, or wrap, the page content and then configure it with the CSS **`margin-left` property**, **`margin-right` property**, and **`width` property**. The margin is the empty space surrounding an element. In the case of the body element, the margin is the empty space between the page content and the edges of the browser window. As you might expect, the `margin-left` and `margin-right` properties configure the space in the left and right margins. The margins can be set to 0, pixel units, em units, percentages, or `auto`. When `margin-left` and `margin-right` are both set to `auto`, the browser calculates the amount of space available and divides it evenly between the left and right margins. The `width` property configures the width of a block-level element. The CSS code sample below sets the width of an `id` named `wrapper` to 700 pixels and centered (using `margin-left:auto` and `margin-right:auto`).

```
#wrapper { width: 700px;
           margin-left: auto;
           margin-right: auto;
}
```

The XHTML code follows:

```
<body>
  <div id="wrapper">
  ... page content goes here
  </div>
</body>
```

HANDS-ON PRACTICE 8

In this Hands-On Practice you will code CSS properties to configure a centered page layout. We'll use the files from Hands-On Practice 7 as a starting point. Create a new folder called trillium2. Locate the Chapter3/3.7 folder in the student files. Copy the index.html, services.html, and trillium.css files to your trillium2 folder. Open the trillium.css file in a text editor. Create an id named `container`. Add the `margin-left`, `margin-right`, and `width` style properties to the style rules as follows:

```
#container { margin-left: auto;
             margin-right: auto;
             width:80%;
}
```

Save the file.

Open the index.html file in a text editor. Add the XHTML code to configure a `<div>` assigned to the id `container` that "wraps" or contains the code within the body section. Save the file. When you test your index.html file in a browser, it should look similar to the one shown in Figure 18. The student files contain a sample solution in the Chapter3/3.8 folder.

10 CSS Validation

The W3C has a free Markup Validation Service (http://jigsaw.w3.org/css-validator/) that will validate your CSS code and check it for syntax errors. **CSS validation** provides students with quick self-assessment—you can prove that your code uses correct syntax. In the working world, CSS validation serves as a quality assurance tool. Invalid code may cause browsers to render the pages slower than otherwise.

HANDS-ON PRACTICE 9

In this Hands-On Practice you will use the W3C CSS Validation Service to validate an external CSS style sheet. This example uses the color.css file completed in Hands-On Practice 6 (student files Chapter3/color.css). Locate color.css and open it in Notepad. We will add an error to the color.css file. Find the `body` selector style rule and delete the first "r" in the `background-color` property. Remove the `#` from the `color` property value. Save the file.

Next, attempt to validate the color.css file. Visit the W3C CSS Validation Service page at http://jigsaw.w3.org/css-validator and select the "by File Upload" tab. Click the Browse button and select the color.css file from your computer. Click the Check button. Your display should be similar to that shown in Figure 19. Notice that two errors were found. The selector is listed followed by the reason an error was noted.

Figure 19
The validation results indicate errors

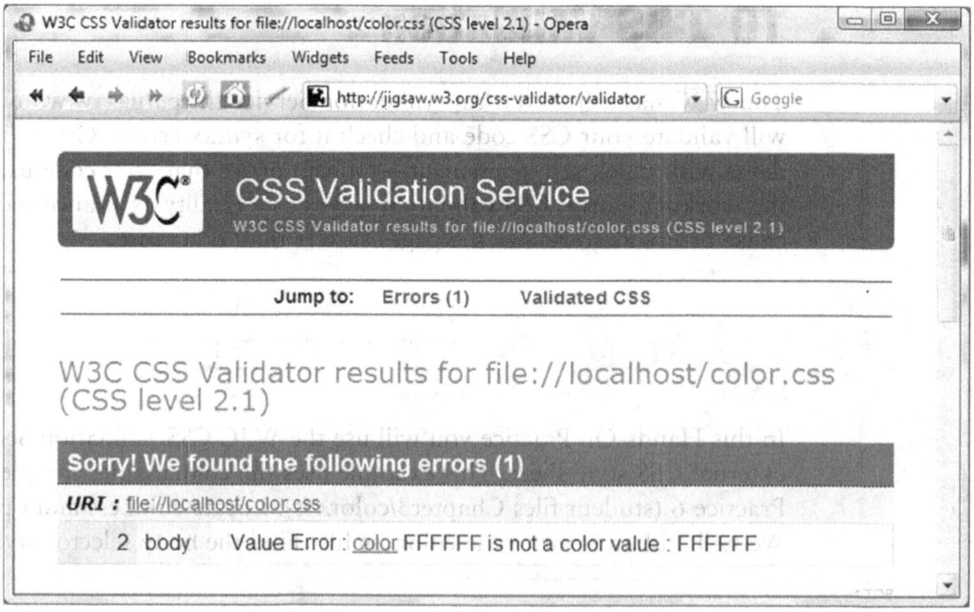

Figure 20
The valid CSS is displayed below the errors (and warnings, if any)

Notice that the first message in Figure 19 indicates that the "backgound-color" property does not exist. This is a clue to check the syntax of the property name. Edit color.css and correct the error. Test and revalidate your page. Your browser should now look similar to the one shown in Figure 20 and report only one error.

The error reminds you that `FFFFFF` is not a color value and expects you to already know that you need to add a "#" character to code a valid color value, **`#FFFFFF`**. Notice how any valid CSS rules are displayed below the error messages. Correct the color value, save the file, and test again.

Your results should look similar to those shown in Figure 21. There are no errors listed. The Valid CSS Information contains all the CSS style rules in color.css. This means your file passed the CSS validation test. Congratulations, your color.css file is valid CSS syntax! It's a good practice to validate your CSS style rules. The CSS validator can help you to identify code that needs to be corrected quickly and indicate which style rules a browser is likely to consider valid. Validating CSS is one of the many productivity techniques that Web developers commonly use.

Figure 21
The CSS is valid!

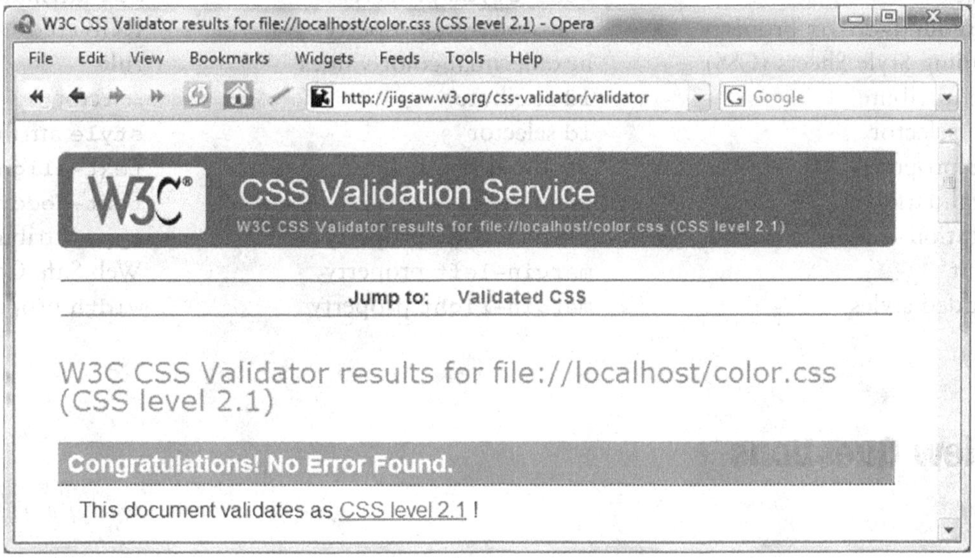

CHAPTER SUMMARY

This chapter introduced Cascading Style Sheet rules associated with color and text on Web pages. There is much more that you can do with CSS: positioning, hiding and showing page areas, formatting margins, and formatting borders. As you continue your study of Web development, you will study these additional uses. To learn more about CSS, check out the tutorials at http://echoecho.com/css.htm and http://www.w3schools.com/css/, or visit the W3C site for official specifications.

Visit http://www.webdevfoundations.net for examples, the links listed in this chapter, and updated information.

Key Terms

`<div>`
`<link />`
`<span>`
`<style>`
`background-color` property
Cascading Style Sheets (CSS)
`class` attribute
`class` selector
`color` property
CSS validation
declaration
em unit
embedded styles
external styles
`font-family` property
`font-size` property
`font-style` property
`font-weight` property
hexadecimal color values
`id` attribute
`id` selector
imported styles
inline styles
`line-height` property
`margin-left` property
`margin-right` property
pixels
point
property
`rel` attribute
RGB color
rule
selector
`style` attribute
`text-align` property
`text-decoration` property
`type` attribute
Web Safe Color Palette
`width` property

Review Questions

Multiple Choice

1. Which of the following can be a CSS selector?
   a. an XHTML element
   b. a class name
   c. an id name
   d. all of the above

2. Which of the following is the CSS property used to set the background color of a Web page?
   a. `bgcolor`
   b. `background-color`
   c. `color`
   d. none of the above

3. Which type of CSS is coded in the body of the Web page as an attribute of an XHTML tag?
   a. embedded
   b. inline
   c. external
   d. imported

4. Which of the following describe two components of CSS rules?
   a. selectors and declarations
   b. properties and declarations
   c. selectors and attributes
   d. none of the above

5. Which of the following associates a Web page with an external style sheet?

a. `<style rel="external" href="style.css">`
b. `<style src="style.css">`
c. `<link rel="stylesheet" type="text/css" href="style.css" />`
d. `<link rel="stylesheet" type="text/css" src="style.css" />`

6. Which of the following is the declaration property used to set the font typeface for an area of a Web page?

a. `font-face`
b. `face`
c. `font-family`
d. `size`

7. Which of the following do you configure to apply a style to only one area on a Web page?

a. group
b. class
c. id
d. none of the above

8. Where do you place the code to associate a Web page with an external style sheet?

a. in the external style sheet
b. in the DOCTYPE of the Web page document
c. in the body section of the Web page document
d. in the head section of the Web page document

9. Which of the following configures a background color of `#FFF8DC` for a Web page using CSS?

a. `body { background-color: #FFF8DC; }`
b. `document { background: #FFF8DC; }`
c. `body {bgcolor: #FFF8DC;}`
d. none of the above

10. Which of the following configures a class called news with red text, large font, and Arial or a sans-serif font using CSS?

a.
```
news {    color: red;
          font-size: large;
          font-family: Arial,
            sans-serif;}
```
b.
```
.news {   color: red;
          font-size: large;
          font-family: Arial,
            sans-serif;}
```
c.
```
.news {   text: red;
          font-size: large;
          font-family: Arial,
            sans-serif;}
```
d.
```
#news {   text: red;
          font-size: large;
          font-family: Arial,
            sans-serif;}
```

Fill in the Blank

11. The ________________ element is useful for creating logical areas on a Web page that are embedded within paragraphs or other block formatting elements.

12. CSS is a technology that is ________________ supported by browsers.

13. The ________________ CSS property can be used to center text on a Web page.

14. The ________________ element is useful for creating areas on a Web page that are physically separated from other areas.

15. CSS was first proposed as a standard by the W3C in ________________.

Apply Your Knowledge

1. Predict the Result. Draw and write a brief description of the Web page that will be created with the following XHTML code:

```
<!DOCTYPE html PUBLIC "-//W3C//DTD XHTML 1.0 Transitional//EN"
  "http://www.w3.org/TR/xhtml1/DTD/xhtml1-transitional.dtd">
<html xmlns="http://www.w3.org/1999/xhtml" lang="en" xml:lang="en">
<head>
<title>Predict the Result</title>
<meta http-equiv="Content-Type" content="text/html; charset=utf-8"/>
<style type="text/css">
```

```
body {  background-color: #000066;
        color: #CCCCCC;
        font-family: Arial,sans-serif;
}
h1 {  background-color: #FFFFFF;
      color: #000066;
}
.footer {  font-size: 80%;
           font-style: italic;
}
</style>
</head>
<body>
  <div>
    <h1>Trillium Media Design</h1>
    <br />
    <p>Home <a href="about.html">About</a>
      <a href="services.html">Services</a>
    </p>
  </div>
<p>Our professional staff takes pride in its working relationship
with our clients by offering personalized services that listen to
their needs, develop their target areas, and incorporate these
items into a well presented Web site that works.</p>
<p> </p>
<p> </p>
  <div>
  <p class="footer">Contact <a
    href="mailto:web@trilliumtechnologies.com">
    web@trilliumtechnologies.com</a><br />
  Copyright &copy; 2011 Trillium Media Design</p>
  </div>
</body>
</html>
```

2. **Fill in the Missing Code.** This Web page should be configured so that the background and text colors have good contrast. The <h2> tag should use Arial. Some CSS properties and values, indicated by "_" (underscore), are missing. Some XHTML tags, indicated by <_>, are missing. Fill in the missing code.

```
<!DOCTYPE html PUBLIC "-//W3C//DTD XHTML 1.0 Transitional//EN"
  "http://www.w3.org/TR/xhtml1/DTD/xhtml1-transitional.dtd">
<html xmlns="http://www.w3.org/1999/xhtml" lang="en" xml:lang="en">
<head>
<title>Trillium Media Design</title>
<meta http-equiv="Content-Type" content="text/html; charset=utf-8"/>
<style type="text/css">
body {  background-color: #0066CC;
        color: "_";
}
h2 {  "_": "_"
}
```

```
<_>
<_>
<body>
  <h2>Trillium Media Design</h2>
  <p> Our professional staff takes pride in its working
relationship with our clients by offering personalized services
that listen to their needs, develop their target areas, and
incorporate these items into a well presented Web site that works.
  </p>
</body>
</html>
```

3. Find the Error. Why won't this page display properly in a browser?

```
<!DOCTYPE html PUBLIC "-//W3C//DTD XHTML 1.0 Transitional//EN"
  "http://www.w3.org/TR/xhtml1/DTD/xhtml1-transitional.dtd">
<html xmlns="http://www.w3.org/1999/xhtml" lang="en" xml:lang="en">
<head>
<title>Trillium Media Design</title>
<meta http-equiv="Content-Type" content="text/html; charset=utf-8"/>
<style type="text/css">
body {  background-color: #000066;
        color: #CCCCCC;
        font-family: Arial,sans-serif;
        font-size: 12px;
}
<style>
</head>
<body>
  <h2>Trillium Media Design</h2>
  <p> Our professional staff takes pride in its working
relationship with our clients by offering personalized services
that listen to their needs, develop their target areas, and
incorporate these items into a well presented Web site that works.
  </p>
</body>
</html>
```

Hands-On Exercises

1. Write the XHTML for a paragraph that uses inline styles to configure the background color of red and the text color of white.
2. Write the XHTML and CSS code for an embedded style sheet that configures a background color of #eaeaea and a text color of #000033.
3. Write the CSS code for an external style sheet that configures the text to be brown, 1.2em in size, and in Arial, Verdana, or a sans-serif font.
4. Write the XHTML and CSS code for an embedded style sheet that configures a class called new, that is bold and italic.

5. Write the XHTML and CSS code for an embedded style sheet that configures links without underlines; background color of white; text color of black; is in Arial, Helvetica, or a sans-serif font; and has a class called `new` that is bold and italic.

6. Write the CSS code for an external style sheet that configures a page background color of `#FFF8DC`; has a text color of `#000099`; is in Arial, Helvetica, or a sans-serif font; and has an id called `new` that is bold and italic.

7. **Practice with External Style Sheets.** In this exercise you will create two external style sheet files and a Web page. You will experiment with linking the Web page to the external style sheets and note how the display of the page is changed.

   a. Create an external style sheet (call it format1.css) to format as follows: document background color of white, document text color of `#000099`, and document font family of Arial, Helvetica, or sans-serif. Hyperlinks should have a background color of gray (`#CCCCCC`). `<h1>` elements should use the Times New Roman font with red text color.

   b. Create an external style sheet (call it format2.css) to format as follows: document background color of yellow, document text color of green. Hyperlinks should have a background color of white. `<h1>` elements should use the Times New Roman font with white background color and green text color.

   c. Create a Web page about your favorite movie that displays the movie name in an `<h1>` tag, a description of the movie in a paragraph, and an unordered (bulleted) list of the main actors and actresses in the movie. The page should also have a hyperlink to a Web site about the movie. Place an e-mail link to yourself on the Web page. This page should be associated with the format1.css file. Save the page as moviecss1.html. Be sure to test your page in more than one browser. Hand in printouts of format1.css, the movieccs1.html source code (print in Notepad), and the browser display of your moviecss1.html to your instructor.

   d. Modify the moviecss1.html page to link to the format2.css external style sheet instead of the format1.css file. Save the page as moviecss2.html and test it in a browser. Notice how different the page looks! Hand in printouts of format2.css, the moviecss2.html source code (print in Notepad), and the browser display of your moviecss2.html.

8. **Practice with the Cascade.** In this exercise you will create two Web pages that link to the same external style sheet. After modifying the configuration in the external style sheet, you will test your pages again and find that they automatically pick up the new style configuration. Finally, you will add an inline style to one of the pages and find that it takes effect and overrides the external style.

   a. Create a Web page that includes an unordered list describing at least three advantages of using CSS. The text `CSS Advantages` should be contained within `<h1>` tags. This page should include a hyperlink to the W3C Web site. Write the XHTML code so that one of the advantages is configured to be a class called `news`. Place an e-mail link to yourself on the Web page. The Web page should use the external style sheet called ex3.css. Save the page as advantage.html.

   b. Create a Web page that includes an unordered list describing at least three disadvantages of utilizing Cascading Style Sheets. The text `CSS Disadvantages` should be contained within `<h1>` tags. This page should include a hyperlink to the W3C Web site. Write the XHTML code so that one of the disadvantages is configured to be a class called `news`. Place an e-mail link to yourself on the Web page. The Web page should use the external style sheet called ex3.css. Save the page as disadvantage.html.

c. Create an external style sheet (call it ex3.css) to format as follows: document background color of white, document text color of `#000099` and document font family of Arial, Helvetica, or sans-serif. Hyperlinks should have a background color of gray (`#cccccc`). `<h1>` elements should use the Times New Roman font with black text color. The news class should use red italic text.

d. Launch a browser and test your work. Display the advantage.html page. It should use the formatting configured in ex3.css. Modify the Web page and/or the css file until your page displays as requested. Display the disadvantage.html page. It should also use the formatting configured in the ex3.css file. Create printouts of ex3.css, advantage.html, disadvantage.html source code (print in Notepad), the browser display of advantage.html, and the browser display of disadvantage.html. Label these printouts Exercise 8d.

e. Change the configuration of the external style sheet (ex3.css) to use a document background color of black, document text color of white, and `<h1>` text color of gray (`#cccccc`). Save the file. Launch a browser and test the advantage.html and disadvantage.html pages. Notice how they each pick up the styles from the external style sheet. Create printouts of the advantage.html and disadvantage.html browser display and label them Exercise 8e.

f. Modify the advantage.html file to use an inline style. The inline style should be applied to the `<h1>` tag and configure it to have red text. Save the advantage.html page and test in a browser. Notice how the `<h1>` text color specified in the style sheet is overridden by the inline style. Print the browser display of advantage.html and label it Exercise 8f.

9. **Practice Validating CSS.** Choose a CSS external style sheet file to validate—perhaps you have created one for your own Web site. Otherwise, use an external style sheet file that you worked with in this chapter. Use the W3C free CSS validator. Visit http://jigsaw.w3.org/css-validator/. If your CSS does not immediately pass the validation test, modify it and test again. Repeat this process until the W3C validates your CSS code. Write a one or two paragraph summary about the validation process. Answer the following questions. Was it easy to use? Did anything surprise you? Did you encounter a number of errors or just a few? How easy was it to determine how to correct the CSS file? Would you recommend this to other students? Why or why not?

Web Research

1. This chapter introduced you to using CSS to configure Web pages. Use a search engine to search for CSS resources. The following resources can help you get started:

   - http://www.w3.org/Style/CSS/
   - http://positioniseverything.net
   - http://www.dezwozhere.com/links.html

Create a Web page that provides a list of at least five CSS resources on the Web. For each CSS resource provide the URL, Web site name, and a brief description. Your Web page should contain a table and use color. Place your name in the e-mail address at the bottom of the Web page. Print the source code (from Notepad) and the browser view of your Web page.

2. There is still much for you to learn about CSS. A great place to learn about Web technology is the Web itself. Use a search engine to search for CSS tutorials. The following resources can help you get started:

   - http://www.echoecho.com/css.htm
   - http://www.w3schools.com/css/
   - http://www.davesite.com/webstation/css/

   Choose a tutorial that is easy to read. Select a section that discusses a CSS technique that was not covered in this chapter. Create a Web page that uses this new technique. The Web page should provide the URL of your tutorial, the name of the Web site, and a description of the new technique you discovered. Place your name in the e-mail address at the bottom of the Web page. Print the external style sheet (if you used one), the Web page source code (from Notepad), and the browser view of your Web page.

Focus on Web Design

In this chapter you learned how to configure color and text with CSS. In this activity you will design a color scheme, code an external CSS file for the color scheme, and code an example Web page that applies the styles you configured. Use any of the following sites to help you get started with color and Web design ideas:

Psychology of Color

- http://www.infoplease.com/spot/colors1.html
- http://coe.sdsu.edu/eet/Articles/wadecolor/start.htm
- http://iit.bloomu.edu/vthc/Design/psychology.htm
- http://www.my-photoshop.com/bydesign/id-tutorials/color-psychology.html

Color Theory

- http://www.colormatters.com/colortheory.html
- http://colortheory.liquisoft.com/
- http://www.digital-web.com/articles/color_theory_for_the_colorblind/

Color Scheme Generators

- http://meyerweb.com/eric/tools/color-blend
- http://colorschemer.com/schemes/
- http://www.colr.org
- http://colorsontheweb.com/colorwizard.asp
- http://kuler.adobe.com/
- http://colorschemedesigner.com/

You have the following tasks:

a. Design a color scheme. List three hexadecimal color values (in addition to white (`#FFFFFF`) or black (`#000000`) in your design.
b. Describe the process you went through as you selected the colors. Describe why you chose these colors. What type of Web site would they be appropriate for? List the URLs of any resources you used.
c. Create an external CSS file name color1.css that configures font properties, text color, and background color selections for the document, `h1` selector, `p` selector, and `footer` class using the colors you have chosen.
d. Create a Web page named color1.html that shows examples of the CSS style rules.

Open your files in Notepad and print the source code for color1.css and color1.html. Display your page in a browser; print the page. Hand in all printouts to your instructor.

WEB SITE CASE STUDY: Implementing CSS

This chapter implements CSS in the following Web sites.

JavaJam Coffee House

See the Chapter "XHTML Basics" for an introduction to the JavaJam Coffee House Case Study. Figure 26 in that chapter shows a site map for the JavaJam Web site. The Home page and Menu page were created in that chapter. You will use the existing Web site as a start while you create a new version that uses an external style sheet to configure text and color.

You have the following tasks:

1. Create an external style sheet named javajam.css that configures the color and text for the JavaJam Web site.
2. Modify the Home page to utilize an external style sheet to configure colors and fonts. The new Home page and color swatches are shown in Figure 22.
3. Modify the Menu page to be consistent with the new Home page.
4. Configure centered page layout.

Figure 22
New JavaJam index.html

Go to the end of the chapter for a full color version of this figure

Hands-On Practice Case

Create a folder called javajamcss. Copy all the files from your javajam folder into the javajamcss folder.

1. **The External Style Sheet.** Launch Notepad. You will create an external style sheet named javajam.css. Code the CSS to configure the following:
   - Global styles for the document background color (`#ffffcc`), text color (`#330000`), and Verdana, Arial, or any sans-serif font
   - Style rules for the `h1` selector that configure background color (`#ccaa66`), text color (`#000000`), 200% line height, and centered text
   - Style rules for the centered navigation area (use an id named `nav`)
   - Style rules for the page footer area (use an id named `footer`) for background color (`#ccaa66`), text color (`#000000`), small font size (.60em), italics, and centered

   Save the file as javajam.css in the javajamcss folder. Check your syntax with the CSS validator (http://jigsaw.w3.org/css-validator). Correct and retest if necessary.
2. **The Home Page.** Launch Notepad and open the index.html file. You will modify this file to apply styles from the javajam.css external style sheet as follows:
   - Add a `<link />` element to associate the Web page with the javajam.css external style sheet file. Save and test your index.html page in a browser and you'll notice that the styles configured with the body and `h1` selectors are already applied!
   - Configure the navigation area. Since the navigation is not semantically a "paragraph" (a collection of sentences about a central topic), replace the `<p>` element with a `<div>` element. Assign this `<div>` to the id named `nav`.
   - Configure the content area with a div assigned to an id named "content". Code the opening div tag on a new line after the navigation div. Code the closing div tag after the end of the paragraph that contains the address and phone number.

- Configure the page footer area. Replace the <p> elements with <div> elements. Remove the <small> and <em> elements because the `font-size` and `font-style` are configured as part of the `footer` id. Assign this <div> to the id named `footer`.
- Save the index.html file and test in a browser. Your page should look similar to the one shown in Figure 22 except that your page content will be left-aligned instead of centered. Don't worry—you'll center your page layout in Step 4 of this case study.

3. **The Menu Page.** Launch Notepad and open the menu.html file. You will modify this file in a similar manner—add the <link /> element, configure the navigation area, configure a div to contain the content, and configure the page footer area. Save and test your new menu.html page. It should look similar to the one shown in Figure 23 except for the alignment.

Figure 23
New menu.html page

4. **Centered Page Layout with CSS.** Modify javajam.css, index.html, and menu.html to configure page content that is centered with width set to 80%. Refer to Hands-On Practice 8 if necessary. Save your files and retest your pages. The index.html and menu.html pages should closely match the samples shown in Figures 22 and 23.

Experiment with modifying the javajam.css file. Change the page background color, the font family, and so on. Test your pages in a browser. Isn't it amazing how a change in a single file can affect multiple files when external style sheets are used?

Fish Creek Animal Hospital

See the Chapter "XHTML Basics" for an introduction to the Fish Creek Animal Hospital Case Study. Figure 30 in that chapter shows a site map for the Fish Creek Web site. The Home page and Services page were created in that chapter. You will use the existing Web site as a start while you create a new version that uses an external style sheet to configure text and color.

You have the following tasks:

1. Create an external style sheet named fishcreek.css that configures the color and text for the Fish Creek Web site.
2. Modify the Home page to use an external style sheet to configure colors and fonts. The new Home page and color swatches are shown in Figure 24 (shown also in the color insert section).

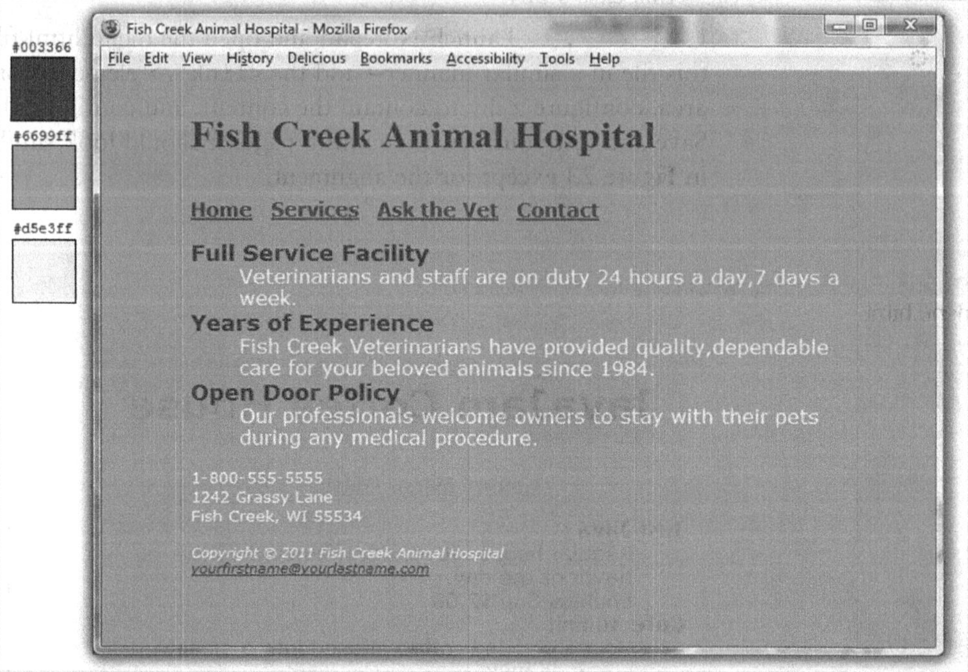

Figure 24
New Fish Creek index.html

Go to the end of the chapter for a full color version of this figure

3. Modify the Services page to be consistent with the new Home page. Configure centered page layout.

Hands-On Practice Case

Create a folder called fishcreekcss. Copy all the files from your fishcreek folder into the fishcreekcss folder.

1. **The External Style Sheet.** Launch Notepad. You will create an external style sheet named fishcreek.css. Code the CSS to configure the following:
   - Global styles for the document background color (`#6699ff`), text color (`#d5e3ff`), and Verdana, Arial, or any sans-serif font
   - Style rules for the `h1` selector that configure background color (`#6699ff`), text color (`#003366`), serif font, and 200% line height
   - Style rules for a navigation area (use an id named `nav`) that displays text in bold
   - Style rules for a class named category with bold font, background-color (`#6699ff`), text color (`#003366`), and larger font size (1.1em)
   - Style rules for the page footer area (use an id named `footer`) with a small font size (.70em) and italic text

   Save the file as fishcreek.css in the fishcreekcss folder. Check your syntax with the CSS validator (http://jigsaw.w3.org/css-validator). Correct and retest if necessary.

2. **The Home Page.** Launch Notepad and open the index.html file. You will modify this file to apply styles from the fishcreek.css external style sheet.
   - Add a `<link />` element to associate the Web page with the fishcreek.css external style sheet file. Save and test your index.html page in a browser and you'll notice that the styles configured with the `body` and `h1` selectors are already applied!
   - Configure the navigation area. Since the navigation is not semantically a "paragraph" (a collection of sentences about a central topic), replace the `<p>` element with a `<div>` element. Assign this `<div>` to the id named `nav`. Remove the `<strong>` element from this area.
   - Configure each `<dt>` element to apply the `category` class. Remove the `<strong>` elements from this area.
   - Configure the page footer area. Replace the `<p>` elements with `<div>` elements. Assign this `<div>` to the id named `footer`. Remove the `<small>` and `<em>` elements because the `font-size` and `font-style` are configured as part of the `footer` id.
   - Save the index.html file and test in a browser. Your page should look similar to the one shown in Figure 24 except that your page content will be left-aligned instead of indented from the margins. Don't worry—you'll configure your page layout in Step 4 of this case study.

3. **The Services Page.** Launch Notepad and open the services.html file. You will modify this file in a similar manner—add the `<link />` element, configure the navigation area, configure the `category` classes (use `<span>` elements), and configure the page footer area. Save and test your new services.html page. It should look similar to the one shown in Figure 25 except for the alignment.

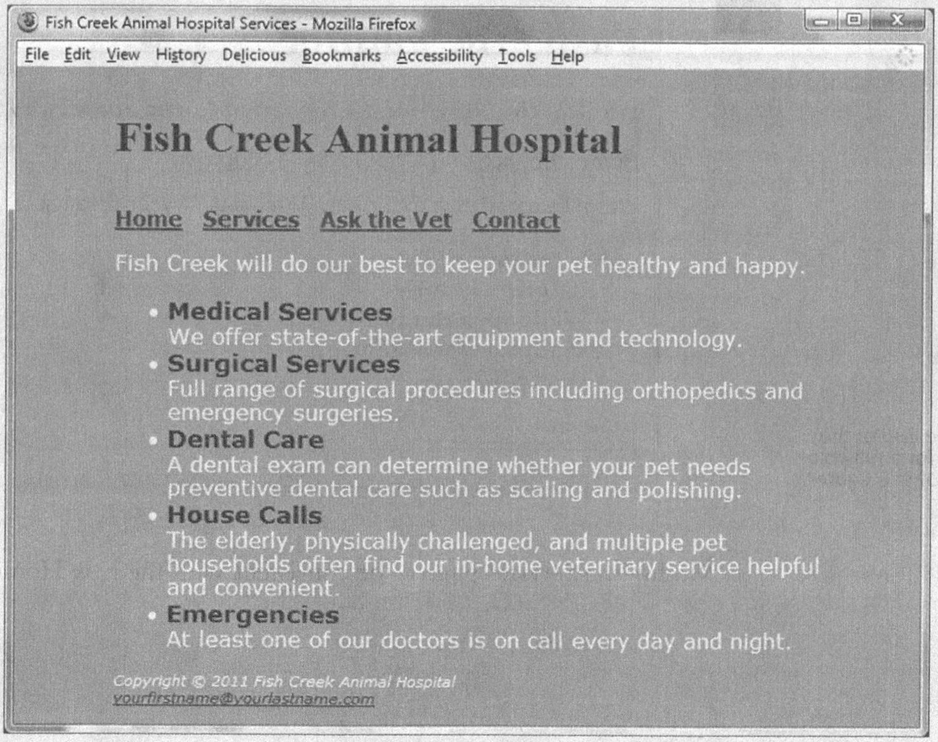

Figure 25
New services.html page

4. **Centered Page Layout with CSS.** Modify fishcreek.css, index.html, and services.html to configure page content that is centered with width set to 80%. Refer to Hands-On Practice 8 if necessary. Save your file and retest your pages. The index.html and services.html pages should closely match the samples shown in Figures 24 and 25.

Experiment with modifying the fishcreek.css file. Change the page background color, the font family, font color, and so on. Test your pages in a browser. Notice that multiple pages display differently because they link to the single file (fishcreek.css) that configures their formatting.

Pasha the Painter

See the Chapter "XHTML Basics" for an introduction to the Pasha the Painter Case Study. Figure 34 in that chapter shows a site map for the Pasha the Painter Web site. The Home page and Services page were created in that chapter. You will use the existing Web site as a start while you create a new version of this Web site that uses an external style sheet to configure text and color.

You have the following tasks:

1. Create an external style sheet named painter.css that configures the color and text for the Pasha the Painter Web site.
2. Modify the Home page to utilize an external style sheet to configure colors and fonts. The new Home page and color swatches are shown in Figure 26 (shown also in the color insert section).

Figure 26
New Pasha the Painter index.html

Go to the end of the chapter for a full color version of this figure

3. Modify the Services page to be consistent with the new Home page.

Hands-On Practice Case

Create a folder called paintercss. Copy all the files from your painter folder into the paintercss folder.

1. **The External Style Sheet.** Launch Notepad. You will create an external style sheet named painter.css. Code the CSS to configure the following:
   - Global styles for the document background color (`#ffffff`), text color (`#000000`), and Verdana, Arial, or any sans-serif font
   - Style rules for the logo class that configure background color (`#ffffff`), text color (`#336633`), and Georgia, Times New Roman, or any serif font
   - Style rules for a navigation area (use an id named `nav`) that displays text in bold
   - Style rules for a class named category with a bold, serif font, background-color (`#ffffff`), text color (`#336633`), and a larger font size (1.2em)
   - Style rules for the page footer area (use an id named `footer`) with a small font size (.60em) and italic text

   Save the file as painter.css in the paintercss folder. Check your syntax with the CSS validator (http://jigsaw.w3.org/css-validator). Correct and retest if necessary.
2. **The Home Page.** Launch Notepad and open the index.html file. You will modify this file to apply styles from the painter.css external style sheet.
   - Add a `<link />` element to associate the Web page with the prime.css external style sheet file. Save and test your index.html page in a browser and you'll notice that the styles configured with the `body` selector are already applied!
   - Configure the logo area. Code a `<div>` element that contains the `<h1>` and `<h3>` elements in the logo area. Assign the `<div>` to the logo class.
   - Configure the navigation area. Since the navigation is not semantically a "paragraph" (a collection of sentences about a central topic), replace the `<p>` element with a `<div>` element. Assign this `<div>` to the id named `nav`. Remove the `<strong>` element from this area.
   - Configure the `<ul>` to apply the `category` class.
   - Configure the page footer area. Replace the `<p>` elements with `<div>` elements. Assign this `<div>` to the id named `footer`. Remove the `<small>` and `<em>` elements because the `font-size` and `font-style` are configured as part of the `footer` id.
   - Save the index.html file and test in a browser. Your page should look similar to Figure 26.
3. **The Services Page.** Launch Notepad and open the services.html file. You will modify this file in a similar manner— add the `<link />` element, configure the logo area, configure the navigation area, configure the `category` classes (use `<span>` elements and remove the `<strong>` element from this area), and configure the page footer area. Save and test your new services.html page. It should look similar to the one shown in Figure 27.

Experiment with modifying the painter.css file. Change the page background color, the font family, and so on. Test your pages in a browser. Notice how a change in a single file can affect multiple files when external style sheets are used.

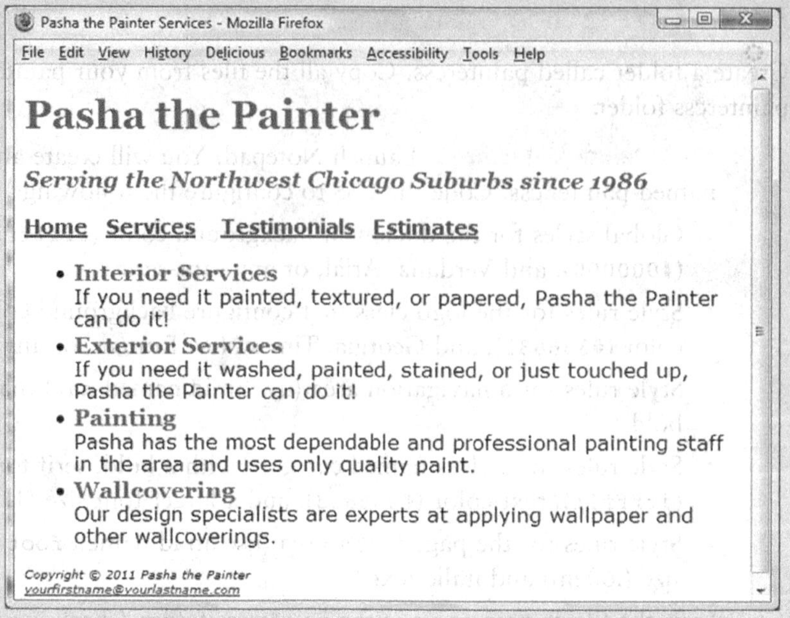

Figure 27
New services.html page

Prime Properties

See the Chapter "XHTML Basics" for an introduction to the Prime Properties Case Study. Figure 38 in that chapter shows a site map for the Prime Properties Web site. The Home page and Financing page were created in that chapter. You will use the existing Web site as a start while you create a new version of this Web site that uses an external style sheet to configure text and color.

You have the following tasks:

1. Create an external style sheet named prime.css that configures the color and text for the Prime Properties Web site.
2. Modify the Home page to use an external style sheet to configure colors and fonts. The new Home page and color swatches are shown in Figure 28 (shown also in the Color Insert Section).
3. Modify the Financing page to be consistent with the new Home page.

Hands-On Practice Case

Create a folder called primecss. Copy all the files from your prime folder into the primecss folder.

1. **The External Style Sheet.** Launch Notepad. You will create an external style sheet named prime.css. Code the CSS to configure the following:
   - Global styles for the document background color (`#ffffcc`), text color (`#003300`), and Arial, Helvetica, or any sans-serif font
   - Style rules for the `h2` selector that configure background color (`#ffffcc`) and text color (`#003366`)
   - Style rules for the `h3` selector that configure background color (`#ffffcc`) and text color (`#006600`)

Figure 28
New Prime Properties index.html

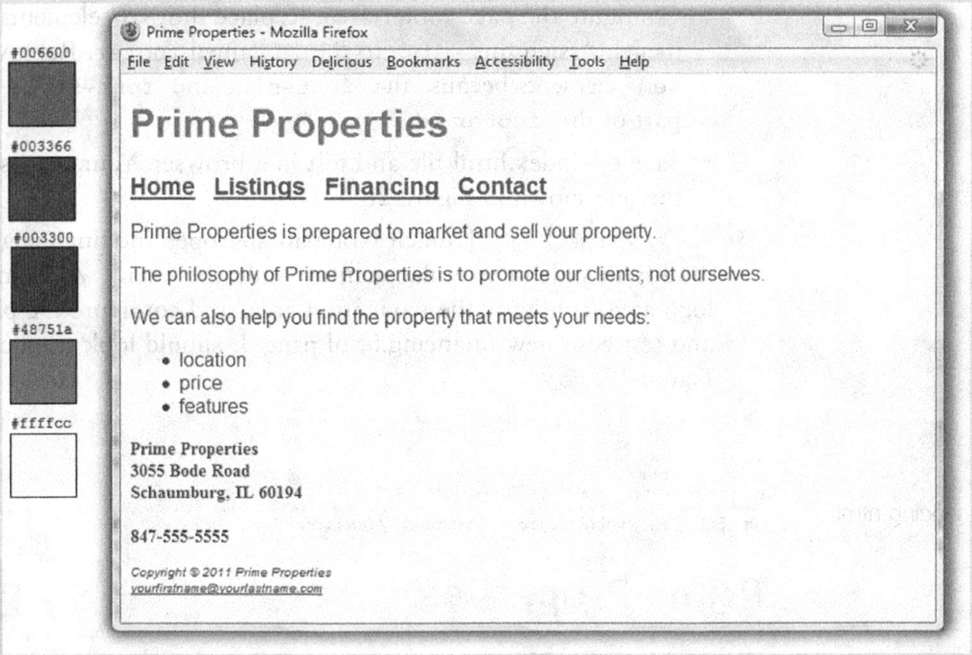

Go to the end of the chapter for a full color version of this figure

- Style rules for the `dd` selector that configure italic, smaller than the default (.90em) font size, with 200% line height
- Style rules for the `logo` class that configure background color (`#ffffcc`) and text color (`#48751A`)
- Style rules for a navigation area (use an id named `nav`) that displays text in bold, large (1.2em) font
- Style rules for a class named contact with bold, smaller than the default (.90em) using the Times New Roman or any serif font
- Style rules for the page footer area (use an id named `footer`) with small font size (.60em) and italic text

Save the file as prime.css in the primecss folder. Check your syntax with the CSS validator (http://jigsaw.w3.org/css-validator). Correct and retest if necessary.

2. **The Home Page.** Launch Notepad and open the index.html file. You will modify this file to apply styles from the prime.css external style sheet.
   - Add a `<link />` element to associate the Web page with the prime.css external style sheet file. Save and test your index.html page in a browser and you'll notice that the styles configured with the `body` selector are already applied!
   - Configure the logo area. Assign the `<h1>` element to the class named `logo`.
   - Configure the navigation area. Since the navigation is not semantically a "paragraph" (a collection of sentences about a central topic), replace the `<p>` element with a `<div>` element. Assign this `<div>` to the `id` named `nav`. Remove the `<strong>` element from this area.
   - Configure the paragraph containing the address and phone information. Assign this area to the class named `contact`. Remove the `<small>` element from this area.

- Configure the page footer area. Replace the `<p>` elements with `<div>` elements. Assign this `<div>` to the `id` named `footer`. Remove the `<small>` and `<em>` elements because the `font-size` and `font-style` are configured as part of the `footer id`.
- Save the index.html file and test in a browser. Your page should look similar to the one shown in Figure 28.

3. **The Financing Page.** Launch Notepad and open the financing.html file. You will modify this file in a similar manner—add the `<link />` element, configure the logo area, configure the navigation area, and configure the page footer area. Save and test your new financing.html page. It should look similar to the one shown in Figure 29.

Figure 29
New financing.html page

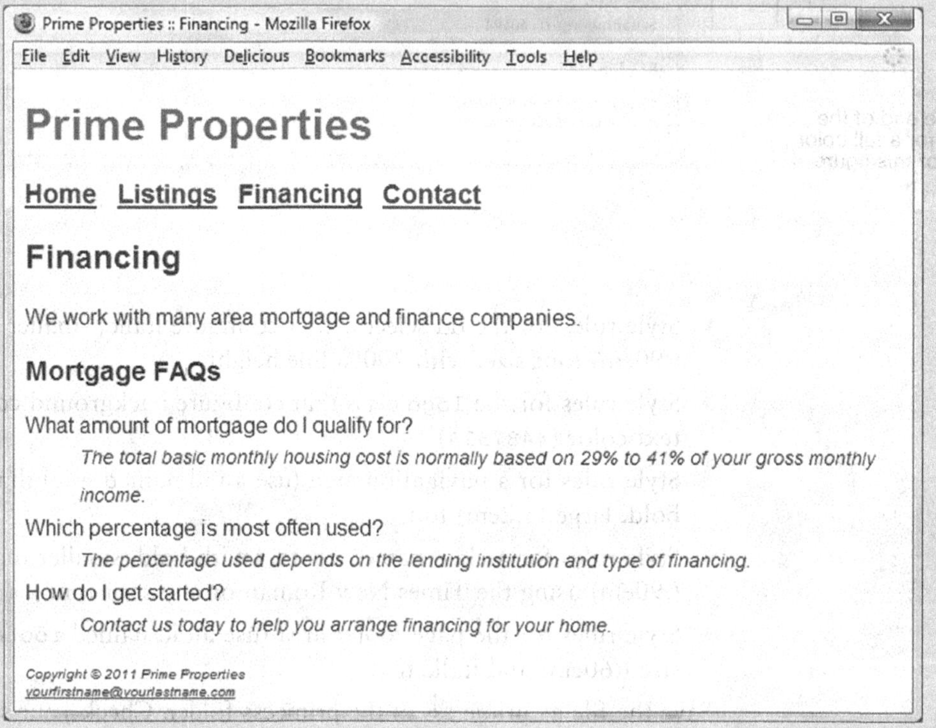

Experiment with modifying the prime.css file. Change the page background color, the font family, and so on. Test your pages in a browser. Notice how a change in a single file can affect multiple files when external style sheets are used.

Answers

Checkpoint 1

1. Reasons to use CSS on a Web page include the following: greater control of typography and page layout, separation of style from structure, potentially smaller Web page documents, and easier site maintenance.
2. Since visitors may set their browsers to certain colors, when changing a text color or a background color it is a good idea to configure the text color and the background color properties to provide good contrast between text and background.
3. Embedded styles are coded once in the header section of the Web page and apply to the entire page. This is more efficient than coding individual styles on HTML elements using inline styles.

Checkpoint 2

1. Embedded styles can be used to configure the text and color formatting for an entire Web page. Embedded styles are placed in the header section of a Web page. The `<style>` tag is used to contain the CSS selectors and properties that configure the embedded styles.
2. External styles can be used to configure the text and color formatting for some or all of the pages on a Web site. This provides a single place for the formatting information. This single file can be changed and all the Web pages associated with it will display the new styles the next time they are rendered in a browser. External styles are placed in a separate text file using a .css file extension. Web pages use the `<link />` tag to indicate that they are using an external style sheet.
3. `<link rel="stylesheet" href="mystyles.css" type="text/css" />`

Review Questions

1. d
2. b
3. b
4. a
5. c
6. c
7. c
8. d
9. a
10. b
11. `<span>`
12. not uniformly
13. `text-align`
14. `<div>`
15. 1996

Visual Elements and Graphics

Chapter Objectives

In this chapter, you will learn how to ...

- Create and format lines and borders on Web pages
- Decide when to use graphics and what graphics are appropriate
- Apply the image element to add graphics to Web pages
- Configure images as backgrounds on Web pages
- Configure images as hyperlinks
- Find free and fee-based graphics sources
- Follow recommended Web design guidelines when using graphics on Web pages

A key component of a compelling Web site is the use of interesting and appropriate graphics. This chapter introduces you to working with visual elements on Web pages.

When you include images on your Web site, it is important to remember that not all Web users are able to view them. Some users may have vision problems and need assistive technology such as a screen reader application that reads the Web page to them. In addition, search engines send out spiders and robots to walk the Web and catalog pages for their indexes and databases; such programs do not access your images. As a Web developer, you should create pages that are enhanced by graphical elements but that are usable without them.

1 Configuring Lines and Borders

Web designers often use visual elements such as lines and borders to separate or define areas on Web pages. In this section you'll explore two coding techniques to configure a line on a Web page: the XHTML horizontal rule element and the CSS `border` and `padding` properties.

The Horizontal Rule Element

A horizontal rule or line visually separates areas of a page. The **`<hr />`** element configures a horizontal line across a Web page. Since the horizontal rule element does not contain any text, it is coded as a stand-alone tag, and not in a pair of opening and closing tags.

HANDS-ON PRACTICE 1

Open the Web page found at chapter4/starter1.html in the student files in a text editor. This file should be familiar to you. Add an `<hr />` tag above the paragraph that contains the page footer (`id="footer"`).

Save your file as hr.html and test it in a browser. The lower portion of your Web page should look similar to the partial screenshot shown in Figure 1. Compare your work with the solution in the student files (Chapter4/hr.html).

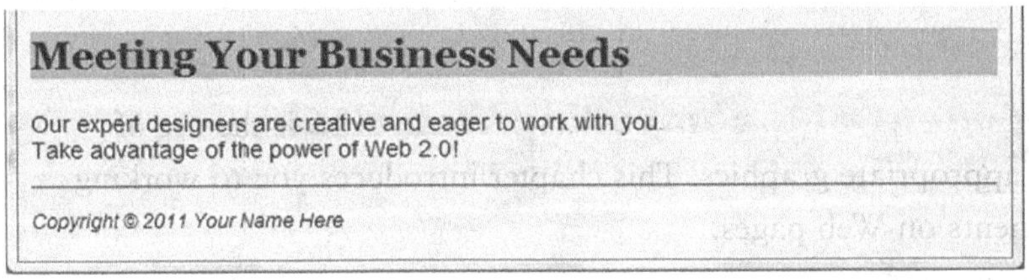

Figure 1
The `<hr />` element configures a horizontal line

Horizontal rules are centered within their container element (in this case the Web page body) by default. A number of attributes exist for the `<hr />` tag but they are deprecated or not officially supported by the W3C.

While a horizontal rule can be easily created using XHTML, a more modern technique is to use CSS to configure a border for a Web page element.

The `border` and `padding` Properties

If you've configured background colors for heading elements, you may have noticed that block-level XHTML elements form the shape of a rectangular box on a Web page. This is known as the CSS box model.

For now, let's focus on two CSS properties that can be configured for the "box"—the `border` and `padding` properties.

The `border` Property. The **`border` property** configures the border, or boundary, around an element. By default, the border has a width set to 0 and does not display. You can set the **`border-width`**, **`border-color`**, and **`border-style`**. And there's more—you can even configure individual settings for `border-top`, `border-right`, `border-bottom`, and `border-left`. You'll get some practice configuring properties for just the top border (`border-top`) in the next Hands-On Practice.

The `border-style` property also offers a variety of formatting options including `inset`, `outset`, `double`, `groove`, `ridge`, `solid`, `dashed`, and `dotted`. Be aware that these property values are not all uniformly applied by browsers. Figure 2 shows how Firefox 3 and Internet Explorer 8 render various `border-style` values.

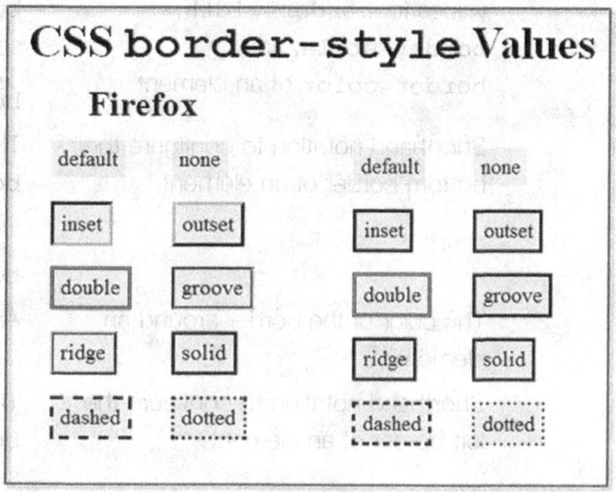

Figure 2 Not all `border-style` properties are rendered the same way by popular browsers

The CSS to configure the borders shown in Figure 2 uses a `border-color` of `#000033`, `border-width` of 3 pixels, and the value indicated for the `border-style` property. For example, the style rule to configure the dashed border follows:

```
.dashedborder { border-color: #000033;
                border-width: 3px;
                border-style: dashed;
}
```

A shorthand notation allows you to configure all the `border` properties in one style rule by listing the values of `border-width`, `border-style`, and `border-color`. An example follows:

```
.dashedborder { border: 3px dashed #000033 }
```

The `padding` Property. The **`padding` property** configures empty space between the content of the XHTML element (usually text) and the border. By default, the padding is set to 0. If you configure a background color for an element, the color is applied to both the padding and the content areas. You'll apply the `padding` property in the next Hands-On Practice. You may want to refer to Table 1, which presents a description of the CSS properties introduced in this chapter, as you work through the Hands-On Practice exercises.

Table 1 New CSS properties introduced in this chapter

Property	Description	Values
`background-image`	Background image on an element	url(imagename.gif) or url(imagename.jpg)
`background-position`	Position of the background image	Two percentage values or numeric pixel values. The first value configures the horizontal position and the second configures the vertical position starting from the upper-left corner of the container's box. Text values can also be used: **`left`**, **`top`**, **`center`**, **`bottom`**, **`right`**.
`background-repeat`	Controls how the background image will repeat	Text values **`repeat`** (default), **`repeat-y`**, (vertical repeat), **`repeat-x`** (horizontal repeat) , **`no-repeat`** (no repeat)
`border`	Shorthand notation to configure the values for **`border-width`**, **`border-style`**, and **`border-color`** of an element	The values for **`border-width`**, **`border-style`**, and **`border-color`** separated by spaces; for example: **`border: 1px solid #000000;`**
`border-bottom`	Shorthand notation to configure the bottom border of an element	The values for **`border-width`**, **`border-style`**, and **`border-color`** separated by spaces; for example: **`border-bottom: 1px solid #000000;`**
`border-color`	The color of the border around an element	Any valid color
`border-left`	Shorthand notation to configure the left border of an element	The values for **`border-width`**, **`border-style`**, and **`border-color`** separated by spaces; for example: **`border-left: 1px solid #000000;`**
`border-right`	Shorthand notation to configure the right border of an element	The values for **`border-width`**, **`border-style`**, and **`border-color`** separated by spaces; for example: **`border-right: 1px solid #000000;`**
`border-style`	The type of border around an element	Text values **`double`**, **`groove`**, **`inset`**, **`none`** (the default), **`outset`**, **`ridge`**, **`solid`**, **`dashed`**, **`dotted`**, **`hidden`**
`border-top`	Shorthand notation to configure the top border of an element	The values for **`border-width`**, **`border-style`**, and **`border-color`** separated by spaces; for example: **`border-top: 1px solid #000000;`**
`border-width`	The width of a border around an element	A numeric pixel value (such as `1px`) or the text values **`thin`**, **`medium`**, **`thick`**
`min-width`	Configures a minimum width for an element	A numeric pixel value or percentage

Table 1 New CSS properties introduced in this chapter *(continued)*

Property	Description	Values
`padding`	Shorthand notation to configure the amount of padding—the blank space between the element and its border	1. A single numeric value (px or em); configure padding on all sides of the element. 2. Two numeric values (px or em); the first value configures the top and bottom padding, the second value configures the left and right padding; for example: `padding: 20px 10px;` 3. Four numeric values (px or em) or percentages. The values configure the padding in the following order: `padding-top`, `padding-right`, `padding-bottom`, `padding-left`.
`padding-bottom`	Blank space between an element and its bottom border	A numeric value (px or em) or percentage
`padding-left`	Blank space between an element and its left border	A numeric value (px or em) or percentage
`padding-right`	Blank space between an element and its right border	A numeric value (px or em) or percentage
`padding-top`	Blank space between an element and its top border	A numeric value (px or em) or percentage

HANDS-ON PRACTICE 2

In this Hands-On Practice you will work with the `border` and `padding` properties. Launch a text editor and open the Web page found at chapter4/starter2.html in the student files. You will modify the CSS style rules for the `h1` selector, `h2` selector and `footer` id. When you are finished, your page should look similar to the one shown in Figure 3.

Modify the CSS style rules as follows:

- Modify the style rules for the `h1` selector. Remove the `line-height` style rule because you will configure the empty space using `padding`. Add a style rule to set the `padding` to 15 pixels. The code follows:

```
padding: 15px;
```

- Add a style rule to the `h2` selector to configure a 2 pixel, dashed, bottom border in the color #191970. The code follows:

```
border-bottom: 2px dashed #191970;
```

- Add style rules to the `footer` id to configure a thin, solid, top border in the color #aeaed4 along with 10 pixels of top padding. The code follows:

```
border-top: thin solid #aeaed4;
padding-top: 10px;
```

Save your file as border.html.

Figure 3
CSS **`border`** and **`padding`** properties add visual interest to the page

Test in multiple browsers. Expect your page to look slightly different in browsers such as Internet Explorer and Firefox. See Figure 3 for a screenshot of the page using Firefox. Figure 4 shows the page displayed in Opera. The student files contain a sample solution (Chapter4/border.html).

Figure 4
Opera renders the dashed border differently than Firefox

FAQ

My page looks different in various browsers. What can I do?

Do not expect your Web pages to always look the same in every browser and every browser version. Web pages that look different in various browsers are a frustrating part of life in the world of Web developers. The good news is that browser manufacturers are finally beginning to be less inventive and more compliant with the W3C standards. Also, organizations such as The Web Standards Project at http://www.webstandards.org have lobbied for standards compliance in browsers. Look for more compliance in the future!

Notice how objects even as simple as dashed borders appear different depending on the way the browsers display the page. To deal with this, remember the following:

- Design for the browser you think most of your visitors will use.
- Design the page so that it looks okay (degrades gracefully) in other browsers.

Perhaps the most exciting way to add visual interest to a Web page is to add graphics. The next section continues with a discussion of types of graphics used on Web pages.

CHECKPOINT 1

1. Is it reasonable to try to code a Web page that looks exactly the same on every browser and every platform? Explain your answer.
2. When a Web page containing the style rules below is rendered in a browser, the border does not display. Describe what is incorrect with the following code:

```
h2 { background-color: #ff0000
     border-top: thin solid #000000
}
```

3. True or False? CSS can be used to configure visual elements such as rectangular shapes and lines on Web pages.

2 Types of Graphics

Graphics help to make Web pages compelling. Unfortunately, they can also make pages very slow to load. This section discusses types and features of graphic files used on the Web: **GIF**, **JPEG**, and **PNG**.

Browsers render, or display, Web page documents in order, line-by-line, starting at the top of the document. They also display standard images as the files are read in order from top to bottom. The top of a standard image begins to display after 50 percent of the image has been read by a browser. As you read about types of images, look for techniques you can use to make your pages load faster.

GIF Images

Graphic interchange format (GIF) is best used for flat line drawings containing solid tones and simple images such as clip art. The maximum number of colors in a GIF file is 256 (although most do not use more than the 216 colors in the Web Color Palette). GIF images have a .gif file extension.

Transparency. The format GIF89A used by GIF images supports image **transparency**. In a graphics application such as Adobe Photoshop or Adobe Fireworks one color (usually the background color) of the image can be set to be transparent. This helps the image to blend in with the Web page background or table background. Figure 5 shows two GIF images, one that does not use transparency and one with a background color configured to be transparent.

Figure 5 Comparison of nontransparent and transparent GIFs

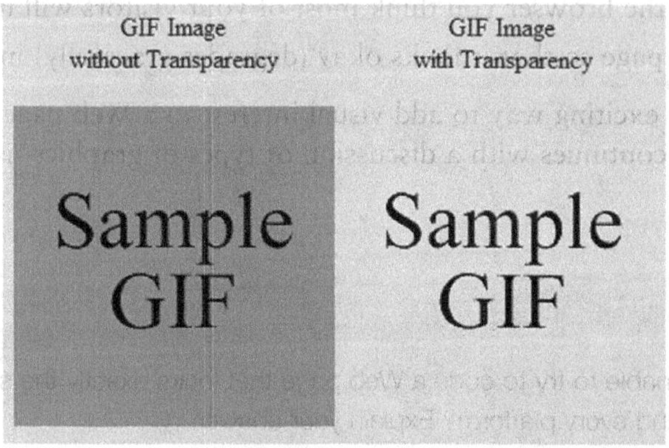

When working with transparent GIFs you should also be aware of the **halo effect**—a fringe of color around parts of the transparent image. Transparent GIFs are usually optimized for display on a particular background color. Displaying them on a background other than the type they were designed for can produce the halo effect.

The GIF used in Figure 6 was created to display on a light background. When it is shown on a dark background, the halo of light pixels is noticeable. This halo can only be fixed by modifying the image in a graphics application such as Adobe Photoshop or Adobe Fireworks and saving a version that is optimized for display on a dark background.

Figure 6 Notice the halo effect on the dark background

Go to the end of the chapter for a full color version of this figure

Animation. Animated GIF images also use the .gif file extension. They are contained in a GIF file that consists of several images or frames, each of which is slightly different. When the frames flash on the screen in order, the image appears animated—**animated GIFs** can be created in a graphics application such as Adobe Fireworks or Adobe

ImageReady. Shareware GIF animation applications such as the GIF Construction Set are also commonly used. There are advantages to using an animated GIF to add action to your Web page. This format is widely supported, does not require a browser plug-in, and is relatively easy to create.

When you decide to add an animated GIF to your Web page, try to use the image for special emphasis only. If you're like most people, at some time you have been annoyed by a flashing ad banner at the top of a Web page. Use animated gifs sparingly.

Compression. When a GIF file is saved, **lossless compression** is used. This means that nothing in the original image is lost and that the compressed image, when rendered by a browser, will contain the same pixels as the original.

Optimization. To avoid slow-loading Web pages, graphic files should be optimized for the Web. **Image optimization** is the process of creating an image with the lowest file size that still renders a good quality image—balancing image quality and file size. GIF images are typically optimized by reducing the number of colors in the image. The image shown in Figure 6 was created using 235 colors and is 12KB in size. A graphics application such as Adobe Photoshop can be used to optimize the image for the Web—reducing the number of colors, which decreases the file size. The image shown in Figure 7 uses only eight colors and has a file size less than 5KB. However, the image quality is unacceptable.

Figure 7 This GIF image is less than 5KB but is poor quality

Figure 8 shows the optimized image with acceptable quality using 128 colors and a file size of 10KB—the best balancing of quality and file size for this particular image.

Figure 8 Optimization is a trade-off between file size and image quality

Interlacing. When a GIF graphic file is created it can be configured as interlaced. This changes the way that browsers render the image. Remember that browsers display standard (noninterlaced) images as the file is read from top to bottom and only begin to display the image after 50 percent of the file has been downloaded by a browser. An **interlaced image** progressively displays and seems to fade in as it downloads. The image first appears fuzzy but gradually becomes clearer and sharper. Interlaced images are repeatedly scanned from left to right. The first time about 13 percent of the image is displayed. The next pass renders about 25 percent. This process continues until the image is completely displayed. When you are using complex GIF images, consider interlacing to improve the perceived load time of your page.

FAQ

Why does my text image look jagged?

If your image looks jagged, your graphic designer did not use **antialiasing** (sometimes called smoothing). Antialiasing is the process of creating a slight blur to smooth the jagged (stair-step) edges found in digital images. In Figure 9, the top image was created using antialiasing and the bottom was not. Note the jagged edges in the bottom image. The only letters not affected are the "l" and "i" because the shapes of these letters are perfectly horizontal and vertical.

Figure 9
Notice the smoother look of the top line of text

JPEG Images

Joint Photographic Experts Group (JPEG) images are best used for photographic images. In contrast to a GIF image, a JPEG image can contain 16.7 million colors. However, JPEG images cannot be made transparent and they cannot be animated. JPEG images usually have a .jpg or .jpeg file extension.

Compression. Another difference between GIF and JPEG images is that when JPEG images are saved **lossy compression** is used. This means that some pixels in the original image are lost or removed from the compressed file. When a browser renders the compressed image, the display is similar but not exactly the same as the original image.

Optimization. There are trade-offs between the quality of the image and the amount of compression. An image with less compression will have higher quality and result in a larger file size. An image with more compression will have lower quality and result in a smaller file size. Most graphics applications allow you to preview the quality/compression trade-off and choose the image that best suits your needs.

When you take a photo with a digital camera, the file size is too large for optimal display on a Web page. Figure 10 shows a JPEG image that is stored in a 205KB file. The same image was saved using a graphics application at various quality levels: Figure 11 was saved with 80 percent quality and is 55KB; Figure 12 was saved with 20 percent quality and is 19KB, but its quality is unacceptable. View these images to gain a perspective on the quality/size trade-off. You should notice that the quality of the image degrades as the file size decreases. The square blockiness you see in Figure 12 is called **pixelation**.

Another method to optimize JPEG images is to use a graphics application to reduce the dimensions of the images. Figure 13 shows a small version, or thumbnail, image of acceptable quality.

Figure 10
Initial JPEG image
(205KB file size)

Go to the end of the chapter for a full color version of this figure

Figure 11
JPEG saved at 80 percent quality
(55KB file size)

Go to the end of the chapter for a full color version of this figure

Figure 12
JPEG saved at 20 percent quality
(19KB file size)

Go to the end of the chapter for a full color version of this figure

Figure 13
This small image is only 5KB

Progressive JPEG. When a JPEG file is created it can be configured as progressive. A **progressive JPEG** is similar to an interlaced GIF in that the image progressively displays and seems to fade in as it downloads. Consider using this for complex images since the general shapes will initially appear and then sharpen as the file is progressively scanned and displayed by the browser.

PNG Images

PNG, pronounced "ping," stands for portable network graphic. Browsers have only recently begun to support this type of image. It combines the best of GIF and JPEG images and will be a replacement for the GIF in the future. PNG graphics can support millions of colors. They can support variable transparency levels and use lossless compression. PNG images also support interlacing. PNG is the native file format of some graphics applications, such as Adobe Fireworks.

3 Using Graphics

Now that you've been introduced to the types of graphic files displayed on Web pages, we'll discuss how to place graphics on your Web pages.

The Image Element

The **`<img />`**, pronounced image, element is used to place graphics on a Web page. These graphics can be photographs, banners, company logos, navigation buttons—you are limited only by your creativity and imagination.

The image tag is used alone, not in a pair of opening and closing tags. The image file should be either in the same folder as your Web site or in a subfolder of your site. For example, to place an image called logo.gif on your Web page, you would use the following XHTML code:

```
<img src="logo.gif" height="200" width="500" alt="My Company Name" />
```

The **`src` attribute** is used to specify the file name of the image. A number of optional attributes can be applied to images. It is a good idea to include the `height`, `width`, and `alt` attributes. The **`height` attribute** and **`width` attribute** can cause the Web page to load more efficiently and quickly. The **`alt` attribute** provides a text replacement, typically a text description, of the image. Table 2 lists attributes and their values. Commonly used attributes are shown in bold.

Table 2 Attributes of the `<img />` tag

Attribute	Value
`align`	`right`, `left` (default), `top`, `middle`, `bottom` (Deprecated)
`alt`	Text phrase that describes the image
`border`	Image border size in pixels (Deprecated) 0 will prevent the border from being displayed.
`height`	Height of image in pixels
`hspace`	Amount of space that is blank to the left and right of the image in pixels (Deprecated)
`id`	Text name, alphanumeric, beginning with a letter, no spaces—the value must be unique and not used for other id values on the same XHTML document
`longdesc`	URL of a Web page that contains a text description of the image
`name`	Text name, alphanumeric, beginning with a letter, no spaces—this attribute names the image so that it can be easily accessed by client-side scripting languages such as JavaScript. This attribute is deprecated in XHTML but is used to provide backward compatibility with browsers that support HTML.
`src`	The URL or file name of the image
`title`	A text phrase containing advisory information about the image—typically more descriptive than the `alt` text
`vspace`	Amount of space that is blank above and below the image in pixels (Deprecated)
`width`	Width of image in pixels

Use `height` and `width` attributes to help the browser render your page more efficiently. If you omit the attributes, the browser must often adjust and shift the other page elements after your images load. This slows down the loading of your Web page. The browser reserves the correct amount of space for your image if you use the `height` and `width` attributes with values either equal to or approximately the size of the image.

FAQ

What if I don't know the height and width of an image?

Most graphics applications can display the height and width of an image. If you have a graphics application such as Adobe Photoshop or Adobe Fireworks handy, launch the application and open the image. These applications include options that will display the properties of the image, such as height and width.

If you don't have a graphics application available, you can determine the dimensions of an image using a browser. Display the image on a Web page. Right-click on the image to display the context-sensitive menu. Select properties and view the dimensions (height and width) of the image. (*Warning*: if the height and width are specified on the Web page, those values will be displayed even if the image's actual height and width are different.)

Focus on Accessibility

WWW

Accessibility and Images

Use the `alt` attribute to provide accessibility. Section 508 of the Rehabilitation Act requires the use of accessibility features for new information technology (including

Web sites) associated with the federal government. The `alt` attribute configures an alternative text description of the image. This `alt` text is used by the browser in two ways. The browser will show the `alt` text in the image area before the graphic is downloaded and displayed. Some browsers will also show the `alt` text as a tool tip whenever the Web page visitor places a mouse over the image area. Applications such as screen readers will read the text in the `alt` attribute out loud.

Standard browsers such as Internet Explorer and Safari are not the only type of application or user agent that can access your Web site. Major search engines run programs called spiders or robots; these programs index and categorize Web sites. They cannot process images, but some process the value of the `alt` attributes in image tags.

Focus on Accessibility

WWW

The **`longdesc` attribute** is used to provide accessibility when the `alt` text description is too short to convey the meaning of the image. The value of the `longdesc` attribute is the URL of a Web page that contains a detailed text description and explanation of the image. Most current browsers do not support this attribute but you can expect expanded support in the future.

Legacy Alert. The `align`, `vspace`, and `hspace` attributes help position the image on the page relative to text. Examples of formatting images and text using vertical alignment properties are shown in Figure 14.

Figure 15 provides examples of horizontal alignments, the **`hspace` attribute**, and the **`vspace` attribute**. The `hspace` and `vspace` attributes are used to add space around an image symmetrically.

Since you'll find many pages on the Web coded using the deprecated attributes of the image element (`align`, `hspace`, `vspace`, `border`), it's a good idea to become familiar with them.

Figure 14
Examples of vertical alignment

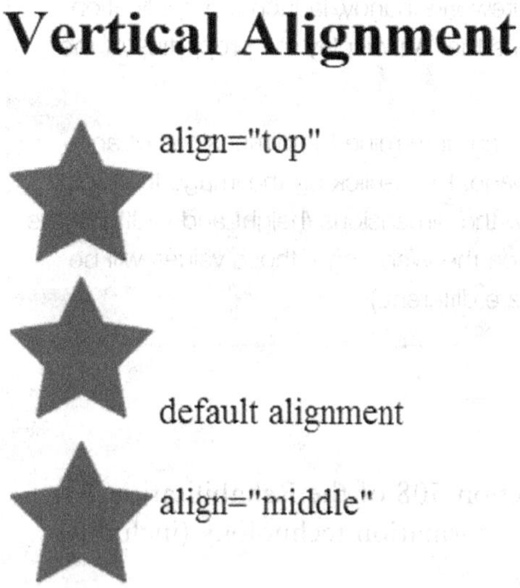

Figure 15
Examples of horizontal alignment

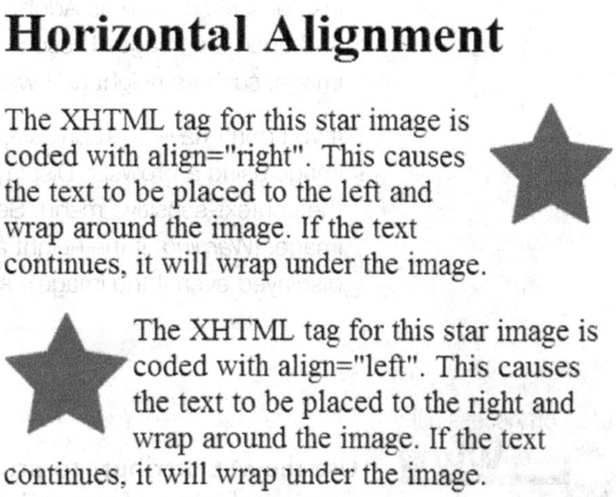

HANDS-ON PRACTICE 3

In this Hands-On Practice you will place a graphical logo banner on a Web page. Create a new folder called trilliumch4. The graphic used in this Hands-On Practice is located in the student files: Chapter4/starters folder. Save trilliumbanner.jpg file in your trilliumch4 folder. A starter version of the Trillium Media Design Home page is ready for you in the student files. Save the chapter4/starter3.html file to your trilliumch4 folder. Launch a browser to display the starter3.html Web page—notice a monochromatic green color scheme has been configured with CSS. When you are finished with this Hands-On Practice, your page will look similar to the one shown in Figure 16—with a logo banner.

Figure 16
The new Trillium Home page with a logo banner

Go to the end of the chapter for a full color version of this figure

Launch a text editor and open starter3.html in the Chapter4 folder.
Configure the image as follows:

Replace the text contained between the <h1> opening and closing tags. Code an <img /> element to display trilliumbanner.jpg in this area. Remember to include the `src`, `alt`, `height`, and `width` attributes. Sample code follows:

```
<img src="trilliumbanner.jpg" alt="Trillium Media Design"
width="700" height="86" />
```

Modify the h2 selector as follows:

Let's review working with the CSS `padding` property. Add a style rule to configure 10 pixels of padding on the left side of the h2 element. The new style rule follows:

```
padding-left: 10px;
```

Save your page as index.html in the trilliumch4 folder. Launch a browser and test your page. It should look similar to the one shown in Figure 16. *Note*: if the image did not display on your Web page, verify that you have saved the trilliumbanner.jpg file in the trilliumch4 folder and that you have spelled the file name correctly in the `<img />` element. The student files contain a sample solution in the Chapter4/4.3 folder. Isn't it interesting how just one image can add visual interest to a Web page?

Image Links

The XHTML to make an image function as a hyperlink is very easy. To create an **image link** all you need to do is surround your `<img />` element with anchor tags. For example, to place a link around an image called home.gif, use the following XHTML code:

```
<a href="index.html"><img src="home.gif" height="19" width="85"
alt="Home" /></a>
```

When an image is used as a hyperlink, the default is to show a blue outline (border) around the image. If you would prefer not to display this outline, you could use the `border="0"` attribute in your image tag as follows:

```
<a href="index.html"><img src="home.gif" height="19"
width="85"alt="Home" border="0" /></a>
```

A more modern approach is to use CSS to configure the border on the `img` selector. The next Hands-On Practice will demonstrate this technique as you add image links to a Web page.

HANDS-ON PRACTICE 4

You will add image links to the Trillium Media Design Home page in this Hands-On Practice. You should already have the index.html and trilliumbanner.jpg files in your trilliumch4 folder. The graphics used in this Hands-On Practice are located in the student files: Chapter4/starters folder. Save the home.gif, services.gif, and contact.gif files to your trilliumch4 folder. View Figure 17 to see how your page should look after you are done with this Hands-On Practice.

Focus on Accessibility
WWW

Let's get started. Launch a text editor and open index.html. Notice that the anchor tags are already coded—you'll just need to convert the text links to image links! However, before you start changing the code, let's take a minute to discuss accessibility. Whenever the main navigation consists of media, such as an image, some individuals may not be able to see the images (or may have images turned off in their browser). To provide

Figure 17
The new Trillium Home page navigation with image links

navigation that is accessible to all, configure a set of plain text navigation links in the page footer area as follows:

1. Copy the `<div>` element containing the navigation area to the lower portion of the page and paste it above the page footer.
2. Modify the style rules in the `nav` class. Change the font size to `.75em`.
3. Now, focus on the top navigation area. Replace the text contained between each pair of anchor tags with an image element. Use home.gif for the link to index.html, services.gif for the link to services.html, and contact.gif for the link to contact.html. A sample follows:
```
<a href="index.html"><img src="home.gif" alt="Home" width="120"
height="40" /></a>
```
4. Create a new style rule that configures no border for the `img` selector. The code follows:
```
img {border:none}
```
5. Save your page as index.html. Launch a browser and test your page. It should look similar to the one shown in Figure 17. As you test your page, resize the browser window—make it smaller—and note how the image links move around. To prevent this, add a new style rule to the body selector that sets a minimum width for the page. This will cause the browser to automatically display a horizontal scroll bar if the Web page visitor resizes the browser window below the size specified:
```
min-width: 700px;
```
Save and test your page again.

The student files contain a sample solution in the Chapter4/4.4 folder.

FAQ

What if my images don't show?

The following are common reasons for images not displaying on a Web page:

- Are your images really in the Web site folder? Use Windows Explorer to double-check.
- Did you code the XTHML and CSS correctly? Check for common mistakes such as typing `scr` instead of `src` and missing quotation marks.
- Do your images have the exact file names that you have used in the background or `src` attributes in your XHTML code? Attention to detail and consistency will be very helpful here.

Hints for naming image files:

- Use all lowercase letters.
- Do not use punctuation symbols and spaces.
- Do not change the file extensions (should be .gif, .jpg, .jpeg, or .png).
- Keep your file names short but descriptive.

    i1.gif is probably too short

    myimagewithmydogonmybirthday.gif is too long

    dogbday.gif may be just about right

Background Images

The CSS `background-color` property can be used to configure the background color of a Web page. The W3C recommends that Web developers use the hexadecimal numeric value rather than the color name when setting a background color. For example, the following CSS code configures the background of a Web page to be a soft yellow:

```
body { background-color: #ffff99; }
```

In addition to a background color, you can also choose to use an image for the background of a Web page. Be careful not to choose an image that is too busy; it could interfere with your text and graphics. Use the CSS **`background-image`** **property** to configure a background image for a Web page. For example, the following CSS code configures the background of a Web page to be the image background1.gif located in the same folder as the Web page:

```
body { background-image: url(background1.gif); }
```

You can use a graphics application to create your own backgrounds or find a free background image on the Web.

Legacy Alert. If you work with Web pages created by others you may find that the XHTML attributes `bgcolor` and `background` have been used to configure the page instead of CSS properties.

FAQ: Can I use both a `background-color` and a `background-image` attribute on the `body` selector?

Yes, you can! The background color (specified by the **background-color** property) will display first. Then the image specified as the Web page background will be loaded and tiled across the page. It's a good idea to choose a background color of a hue similar to the major color in your Web page background image. By coding both a background color and a background image you provide your visitor with a more pleasing visual experience. If the background image does not load for some reason, the page background will still have the expected contrast with your text color. If the background image is smaller than the Web browser window and the Web page is configured with CSS to not automatically tile (repeat), the page background color will display in areas not covered by the background image. The CSS for a page with both a background color and a background image is as follows:

```
body {  background-color: #cccccc;
        background-image: url(mybackground.gif);
}
```

You may think that a graphic created to be the background of a Web page would always be about the size of a browser window. This can be done; however, often the background image is actually much smaller than the typical browser window. The shape of a background image is usually either a long, thin rectangle or a small rectangular block. Unless otherwise specified in a style rule, Web browsers repeat, or tile, these images to cover the page background. The images have small file sizes so that they download as quickly as possible. Figure 18 shows a long, thin rectangular image that will repeat down the page. The Web page shown in Figure 19 uses a small rectangular image that is repeated or tiled on the page. In each of these cases, the small background image has the effect of a much larger image that fills the screen.

Figure 18
A long, thin background image tiles down the page

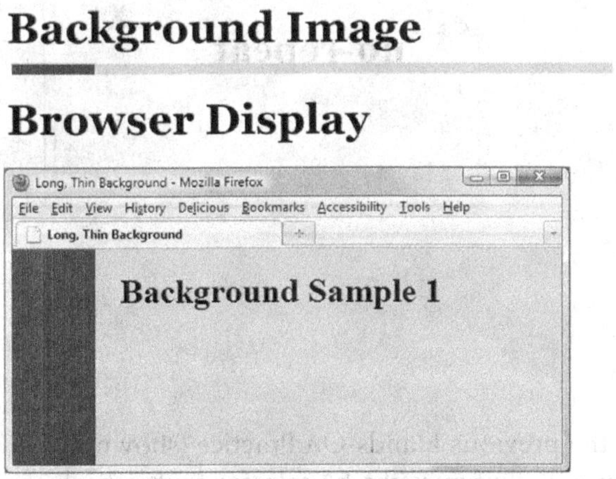

Figure 19
A small rectangular background is repeated to fill the Web page window

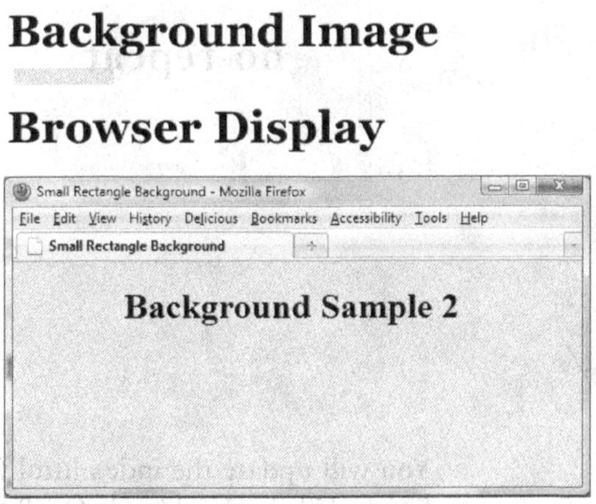

Configuring Background Images with CSS

The default behavior of a browser is to repeat, or tile, background images to cover the entire element's background. Figures 18 and 19 display examples of this type of tiling for a Web page background. This behavior also applies to other elements, such as backgrounds for headings, paragraphs, and so on. You can change this tiling behavior with the CSS **`background-repeat` property**. The `background-repeat` property has a number of values: `repeat` (default), `repeat-y` (vertical repeat of background image), `repeat-x` (horizontal repeat of background image), and `no-repeat` (background image does not repeat). Figure 20 provides examples of the actual background image and the result of applying various `background-repeat` property values.

You will explore configuring image backgrounds in the next Hands-On Practice.

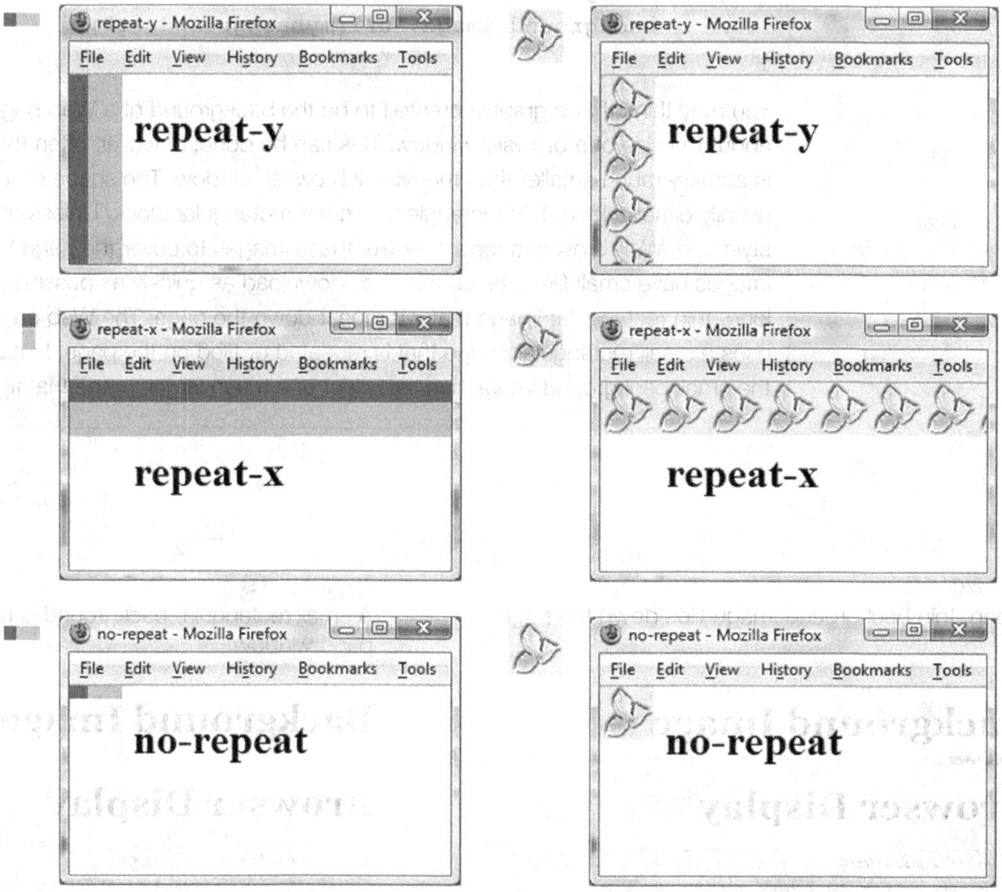

Figure 20 Examples of the CSS `background-repeat` property

HANDS-ON PRACTICE 5

You will update the index.html file from the previous Hands-On Practice (shown in Figure 17). In this Hands-On Practice you will configure the `h2` selector with a background image that does not repeat. Obtain the trilliumbullet.gif image from the student files in the Chapter4/starters folder. Save the images in your trilliumch4 folder. When you are completed with this exercise, your page should look similar to the one shown in Figure 21.

Figure 21
The background image in the <h2> areas is configured with `background-repeat: no-repeat`

Launch Notepad and open index.html.

Modify the style rule for the `h2` selector and configure the `background-image` and `background-repeat` properties. Set the background image to be trilliumbullet.gif. Set the background to not repeat. The `h2` selector style rules follow:

```
h2 { background-color: #d5edb3;
     color: #5c743d;
     font-family: Georgia, "Times New Roman", serif;
     padding-left: 30px;
     background-image: url(trilliumbullet.gif);
     background-repeat: no-repeat;
}
```

Save your page as index.html. Launch a browser and test your page. It should look similar to the one shown in Figure 21. The student files contain a sample solution in the Chapter4/4.5 folder.

FAQ

What if my images are in their own folder?

It's a good idea to organize your Web site by placing all your images in a folder separate from your Web pages. Notice that the CircleSoft Web site shown in Figure 22 has a folder called images, which contains a number of GIF files. To refer to these files in XHTML or CSS code, you also need to refer to the images folder. The following are some examples:

- The CSS code to configure the background.gif file from the images folder as the page background is as follows:

```
body { background-image: url(images/background.gif); }
```

- XHTML to display the logo.jpg file from the images folder is as follows:

```
<img src="images/logo.jpg" alt="CircleSoft" width="588"
height="120" />
```

Figure 22
A folder named "images" contains the graphic files

CHECKPOINT 2

1. Describe the CSS to configure a graphic named circle.jpg to display once in the background of all <h1> elements. Code sample CSS to demonstrate this.
2. Describe the CSS that configures a file named bg.gif to repeat vertically down the background of a Web page. Code sample CSS to demonstrate this.
3. Explain how the browser will render the Web page if you use CSS to configure both a background image and a background color.

4 XHTML Images and More

This section introduces additional XHTML coding techniques associated with using images on Web pages. Topics discussed include image maps, thumbnail images, and image slicing.

Image Maps

An **image map** is an image that can be used as one or more hyperlinks. An image map will have at least one clickable area and usually multiple clickable areas that link to another Web page or Web site. The clickable areas are sometimes called **hotspots**. You have probably used image maps many times but never realized it. One common use of image maps is to create real clickable maps that Web site visitors can manipulate to choose a location. Figure 23 shows the home page of Recreation.gov with a map of the United States. Visitors use the map to select the state they are interested in. You can also visit the textbook's Web site at http://webdevfoundations.net to try out an image map.

Figure 23 An image map is used to select a location on this Web site

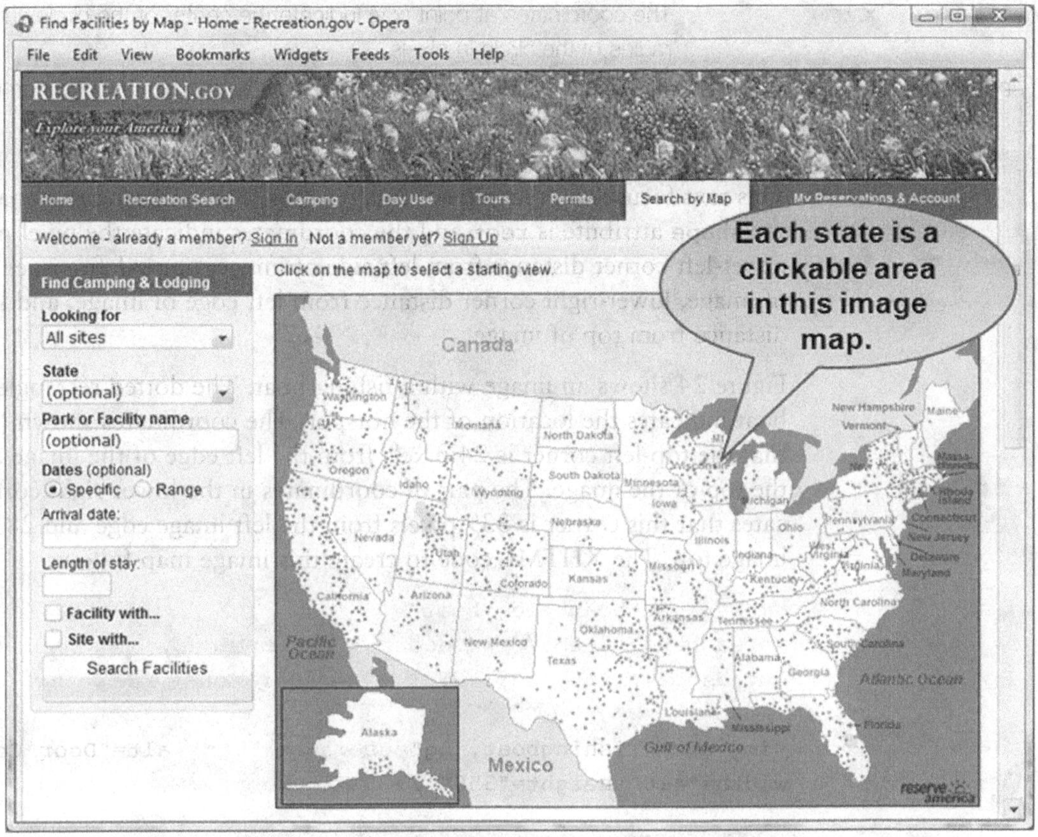

Most Web authoring software, such as Adobe Dreamweaver, have wizards or other tools to help you create image maps quickly and easily. If you don't have access to a Web authoring tool to create an image map, the most difficult part is determining the pixel coordinates of the hyperlink area. The coordinates are in pairs of numbers that signify the number of pixels from the top and the number of pixels from the left edge of the image. If you are working with a graphic artist, he or she may be able to supply you with the coordinates. Another option is to open the image in a graphics application such as Adobe Fireworks, Adobe Photoshop, or even MS Paint to obtain approximate coordinates. You can modify these coordinate values as you work with the XHTML on your Web page. Image maps can be used to create clickable areas in three shapes: rectangles, circles, and polygons.

An image map uses two new elements: <map> and <area />. The **<map>** tag is a container tag and is used to begin and end the image map. The name attribute is used to correspond the <map> tag with its associated image. The image tag uses the **usemap attribute** to indicate which <map> to use. For example, <img src="fishingboat.jpg" usemap="#boat" /> will be associated with the image map described by <map name="boat" id="boat">. The id attribute is part of XHTML. The name attribute is required for backward compatibility with older browsers that were written to process HTML.

The **<area />** tag is used to define the coordinates or edges of the map area and uses shape, coords, alt, and href attributes. Table 3 describes the type of coordinates (coords) needed for each shape value.

Table 3 Shape coordinates

Shape	Coordinates	Meaning
`rect`	"x1,y1, x2,y2"	The coordinates at point (x1,y1) represent the upper-left corner of the rectangle. The coordinates at point (x2,y2) represent the lower-right corner of the rectangle.
`circle`	"x,y,r"	The coordinates at point (x,y) indicate the center of the circle. The value of r is the radius of the circle in pixels.
`polygon`	"x1,y1, x2,y2, x3,y3", etc.	The values of each (x,y) pair represent the coordinates of a corner point of the polygon.

This text focuses on rectangular image maps. For a rectangular image map, the value of the `shape` attribute is `rect` and the coordinates indicate the pixel positions as follows: upper-left corner distance from left side of image, upper-left corner distance from top of image, lower-right corner distance from left edge of image, and lower-right corner distance from top of image.

Figure 24 shows an image with a fishing boat. The dotted rectangle around the fishing boat indicates the location of the hotspot. The coordinates shown (24, 188) indicate that the top-left corner is 24 pixels from the left edge of the image and 188 pixels from the top of the image. The pair of coordinates in the lower-right corner (339, 283) indicates that this corner is 339 pixels from the left image edge and 283 pixels from the image top. The XHTML code to create this image map follows:

```
<map name="boat" id="boat">
<area href="http://www.doorcountyvacations.com" shape="rect"
coords="24, 188, 339, 283" alt="Door County Fishing" />
</map>
<img src="fishingboat.jpg" usemap="#boat" alt="Door County"
width="416" height="350" />
```

Figure 24
Sample image map

This example is for a client-side image map. No special Web server processing is needed for this image map to work. Another, more complex type of image map is a server-side image map. This type requires a program on the Web server to coordinate the linking.

Server-side maps are no longer commonly used because they require resources on the Web server. It is more efficient to distribute processing to be on the Web browser client whenever possible. This way, the resources of the Web server can be reserved for the tasks that only it can perform.

Most Web developers do not hand-code image maps. As mentioned previously, the easiest way to create a client-side image map is to use a Web authoring tool. Some shareware programs, such as CoffeeCup Image Mapper (http://www.coffeecup.com) and HTML Map Designer Pro (http://www.imagecure.com/) also provide this feature.

Thumbnail Images

A **thumbnail image** is a smaller version of an image you would like to include on a Web site. It is usually placed within anchor tags that link to the larger, more detailed version of the image. Large images can significantly increase the load time of a Web page. If you are creating a page with multiple detailed images, consider displaying thumbnail images instead. This way, visitors who are interested in the images and willing to wait can use the thumbnail image to link to the larger image. Most graphics applications can create thumbnail images.

The Favorites Icon

Ever wonder about the small icon you sometimes see in the address bar or tab of a browser? That's a favorites icon, usually referred to as a **favicon**, which is a square image (either 16×16 pixels or 32×32 pixels) associated with a Web page. The favicon, shown in Figure 25, may display in the browser address bar, tab, or the favorites/bookmarks list.

Figure 25
The favorites icon displays in the browser tab and address bar

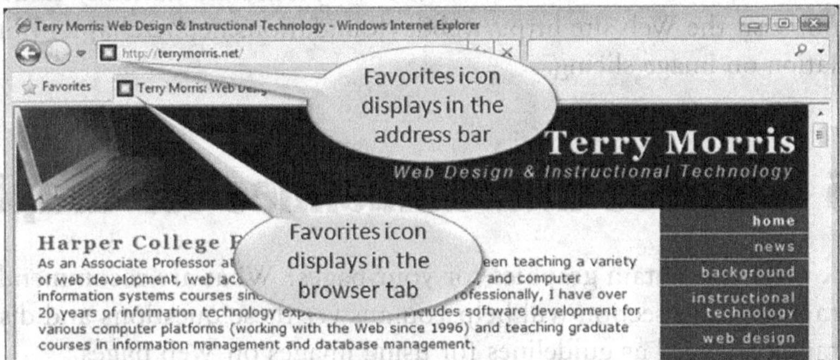

Go to the end of the chapter for a full color version of this figure

You can create a favicon in a graphics application, such as Adobe Fireworks, or at a number of Web sites including http://www.favicongenerator.com, http://www.favicon.cc, and http://www.freefavicon.com. While earlier versions of Internet Explorer (such as version 5 and 6) expected the file to be named favicon.ico and to reside in the root directory of the Web server, a more modern approach is to associate the favicon.ico file with a Web page using the link element. Coding the `<link />` tag in the header section of a Web page associates an external style sheet file with a Web page file. You can also use the `<link />` tag associates a favorites icon with a Web page. Three attributes are used to associate a Web page with a favorites icon: `rel`, `href`, and `type`. The value of the `rel` attribute is `icon`. The value of the `href` attribute is the name of the image file. The value of the `type` attribute describes the MIME type of the image—which defaults to `image/x-icon` for .ico files. The XHTML code to associate a favorites icon named favicon.ico to a Web page is as follows:

```
<link rel="icon" href="favicon.ico" type="image/x-icon" />
```

Note that to be compatible with Internet Explorer and follow Microsoft's proprietary syntax, you'll also need to code a second link tag:

```
<link rel="shortcut icon" href="favicon.ico" type="image/x-icon" />
```

Be aware that Internet Explorer's support of the favorites icon is somewhat buggy. You may need to publish your files to the Web (see the FTP tutorial in the student files) in order for the favicon to display in even current versions of Internet Explorer. Other browsers, such as Firefox, Safari, Google Chrome, and Opera, display favicons more reliably and also support GIF and PNG image formats. You'll get a chance to practice using a favicon in Hands-On Exercise #6 at the end of the chapter.

Advanced Techniques: Image Slicing

Graphic artists and designers can create complex Web page images. Sometimes parts of these images are better optimized as GIFs than as JPEGs. Some parts of these images may be better optimized as JPEGs than as GIFs. By **image slicing** the single, complex images into multiple, smaller images, you can optimize all portions for the most efficient display. There may be times when you plan special mouse rollover effects for parts of a large, complex image. In this case, parts of the image need to be individually accessible to scripting languages and the image needs to be sliced. When an image is sliced, it is broken into multiple graphic files. These multiple graphic files are formatted using an XHTML table. Most graphics applications, such as Adobe Fireworks and Adobe Photoshop, have features for image slicing that automatically create the XHTML for you. Visit the Web site http://webdevfoundations.net/5e/chapter4.html for more information on image slicing.

5 Sources and Guidelines for Graphics

How do you obtain graphics for your pages? What are recommended ways to use graphics? This section will help you answer these questions and discuss sources of graphics as well as guidelines for using images on Web pages.

Sources of Graphics

There are many ways to obtain graphics: you can create them using a graphics application, download them from a free site, purchase and download them from a graphics site, purchase a graphics collection on a CD, take digital photographs, scan photographs, scan drawings, or hire a graphic designer to create graphics for you. Popular graphic applications include Adobe Photoshop, Adobe Fireworks, and Jasc Paint Shop Pro. These applications usually include tutorials and sample images to help you get started. Visit the textbook Web site at http://webdevfoundations.net/5e/chapter4.html, for tutorials on using Adobe Fireworks and Adobe Photoshop to create a logo banner image.

Focus on Ethics

However, one thing that you should definitely not do is right-click and download graphics that others have created without first obtaining their permission. Materials on a Web site are copyrighted (even if a copyright symbol or notice does not appear) and are not free to use unless the owner of the site permits it.

There are many Web sites that offer free graphics, although some graphics are free for nonprofit use only. Choose a search engine and search for "free graphics"—you'll get more results than you have time to view. The following are a few sites that you may find helpful when looking for images:

- Microsoft Clip Art: http://office.microsoft.com/clipart/default.aspx
- FamFamFam: http://www.famfamfam.com
- Free Stock Photo Search Engine: http://www.everystockphoto.com
- Free Images: http://www.freeimages.co.uk
- The Stock Solution: http://www.tssphoto.com
- SuperStock: http://www.superstock.com
- iStockphoto: http://www.istockphoto.com

It is also possible to create a banner or button image online. There are a number of sites that offer this feature—some include advertising with your free image, some offer paid memberships, others are simply free. Search for "create free online banner" to find sites offering this service.

- Animation Online: http://www.animationonline.com
- Web 2.0 LogoCreator: http://creatr.cc/creatr
- Cooltext.com: http://www.cooltext.com
- Ad Designer.com: http://www.addesigner.com

Guidelines for Using Images

Images can help your Web page by creating an engaging, interesting user experience. Images can hurt your Web pages by slowing down their performance to a crawl and discouraging visitors.

Consider Image Load Time. Be careful when using images on Web pages—it takes time for them to load. A suggested maximum file size for both the Web page and all the media files used by it is 60KB. If your banner graphic is 25KB, that does not leave much room for other images or even for your Web page XHTML. Use images when they are necessary to convey a message or complement a Web site's look and feel. Table 4 lists the download time for file sizes of 30KB, 60KB, and 90KB at various connection speeds.

Table 4 Download times

File Size	Approximate Connection Speed				
	28.8KB	33.6KB	56KB	ISDN (128KB)	T-1 (1.544MB)
30KB	8 seconds	7 seconds	4 seconds	1 second	Less than 1 second
60KB	17 seconds	14 seconds	8 seconds	3 seconds	Less than 1 second
90KB	25 seconds	21 seconds	13 seconds	5 seconds	Less than 1 second

Reuse Images. Once an image from your site is requested for a Web page, it is stored in the cache on your visitor's hard drive. Subsequent requests for the image will use the file from the hard drive instead of another download. This results in faster page loads for all pages that also use the image. It is recommended that you reuse common graphics such as logos and navigation buttons on multiple pages instead of creating different versions of these common graphics.

Consider the Size/Quality Issue. When using a graphics application to create an image, you can choose among varying levels of image quality. There is a correspondence between the quality of the image and the size of the image file—the higher the quality, the larger the file size. Choose the smallest file that gives you appropriate quality. You may need to experiment until you get the right match. Also be aware of the file size when using graphics created by others—the image may look great but if it is 300KB, you really shouldn't use it on a Web page.

Use Appropriate Resolution. Web browsers display images at relatively low resolution—72ppi (pixels per inch) or 96ppi. Many digital cameras and scanners can create images with much higher resolution. Of course, higher resolution means larger file size. Even though the browser does not display the depth of resolution, more bandwidth is still used for the large file size. Be careful when taking digital photographs or scanning. Use a resolution setting appropriate for Web pages. A one-inch image saved at 150ppi could appear close to two inches wide on a 72ppi monitor.

Specify Dimensions. Always use accurate `height` and `width` attributes on image tags. This will allow the browser to allocate the appropriate space on the Web page for the image and load the page faster. Do not try to resize the appearance of an image by modifying the settings of the `height` and `width` attributes. While this will work, your page will load slower and your image quality may suffer. Instead, use a graphics application to create a smaller or larger version of the graphic when needed.

Be Aware of Brightness and Contrast. Gamma refers to the brightness and contrast of the monitor display. Monitors used with Macintosh and Windows operating systems use a different default gamma setting (Macintosh 1.8, Windows 2.2). Images that have good contrast on a computer running Windows may look slightly washed out on a Macintosh. Images created on a Macintosh may look darker with less contrast when displayed on a computer with a Windows operating system. Be aware that even monitors on the same operating system may have slightly different gamma values than the default for the platform. A Web developer cannot control gamma, but should be aware that images will look different on various platforms because of this issue.

Accessibility and Visual Elements

Focus on Accessibility

Even though images help to create a compelling, interesting Web site, remember that not all your visitors will be able to view your images. The Web Accessibility Initiative has a number of guidelines for Web developers in the use of color and images.

- Don't rely on color alone. Some visitors may have color perception deficiencies. Use high contrast between background and text color.

- Provide a text equivalent for every nontext element. Use the `alt` attribute on your image tags.
- If your site navigation uses image links, provide simple text links at the bottom of the page.

Vinton Cerf, the coinventor of TCP/IP and the former Chairman of the Internet Society, said, "The Internet is for everyone." Follow Web accessibility guidelines to ensure that this is true.

CHECKPOINT 3

1. Search for a site that uses image links to provide navigation. List the URL of the page. What colors are used on the image links? If the image links contain text, is there good contrast between the background color and letters on the image links? Would the page be accessible to a visitor who is sight-challenged? How have accessibility issues been addressed? Is the `alt` attribute used to describe the image link? Is there a row of text links in the footer section of the page? Answer these questions and discuss your findings.
2. When configuring an image map, describe the relationship between the image, map, and area tags.
3. True or False? Save your images using the smallest file size possible.

CHAPTER SUMMARY

This chapter introduced the use of visual elements and graphics on Web pages. As you continue to create Web pages, refer to the guidelines and accessibility issues related to graphics. The number one reason visitors leave Web pages is long download times. When using images, be careful to minimize download time. Also, provide alternatives to images (such as text links) and use the `alt` attribute on your pages.

Visit http://www.webdevfoundations.net for examples, the links listed in this chapter, and updated information.

Key Terms

`<area />`
`<hr />`
`<img />`
`<map>`
`alt` attribute
animated GIFs
antialiasing
`background-image` property
`background-repeat` property
`border` property
`border-color` property
`border-style` property
`border-width` property
favicon
gamma
GIF
halo effect
`height` attribute
hotspots
`hspace` attribute
image link
image map
image optimization
image slicing
interlaced image
JPEG
`longdesc` attribute
lossless compression
lossy compression
min-width property
`padding` property
pixelation
PNG
progressive JPEG
resolution
`src` attribute
thumbnail image
transparency
`usemap` attribute
`vspace` attribute
`width` attribute

Review Questions

Multiple Choice

1. Which CSS property is used to change the background color?
   a. bgcolor
   b. background-color
   c. color
   d. none of the above

2. Which is the correct CSS syntax to configure the text color dark blue (#000033)?
   a. `body: color=#000033`
   b. `{ body color:#000033 }`
   c. `body { color:#000033 }`
   d. `body { text-color:#000033 }`

3. Which of the following creates an image link to the index.html page when the home.gif graphic is clicked?
   a. `<a href="index.html" src="home.gif" alt="Home"></a>`
   b. `<a href="index.html"><img src="home.gif" alt="Home" /></a>`
   c. `<img src="home.gif" href="index.html" alt="Home">`
   d. none of the above

4. Why should you include height and width attributes on an <img /> tag?
   a. They are required attributes and must always be included.
   b. They help the browser render the page faster because it reserves the appropriate space for the image.
   c. They help the browser display the image in its own window.
   d. none of the above

5. Which attribute specifies text that is available to browsers and other user agents that do not support graphics?
   a. alt
   b. text
   c. src
   d. none of the above

6. What is the term used to describe a square icon that is associated with a Web page and is displayed in the browser address bar or tab?
   a. background
   b. bookmark icon
   c. favicon
   d. logo

7. Which of the following graphic types is best suited to photographs?
   a. GIF
   b. photo
   c. BMP
   d. none of the above

8. Which of the following graphic types can be made transparent?
   a. GIF
   b. JPG
   c. BMP
   d. photo

9. Which of the following configures empty space between the content of the XHTML element (usually text) and the border?
   a. vspace property
   b. padding property
   c. margin property
   d. none of the above

10. Which of the following configures a graphic to repeat vertically down the side of a Web page?
    a. hspace="10"
    b. background-repeat:repeat;
    c. valign="left"
    d. background-repeat: repeat-y;

Fill in the Blank

11. A background image will automatically be repeated, or ________________, by a Web browser.

12. If your Web page uses graphic links, include ________________ at the bottom of the page to increase accessibility.

13. A ________________ image is a smaller version of a larger image that usually links to the larger image.

14. One method to obtain graphics for your Web site is to ________________.

15. A(n) ________________ is an image that can be used as one or more hyperlinks.

Apply Your Knowledge

1. **Predict the Result.** Draw and write a brief description of the Web page that will be created with the following XHTML code:

```
<!DOCTYPE html PUBLIC "-//W3C//DTD XHTML 1.0 Transitional//EN"
  "http://www.w3.org/TR/xhtml1/DTD/xhtml1-transitional.dtd">
<html xmlns="http://www.w3.org/1999/xhtml" lang="en" xml:lang="en">
```

```
<head>
<title>Predict the Result</title>
<meta http-equiv="Content-Type" content="text/html; charset=utf-8" />
</head>
<body>
  <div>
    <img src="logo.gif" alt="CircleSoft Design"
    height="150" width="600" />    <br />
    <p>Home <a href="about.html">About</a>
      <a href="services.html">Services</a>
    </p>
  </div>
  <p><img src="people.jpg" alt="Professionals at CircleSoft
Design" height="300" width="300" align="right" /> Our professional
staff takes pride in its working relationship with our clients by
offering personalized services which listen to their needs,
develop their target areas, and incorporate these items into a
well presented Web Site that works.</p>
  </div>
</body>
</html>
```

2. **Fill in the Missing Code.** This Web page contains an image link and should be configured so that the background and text colors have good contrast. The image used on this Web page should link to a page called services.html. Some XHTML attribute values, indicated by "_" are missing. Some CSS style rules indicated by "_" are incomplete.

```
<!DOCTYPE html PUBLIC "-//W3C//DTD XHTML 1.0 Transitional//EN"
  "http://www.w3.org/TR/xhtml1/DTD/xhtml1-transitional.dtd">
<html xmlns="http://www.w3.org/1999/xhtml" lang="en" xml:lang="en">
<head>
<title>CircleSoft Design</title>
<meta http-equiv="Content-Type" content="text/html; charset=utf-8" />
<style type="text/css">
.body { "_": "_";
        color: "_";
}
</style>
</head>
<body>
<div>
  <a href="_"><img src="logo.gif" alt="_" height="100" width="600"/>
  <br />Enter CircleSoft Design</a>
</div>
</body>
</html>
```

3. **Find the Error.** This page displays an image called trillium.jpg. The image is 100 pixels wide by 200 pixels high. When this page is displayed, the image does not look right. Find the error. Describe the attributes that you would code in the <img /> tag to provide accessibility.

```
<!DOCTYPE html PUBLIC "-//W3C//DTD XHTML 1.0 Transitional//EN"
  "http://www.w3.org/TR/xhtml1/DTD/xhtml1-transitional.dtd">
<html xmlns="http://www.w3.org/1999/xhtml" lang="en" xml:lang="en">
<head>
<title>Find the Error<title>
<meta http-equiv="Content-Type" content="text/html; charset=utf-8" />
</head>
<body>
<img src="trillium.jpg" height="100" width="100" alt="Trillium
flower" />
</body>
</html>
```

Hands-On Exercises

1. Write the XHTML to place an image called primelogo.gif on a Web page. The image is 100 pixels high by 650 pixels wide.
2. Write the XHTML to create an image hyperlink. The image is called schaumburgthumb.jpg. It is 100 pixels high by 150 pixels wide. The image should link to a larger image called schaumburg.jpg. There should be no border on the image.
3. Write the XHTML to create a <div> containing three images used as navigation links. Table 5 provides information about the images and their associated links.

Table 5

Image Name	Link Page Name	Image Height	Image Width
home.gif	index.html	50	200
products.gif	products.html	50	200
order.gif	order.html	50	200

4. Experiment with page backgrounds.
   a. Locate the twocolor.gif file in the student files chapter4/starters folder. Design a Web page that uses this file as a background image that repeats down the left side of the browser window. Save your file as bg1.html. Hand in printouts of the source code (print in Notepad) and the browser display of your page to your instructor.
   b. Locate the twocolor1.gif file in the student files chapter4/starters folder. Design a Web page that uses this file as a background image that repeats across the top of the browser window. Save your file as bg2.html. Hand in printouts of the source code (print in Notepad) and the browser display of your page to your instructor.
5. Visit one of your favorite Web sites. Note the colors used for background, text, headings, images, and so on. Write a paragraph that describes how the site uses color for these elements and if the Web Safe Color Palette is used. Code a Web page (either a new page or you can use the index.html file from the student files, Chapter4/index.html) that uses colors in a similar manner.
6. **Practice with Favicon.** Obtain the favicon.ico file from the student files in the Chapter4/starters folder. In this exercise you will use your files from Hands-On Practice 5 (see the student files Chapter4/4.5 folder) as a starting point. You are

going to associate the favorites icon, favicon.ico, with the index.html page—you'll need to use the link tag (refer back to Section 4). Hand in printouts of the source code to your instructor.

7. Design a new Web page about your favorite movie. Configure a background color for the page, and either background images or background colors for at least two sections of the page. Search the Web for a photo of a scene from the movie, an actress in the movie, or an actor in the movie.

   Include the following information on your Web page:

   - Title of the movie
   - Director or producer
   - Leading actor
   - Leading actress
   - Rating (R, PG-13, PG, G, NR)
   - A brief description of the movie
   - An absolute link to a review about the movie

   Save the page as movie3.html. Hand in printouts of both the source code (print in Notepad) and the browser display of your page to your instructor.

   Focus on Ethics

   (*Note*: It is unethical to steal an image from another Web site. Some Web sites have a link to their copyright policy. Most Web sites will give permission for you to use an image in a school assignment. If there is no available policy, e-mail the site's contact person and request permission to use the photo. If you are unable to obtain permission, you may substitute with clip art or an image from a free site instead.)

8. Design a Web page that provides a list of resources for free clip art and free photographs. The list should contain at least five different Web sites. Use your favorite graphic sites, the sites suggested in this chapter, or sites you have found on the Web. Save the page as freegraphics.html. Hand in printouts of both the source code (print in Notepad) and the browser display of your page to your instructor.

9. Design a Web page about your favorite musical group. Use a background color for the page and either background images or background colors for at least two sections of the page. Search the Web for a photo of the group.

   Include the following information about the group on your Web page:

   - Name of group
   - Type of music
   - Names of principle group members
   - Photo of group
   - Link to another Web page with information about the group.

   Save the page as band3.html. Hand in printouts of the source code (print in Notepad) and the browser display of your page to your instructor.

   Focus on Ethics

   (*Note*: It is unethical to steal an image from another Web site. Some Web sites have a link to their copyright policy. Most Web sites will give permission for you to use an image in a school assignment. If there is no available policy, e-mail the site's contact person and request permission to use the photo. If you are unable to obtain permission, you may substitute clip art or an image from a free site.)

10. Visit http://webdevfoundations.net/5e/chapter4.html and follow the link to the Adobe Fireworks or Adobe Photoshop tutorial. Follow the instructions to create a logo banner. Hand in the printouts described in the tutorial to your instructor.

Web Research

Providing access to the Web for all people is an important issue. Visit the W3C's Web Accessibility Initiative and explore their WCAG 2.0 Quick Reference at http://www.w3.org/WAI/WCAG20/quickref/ (http://webdevfoundations.net/5e/chapter4.html has an updated link if needed). View additional pages at the W3C's site as necessary. Explore the checkpoints that are related to the use of color and images on Web pages. Create a Web page that uses color, uses images, and includes the information that you discovered. Print both the source code (from Notepad) and the browser view of your Web page.

Focus on Web Design

Visit a Web sites that interests you. Print the home page or one other pertinent page from the site. Write a one-page summary and reaction to the Web site you chose to visit. Address the following topics:

a. What is the purpose of the site?

b. Who is the intended audience?

c. Do you believe the site reaches its audience?

d. Was this site useful to you? Why or why not?

e. List the colors that were used on the home page of this Web site: background, backgrounds of page sections, text, logo, navigation buttons, and so on.

f. How did the use of color enhance the Web site?

WEB SITE CASE STUDY: Using Graphics

Each of the following case studies in this chapter adds images to the following Web sites, creates a new page, and modifies existing pages.

JavaJam Coffee House

See the Chapter "XHTML Basics" for an introduction to the JavaJam Coffee House Case Study. Figure 26 in that chapter shows a site map for the JavaJam Web site. The Home page and Menu page were created in earlier chapters. You will continue to work with this Web site here.

You have the following tasks:

1. Modify the Home page to display a logo, a JPEG image, and additional text, as shown in Figure 26 (shown also in the color insert section).

Figure 26
New JavaJam Home page

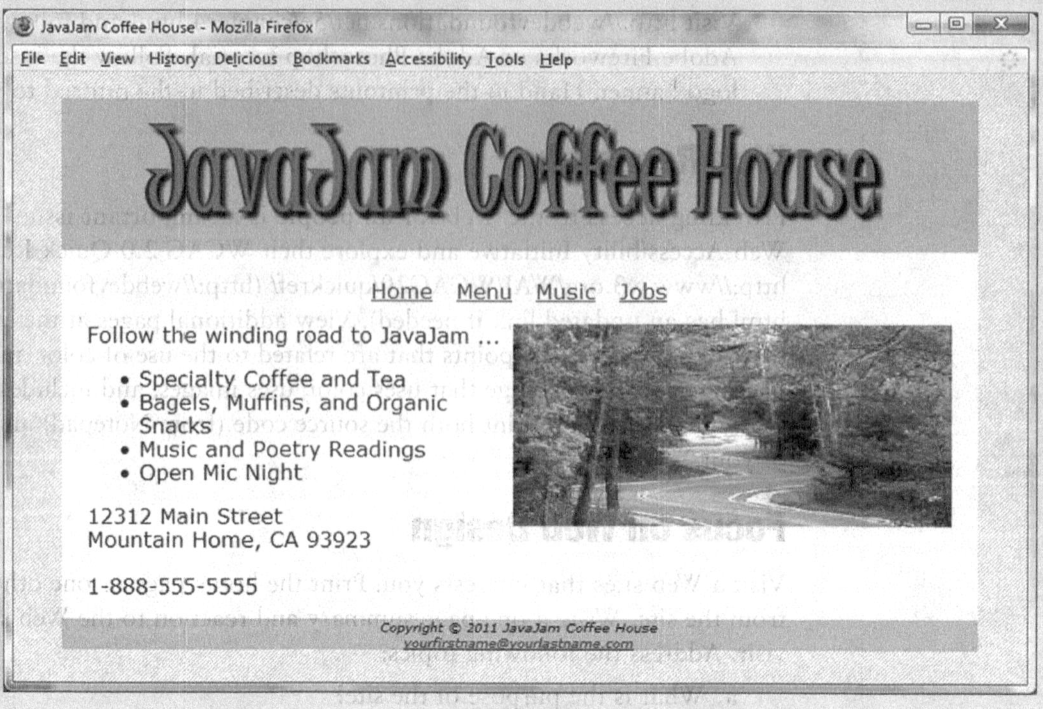

Go to the end of the chapter for a full color version of this figure

2. Modify the Menu page to be consistent with the Home page.
3. Create a new Music page, as shown in Figure 27.
4. Modify the style rules in the javajam.css file as needed.

Figure 27
JavaJam music.html

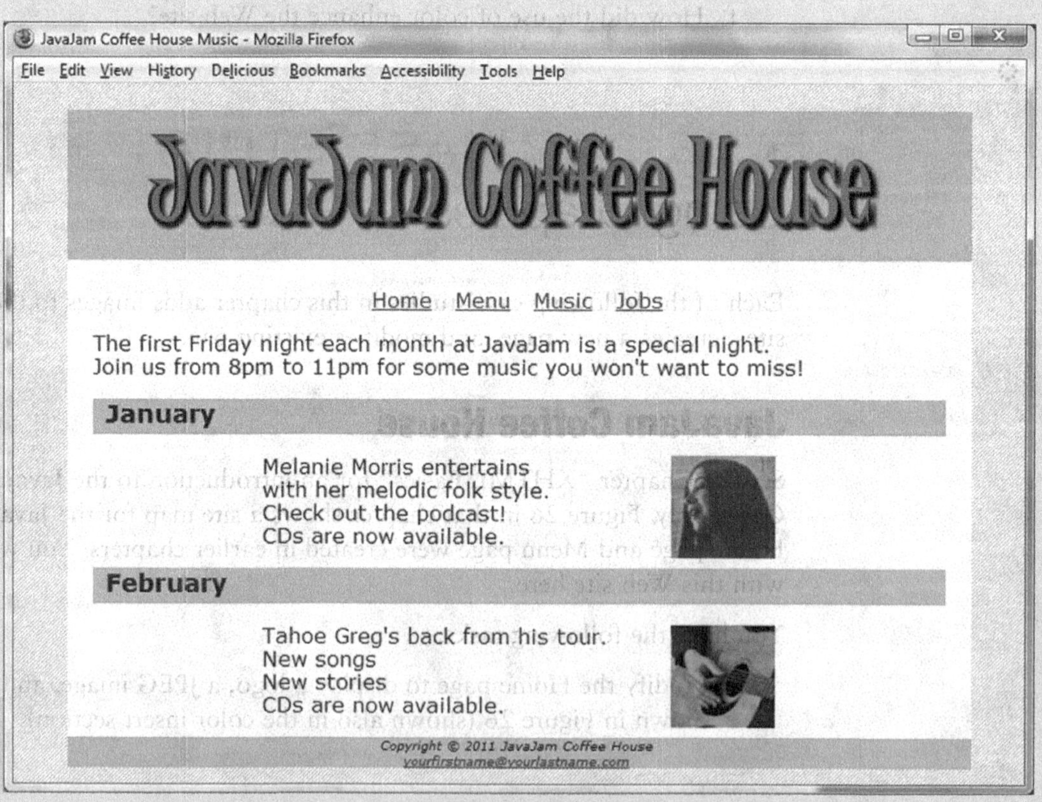

Go to the end of the chapter for a full color version of this figure

Hands-On Practice Case

Obtain the images used in this case study from the student files. The images are located in the Chapter4/CaseStudyStarters/JavaJam folder. The images are: melanie.jpg (Figure 28), melaniethumb.jpg (Figure 29), greg.jpg (Figure 30), gregthumb.jpg (Figure 31), javalogo.gif (Figure 32), windingroad.jpg (Figure 33), and background.gif (Figure 34). Save them in your javajam folder.

Figure 28
Melanie Morris (melanie.jpg)

Figure 29
Melanie Morris thumbnail (melaniethumb.jpg)

Figure 30
Greg (greg.jpg)

Figure 31
Greg thumbnail (gregthumb.jpg)

Figure 32
JavaJam logo (javalogo.gif)

Figure 33
Winding road (windingroad.jpg)

Figure 34
Background (background.gif)

1. **The Home Page.** Launch Notepad and open the index.html file from your javajam folder. Modify the index.html file to look similar to the Web page shown in Figure 26.
   - Replace the JavaJam Coffee House heading with the javalogo.gif, Figure 32. Be sure to include the `alt`, `height`, and `width` attributes on the `<img />` tag for the graphic.
   - Configure windingroad.jpg, Figure 33, to display on the right side of the paragraph. Be sure to include the `alt`, `height`, and `width` attributes. *Hint*: Use the `align="right"` attribute on the `<img />` tag.

   Save and test your new index.html page.
2. **The Menu Page.** Launch Notepad and open the menu.html page from your javajam folder. Modify the menu.html page in a similar manner—adding the logo banner. Save and test your new menu.html page.

3. **The Music Page.** Use the Menu page as the starting point for the Music page. Launch Notepad and open the menu.html file in the javajam folder that you previously created. Save the file as music.html.

   Modify the music.html file to look similar to the Music page, as shown in Figure 27:

   - Change the page title to an appropriate phrase.
   - Delete the definition list from the page.
   - The main content in the page will consist of an introductory paragraph below the navigation and two sections describing music performances.
   - The content of the paragraph is as follows:

     The first Friday night each month at JavaJam is a special night. Join us from 8pm to 11pm for some music you won't want to miss!

     Place a line break tag after the first sentence.
   - The section describing each music performance consists of an `<h3>` element, a paragraph, and an image link. You'll need to configure the paragraph, so assign it to a class named `content`.
   - January Music Performance:

     Configure an `<h2>` with the following text: January

     Configure a paragraph assigned to the `content` class with the following text:

     Melanie Morris entertains

     with her melodic folk style.

     Check out the podcast!

     CDs are now available.

     Add line breaks as indicated above.
   - Configure the melaniethumb.jpg as an image link to melanie.jpg. Code appropriate attributes on the `<img />` element, including `align="right"`
   - February Music Performance:

     Configure an `<h2>` with the following text: February

     Configure a paragraph assigned to the `content` class with the following text:

     Tahoe Greg's back from his tour.

     New songs

     New stories

     CDs are now available.

     Add line breaks as indicated above.
   - Configure the gregthumb.jpg as an image link to greg.jpg. Code appropriate attributes on the `<img />` element, including `align="right"`
   - Save the music.html file. If you test your page in a browser you'll notice that it looks different from Figure 27—you still need to configure style rules.

4. **Configure the CSS.** Open javajam.css in Notepad. Edit the style rules as follows:

   - Modify the body selector style rules. Configure background.gif (see Figure 34) as the background image.
   - Modify the container id. Configure the background color to be #ffffcc. Configure a minimum width of 700px (use min-width).

- Modify the content id. Now that the page has a background image, the content seems to be crowding the left and right sides. Configure 20 pixels of left and right padding (use padding-left and padding-right).
- Modify the `h1` selector. Remove the line-height style rule.
- Add a new style rule for the `h2` selector that configures a background color (#ccaa66), font size (1.2em), left padding (10px) and bottom padding (5px). The style rules follow:

```
background-color: #ccaa66;
font-size: 1.2em;
padding-left: 10px;
padding-bottom: 5px;
```

- Configure the class named `details` to add 20 percent left and right padding (use `padding-left` and `padding-right`). Notice how this adds empty space either side of the music performance description and image.
- Configure the `img` selector not to display a border.

Save the javajam.css file. Test it in a browser. If your images do not appear or your image links do not work, examine your work carefully. Use Windows Explorer to verify that the images are saved in your javajam folder. Examine the `src` attribute on the <img /> tags to be sure you spelled the image names correctly. Another useful troubleshooting technique is to validate the XHTML and CSS code.

Fish Creek Animal Hospital

See the chapter "XHTML Basics" for an introduction to the Fish Creek Animal Hospital Case Study. Figure 30 in that chapter shows a site map for Fish Creek. The Home page and Services page were created in earlier chapters. You will continue to work with this Web site in this case study, creating the Ask the Vet page, shown in Figure 35. You will then modify the other pages so they are consistent with the new design.

Figure 35
Fish Creek askvet.html

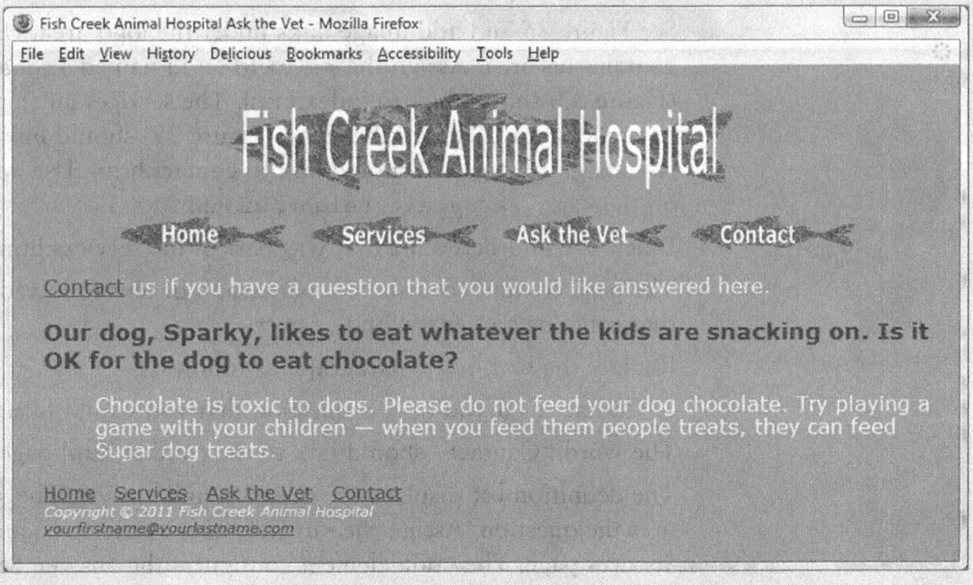

Go to the end of the chapter for a full color version of this figure

Hands-On Practice Case

Obtain the images used in this case study from the student files. The images are located in the Chapter4/CaseStudyStarters/FishCreek folder. The images are: fishcreeklogo.gif (Figure 36), home.gif (Figure 37), services.gif (Figure 38), askthevet.gif (Figure 39), and contact.gif (Figure 40). Save the files in your fishcreek folder.

Figure 36
Fish Creek logo
(fishcreeklogo.gif)

Figure 37
Home button
(home.gif)

Figure 38
Services button
(services.gif)

Figure 39
Ask the Vet button
(askthevet.gif)

Figure 40
Contact button
(contact.gif)

1. **The Ask the Vet Page.** Use the Services page as the starting point for the Ask the Vet page. Launch Notepad and open the services.html file in the fishcreek folder that you previously created. Save the file as askvet.html.

   Modify your file to look similar to the Ask the Vet page, as shown in Figure 33.

   - Change the page title to an appropriate phrase.
   - Replace the Fish Creek Animal Hospital heading with the fishcreeklogo.gif, as shown in Figure 36. Be sure to include the `alt`, `height`, and `width` attributes on the `<img />` tag for the graphic.
   - Move the text links to the bottom of the page right above the copyright information (see Figure 35).
   - See Figure 35 and add image links under the logo area. Use a `<div>` element to contain this area. Assign the `<div>` to an id named `imgnav`. The home.gif (Figure 37) should link to index.html. The services.gif (Figure 38) should link to services.html. The askthevet.gif (Figure 39) should link to askvet.html. The contact.gif (Figure 40) should link to contact.html. Use appropriate attributes on the `<img />` tag: `alt`, `height`, `width`.
   - Delete the unordered list that was part of the services.html page.
   - The page content consists of a paragraph of text followed by a definition list that contains a question and answer.
   - Replace the text in the paragraph as follows:

     Contact us if you have a question that you would like answered here.

     The word "Contact" should link to the contact.html page.
   - The definition list displays the question and answer. The `<dt>` element configures the question. Assign the `<dt>` element to the `category` class used on the Services page. The `<dd>` element configures the answer. See Appendix B Special Characters for the character code to display the em dash (—).

- The content of the definition list is as follows:

  Question: Our dog, Sparky, likes to eat whatever the kids are snacking on. Is it OK for the dog to eat chocolate?"

  Answer: Chocolate is toxic to dogs. Please do not feed your dog chocolate. Try playing a game with your children—when you feed them people treats they can feed Sparky dog treats.

2. **Configure the CSS.** Open fishcreek.css in Notepad. Edit the style rules as follows:
   - The fish navigation image area is quite wide. Modify the style rules and change the width of the page content `container` id from 80 percent to 700 pixels.
   - Modify the style rules for the `h1` selector. Delete the existing style rules. Add a new style rule to center the image (use `text-align:center`).
   - Configure the id named `imgnav` to be centered (use `text-align:center`).
   - Configure the `img` selector not to display a border.

   Save the fishcreek.css file.
3. **Save and Test.** Save your page and test it in a browser. If your images do not appear or your image links do not work, examine your work carefully. Use Windows Explorer to verify that the images are saved in your fishcreek folder. Examine the `src` attribute on the image tags to be sure you spelled the image names correctly. Another useful troubleshooting technique is to validate the XHTML and CSS code.

Focus on Accessibility

4. **The Home and Services Pages.** Modify the Home page (index.html) and Services page (services.html) to look similar to the Ask the Vet page you just created. Save and test your pages. Notice how the use of coordinating logo and navigation images helped to unite the Web site visually. To provide accessibility, the original text navigation links were not deleted. Instead, they were moved to the bottom of the page. It is common for sites that use images for main navigation to provide simple text links at the lower portion of each Web page.

Pasha the Painter

See the chapter "XHTML Basics" for an introduction to the Pasha the Painter Case Study. Figure 34 in that chapter shows a site map for Pasha the Painter. The Home page and Services page were created in earlier chapters. You will continue to work with this Web site in this case study and create the Testimonials page, as shown in Figure 41. You will then modify the other pages so they are consistent with the new design.

Hands-On Practice Case

Obtain the images used in this case study from the student files. The images are located in the Chapter4/CaseStudyStarters/Painter folder. The images are: painterlogo.gif (Figure 42), paintroom.jpg (Figure 43), paintroom_small.jpg (Figure 44), undecorated.jpg (Figure 45), and undecorated_small.jpg (Figure 46). Save the files in your painter folder.

1. **The Testimonials Page.** Use the Services page as the starting point for the Testimonials page. Launch Notepad and open the services.html file in the painter

Figure 41
Pasha the Painter testimonials.html

Go to the end of the chapter for a full color version of this figure

Figure 42
Pasha the Painter logo (painterlogo.gif)

Figure 43
Painted room (paintroom.jpg)

Figure 44
Painted room thumbnail (paintroom_small.jpg)

Figure 45
Undecorated room
(undecorated.jpg)

Figure 46
Undecorated room thumbnail
(undecorated_small.jpg)

folder that you previously created. Save the file as testimonials.html Modify your file to look similar to the Testimonials page, as shown in Figure 41:

- Change the page title to an appropriate phrase.
- Replace the Pasha the Painter heading with the painterlogo.gif, Figure 42. Be sure to include the `alt`, `height`, and `width` attributes on the `<img />` tag for the graphic.
- Delete the unordered list that was copied as part of the services.html page.
- The main content consists of two sections describing testimonials with an `<h2>` element, a paragraph, and an image hyperlink. See Appendix B Special Characters for the character code to display the em dash (—).

Painting Testimonial

- Configure an `<h2>` with the following text: Painting
- Configure a paragraph with the following text:

  We were selling our home and needed a room painted quickly. Pasha's team promptly came out and gave an estimate. It was quite reasonably priced.

  They started and finished the very next day!—The Morris Family.
- Configure the paintroom_small.jpg as an image link to paintroom.jpg. Code appropriate attributes on the `<img />` element, including `align="left"`.

Remodeling Testimonial

- Configure an `<h2>` with the following text: Remodeling
- Configure a paragraph with the following text:

  We needed to "undecorate" a room—the previous owners had been a little too creative. Pasha's team provided an estimate, promptly began work, and within a few days our room was looking great!—The Felkes.
- Configure the undecorated_small.jpg as an image link to undecorated.jpg. Code appropriate attributes on the `<img />` element, including `align="left"`.

Save the testimonials.html file. If you test your page in a browser you'll notice that it looks different from Figure 41—you still need to configure style rules.

2. **Configure the CSS.** Open painter.css in Notepad. Edit the style rules as follows:
   - Add a new style rule for the `h2` selector that configures a background color (#336633), text color (#ffffff), font typeface (Georgia, Times New Roman, or serif), font size of 1.2em, left padding (10px), and bottom padding (5px).
   - Modify the CSS to configure an id named `container` with width set to 620 pixels.
   - Configure the `img` selector as follows: 10 pixels of right padding and do not display a border.

   Save the painter.css file.
3. **Configure the `container` id on each page.** Modify the index.html, services.html, and testimonials.html pages to utilize a wrapper `<div>` that configures the page width as indicated. On each page, assign the `container` id to a `<div>` element that contains the page content (see Section 3.9 for a review). Configure this `<div>` on each page as follows:

```
<body>
  <div id="container">
  ... page content goes here
  </div>
</body>
```

4. **Test.** Test your pages in a browser. If your images do not appear or your image links do not work, examine your work carefully. Use Windows Explorer to verify that the images are saved in your painter folder. Examine the `src` attribute on the `<img />` tags to be sure you spelled the image names correctly. Another useful troubleshooting technique is to validate the XHTML and CSS code. See Chapters 2 and 3 for Hands-On Practice exercises that describe how to use these validators.
5. **The Home and Services Pages.** Modify the Home page (index.html) and Services page (services.html) to display the Pasha the Painter logo (painterlogo.gif) image and look similar to the Testimonials page you just created. A cohesive Web site uses color and images in a consistent manner. Save and test your pages.

Prime Properties

See the Chapter "XHTML Basics" for an introduction to the Prime Properties Case Study. Figure 38 in that chapter shows a site map for Prime Properties. A Home page and Financing page were created in earlier chapters. You will continue to work with this Web site in this case study and create the Listings page, as shown in Figure 47. You will then modify the other pages so that they are consistent with the new design.

Hands-On Practice Case

Obtain the images used in this case study from the student files. The images are located in the Chapter4/CaseStudyStarters/Prime folder. The images are: primelogo.gif (Figure 48), primehomenav.gif (Figure 49), primehomebtn.gif (Figure 50), primelist-ingsnav.gif (Figure 51), primelistingsbtn.gif (Figure 52), primefinancingnav.gif (Figure 53), primefinancingbtn.gif (Figure 54), primecontactnav.gif (Figure 55), primecontactbtn.gif (Figure 56), schaumburg.jpg (Figure 57), schaumburgthumb.jpg (Figure 58), liber-tyville.jpg (Figure 59), libertyvillethumb.jpg (Figure 60). Save the files in your prime folder.

Figure 47
Prime Properties
listings.html

Go to the end of the chapter for a full color version of this figure

Figure 48
Prime Properties
logo (primelogo.gif)

Figure 49
Home navigation
button
(primehomenav.gif)

Figure 50
Home page
placeholder button
(primehomebtn.gif)

Figure 51
Listings navigation
button
(primelistingsnav.gif)

Figure 52
Listings page
placeholder button
(primelistingsbtn.gif)

Figure 53
Financing
navigation button
(primefinancingnav.gif)

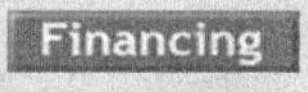

Figure 54
Financing page
placeholder button
(primefinancingbtn.gif)

Figure 55
Contact navigation button (primecontactnav.gif)

Figure 56
Contact page placeholder button (primecontactbtn.gif)

Figure 57
Schaumburg listing photo (schaumburg.jpg)

Figure 58
Schaumburg listing thumbnail (schaumburgthumb.jpg)

Figure 59
Libertyville listing photo (libertyville.jpg)

Figure 60
Libertyville listing thumbnail (libertyvillethumb.jpg)

1. **The Listings Page.** Use the Financing page as the starting point for the Listings page. Launch Notepad and open the financing.html file in the prime folder that you previously created. Save the file as listings.html. Modify your file to look similar to the Listings page, as shown in Figure 47.
   - Change the title to an appropriate phrase.
   - Replace the Prime Properties heading with the primelogo.gif, Figure 48. Be sure to include the `alt`, `height`, and `width` attributes on the `<img />` tag for the graphic.

     Move the `div` with the navigation links to the bottom of the page right above the copyright information (see Figure 47).
   - See Figure 47 and add a `div` with image links under the logo area. The navigation buttons use color as a visual cue for visitors. The navigation button links use a green background. The button for the current page is not a link and uses a blue background. To configure this area for the Listings page, use primehomenav.gif (link to index.html), primelistingsbtn.gif (no link), primefinancingnav.gif (link to financing.html), and primecontactnav.gif (link to contact.html). Use appropriate attributes on the `<img />` tag: `alt`, `height`, and `width`.
   - Replace the heading Financing with the heading Listings.
   - Delete the text between the Listings heading and the text navigation near the footer section of the Web page.
   - The section describing each listing consists of an `<h3>` element, a paragraph, an image link, and an unordered list.

   Schaumburg Colonial Listing
   - Configure an `<h3>` with the following text: Schaumburg Colonial
   - Configure a paragraph with the following text:

     This single family home is a two-story colonial on a large lot.
   - Configure the schaumburgthumb.jpg as an image link to schaumburg.jpg. Assign the `<img />` element to a class named property. Code appropriate attributes on the `<img />` element, including `align="left"`. *Note*: In Chapter 6 you'll learn to use CSS to configure this alignment.
   - Configure an unordered list with the following text:

     Four bedrooms

     Two and 1/2 baths

     Finished family room

     Two car garage

     Listing #3432535
   - Code a line break between the two listings.

   Libertyville Condo Listing
   - Configure an `<h3>` with the following text:

     Libertyville Condo
   - Configure a paragraph with the following text:

     New construction condo in downtown Libertyville.

- Configure the libertyvillethumb.jpg as an image link to libertyville.jpg. Assign the `<img />` element to a class named property. Code appropriate attributes on the `<img />` element, including `align="left"`.
- Configure an unordered list with the following text:

  Close to train

  Two bedrooms

  Two baths

  Two indoor parking spaces

  Listing #3432432
- Configure a line break after the unordered list.

Save the listings.html file. If you test your page in a browser you'll notice that it looks different from Figure 47—you still need to configure style rules.

2. **Configure the CSS.** Open prime.css in Notepad. Edit the style rules as indicated.
   - Configure the `img` selector to not display a border.
   - Configure the nav id for the new page design. Remove the existing style rules. Configure .70em font size.
   - Configure a class named property to have 30 pixels of right padding, and 5 pixels of top padding.

   Save the prime.css file.
3. **Test.** Test the listings.html page in a browser. If your images do not appear or your image links do not function, examine your work carefully. Use Windows Explorer to verify that the images are saved in your prime folder. Examine the `src` attributes on the `<img />` tags to be sure you spelled the image names correctly.
4. **The Home and Financing Pages.** Modify the Home page (index.html) and Financing page (financing.html) to be similar to the Listings page you just created. Pay close attention to the navigation buttons. Refer to Step 2 if necessary. Save and test your pages. Isn't it interesting how just a few images can add a professional look to a Web site?

Answers

Checkpoint 1

1. It is reasonable to code pages that look similar on various browsers; it is not reasonable to try to code pages that look exactly the same on various browsers and operating systems. As shown in this chapter, even a simple horizontal rule displays differently. Typically, Web developers code pages that look best on the browser and operating system most often used by their visitors. These pages should also look acceptable on other platforms. This is called "degrading gracefully."
2. The first style rule is missing an ending semicolon (;).
3. True. CSS can be utilized to configure color, text, and even visual elements such as rectangular shapes and lines (with the `border` property).

Checkpoint 2

1. CSS `background-image` property configures the file that is displayed. The CSS `background-repeat` property configures the way the image is displayed on the page.

   Suggested solution:

   ```
   h1 { background-image: url(circle.jpg);
        background-repeat: no-repeat;
   }
   ```
2. The CSS `background-image` property configures the file that is displayed. The CSS `background-repeat` property configures the way the image is displayed on the page.

   Suggested solution:

   ```
   body { background-image: url(bg.gif);
          background-repeat: repeat-y;
   }
   ```
3. The browser will display the background color immediately. Then, the browser will render the background image and repeat the image as specified in the CSS. The background color will appear in areas not covered by the background image.

Checkpoint 3

1. Answers will vary depending on the site that you choose to review. Suggested solution: The page reviewed is the home page of a travel soccer league. The URL is http://www.alithsa.org. Image links are used for the main navigation of the site. Each image link contains a rectangle with text and a soccer ball. There is good contrast between the black text and the background color of either yellow or green. Yellow background is used to indicate the current page. This page would not be easily accessible to a visitor who is site-challenged because of the `alt` attribute values used. Currently, every graphic has the same value for the `alt` attribute, "Picture". To improve accessibility the `alt` attribute values on each image tag should be modified to contain brief, descriptive phrases. On the plus

side, the page does display plain text links in the footer section. The images used as navigation links on this page contribute to the fun, sporty attitude of the site. The accessibility of the page needs to be improved.

2. The elements `<img />`, `<map>`, and `<area />`—work together to create a functioning image map. The `<img />` tag configures the image that will be used for the map and contains a `usemap` attribute whose value corresponds to the `id` value on the `<map>` tag associated with the image. The `<map>` tag is a container tag and surrounds one or more `<area />` tags. There is one self-contained `<area />` tag for each clickable hotspot on the image map. See the working example on the textbook Web site at http://webdevfoundations.net/5e/chapter4.html.
3. False. There is a trade-off between the quality of the image and the file size. The goal should be to save images using the smallest file size that provides acceptable display quality.

Review Questions

1. b
2. c
3. b
4. b
5. a
6. c
7. d
8. a
9. b
10. d
11. tiled
12. text links
13. thumbnail
14. Create them using a graphics application, download them from a free site, purchase and download them from a graphics site, purchase a graphics collection on CD, take digital photographs, scan photographs, scan drawings, or hire a graphic designer to create graphics.
15. image map

Web Design

Chapter Objectives

In this chapter, you will learn how to ...

- Describe the most common types of Web site organization
- Create clear, easy Web site navigation
- Design user-friendly Web pages
- Improve the readability of the text on your Web pages
- Use graphics appropriately
- Create accessible Web pages
- Describe design principles
- Describe Web page design techniques
- Apply best practices of Web design

As a Web site visitor, you have probably found that certain Web sites are appealing and easy to use while others seem awkward or just plain annoying. What separates the good from the bad? This chapter discusses recommended Web site design practices. The topics include site organization, site navigation, page design, text design, graphic design, and accessibility considerations.

Whatever your personal preferences, your Web site should be designed to appeal to your **target audience**—the people who will use your Web site. They may be teens, shoppers, college students, young couples, the list goes on and on. You should follow all of the recommended Web site design practices with an eye toward your target audience.

For example, NASA's site, http://www.nasa.gov (Figure 1), features compelling graphics and has a different look and feel from the text-based, link-intensive Web site of the Agency for Healthcare Research and Quality (see http://www.ahrq.gov, Figure 2).

Figure 1
The compelling graphic draws you in

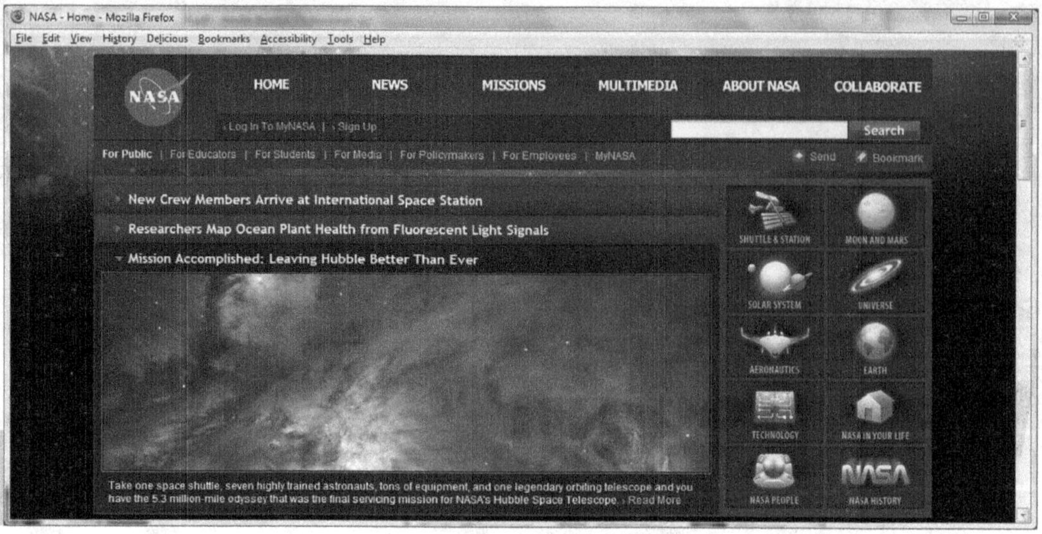

Go to the end of the chapter for a full color version of this figure

Figure 2
This text-intensive Web site offers numerous choices

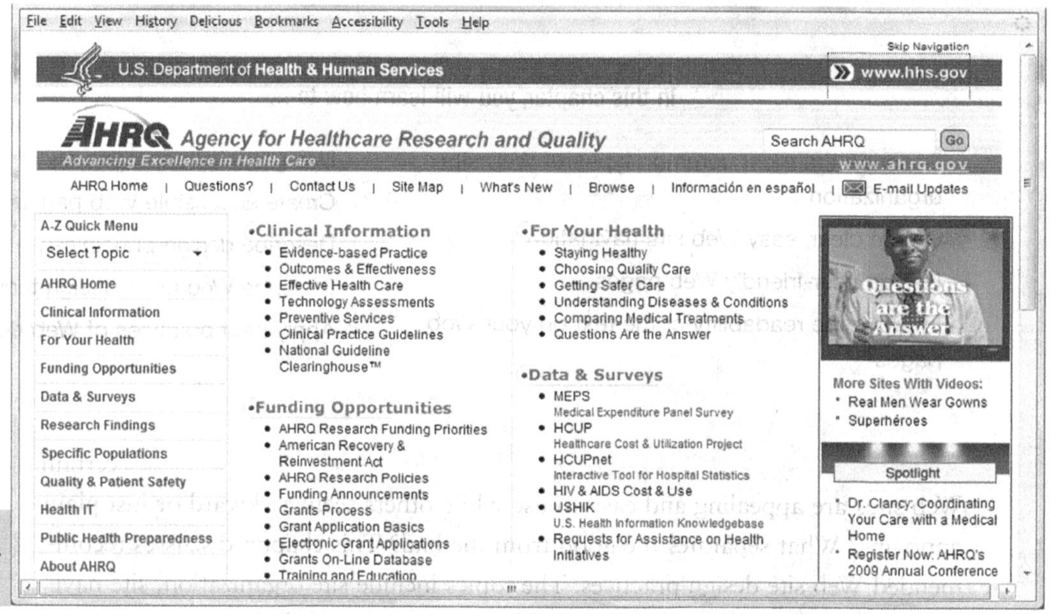

Go to the end of the chapter for a full color version of this figure

The first site engages you and draws you in. The second site provides you with a wide range of choices so that you can quickly get down to work. With your target audience in mind, take a look at some common recommended Web site design practices.

1 Web Site Organization

How will visitors move around your site? How will they find what they need? This is largely determined by the Web site's organization or architecture. There are three common types of Web site organization:

- Hierarchical
- Linear
- Random (sometimes called Web organization)

A diagram of the organization of a Web site is called a **site map** or **storyboard**. Creating the site map is one of the initial steps in developing a Web site.

Hierarchical Organization

Most Web sites use **hierarchical organization**. A site map for hierarchical organization, such as the one shown in Figure 3, is characterized by a clearly defined home page with links to major site sections. Web pages within sections are placed as needed.

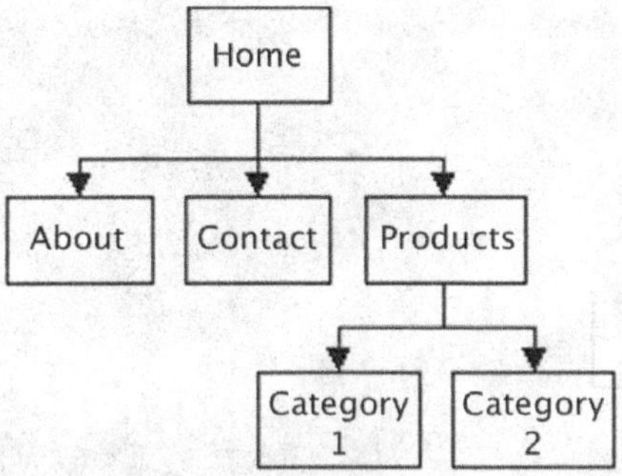

Figure 3
Hierarchical site organization

It is important to be aware of pitfalls of hierarchical organization. Figure 4 shows a site design that is too shallow—there are too many major site sections.

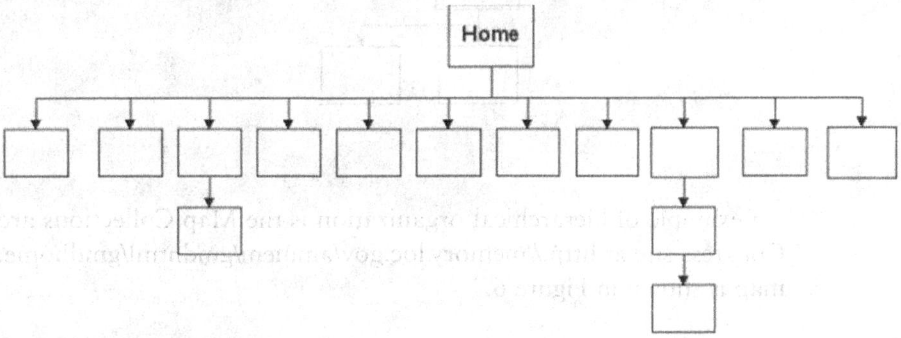

Figure 4
This site design uses a shallow hierarchy

This site design needs to be broken down into small, easily managed topics or units, a process called **chunking.** In the case of Web page design, each unit of information is a page. George A. Miller, a research psychologist for Princeton University's WorldNet (http://www.cogsci.princeton.edu/~wn/) found that humans can store only five to nine chunks of information at a time in short-term memory (see http://www.nwlink.com/~donclark/hrd/learning/memory.html). He called this the "seven plus or minus two" principle. Following this principle, many Web designers try not to place more than nine major navigation links on a page, unless they are creating a very large site. Even then, they may try to chunk the navigation links into visually separate sections on the page with each group having no more than nine links.

Another design pitfall is designing a site that is too deep. Figure 5 shows an example of this. The interface design "three click rule" says that a Web page visitor should be able to get from any page on your site to any other page on your site with a maximum of three hyperlinks. In other words, a visitor who cannot get what they want in three mouse clicks will begin to feel frustrated and may leave your site. This rule may be very difficult to satisfy on a large site, but in general, the goal is to organize your site so that your visitors can easily navigate from page to page within the site structure.

Figure 5
This site design uses a deep hierarchy

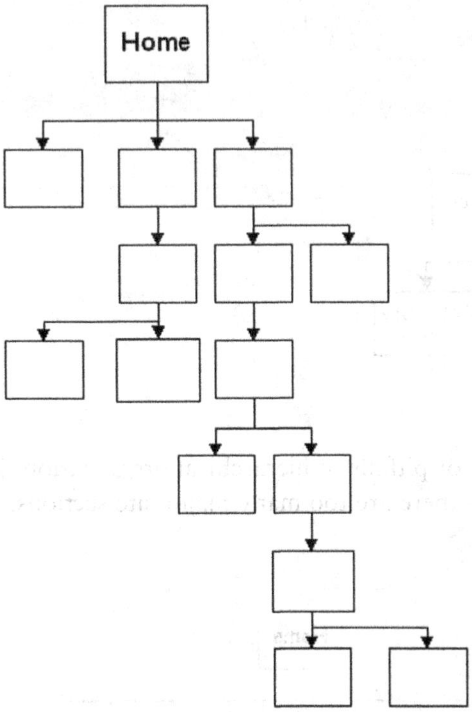

An example of hierarchical organization is the Map Collections area of the Library of Congress site at http://memory.loc.gov/ammem/gmdhtml/gmdhome.html. A partial site map is shown in Figure 6.

Figure 6
Map Collections site map

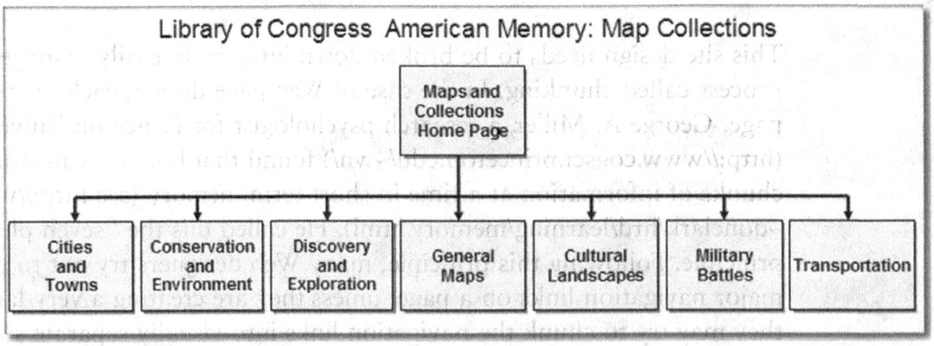

The Map Collections Home Page contains navigation to the main map areas. It functions as a map to the site (see Figure 7) and it is intentionally different from the content pages.

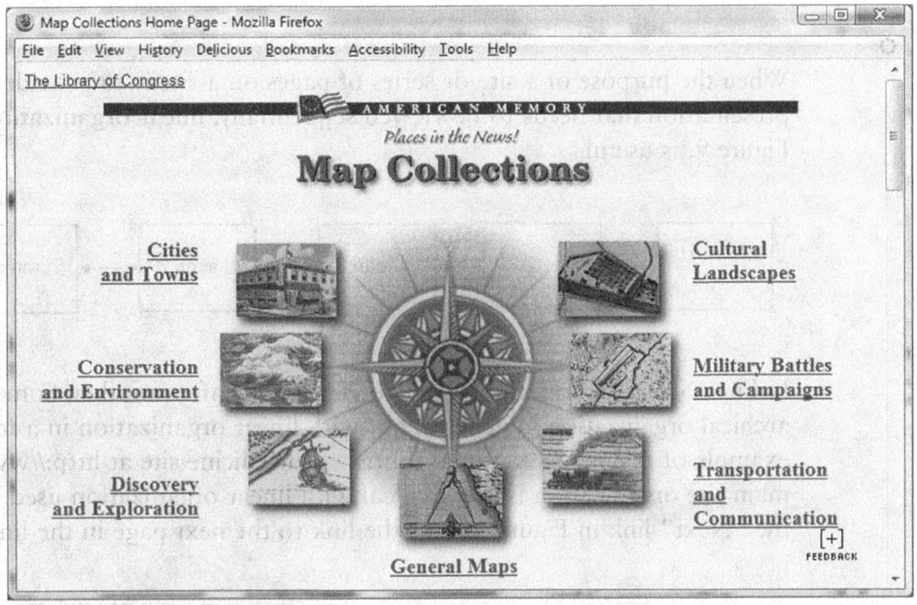

Figure 7
Map Collections Home page

The main section content pages of a site usually have a similar look and feel. Two content pages are shown in Figure 8.

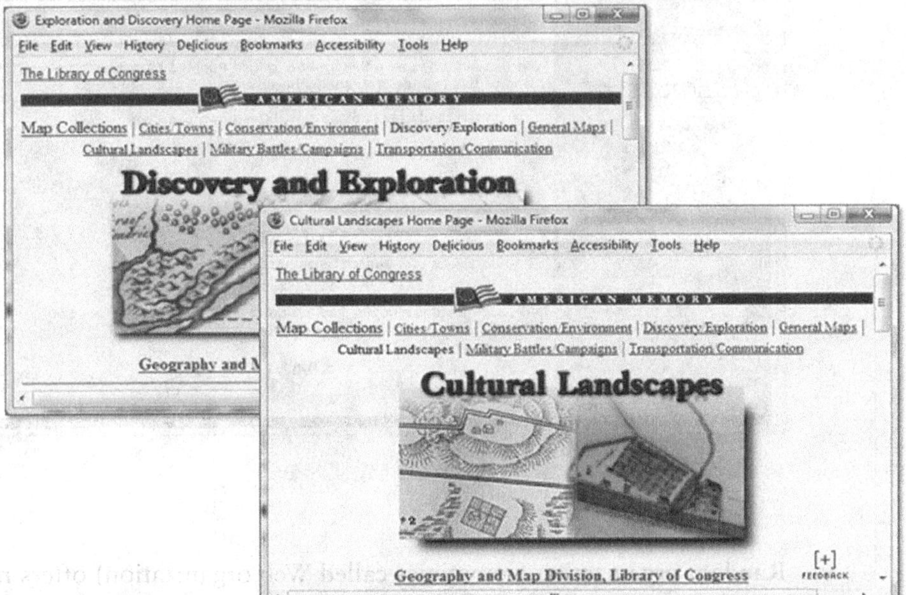

Figure 8
Sample content pages

Each main section may have one or more subpages. Some sites with a hierarchical organization may use a consistent design for the home page and the content pages. Either method is acceptable. Most commercial sites, such as http://amazon.com and http://ebay.com use hierarchical site organization.

Linear Organization

When the purpose of a site or series of pages on a site is to provide a tutorial, tour, or presentation that needs to be viewed sequentially, **linear organization**, as shown in Figure 9, is useful.

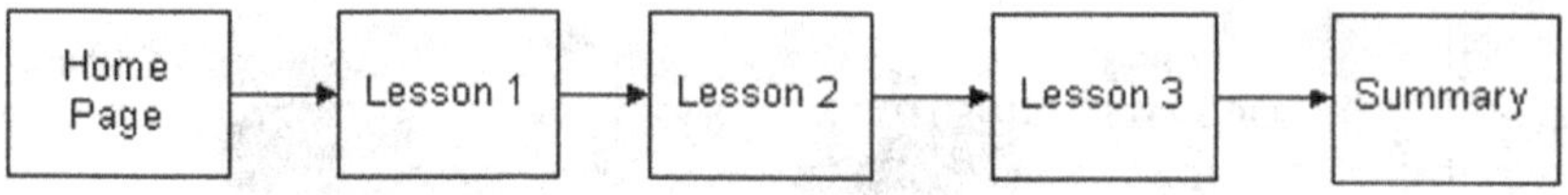

Figure 9
Linear site organization

In linear organization, the pages are viewed one after another. Some Web sites use hierarchical organization in general, but with linear organization in a few small areas. An example of this is the National Library of Medicine site at http://www.nlm.nih.gov. The main site organization is hierarchical with linear organization used for tutorials. Notice the "Next" link in Figure 10; it's the link to the next page in the linear presentation.

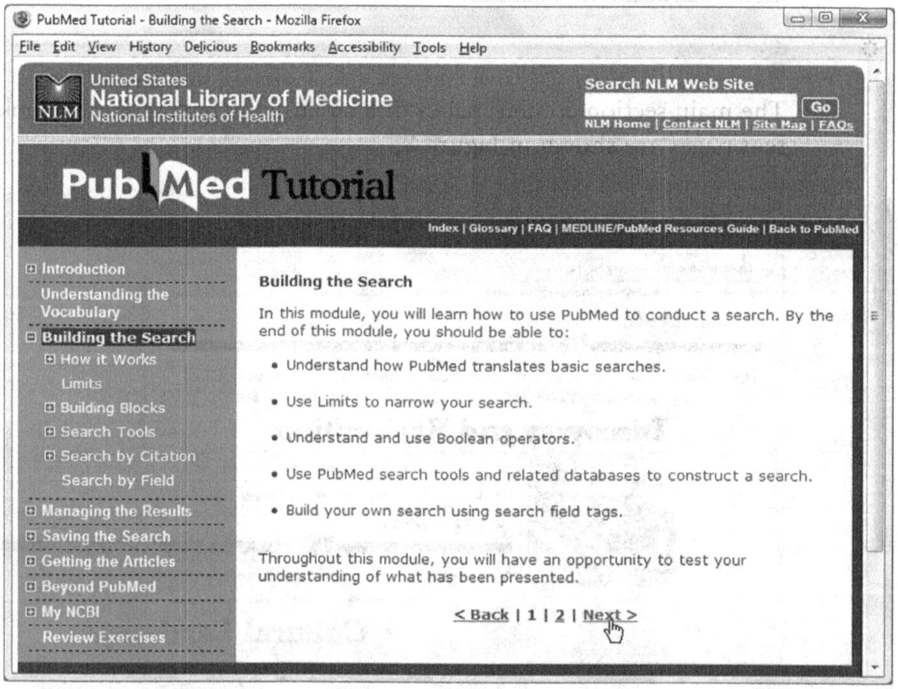

Figure 10
Tutorial linear organization using the "Next" link

Random Organization

Random organization (sometimes called Web organization) offers no clear path through the site, as shown in Figure 11 There is often no clear home page and no discernable structure. Random organization is not as common as hierarchical or linear organization and is usually found only on artistic sites or sites that strive to be especially different and original. This type of organization is typically not used for commercial Web sites.

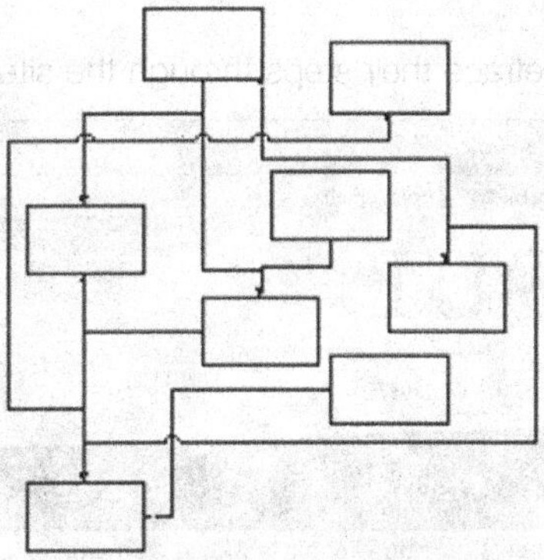

Figure 11
Random site organization

FAQ

Where do I begin?

Sometimes it is difficult to begin creating a site map for a Web site. Some design teams meet in a room with a blank wall and a package of large Post-it® Notes. They write the titles of topics and subtopics needed on the site on the Post-it® Notes. They arrange the notes on the wall and discuss until the site structure becomes clear and there is consensus within the group. If you are not working in a group, you can try this on your own and then discuss the way you have chosen to organize the Web site with a friend or fellow student.

2 Web Site Navigation—Best Practices

Ease of Navigation

Sometimes Web developers are so close to their sites that they can't see the forest for the trees. A new visitor will wander on to the site and not know what to click or how to find out what it offers. Clearly labeled navigation on each page is helpful—it should be in the same location on each page for maximum usability. A visitor should not feel lost in the site. Jakob Nielsen, a well-known Web usability and Web design professional, favors what he calls **breadcrumb trails** for larger sites. Figure 12 shows a page from http://www.cabq.gov, a site that has a well-organized main navigation area below the logo area in addition to personalized breadcrumb trails for each visitor. To access the What is Global Warming page currently displayed, the visitor has already viewed the Home, Albuquerque Green, and Stop Global Warming pages. Note the breadcrumb navigation at the top of the main content area: Home > Albuquerque Green > Stop Global Warming > What is Global Warming? Visitors can easily retrace their steps or jump back to a previously viewed page. The left side of this page also contains a vertical navigation bar with links for the Albuquerque Green section.

Navigation Bars

Clear navigation bars, either graphic- or text-based, make it obvious to Web site users where they are and where they can go next. The site shown in Figure 13 includes a vertical text navigation bar down the left side of the page.

Figure 12

Visitors can follow the "breadcrumbs" to retrace their steps through the site

Figure 13

Vertical text-based navigation is used at http://www.usdoj.gov

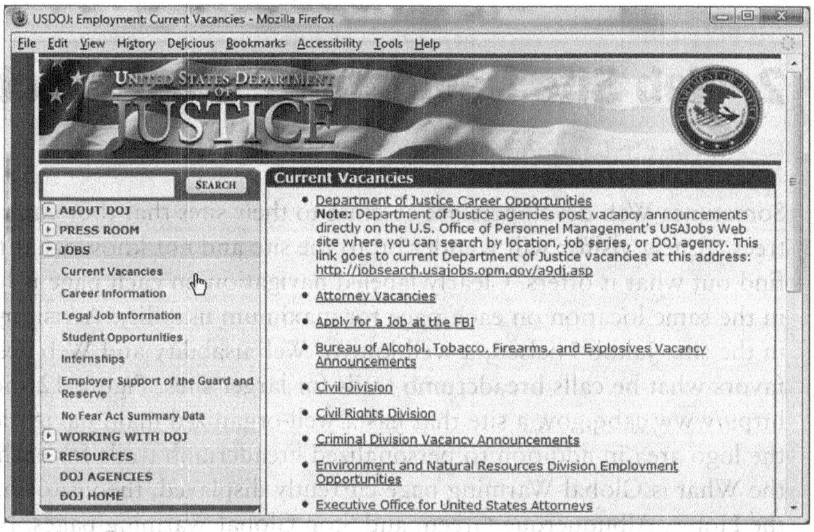

The display of the Current Vacancies link shown on a contrasting background color, provides a visual cue that the visitor is at that location. The page header and page title also display the text "Current Vacancies." The **navigation bar** indicates other choices available to the Web site visitor.

Sometimes graphics are used to convey navigation, as in the Web site for the Department of Transportation (http://www.dot.gov), as shown in Figure 14.

The "text" for the navigation is actually stored in image files. This technique of placing text in navigation images is used to create interactive Web pages. In this case, JavaScript is used to detect when the Web page visitor has placed the mouse over an image of text,

Figure 14
The tabs provide horizontal graphics-based navigation

which then displays an alternate image. Even though images provide the main navigation of the site, the site is still accessible: a row of text links appear in the footer section of the page (not shown in Figure 14) and the image tags are configured with text descriptions using the `alt` attribute. Combinations of text with graphic images can be helpful to your visitors and add visual interest. Figure 15 shows a graphical navigation bar at http://www.genome.gov.

Figure 15
The graphical navigation bar adds visual interest

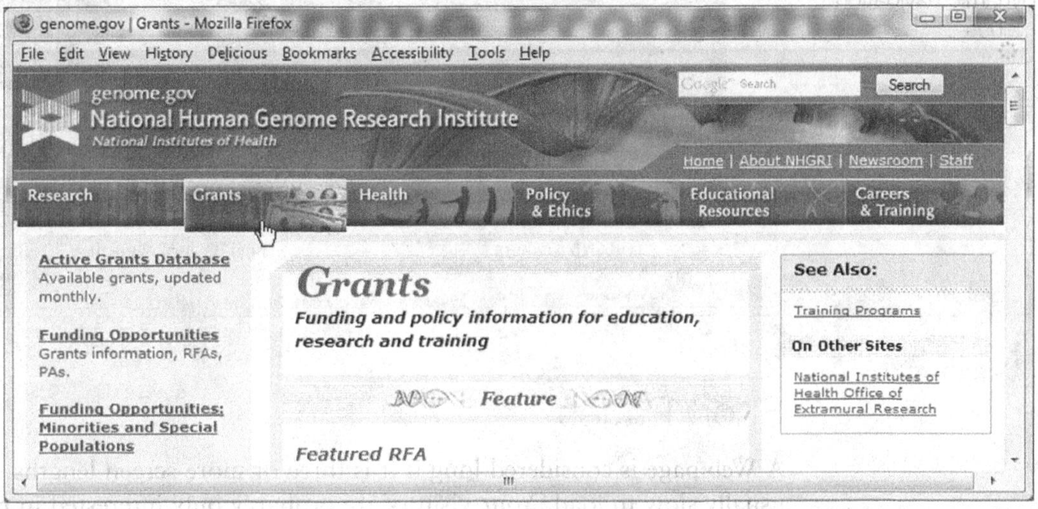

Technologies such as Adobe Flash can be combined with XHTML to create interactive, interesting navigation. See the screenshot in Figure 16 of http://www.loc.gov/wiseguide. The designers of this site used Flash to create the dynamic navigation and interactive images.

Java applets and Dynamic HTML (DHTML) can also be used to create similar interactive effects.

In Figure 17, "For Visitors" has been selected causing the vertical menu to appear. This type of navigation on a large complex site keeps the visitor from feeling overwhelmed by choices. The visitor first chooses a major menu category, and then sees the individual additional choices that can be made.

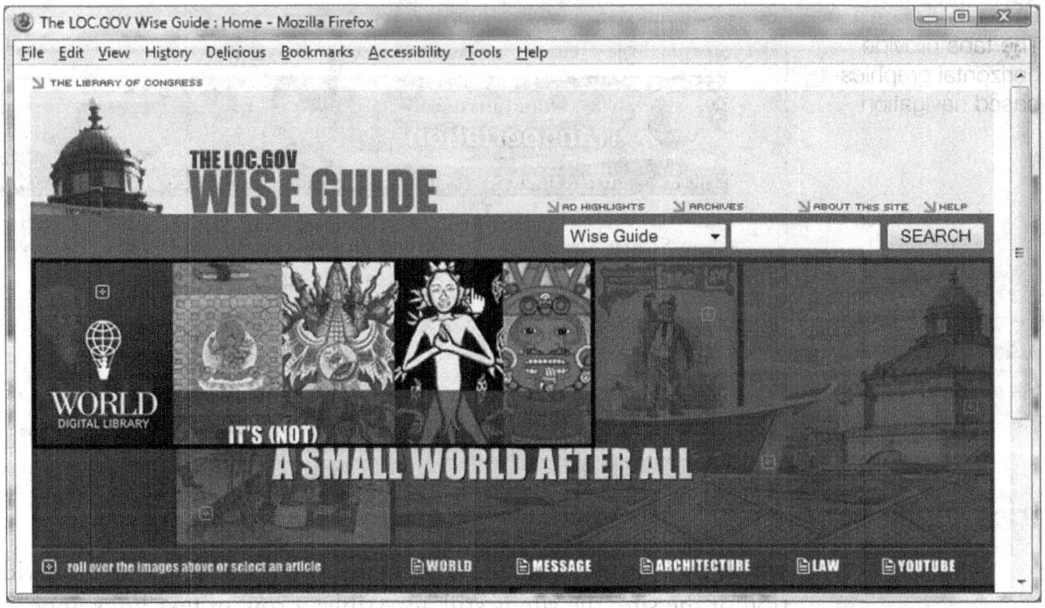

Figure 16
Flash navigation

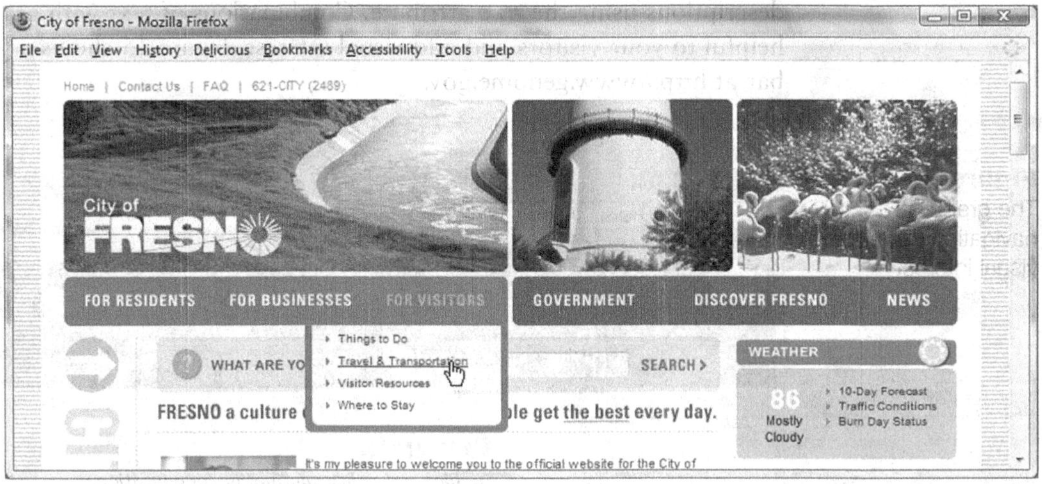

Figure 17
The City of Fresno (http://www.fresno.gov) Web site uses DHTML to create dynamic navigation menus

Short Pages

A Web page is considered long if it is three or more screen lengths. Long pages are usually slow to load. Your visitors are probably only interested in portions of a long page, so consider breaking a long page into multiple short pages—possibly using linear organization to link the ideas.

Table of Contents

When a long Web page must be kept as a single file, a **table of contents** or bulleted list at the top of the page can provide links to specific parts of the page. This will help visitors find exactly what they need. An example of this is the page shown in Figure 18. Note the list of questions—they all link to corresponding answers at another location on the same page.

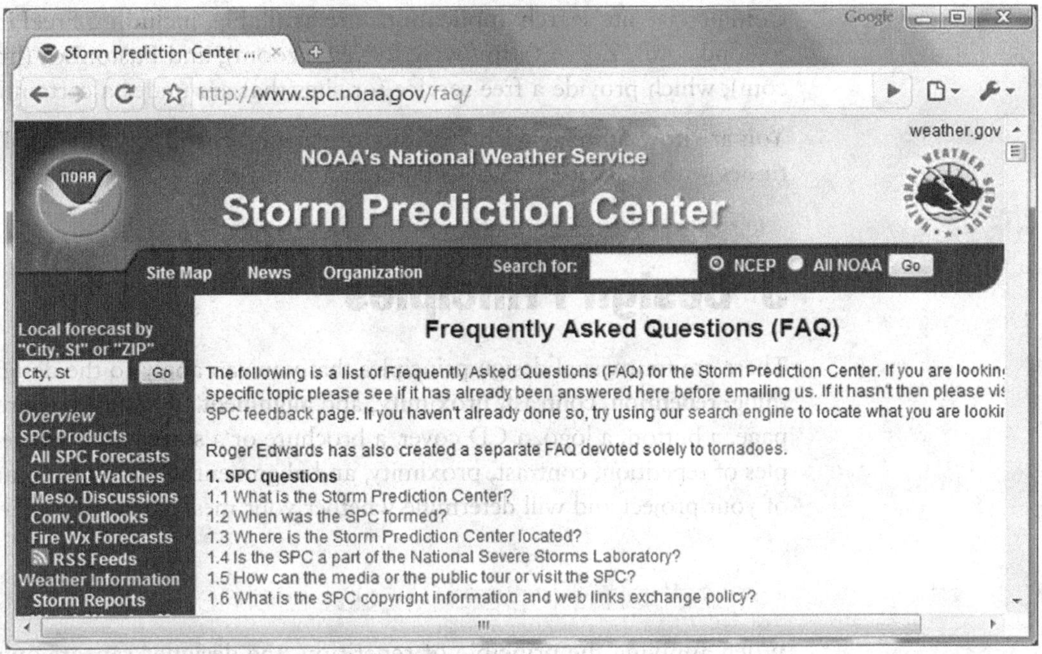

Figure 18
A list of FAQ links to answers on the page

Site Map and Site Search Features

The Ready.gov Web site shown in Figure 19 has a **site search** and site map on the same page. The site map allows a visitor to scan the contents of the site visually. The search helps visitors find information that is not apparent from the navigation or the site map features. A Web developer could add the `title` attribute to these anchor tags to provide a brief text description.

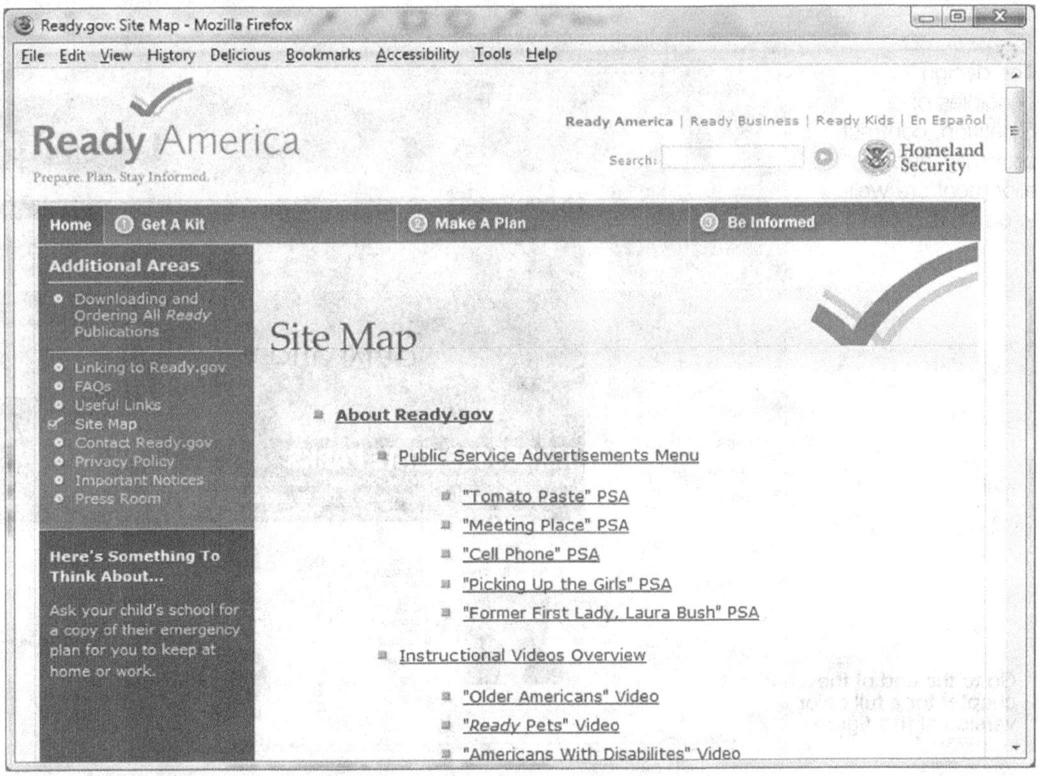

Figure 19
This large site offers a site search and a site map to visitors

Commercial site search applications are available, including FreeFind (http://www.freefind.com), Zoom (http://wrensoft.com/zoom), and FusionBot (http://www.fusionbot.com), which provide a free service for sites that are under a certain number of pages.

You are now familiar with Web site organization and navigation. The next section continues with a discussion of visual design principles.

3 Design Principles

There are four visual design principles that you can apply to the design of just about anything: **repetition, contrast, proximity**, and **alignment.** Whether you are designing a Web page, a button, a logo, a CD cover, a brochure or a software interface—the design principles of repetition, contrast, proximity, and alignment will help to create the "look and feel" of your project and will determine whether your message is effectively communicated.

Repetition: Repeat Visual Elements throughout Design

When applying the principle of repetition, the designer repeats one or more elements through the product. The repeating aspect ties the work together. Figure 20 displays the home page of the Tennesee Web site (http://www.tn.gov). The page design demonstrates the use of repetition in a variety of design components, including shape, color, font, and images. The main navigation links on the left side of the page are the same rectangular shape. Notice how background color is used within the repetition of the navigation rectangles to differentiate the type of link—blue indicates target audience, medium gray indicates site section, and light gray indicates "housekeeping" (site map, contact page, etc.). The gray colors are also repeated in the governor's section in the lower middle of the page and in the bottom border of the right sidebar categories. The

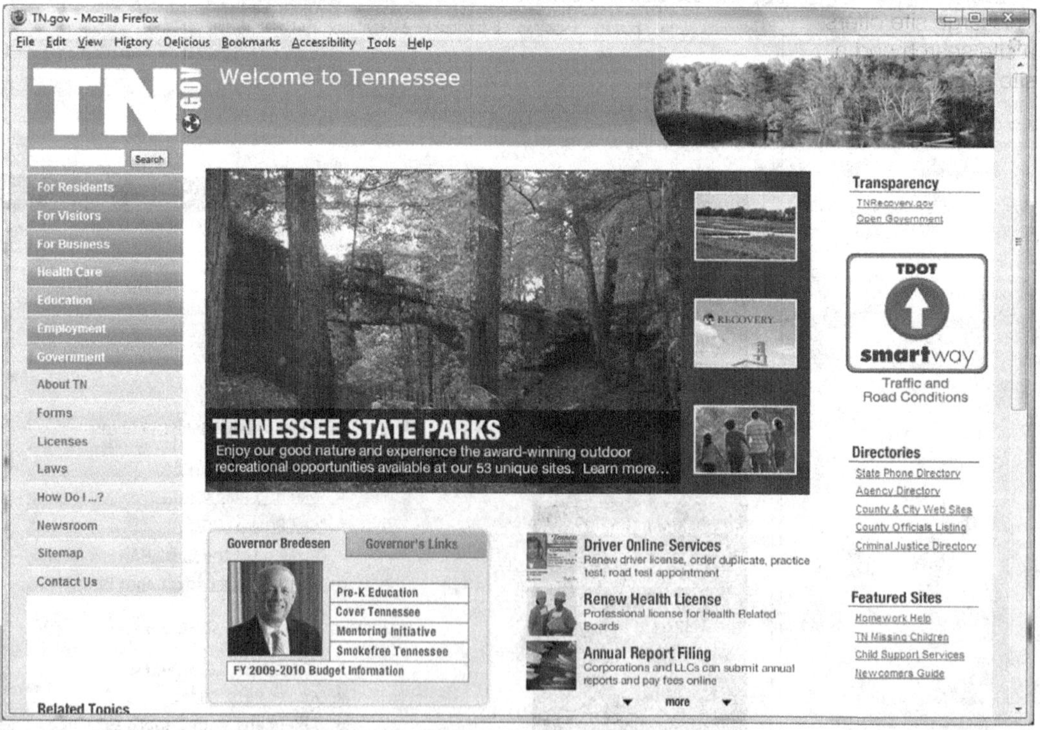

Figure 20
The design principles of repetition, contrast, proximity, and alignment are well used on this site

Go to the end of the chapter for a full color version of this figure

use of only two font typefaces on the page also demonstrate repetitions and helps to create a cohesive look. Arial is the default font. Page headings are configured with Verdana font. The large rectangular visual element in the middle of the page engages the visitor and incorporates repetition of three thumbnail images. The services area also utilizes several thumbnail images. Whether it is color, shape, font, or image, repetition of elements helps to unify a design.

Contrast: Add Visual Excitement and Draw Attention

To apply the principle of contrast, the designer should make elements very different (add contrast) in order to make the design interesting and direct attention. When designing Web pages, there should be good contrast between the background color and the text. Notice how the navigation area in Figure 20 uses text color with good contrast (either light text with the blue and medium gray background or dark text with the light gray background). The main content areas use dark text on a medium or light background to provide good visual contrast and easy reading.

Proximity: Group-Related Items

When designers apply the principle of proximity, related items are placed physically close together. Unrelated items should have space separating them. The placing of interface items close together gives visual clues to the logical organization of the information or functionality. In Figure 20, the vertical navigation links are all placed in close proximity to each other. This creates a visual group on the page and makes the navigation easier to use. Notice the proximity of the options in the governor's section, services options, and right-sidebar links. Proximity is used well on this page to group related elements.

Alignment: Align Elements to Create Visual Unity

Another principle that helps to create a cohesive Web page is alignment. When applying this principle, the designer organizes the page so that each element placed has some alignment (vertical or horizontal) with another element on the page. The page shown in Figure 20 also applies this principle. Notice how the page components are vertically aligned in columns. Examine the services area (Driver Online Services, Renew Health License, Annual Report Filing) and observe the alignment of the thumbnail images, headings, and text.

Repetition, contrast, proximity, and alignment are four principles that can greatly improve your Web page designs. If you apply these principles effectively, your Web pages will look more professional and you will communicate your message more clearly. Keep these visual design principles in mind as you explore recommended Web site design practices related to **page layout**, text, graphic, and accessibility in the next section.

4 Web Page Design—Best Practices

The major components of Web page design are as follows:

- Page layout design
- Text design

- Graphic design
- Accessibility considerations

Web sites that look great and are easy to use don't happen by accident. Outstanding Web sites are carefully planned and created by using recommended design practices. (They also require a little bit of talent!) There are a number of factors to consider when designing a Web page. Some factors relate to the usability, accessibility, and appeal of the site to the target audience—use of color, text, graphics, and animations. Other factors relate to the medium of the Web itself—**load time** issues, browser support, and monitor **screen resolution.**

Load Time

The last thing you want to happen is for your visitors to leave your page before it has even finished loading! Make sure your pages load as quickly as possible. How long do you generally wait for a page to load? Many Web page visitors will not wait more than several seconds. It's a good practice to limit the total file size of a Web page and all of its associated images and media files to under 60KB. It takes about eight seconds at 56KB for a browser to display a Web page and associated files of 60KB.

According to a recent study by the PEW Internet and American Life Project, the percentage of U.S. Internet users with a broadband (cable, DSL, and so on) connection at home or at work is rising. Fifty-five percent of adult Americans have access to broadband at home. Even with the trend of increasing bandwidth available to your visitors, keep in mind that 45% of households do not have broadband Internet access. For the most up-to-date statistics, visit http://www.pewinternet.org and http://www.clickz.com.

The 60KB per page limit is a guideline—it's better if the file size of your home page and associated media files is smaller. Go over the limit for content pages only when you are sure your visitors will be interested enough to wait to see what your site is presenting. The chart shown in Figure 21 (created using the calculator at http://www.t1shopper.com/tools/calculate/downloadcalculator.php) compares file sizes and connection speed download times.

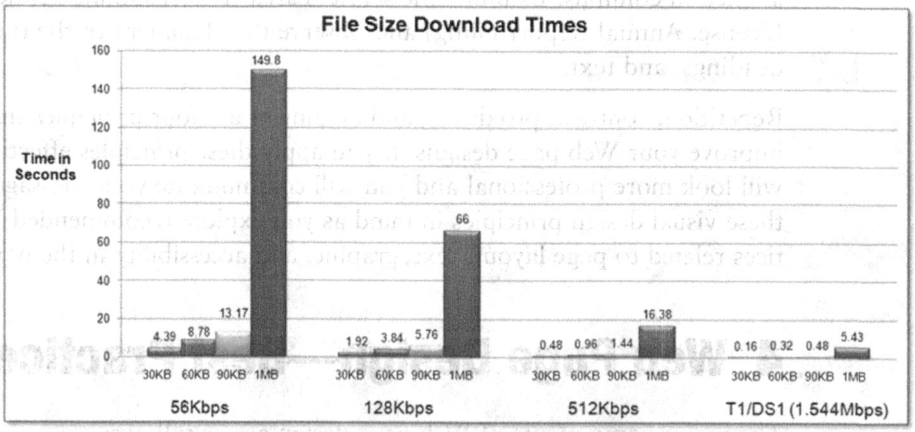

Figure 21 File size download times and Internet connection speeds

One method to help determine if the load time of your page is acceptable is to view the size of your Web site files in Windows Explorer. Calculate the total file size of your Web page plus all its associated images and media. If the total file size for a single page and its associated files is over 60KB and it is likely that your target audience may not be using broadband access, take a closer look at your design. Consider if you really need to use all the images to convey your message. Perhaps the images can be better optimized for the Web or the content of the page should be divided into multiple pages. This is a time for some decision making!

Popular Web authoring tools such as Microsoft Expression Web and Adobe Dreamweaver will calculate load time at various transmission speeds.

Perceived Load Time

Perceived load time is the amount of time a Web page visitor is aware of waiting while your page is loading. Since visitors often leave a Web site if a page takes too long to load, it is important to shorten their perception of waiting. A common technique is to shorten the perceived loading time by breaking the long page into multiple smaller pages using the methods described earlier. This might even aid in the organization of your Web site.

Web pages containing large graphics may appear to load very slowly. Image slicing—dividing or slicing large images into multiple smaller images, divides large images into several smaller graphics. Since each graphic displays as it loads, the perceived load time is shorter than it is for a single large graphic. Even though the total download time is about the same, the visitor sees the browser window changing and perceives the wait as being shorter.

Above the Fold

Placing important information **above the fold** is a technique borrowed from the newspaper industry. When newspapers are placed on counters and in vending machines waiting to be sold, the portion above the fold in the page is viewable. Publishers noticed that more papers were sold when the most important, attention-getting information was placed in this location. You may use this technique to attract and keep visitors on your Web pages. Arrange interesting content above the fold—the area the visitor sees before scrolling down the page. At a screen resolution of 800 pixels wide by 600 pixels high, the amount of screen viewable above the fold (after accounting for Web browser menus and controls) is about 410 pixels. At 1024×768 resolution, you can expect there to be close to 600 pixels above the fold—but keep in mind that the amount of browser chrome (the browser menus, address bar, and scroll bar) varies and that not everyone will be visiting your Web site with a maximized browser viewport.

Web Page "Real Estate"

There is a saying in the real estate field that the three most important factors about a property are location, location, and location. The Web page location you choose for high-profile components such as logo banners, page headings, and navigation is also important. Web page visitor eye tracking studies reported by The Poynter Institute (http://www.poynterextra.org/eyetrack2004/main.htm) indicate that "eyes most often fixated first in the upper-left of the page, then hovered in that area before going left to right." This makes the most valuable Web page "real estate" the upper-left side and top center of the page. Avoid placing important information and navigation on the far right side—this area may not be initially displayed by browsers at some screen resolutions.

Horizontal Scrolling

In order to make it easy for Web page visitors to view and use your Web pages, avoid creating pages that are too wide to be displayed in the browser window. These pages require the user to scroll horizontally. Using the screen resolution of 800 pixels wide by 600 pixels high, the amount of viewable screen (after accounting for area used by the Web browser) is about 760 pixels. However, the most popular screen resolution is currently 1024×768. Cameron Moll (http://www.cameronmoll.com/archives/001220.html) suggests that the optimal Web page width for display at 1024×768 screen resolution is 960 pixels. Be mindful that all your web page visitors will not maximize their browser viewport. One approach when designing a wide page is to place less important content on the right. An easy way to make sure your page will not require **horizontal scrolling** is to place the page contents in a layout table that uses a percentage width of 100 percent or less. Another method is to use a fixed width set to the value you have chosen—760 pixels or less (for 800×600) or 960 pixels or less (for 1024×768). If you expect your pages to be printed often, use CSS to configure styles for printing.

Adequate White Space

This term **white space** is also borrowed from the publishing industry. Placing blank or white space (because paper is usually white) in areas around blocks of text increases the readability of the page. Placing white space around graphics helps them to stand out. Allow for some blank space between blocks of text and images. How much is adequate? It depends—experiment until the page is likely to look appealing to your target audience.

Target Audience

Use of Color. Younger audiences, such as children and preteens, prefer bright, lively colors. The United States Mint's Site for Kids home page (http://usmint.gov/kids) shown in Figure 22, features bright graphics, lots of color, and interactivity.

Figure 22
A typical site for children

Go to the end of the chapter for a full color version of this figure

Individuals in their late teens and early twenties generally prefer dark background colors with occasional use of bright contrast, music, and dynamic navigation. Figure 23 shows http://underatedrock.com, a Web site designed by Michael Martin for this age group.

Figure 23
Many teens and young adults find dark sites appealing

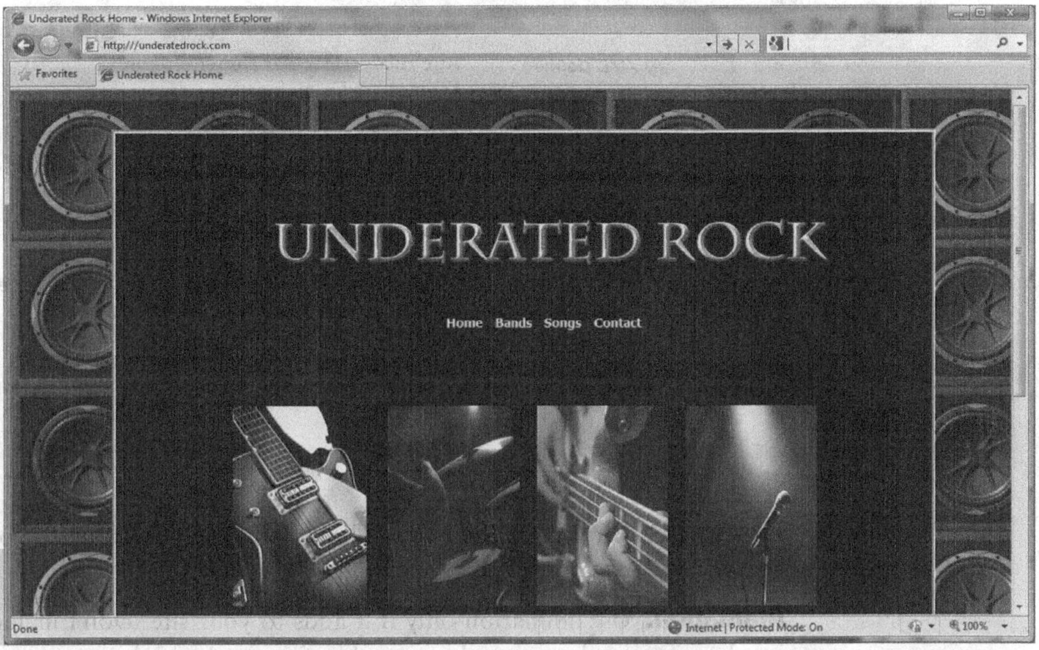

Go to the end of the chapter for a full color version of this figure

Note how it has a completely different look and feel from the site designed for children.

If your goal is to appeal to everyone, follow the example of the popular Amazon.com and eBay.com Web sites in their use of color. These sites use a neutral white background with splashes of color to add interest and highlight page areas. Use of white as a background color was also reported by Jakob Nielsen and Marie Tahir in Homepage Usability: 50 Websites Deconstructed, a book that analyzed 50 top Web sites. According to this study, 84 percent of the sites used white as the background color and 72 percent used black as the text color. This maximized the contrast between text and background—providing maximum readability.

For an older target audience, light backgrounds, well-defined images, and large text are appropriate. The screenshot of the Senior Health site (http://nihseniorhealth.gov) shown in Figure 24 is an example of a Web page intended for the over 55 group.

Focus on Accessibility

Another issue related to color is the fact that many individuals experience color deficiency (color blindness). The inability to differentiate between red and green, called deuteranopia, is the most common type of color deficiency. To increase the accessibility of Web pages for these individuals, a Web designer can use high contrast between background and text. The choice of colors is important—avoid using red, green, brown, gray, or purple next to each other. White, black, and shades of blue and yellow are easier for these individuals to differentiate. To see what your pages look like to a person with color blindness, try the online simulator at http://www.vischeck.com/vischeck/.

Figure 24
A site designed specifically for the 55 and over age range

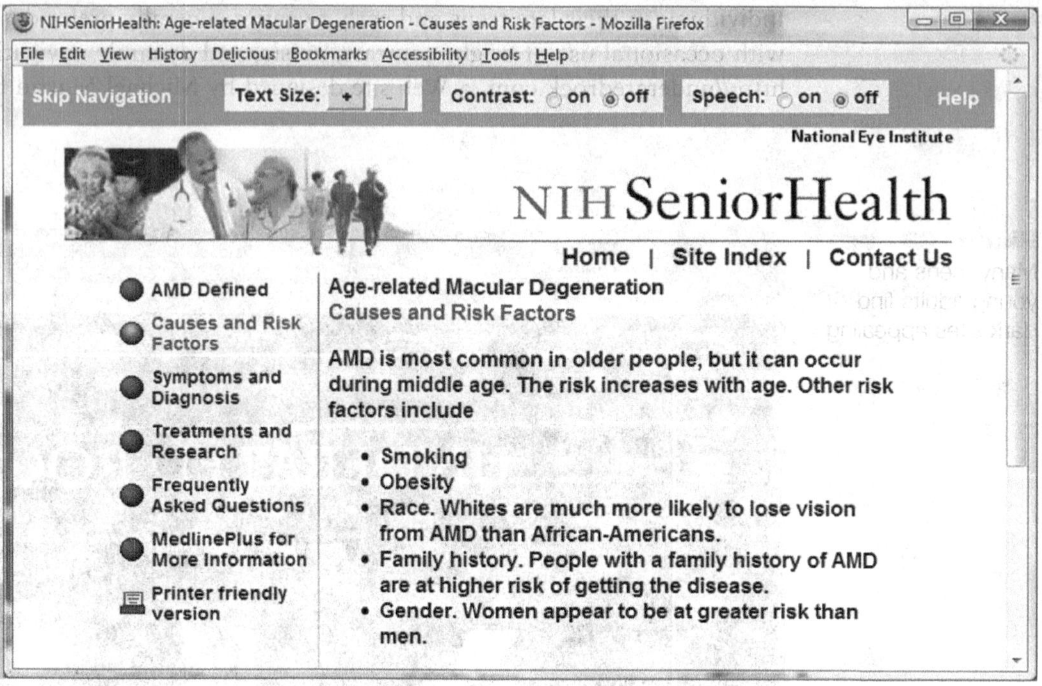

Go to the end of the chapter for a full color version of this figure

Reading Level. Match the reading level and style of writing to your target audience. Use vocabulary that they will be comfortable with.

Animation. Use animation only if it adds to your site. Don't include an animated GIF just because you have one. In general, animation appeals more to younger audiences than to older audiences. The United States Mint's Site for Kids (Figure 22) is geared to children and uses lots of animation. This would be too much animation for a Web site targeted to adult shoppers. However, a well-done navigation animation or an animation that describes a product could be appealing to almost any target group. Adobe Flash is frequently used on the Web to add animation to Web pages and even to create entire animated Web sites.

FAQ

Which browser is everyone using?

A recent survey by Net Applications (http://marketshare.hitslink.com/browser-market-share.aspx?qprid=0) indicates that while Microsoft's Internet Explorer is still the most popular Web browser, the Firefox open source browser has been gaining ground. The survey reports that about 65 percent of users use Internet Explorer and 24 percent use Firefox (http://www.mozilla.org/products/firefox/). It is important to test your site in the major browsers (and versions). You never know which browser your next client will favor!

If you are developing for an intranet, ask what browser (and version) is installed at the organization. If you are developing for a client, ask what browser he or she regularly uses.

Browser-Friendly

Just because your Web page looks great in your favorite browser, doesn't automatically mean that all browsers will render it well. Determine the browser most likely to be used by your target audience. A good source of statistics is http://www.thecounter.com/stats. Develop the site so that it looks great in your target audience's most popular browser and looks acceptable (degrades gracefully) in other browsers. Visit http://www.upsdell.com/BrowserNews for timely information about current browsers.

Always try to test your pages in the most popular versions of browsers and in the newest versions. At the time of this writing, these are Firefox 3, Internet Explorer 8, Safari (both Mac and Windows versions), Opera 10, and Google's Chrome browser. While it is possible to install multiple versions of Firefox on the same computer, dual installs cannot easily be done with Internet Explorer. Unless you have multiple computers to work with, test with the most popular version of Internet Explorer. If you can, it is also a good idea to test your pages on both the Mac and PC platforms.

Large information technology departments and Web design firms will dedicate a number of computers with various operating systems and browser versions for compatibility testing. Many Web page components, including default text size and default margin size, are different among browsers, browser versions, and operating systems.

Screen Resolution

Higher resolutions are becoming more popular. The most commonly used screen resolutions are currently 1024×768, 1280×800, and 1280×1024. Design your pages to avoid horizontal scrolling at these resolutions. However, depending on your target audience, you still may have some visitors using 640×480 screen resolution! Also, be mindful that mobile web browsers have very low screen resolution. One way to create a page that looks good in multiple screen resolutions is to center the entire page.

FAQ

Which screen resolution is everyone using?

A recent survey by Net Applications (http://marketshare.hitslink.com/report.aspx?qprid=17) reported that 1024×768 is currently the most popular screen resolution. Of visitors surveyed, 30 percent use 1024×768, 20 percent use 1280×800, 11 percent use 1280×1024, 9 percent use 1440×900, 6 percent use 1680×1050, and less than 4 percent use 800×600.

Wireframes and Page Layout

A **wireframe** is a sketch or blueprint of a Web page that shows the structure (but not the detailed design) of basic page elements such as the logo, navigation, content, and footer. Depending on the purpose of a particular Web site, the wireframe may incorporate additional components including pull quotes, news items, and interactive features such as a login or search function. Wireframes are used as part of the design process to experiment with various page layouts, develop the structure and navigation of the site, and provide a basis for communication among project members. Figures 25 through 27 can be considered very basic wireframes. Visit the website http://www. webdevfoundations.net/5e/chapter5.html, for more detailed examples.

Figure 25
An adequate page layout

Figures 25, 26, and 27 show diagrams of three possible Web page layouts. Note that the exact content (text, images, logo, and navigation) does not need to be placed in the diagram in order to illustrate this concept. The page area where the content will appear is indicated. This type of sketch, called a wireframe, can be used to experiment with page structures and find the one that will work best for a site. Figure 25 shows a diagram of a Web page with a logo, navigation area, content area, and a footer area.

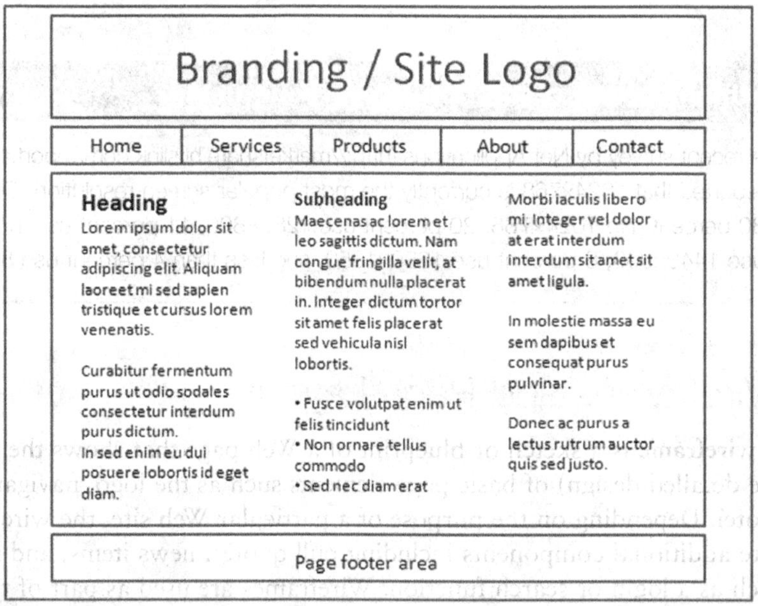

Figure 26
The columns make this page layout more interesting

This layout is adequate and may be appropriate for some content, but it's not very interesting. Figure 26 shows a diagram of a Web page containing about the same content, but formatted in three-columns.

This is an improvement, but something is still missing. Figure 27 shows a diagram of the same content but formatted in three columns of varying widths, with graphics interspersed.

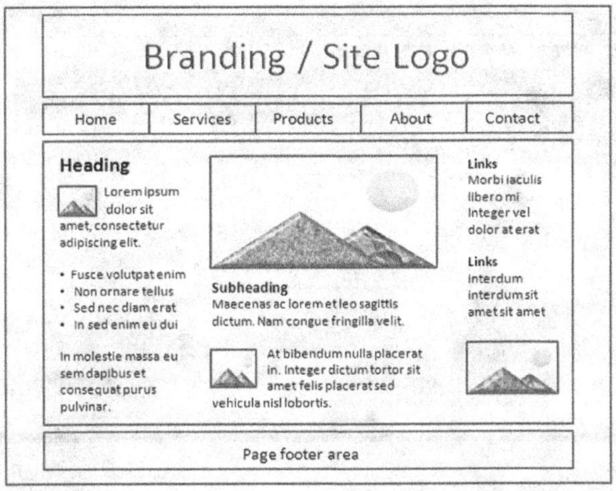

Figure 27
This page layout uses images and columns of varied widths

This is the most interesting page layout of the three. Notice how images and tables make the same content more appealing. Try using this concept when designing your pages.

Often the page layout (sometimes called a storyboard) for the home page is different from the page layout used for the content pages. Even when this is the case, a consistent logo and color scheme will produce a more cohesive Web site. Using style sheets to create interesting page layouts can keep visitors engaged in your Web site. Web authoring tools such as Microsoft Expression Web and Adobe Dreamweaver offer templates and example sites to assist you with layout ideas.

5 Page Layout Design Techniques

Now that you have been introduced to Web page design best practices and page layout, it's time to consider three popular techniques of Web page layout design: ice, jello, and liquid.

Ice Design

The **ice design** technique is sometimes referred to as a solid or fixed design. The page hugs the left margin and generally either CSS is used to configure a fixed-width block-level element or an XHTML table is used to format the page. A CSS style rule is shown below that configures an id named `wrapper` in this manner.

```
#wrapper { width: 700px; }
```

Due to the fixed width, the designer has much control over the layout and formatting—configuring the page to look best at a certain screen resolution (often 1024×768) and degrade gracefully when other screen resolutions are used. The right-hand side of the browser window will often contain much empty space—especially at higher screen resolutions.

The Energy Star site (http://www.energystar.gov), shown in Figure 28, is an example of ice design. This particular page is formatted with a fixed width. Other sites that currently use this technique include http://www.cabelas.com and http://www.league.org.

Figure 28 This page is configured with a fixed width and demonstrates ice design

Jello Design

The **jello design** technique configures content that is centered and may be of a fixed width or a percentage width such as 80 percent. A CSS style rule that configures an id named `wrapper` in this manner follows:

```
#wrapper { width: 80%;
           margin-left: auto;
           margin-right: auto;
}
```

Jello design pages typically are more pleasing to view at higher screen resolutions than ice design pages. No matter the screen resolution, the content is centered in the page with even margins on both sides. The Department of Energy site (http://energy.gov), as shown in Figure 29, uses jello design. Other sites currently using this technique include http://www.pbs.org and http://www.officedepot.com.

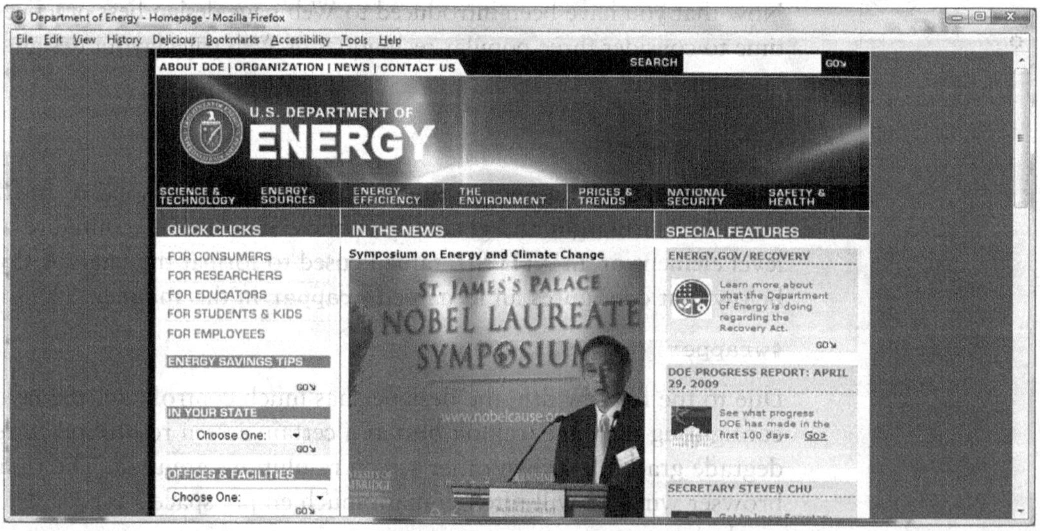

Figure 29 The left and right margins are balanced on this page using jello design

Liquid Design

The **liquid design** technique results in a fluid Web page with content that takes up 100 percent of the browser window regardless of the screen resolution. There is no blank margin on the left or right—the multicolumn content will flow to fill whatever size window is used to display it. This type of design can be created with CSS or with XHTML using a table with width set to 100 percent. Using CSS instead of a table to configure Web page layout has a number of advantages, including smaller Web page document file sizes, quicker loading pages, and more accessible pages that are easier for screen readers to access. Figure 30 shows a page from the State of Illinois site at http://www.illinois.gov/tech/. Other sites currently using this technique include http://www.amazon.com and http://moodle.org.

Figure 30
This page uses liquid design to adjust content to fill the browser window

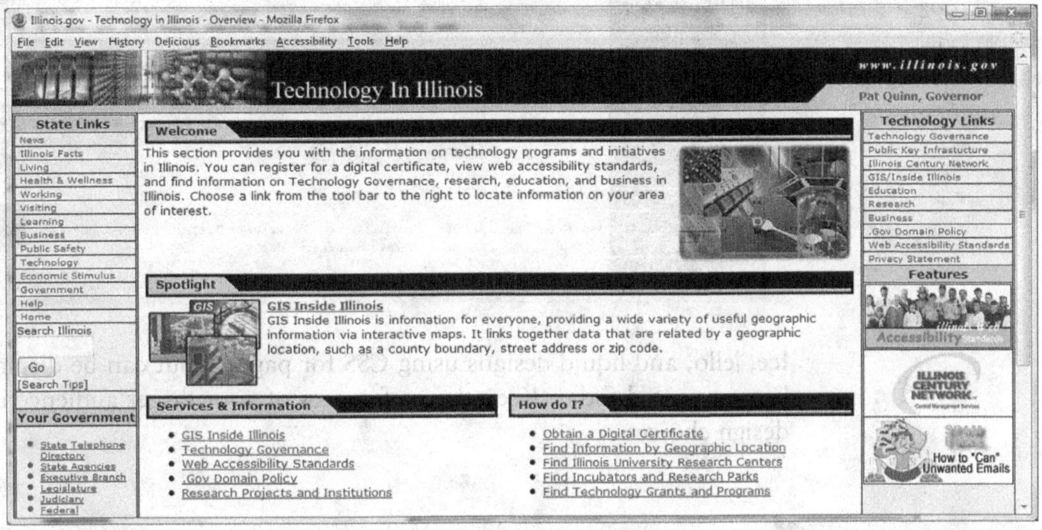

Sites designed using ice, jello, and liquid techniques can be found throughout the Web. Ice and jello designs using a fixed-width layout provide the Web developer the most control over the page configuration but result in pages with large empty areas when viewed at higher screen resolutions.

Figure 31 shows the National Park Service (http://nps.gov) site viewed using 1280×1024 screen resolution. Note how more than one-third of the browser window is empty. Liquid design avoids this awkwardness and takes advantage of the entire browser window.

Figure 31
At 1280×1024 resolution the right side of this page is mostly empty

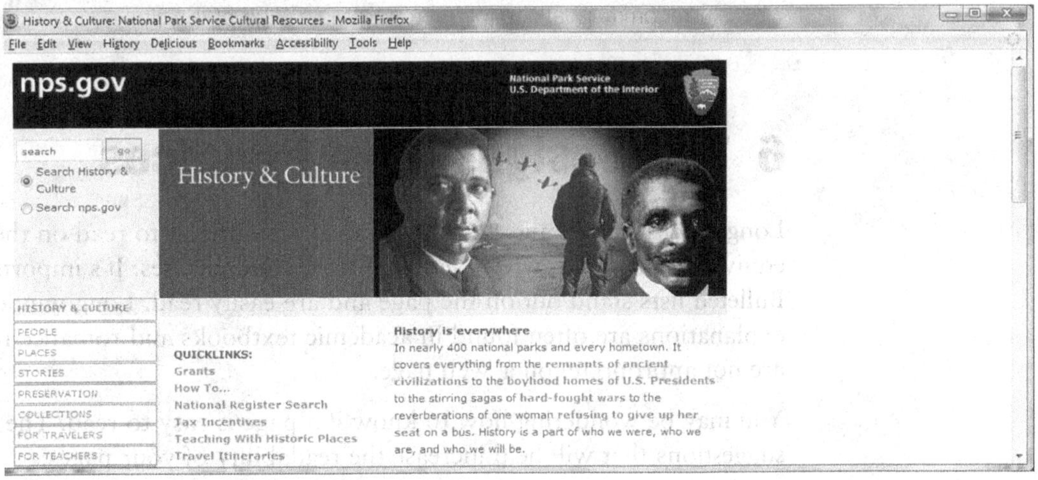

See the liquid-designed Census Bureau (http://www.census.gov) site using 1280×1024 screen resolution in Figure 32—the site still fills the browser window. Since liquid design pages are intended to stretch, it's very important to test pages using this technique at various screen resolutions.

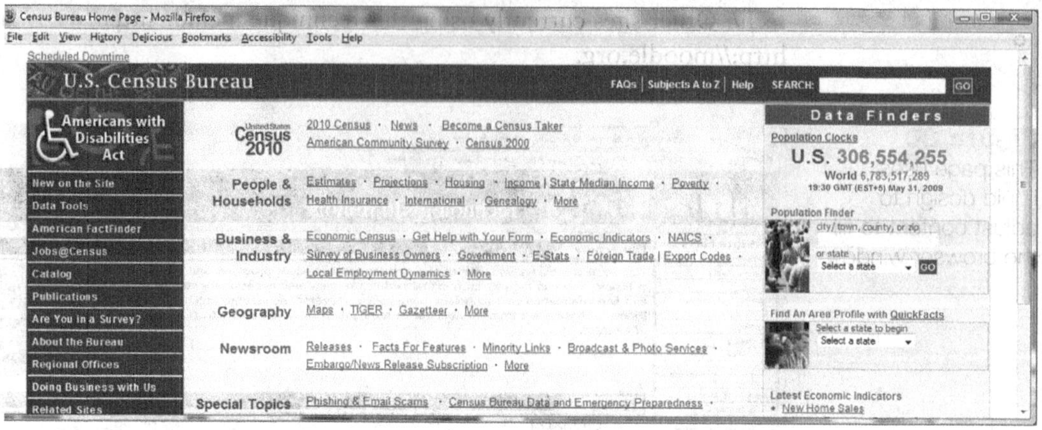

Figure 32 This page stretches to fill the browser window—even at 1280×1024 resolution

Ice, jello, and liquid designs using CSS for page layout can be displayed on most browsers used today. Keep the preferences of your target audience in mind as you make design choices.

CHECKPOINT 1

1. List the four basic principles of design. View the home page of your school and describe how each principle is applied.
2. View http://www.walmart.com, http://www.mugglenet.com/, and http://www.sesamestreet.org/muppet. Describe the target audience for each site. How do their designs differ? Do the sites meet the needs of their target audiences?
3. View your favorite Web site (or a URL provided by your instructor). Maximize and resize the browser window. Decide whether the site uses ice, jello, or liquid design. Adjust the screen resolution on your monitor (Start, Control Panel, Display, Settings) to a different resolution than you normally use. Does the site look similar or very different? List two recommendations for improving the design of the site.

6 Text Design—Best Practices

Long blocks of text and long paragraphs are difficult to read on the Web. Use the text equivalent of sound bytes—short sentences and phrases. It's important to be concise. Bulleted lists stand out on the page and are easily read. Long-winded sentences and explanations are often found in academic textbooks and romance novels, but they really are not appropriate on a Web page.

You may be wondering how to know if a page is easy to read. The following are some suggestions that will help increase the readability of your pages:

- Use common fonts such as Arial, Verdana, or Times New Roman. Remember that the Web page visitor must have the font installed on his/her computer in order for that particular font to appear. Your page may look great with Gill Sans Ultra Bold Condensed, but if your visitor doesn't have the font, the browser's default font will be displayed. Explore the list of "Web-safe" fonts at http://www.ampsoft.net/webdesign-l/WindowsMacFonts.html.

- Serif fonts, such as Times New Roman, were originally developed for printing text on paper—not for displaying text on a computer monitor. Research shows that sans serif fonts, such as Arial, are easier to read than serif fonts when displayed on a computer screen (see http://www.alexpoole.info/academic/literaturereview.html or http://www.wilsonweb.com/wmt6/html-email-fonts.htm for details). The sans serif Verdana font, designed by Microsoft specifically for display on a computer screen, may be more readable than Arial due to the increased width and openness of the letters.
- Be careful with the size of the fonts—12 point font size is the same as "Medium" size and is the same as `1 em`. Be aware that fonts display smaller on a Mac than on a PC. Even within the PC platform, the default font size displayed by browsers may not be the same. Consider creating prototype pages of your font size settings to test on a variety of browsers and screen resolution settings.
- Use appropriate color combinations. Students often choose color combinations for Web pages that they would never dream of using in their wardrobe. An easy way to choose colors that contrast well and look good together is to select colors from an image or logo you will use for your site. Make sure your page background color properly contrasts with your text and hyperlink colors.
- Be aware of line length and alignment—use white space and multiple columns if possible. Review Figures 25, 26, and 27 for examples of text placement on a Web page.
- Bold (use the `<strong>` element) or emphasize (use the `<em>` element to configure italics) important text.
- Hyperlink keywords or phrases—do not hyperlink entire sentences.
- Avoid the use of the words "click here"—users know what to do by now.

Finally, check spelling and grammar. Many Web sites every day contain misspelled words. Most Web authoring tools have built-in spell checkers; consider using this feature. Also, be sure that you proofread and test your site thoroughly. It is very helpful if you can find Web developer buddies—you check their sites and they check yours. It's always easier to see someone else's mistake than your own.

7 Graphic Design—Best Practices

- If you would like your site to have the most consistent display on various monitors using various computer platforms, choose from the 216 colors on the Web Color Palette.
- Use **antialiased text** in images. Antialiasing introduces intermediate colors to smooth jagged edges in digital images. Graphic applications such as Adobe Photoshop and Adobe Fireworks can be used to create antialiased text images. The graphic shown in Figure 33 was created using antialiasing.

Figure 33
Antialiased text

Figure 34 contains an image that did not use antialiasing; note the jagged edges.

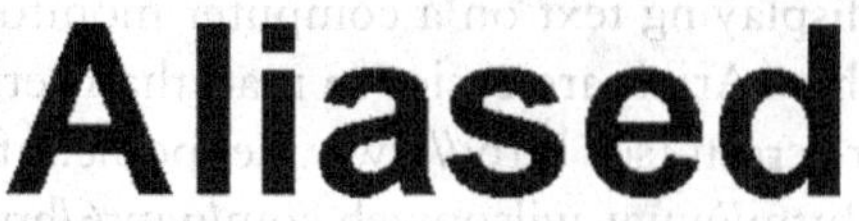

Figure 34
This graphic has a jagged look and was not saved using antialiasing

The only letters not affected are the i and l because the edges of these letters are perfectly horizontal and vertical.

- Use only necessary images. Don't use extra images, just because you have them. Oh, by the way, isn't my dog (see Figure 35) cute?

Figure 35
This is Sparky—but do you really need to see a picture of my dog in this book? Use necessary images only.

- Keep both the file size and the dimensions of images as small as possible. Try to display only exactly what is needed to get your point across. Use a graphic application to crop an image or create a thumbnail image that links to a larger version of the image.
- Make sure the site is usable if images are not displayed. If a Web page visitor is using an assistive technology, such as screen reader, he or she will not see your images but will still want to navigate through your Web site. If your main navigation uses images, DHTML, Flash, or other interactive technologies, place a plain text navigation bar at the bottom of each page. The Studentjobs.gov Web site, http://www.studentjobs.gov, shown in Figure 36, uses this technique.

Focus on Accessibility

WWW

Figure 36
Scrolling to the bottom of this page will display simple text links, which provide accessibility

Image links are used for the main navigation in the tabs below the logo area. There are plain text links to the main site categories at the bottom of the page. These text links provide for accessibility.

Focus on Accessibility

It is also a good idea to include text descriptions of important concepts or key points that your site is trying to communicate. Don't rely on images alone—some individuals may not be able to see them—they may have set their browser not to display images or use an assistive technology such as a screen reader to visit your page.

- Use alternate text for images. Place the `alt` attribute with descriptive text on each `<img />` tag.
- Limit the use of animated items. Only use animation if it makes the page more effective. Consider limiting how long an animation plays.
- Create a text only version of the page. If there are a large number of images, or the images are integral to your content, consider creating an alternate version of the page that contains text only. Keep in mind that this means double maintenance for all future page modifications. Figure 37 displays both the standard and text-only versions of the National Hurricane Center page, http://www.nhc.noaa.gov.

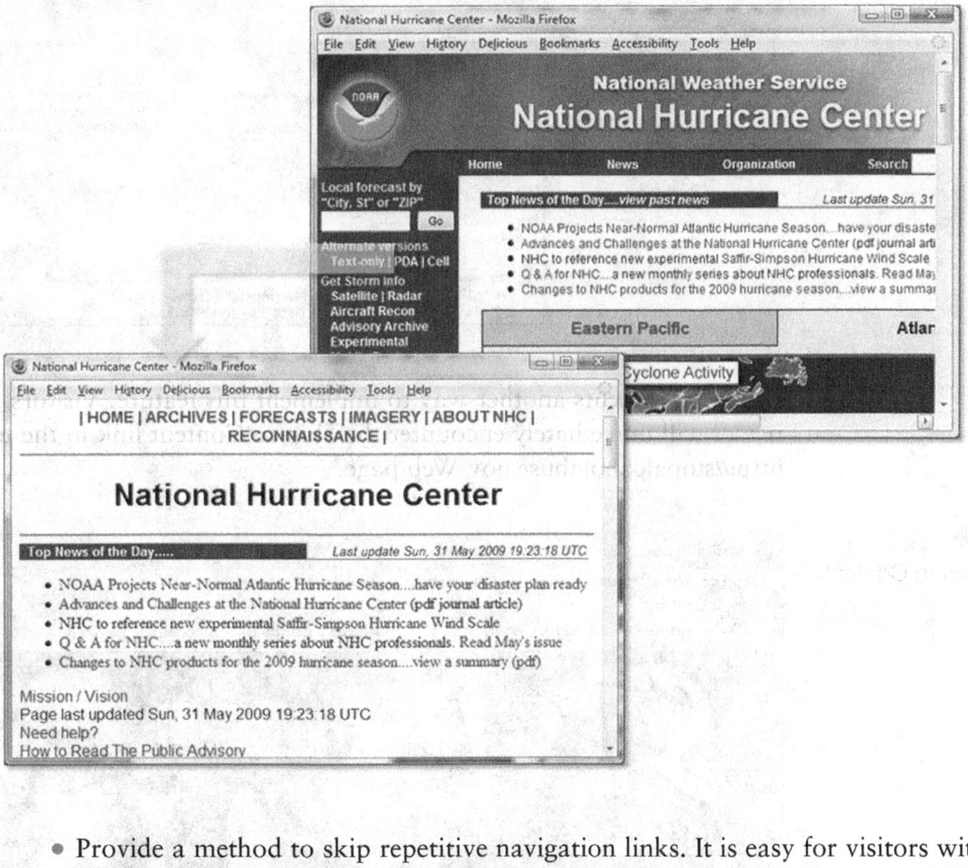

Figure 37
The standard page provides a link to the text-only version

Focus on Accessibility

- Provide a method to skip repetitive navigation links. It is easy for visitors without vision and mobility challenges to scan a Web page and quickly focus on the page content. However, long, repetitive navigation bars quickly become tedious to access when utilizing a screen reader or a keyboard to visit a Web page. Consider adding a Skip Navigation or Skip to Content hyperlink before your main navigation bar that links to a named fragment at the beginning of the content section of your page. The Senior Health site (see Figure 24) displays a "Skip Navigation" link in the upper left corner—this could be accessed by a person using a screen reader to jump directly to the page content. The Department of Transportation site, as shown in Figure 14, uses a transparent image link to provide this feature. Since the image is "invisible," visitors using a graphical browser are not even aware of the additional functionality.

Figure 38 contains comparison screenshots of the page when viewed with Internet Explorer and Firefox's Web Developer extension (available at https://addons.mozilla.org/en-US/firefox/addon/60) to display image `alt` attribute text instead of images. Notice the Skip Navigation alternate text displayed in the upper-right-hand corner—convenient for visitors using screen readers or nongraphical browsers.

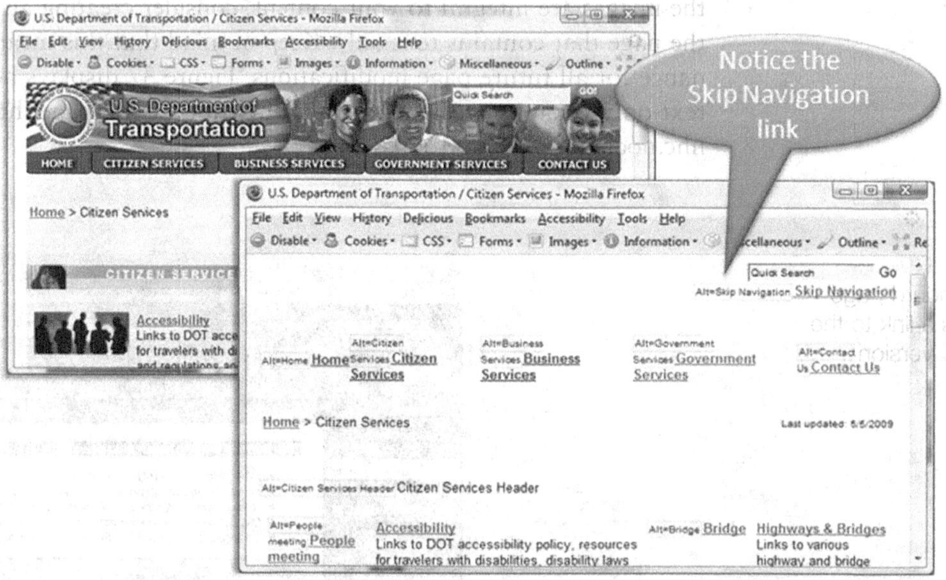

Figure 38
The Firefox Web Developer extension can display the text descriptions of each image

Figure 39 presents another way to implement this feature. Visitors using a screen reader will immediately encounter the Skip to Content link in the upper-left side of the http://stopalcoholabuse.gov Web page.

Figure 39
The Skip to Content link

8 Design to Provide Accessibility

Focus on Accessibility

Vinton Cerf, the coinventor of TCP/IP and the former chairman of the Internet Society, proclaimed that "The Internet is for everyone" (see http://www.isoc.org/isoc/media/speeches/foreveryone.shtml). Tim Berners-Lee, the inventor of the World Wide Web, states that "The power of the Web is in its universality. Access by everyone regardless of disability is an essential aspect" (see http://www.w3.org/WAI).

Who benefits from increased accessibility? Consider the following scenarios:

- Maria, a young woman in her twenties with physical challenges who cannot manipulate a mouse and who uses a keyboard with much effort
- Leotis, a college student who is deaf and wants to be a Web developer
- Jim, a middle-aged man who has a dial-up Internet connection and is using the Web for personal enjoyment
- Nadine, a mature woman with age-related macular degeneration who has difficulty reading small print
- Karen, a college student using a different type of user-agent, such as a cell phone, to access the Web
- Prakesh, a man in his thirties who is legally blind and needs access to the Web to do his job

All these individuals benefit from Web pages designed with accessibility in mind. A Web page that is designed to be accessible is typically more usable for all—even a person who has no physical challenges and is using a broadband connection benefits from the improved presentation and organization of a well-designed Web page.

The Internet and Web are such a pervasive part of our culture that accessibility is protected by laws in the United States. Section 508 of the Rehabilitation Act requires electronic and information technology, including Web pages, used by federal agencies to be accessible to people with disabilities.

The accessibility recommendations presented in this text are intended to satisfy the Section 508 standards and the W3C Web Accessibility Initiative guidelines See http://www.access-board.gov/sec508/guide/1194.22.htm for an informative, descriptive list of the Section 508 Standards for Web pages (Web-based intranet and Internet information and applications).

The federal government is promoting accessibility by law and the private sector is following its lead.

The W3C is also active in this cause and has created the Web Accessibility Initiative (WAI) (see http://www.w3.org/WAI/) to create guidelines and standards applicable to Web content developers, authoring tool developers, and browser developers. The most recent version of the WAI's guidelines are the Web Content Accessibility Guidelines 2.0 (WCAG 2.0). The following four principles are essential to conformance with WCAG 2.0—Perceivable, Operable, Understandable, and Robust. Use the acronym **POUR** to remember them.)

1. Content must be Perceivable
2. Interface components in the content must be Operable
3. Content and controls must be Understandable
4. Content should be Robust enough to work with current and future user agents, including assistive technologies

See http://www.w3.org/TR/WCAG20/Overview for a description of the WCAG 2.0 guidelines. These guidelines are segmented into three levels of conformance: Level A, Level AA, and Level AAA.

In addition to satisfying the Section 508 guidelines, the accessibility recommendations discussed in this text are also intended to fully satisfy the WCAG 2.0 Level AA (includes Level A) guidelines and partially satisfy the Level AAA guidelines. Visit http://www.w3.org/WAI/WCAG20/quickref for an interactive checklist of these guidelines. You're already well on your way to creating accessible web pages—see the list of Level AA guidelines below:

WCAG 2.0 Quick Reference List

Perceivable

- **1.1 Text Alternatives:** Provide text alternatives for any non-text content so that it can be changed into other forms people need, such as large print, braille, speech, symbols, or simpler language. *You've already begun to satisfy this guideline if you've coded the alt attribute on img tags.*
- **1.2 Time-based Media:** Provide alternatives for time-based media. *We won't be creating time-based media in this text, but keep this in mind for the future—if you create animation or use client-side scripting for features such as interactive slide shows.*
- **1.3 Adaptable:** Create content that can be presented in different ways (for example, simpler layout) without losing information or structure. *You've probably already used block elements (such as divs, headings, paragraphs, and lists) to create single-column Web pages. You'll continue to expand your CSS skills as you create multi-column Web pages AND explore the use of XHTML tables to configure information. You are aware that text-only Web pages can be created if needed.*
- **1.4 Distinguishable:** Make it easier for users to see and hear content including separating foreground from background. *You should be aware of the importance of good contrast between text and background.*

Operable

- **2.1 Keyboard Accessible:** Make all functionality available from a keyboard. *Examples include configuring a skip to content link and configuring the tabindex to help a visitor move around in a Web page form.*
- **2.2 Enough Time:** Provide users enough time to read and use content. *We won't be creating time-based media in this text, but keep this in mind for the future—if you create animation or use client-side scripting for features such as interactive slide shows.*
- **2.3 Seizures:** Do not design content in a way that is known to cause seizures. *You won't learn to create animation in this text, but be careful when you use*

animation created by others; Web pages should not contain elements that flash more than three times in a one-second period.

- **2.4 Navigable:** Provide ways to help users navigate, find content and determine where they are. *You've explored many ways to configure navigation in this chapter, including the importance of providing text navigation links in the footer section of a Web page when media such as images or Flash are used for main navigation.*

Understandable

- **3.1 Readable:** Make text content readable and understandable. *You've begun to explore methods of writing for the Web in this chapter.*
- **3.2 Predictable:** Make Web pages appear and operate in predictable ways. *The Web pages you create are predictable with clearly labeled and functioning hyperlinks.*
- **3.3 Input Assistance:** Help users avoid and correct mistakes. *Client-side scripting can be used to edit Web page forms and provide feedback to users.*

Robust

- **4.1 Compatible:** Maximize compatibility with current and future user agents, including assistive technologies. *If you have learned to write code that follows XHTML and CSS standards; this will provide for future compatibility.*

Developing accessible Web sites is an important aspect of Web site design. Web authoring tools such as Adobe Dreamweaver provide extensions that will help you create accessible sites. WebAim has created a WCAG 2.0 checklist with helpful tips at http://webaim.org/standards/wcag/checklist. Worldspace Online (http://worldspace.deque.com) is a free Web page validator that will check your Web page for common accessibility issues. The University of Toronto (http://achecker.ca/checker/index.php) also provides a free accessibility validation service. Both online validators test one page at a time.

Finally, the Section 508 Standards require that if a Web page cannot comply with accessibility requirements, then a separate text-only version of the Web page must be provided and regularly updated. Although the text pages could be coded manually, other options exist to provide this functionality. The LIFT Text Transcoder server, available from UsableNet (http://www.usablenet.com), dynamically generates text-only, accessible pages that comply with accessibility standards. For a live example of this technology in action, compare the graphical University of Illinois home page (http://www.uiuc.edu) with the text-only version generated by UsableNet at (http://transcoder.usablenet.com/tt/http://www.uiuc.edu).

9 Best Practices Checklist

Table 1 contains a checklist of recommended Web design practices. Use this as a guide to help you create easy to read, usable, and accessible Web pages.

Table 1 Web Design Best Practices Checklist

Page Layout		
❑	1.	Appealing to target audience
❑	2.	Consistent site header/logo
❑	3.	Consistent navigation area
❑	4.	Informative page title that includes the company/organization/site name
❑	5.	Page footer area—copyright, last update, contact e-mail address
❑	6.	Good use of basic design principles: repetition, contrast, proximity, and alignment
❑	7.	Displays without horizontal scrolling at 1024×768 and higher resolutions
❑	8.	Balance of text/graphics/white space on page
❑	9.	Good contrast between text and background
❑	10.	Repetitive information (header/logo and navigation) takes up no more than one-quarter to one-third of the browser window at 1024×768 resolution
❑	11.	Home page has compelling, interesting information above the fold (before scrolling down) at 1024×768 resolution
❑	12.	Home page downloads within 10 seconds on dial-up connection
Browser Compatibility		
❑	1.	Displays on current versions of Internet Explorer (7+)
❑	2.	Displays on current versions of Firefox (3+)
❑	3.	Displays on current versions of Opera (9+)
❑	4.	Displays on current versions of Safari (both Mac and Windows)
❑	5.	Displays on current versions of Google Chrome
Navigation		
❑	1.	Main navigation links are clearly and consistently labeled
❑	2.	Navigation is easy to use for target audience
❑	3.	If image, Flash, or DHTML is the main navigation, clear text links are in the footer section of the page (accessibility)
❑	4.	Navigational aids, such as site map, skip to content link, or breadcrumbs, are used
❑	5.	All navigation hyperlinks work
Color and Graphics		
❑	1.	Use of different colors in page backgrounds/text is limited to a maximum of three or four
❑	2.	Color is used consistently
❑	3.	Color has good contrast with associated text
❑	4.	Color is not used alone to convey meaning (accessibility)
❑	5.	Use of color and graphics enhances rather than distracts from the site
❑	6.	Graphics are optimized and do not slow download significantly
❑	7.	Each graphic used serves a clear purpose
❑	8.	Image tags use the `alt` attribute to configure alternate text to display if the browser or user agent does not support images (accessibility)
❑	9.	Animated images do not distract from the site and either do not repeat or only repeat a few times

Table 1 Web Design Best Practices Checklist (*continued*)

Multimedia		
❑	1.	Each audio/video/Flash file used serves a clear purpose
❑	2.	The audio/video/Flash files used enhance rather than distract from the site
❑	3.	Captions are provided for each audio or video file used (accessibility)
❑	4.	Download times for audio or video files are indicated
❑	5.	Links to downloads for media plug-ins are provided
Content Presentation		
❑	1.	Common fonts such as Arial or Times New Roman are used
❑	2.	Techniques of writing for the Web are used: headings, bullet points, short sentences in short paragraphs, use of white space, and so on
❑	3.	Fonts, font sizes, and font colors are consistently used
❑	4.	Content provides meaningful, useful, information
❑	5.	Content is organized in a consistent manner
❑	6.	Information is easy to find (minimal clicks)
❑	7.	Timeliness: The date of the last revision and/or copyright date is accurate
❑	8.	Content does not include outdated material
❑	9.	Content is free of typographical and grammatical errors
❑	10.	Content provides links to other useful sites
❑	11.	Avoids the use of "Click here" when writing text for hyperlinks
❑	12.	If standard link colors are not used, all links use a consistent set of colors to indicate visited/nonvisited status
❑	13.	If graphics and/or media is used to convey meaning, the alternate text equivalent of the content is provided (accessibility)
Functionality		
❑	1.	All internal hyperlinks work
❑	2.	All external hyperlinks work
❑	3.	All forms function as expected
❑	4.	No JavaScript errors are generated by the pages
Accessibility		
❑	1.	If image, Flash, or DHTML is the main navigation, clear text links are in the footer section of the page
❑	2.	Color is not used alone to convey meaning
❑	3.	Image tags use the `alt` attribute to configure alternate text replacement
❑	4.	Captions are provided for each audio or video file used
❑	5.	Use attributes designed to improve accessibility such as `alt`, `longdesc`, `title`, and `summary` where appropriate
❑	6.	If the site uses frames, use frame titles and place meaningful content in the noframes area
❑	7.	To assist screen readers, the html element's lang and xml:lang attributes indicate the spoken language of the page.

Note: Web Design Best Practices Checklist is copyrighted by http://terrymorris.net. Used by permission.

CHECKPOINT 2

1. View the home page of your school. Use the Best Practices Checklist (Table 1) to evaluate the page. Describe the results.
2. List three best practices of writing text for the Web. The following text was found on a real Web site. The company name and city have been changed. Use the hints in the text design best practices described earlier in the chapter to rewrite the following content for the Web:

   "Acme, Inc. is a new laboratory instrument repair and service company. Our staff at this time has a combined total of 30 plus years of specimen preparation instrumentation service and repair.

   Our technicians are EPA refrigeration certified. We are fully insured and all of our workers are fully covered by workman's compensation insurance. A proof of insurance certificate can be provided upon request.

   We are located in Chicago, Illinois. Which houses shop repair facilities and offices. Acme, Inc. technicians are factory trained and equipped with the best diagnostic and repair equipment available.

   We keep a separate file on every piece of equipment we work on. When a technician is sent on a repair, he has a file which lists the whole repair history on that piece of equipment. These files also help us answer any of your questions about past repairs.

   Our rates are $100.00 per hour for Labor and Travel with a 2 hour minimum. $0.40 per mile and all related expenses PARTS are not included."
3. List three best practices of using graphics on Web pages. View the home page of your school. Describe the use of graphic design best practices on this page.

CHAPTER SUMMARY

This chapter introduced recommended Web site design practices. The choices you make in the use of color, graphics, and text should be based on your particular target audience. Developing an accessible Web site should be the goal of every Web developer.

Visit http://www.webdevfoundations.net for examples, the links listed in this chapter, and updated information.

Key Terms

above the fold
alignment
antialiased text
breadcrumb trails
chunking
contrast
hierarchical organization
horizontal scrolling
ice design
jello design
linear organization
liquid design
load time
navigation bar
page layout
perceived load time
proximity
random organization
repetition
screen resolution
site map
site search
storyboard
table of contents
target audience
WAI (Web Accessibility Initiative)
WCAG 2.0 (Web Content Accessibility Guidelines 2.0)
white space
wireframe

Review Questions

Multiple Choice

1. Which of the following would a consistent Web site design *not* have?
   a. a similar navigation area on each content page
   b. the same fonts on each content page
   c. a different background color on each page
   d. the same logo in the same location on each content page

2. Which of the following are the three most common methods of organizing Web sites?
   a. horizontal, vertical, and diagonal
   b. hierarchical, linear, and random
   c. accessible, readable, maintainable
   d. none of the above

3. Which of the following is not a Web design recommended practice?
   a. design your site to be easy to navigate
   b. colorful pages appeal to everyone
   c. design your pages to load quickly
   d. limit the use of animated items

4. Which are the four principles of the Web Content Accessibility Guidelines?
   a. contrast, repetition, alignment, proximity
   b. perceivable, operable, understandable, robust
   c. accessible, readable, maintainable, reliable
   d. hierarchical, linear, random, sequential

5. Which of the following is a sketch or blueprint of a Web page that shows the structure (but not the detailed design) of basic page elements?
   a. drawing
   b. HTML code
   c. site map
   d. wireframe

6. Which of the following are influenced by the intended or target audience of a site?
   a. the amount of color used on the site
   b. the font size and styles used on the site
   c. the overall look and feel for the site
   d. all of the above

7. Which of the following recommended design practices apply to a Web site that uses images for its main site navigation?
   a. provide alternative text for the images
   b. place text links at the bottom of the page
   c. both a and b
   d. no special considerations are needed

8. Which of the following is known as white space?
   a. the empty screen area around blocks of text and images
   b. the background color of white used for a page
   c. both a and b
   d. none of the above

9. Which of the following should you do when creating text hyperlinks?
   a. create the entire sentence as a hyperlink
   b. include the words "click here" in your text
   c. use a key phrase as a hyperlink
   d. none of the above

10. Which of the following is the design technique used to create pages that stretch to fill the browser window?
   a. ice
   b. liquid
   c. jello
   d. none of the above

Fill in the Blank

11. The most common Web site structure used for commercial Web sites is ___________ Web site organization.

12. Animation should be used only if it ___________ to your Web site.

13. All browsers and browser versions ___________ display Web pages in exactly the same way.

14. The ___________ is a group whose mission is to create guidelines and standards for Web accessibility.

Short Answer

15. Describe one of the four principles of WCAG 2.0.

Hands-On Exercises

1. **Web Design Evaluation.** In this chapter you've explored Web page design, including navigation design techniques and the design principles of contrast, repetition, alignment, and proximity. In this Hands-On Exercise, you'll review and evaluate screenshots of Web pages.
   a. Review Figure 40 and complete the following information.

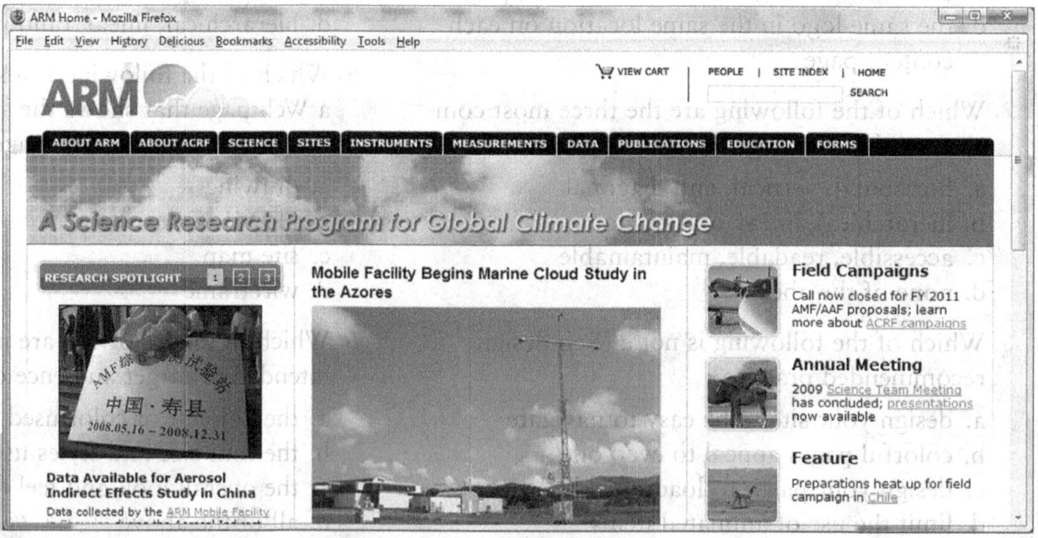

Figure 40 The Atmospheric Radiation Measurement (ARM) Program Web site at http://www.arm.gov

Go to the end of the chapter for a full color version of this figure

Indicate the type(s) of navigation evident.

____

Describe how the design principles of contrast, repetition, alignment, and proximity are applied. Be specific.

____

____

____

____

b. Review Figure 41 and complete the following information.

Figure 41
SmokeFree.gov's site for women at http://women.smokefree.gov

Go to the end of the chapter for a full color version of this figure

Indicate the type(s) of navigation evident.

____

Describe how the design principles of contrast, repetition, alignment, and proximity are applied. Be specific.

____

____

____

____

c. Review Figure 42 and complete the information below.

Figure 42
Telework.gov at http://www.telework.gov

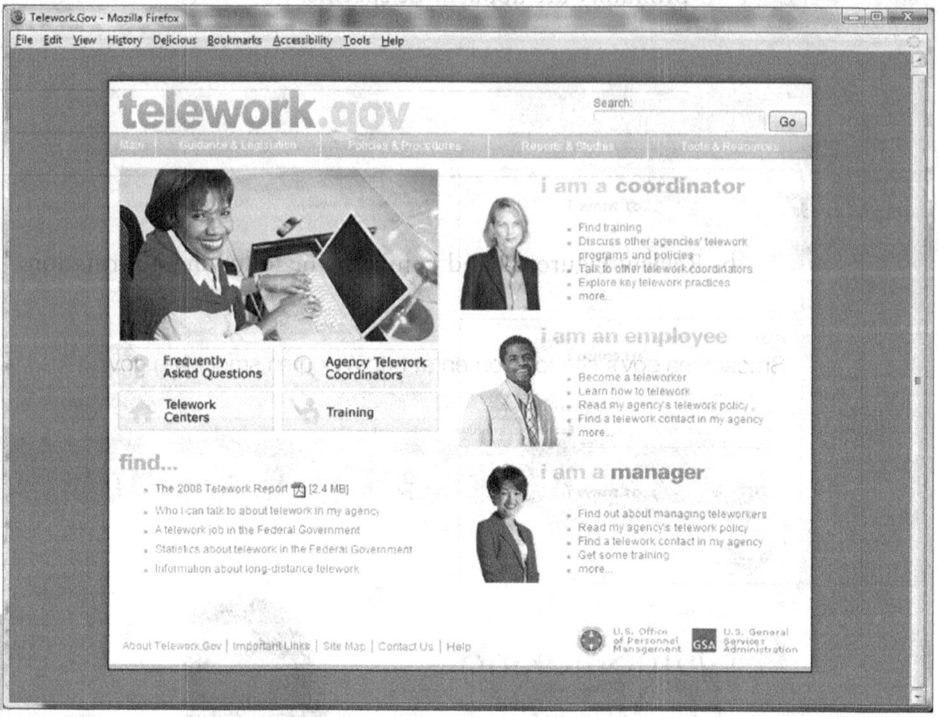

Go to the end of the chapter for a full color version of this figure

Indicate the type(s) of navigation evident.

Describe how the design principles of contrast, repetition, alignment, and proximity are applied. Be specific.

2. Practice creating site maps for the following situations. You may either draw your site map using a pencil and a ruler or use software such as Microsoft Visio, Microsoft Word, or Microsoft PowerPoint.

a. Doug Kowalski is a freelance photographer specializing in nature photography. He often gets work on contract, shooting photos for textbooks and journals. Doug would like a Web site that showcases his talents and that provides publishers with an easy way to contact him. He would like a home page, a few pages with samples of his nature photographs, and a contact page. Create a site map based on this scenario.

b. Mary Ruarez owns a business, named Just Throw Me, that handcrafts specialty pillows. She currently sells at craft fairs and local gift shops but would like to expand her business to the Web. She would like a Web site with a home page, a page that describes her products, a page for each of her seven pillow styles, and an order page. She has been advised that since she is collecting information from individuals, a page describing her privacy policy would be a good idea. Create a site map based on this scenario.

c. Prakesh Khan owns a dog-grooming business named A Dog's Life. He would like a Web site that includes a home page, a page about grooming services, a page with a map to his shop, a contact page, and a section that explains how to select a good pet. The content for the part of the Web site on selecting a pet will be a step-by-step presentation. Create a site map based on this scenario.

3. Practice creating wireframe page layouts with the following situations. Use the style for page layout composition shown in Figures 25, 26, and 27, where places for logo, navigation, text, and images are indicated. Do not worry about exact wording or exact images. If you prefer, use an application such as PowerPoint to create the wireframes, otherwise use a pencil, ruler, and paper to draw the diagrams.

   a. Create sample page layout wireframes for Doug Kowalski's photography business, described in 2(a). Create one page layout wireframe for the home page. Create another page layout diagram for the content pages.

   b. Create sample page layout wireframes for the Just Throw Me Web site described in 2(b). Create one page layout wireframe for the home page. Create another page layout wireframe for the content pages.

   c. Create sample page layout wireframes for the A Dog's Life Web site described in 2(c). Create one page layout wireframe for the home page and the regular content pages. Create another page layout wireframe for the presentation pages.

4. Choose two sites that are similar in nature or have a similar target audience such as the following:

   - http://amazon.com and http://bn.com
   - http://kohls.com and http://jcpenney.com
   - http://cnn.com and http://msnbc.com

   Describe how the two sites you chose to review exhibit the design principles of repetition, contrast, alignment, and proximity.

5. Choose two sites that are similar in nature or have a similar target audience such as the following:

   - http://www.crateandbarrel.com and http://www.potterybarn.com
   - http://www.harpercollege.edu and http://www.clcillinois.edu
   - http://chicagobears.com and http://greenbaypackers.com

   Describe how the two sites you chose to review exhibit Web design best practices. How would you improve these sites? Recommend three improvements for each site.

6. Think about the following scenarios and how you would design a home page using the ice design technique. Describe the advantages this technique provides for the Web developer. Describe the advantages this technique provides for the Web site visitor. Create a wireframe page layout for the home page.

   a. See 2(a) for the description of Doug Kowalski's photography business.

   b. See 2(b) for the description of Just Throw Me.

   c. See 2(c) for the description of A Dog's Life.

7. Think about the following scenarios and how you would design a home page using the jello design technique. Describe the advantages this technique provides for the

Web developer. Describe the advantages this technique provides for the Web site visitor. Create a wireframe page layout for the home page.

a. See 2(a) for the description of Doug Kowalski's photography business.
b. See 2(b) for the description of Just Throw Me.
c. See 2(c) for the description of A Dog's Life.

8. Think about the scenarios described below and how you would design a home page using the liquid design technique. Describe the advantages this technique provides for the Web developer. Describe the advantages this technique provides for the Web site visitor. Create a wireframe page layout for the home page.

a. See 2(a) for the description of Doug Kowalski's photography business.
b. See 2(b) for the description of Just Throw Me.
c. See 2(c) for the description of A Dog's Life.

Web Research

This chapter offered suggestions for organizing text on Web pages. In this research exercise, take this topic a step further and investigate writing for the Web. A few resources are listed here:

- http://www.useit.com/papers/webwriting
- http://www.efuse.com/Design/web_writing_basics.html. Explore the article "Writing for the Web."
- http://www.webreference.com/content/writing. If you cannot find that page, visit webreference.com and search for "writing for the Web."
- http://www.webwritingthatworks.com
- http://www.alistapart.com/articles/writeliving

If these resources are no longer available, search the Web for information on "writing for the Web." Read one or more articles. Select five techniques that you would like to share with others. Write a one-page summary of your findings. Include the URLs of your resources.

Focus on Web Design

1. This chapter discusses recommended Web design practices. Sometimes it is helpful to learn about good design by examining poor design. Visit http://www.webpagesthatsuck.com and read about their examples of poor design. Try to think of Web sites that you have visited on the Web. Do any of them have similar qualities? Find two Web sites that use poor Web design practices. Write a one-page report that includes an introduction about the design practices not followed at the Web sites, a link to each site, and a description of how each site has practiced poor Web site design.
2. Visit any of the Web sites referenced in this chapter that interested you. Print the home page or one other pertinent page from the site. Write a one-page summary and reaction to the Web site you chose to visit. Address the following topics:
   - What is the purpose of the site?
   - Who is the intended audience?
   - Do you think the site reaches the intended audience?
   - List three examples of how this Web site uses recommended Web design guidelines.
   - How could this site be improved?

WEB SITE CASE STUDY: Web Design Best Practices

This chapter asks you to analyze the design of the following Web sites.

JavaJam Coffee House

See the Chapter "XHTML Basics" for an introduction to the JavaJam Coffee House case. Figure 26 in that chapter shows a site map for the JavaJam Web site. Three pages for this site were created in earlier chapters. In this case study you will review the site for recommended Web site design practices.

Hands-On Practice Case

1. Examine the site map in Figure 26 of the Chapter "XHTML Basics". What type of site organization is used for the JavaJam Web site? Is it the most appropriate organization for the site? Why or why not?
2. Review the recommended Web page design practices from this chapter. Use the Web Design Best Practices Checklist (Table 1) to evaluate the JavaJam site that you created in earlier chapters. Cite three design practices that have been well implemented. Cite three design practices that could be implemented in a better way. How else would you improve the Web site?

Fish Creek Animal Hospital

See the Chapter "XHTML Basics" for an introduction to the Fish Creek Animal Hospital Case. Figure 30 in that chapter shows a site map for the Fish Creek Web site. Three pages for the site were created in earlier chapters. In this case study you will review the site for recommended Web site design practices.

Hands-On Practice Case

1. Examine the site map in Figure 30 of the Chapter "XHTML Basics". What type of site organization is used for the Fish Creek Web site? Is it the most appropriate organization for the site? Why or why not?
2. Review the recommended Web page design practices from this chapter. Use the Web Design Best Practices Checklist (Table 1) to evaluate the Fish Creek site that you created in earlier chapters. Cite three design practices that have been well implemented. Cite three design practices that could be implemented in a better way. How else would you improve the Web site?

Pasha the Painter

See the Chapter "XHTML Basics" for an introduction to the Pasha the Painter Case. Figure 34 of that chapter shows a site map for the Pasha the Painter Web site. Three pages for the site were created in earlier chapters. During this case study you will review the site for recommended Web site design practices.

Hands-On Practice Case

1. Examine the site map in Figure 34 of the Chapter "XHTML Basics". What type of site organization is used for the Pasha the Painter Web site? Is it the most appropriate organization for the site? Why or why not?
2. Review the recommended Web page design practices from this chapter. Use the Web Design Best Practices Checklist (Table 1) to evaluate the Pasha the Painter site that you created in earlier chapters. Cite three design practices that have been well implemented. Cite three design practices that could be implemented in a better way. How else would you improve the Web site?

Prime Properties

See the Chapter "XHTML Basics" for an introduction to the Prime Properties Case. Figure 38 in that chapter shows a site map for the Prime Properties Web site. Three pages for the site have already been created. During this case study you will review the site for recommended Web site design practices.

Hands-On Practice Case

1. Examine the site map in Figure 38 of the Chapter "XHTML Basics". What type of site organization is used for the Prime Properties Web site? Is it the most appropriate organization for the site? Why or why not?
2. Review the recommended Web page design practices from this chapter. Use the Web Design Best Practices Checklist (Table 1) to evaluate the Prime Properties site you created in earlier chapters. Cite three design practices that have been well implemented. Cite three design practices that could be implemented in a better way. How else would you improve the site?

Web Project

The purpose of this Web Project Case Study is to design a Web site using recommended design practices. Your Web site might be about a favorite hobby or subject, your family, a church or club you belong to, a company that a friend owns, the company you work for, and so on. Your Web site will contain a home page and at least six (but no more than ten) content pages. In this Chapter's Web Project Case Study you will complete the following documents: Topic Approval, Site Map, and Page Layout Design. You will not develop Web pages as part of this chapter's Web Project Case Study.

Hands-On Practice Case

1. **Web Project Topic Approval.** The topic of your Web site must be approved by your instructor. Complete the following:
   - What is the purpose of the site?

     List the reason you are creating the site.
   - What do you want the site to accomplish?

     List the goals you have for the site.

     Describe what needs to happen for you to consider your site a success.

- Who is your target audience?

  Describe your target audience by age, gender, socio-economic characteristics, and so on.
- What opportunity or issue is your site addressing? *Note*: Your site might be addressing the opportunity of providing information about a topic to others, creating an initial Web presence for a company, and so on.
- What type of content might be included in your site?

  Describe the type of text, graphics, and media you will need for the site.
- List at least two related or similar sites found on the Web.

  Hand in this document to your instructor for approval of your Web project topic.

2. **Web Project Site Map.** Use the drawing features of a word processing program, a graphic application, or paper and pencil to create a site map of your Web site that shows the hierarchy of pages and relationships between pages. Hand in this document to your instructor.
3. **Web Project Page Layout Design.** Use the drawing features of a word processing program, a graphic application, or paper and pencil to create wireframe page layouts for the home page and content pages of your site. Unless otherwise directed by your instructor, use the style for page layout composition shown in Figures 25, 26, and 27. Indicate where the logo, navigation, text, and images will be located. Do not worry about exact wording or exact images. Hand in these documents to your instructor.

Answers

Checkpoint 1

1. The four basic principles of design are repetition, contrast, proximity, and alignment. Descriptions of school home pages and how these principles are applied will vary.
2. http://www.walmart.com is an e-commerce site. It is designed to appeal to the general public—note the white background and high contrast and use of tabbed navigation, product hierarchy, and site search. This meets the needs of its target audience—teen and adult shoppers. http://www.sesameworkshop.org/sesamestreet is geared toward young children and their parents. It is bright and colorful with much interactivity and animation, which is appealing to the target audience. http://www.mugglenet.com is a fan site designed to appeal to teens and young adults. It is a dark, mysterious site with much interaction—the forums are very busy. This site appeals to its niche audience.
3. Answers will vary.

Checkpoint 2

1. Answers will vary.
2. Best practices for writing for the Web include the following: short paragraphs, bullet points, common fonts, white space, multiple columns if possible, bold or emphasized important text, and correct spelling and grammar.

   Answers will vary. The following suggested solution adds interest with bullet points, places emphasis on important phrases, and includes editing of the original text:

   Acme, Inc. is a new laboratory instrument repair and service company. Our staff at this time has a combined total of 30 plus years of specimen preparation instrumentation service and repair.

   - **EPA Refrigeration Certified**

     Acme, Inc. technicians are factory trained and equipped with the best diagnostic and repair equipment available.
   - **Fully Insured**

     Our workers are fully covered by workman's compensation insurance.

     A proof of insurance certificate can be provided upon request.
   - **Convenient Location**

     Repair shop facilities and offices located in Chicago, Illinois.
   - **Service History**

     Your equipment is important to us.

     A detailed repair history is kept and available to our service technicians.
   - **Rates**

     Labor and Travel $100.00 per hour

     2 hour minimum

     $0.40 per mile and all related expenses

     Parts are not included

3. Best practices for using graphics on Web pages include the following: careful choice of colors (Web Safe Color Palette is recommended for the most similar cross-platform display), use of necessary images only, use of images as small as possible, a usable site even if images are not displayed, and use of the `alt` attribute to configure text descriptions for images.

   Recommendations for school home pages will vary.

Review Questions

1. c
2. b
3. b
4. b
5. d
6. d
7. c
8. a
9. c
10. b
11. hierarchical
12. adds value
13. will not
14. Web Accessibility Initiative (WAI)
15. Student answers will vary. The four principles that are essential to complying with WCAG 2.0 are as follows: Perceivable, Operable, Understandable, and Robust.
    1. Content must be Perceivable
    2. Interface components in the content must be Operable
    3. Content and controls must be Understandable
    4. Content should be Robust enough to work with current and future user agents, including assistive technologies

Page Layout with CSS

Chapter Objectives

In this chapter, you will learn how to ...

- Describe reasons to use CSS for page layout
- Use relative and absolute positioning
- Apply the CSS Box Model
- Configure basic page layouts using CSS
- Configure two-column page layouts using CSS
- Locate CSS page layout resources

If you are familiar with using CSS to format text and color, you are ready to explore using CSS to configure Web page layout. This method relies on CSS properties rather than XHTML tables to design a Web page. The technology for this layout is often called CSS-P, for CSS positioning. This chapter introduces you to configuring page layouts using CSS.

1 CSS Page Layout Overview

You've probably used CSS to configure presentation (fonts, colors, and so on) of the structural XHTML elements including headings, paragraphs, divs, and lists. You may have noticed that using CSS results in smaller Web page documents (html files), which saves on bandwidth and eases site maintenance. You will soon see that using CSS to configure page layout enhances these advantages.

First, here is a little background about CSS and some acronyms you should be familiar with. As you probably already know, the W3C produced a recommendation for CSS (http://www.w3.org/TR/REC-CSS1–961217.html), now called CSS Level 1 (CSS1), in 1996. They continued their work and produced a recommendation for CSS Level 2 or CSS2, (http://www.w3.org/TR/1998/REC-CSS2–19980512/) in 1998. CSS2 built on CSS1 and introduced new properties needed for positioning—known as CSS-P. CSS3 is currently under development (http://www.w3.org/Style/CSS/current-work).

Even though CSS2 was introduced in the last millennium, commercial Web sites have only recently begun to utilize its features. You may wonder why it has taken so long. The reason is lack of browser support of the W3C recommendations. Only very recently have the most current versions of commonly used browsers begun to support these recommendations reliably and consistently. Even so, you will encounter differences in rendering when displaying pages coded using CSS-P page layout techniques in various browsers. Keep in mind that not all Web page visitors will be using the most current browser version. There are a number of ways to handle this issue—including coding alternate pages or allowing the browser display to degrade gracefully. Visitors using an older browser will see a usable, but not highly formatted Web page. Let's take a look at an example of a Web site that uses CSS to configure page layout.

Figure 1 shows the DisabilityInfo.gov (http://www.disabilityinfo.gov) home page rendered by Firefox. The Web site uses CSS for page layout to configure a page with multiple columns.

Figure 1 The DisabilityInfo.gov home page displayed in Firefox, a modern browser

A visitor using an outdated, older browser such as Netscape 4.7 experiences a plain vanilla version of the site, as shown in Figure 2. The content is displayed in the order

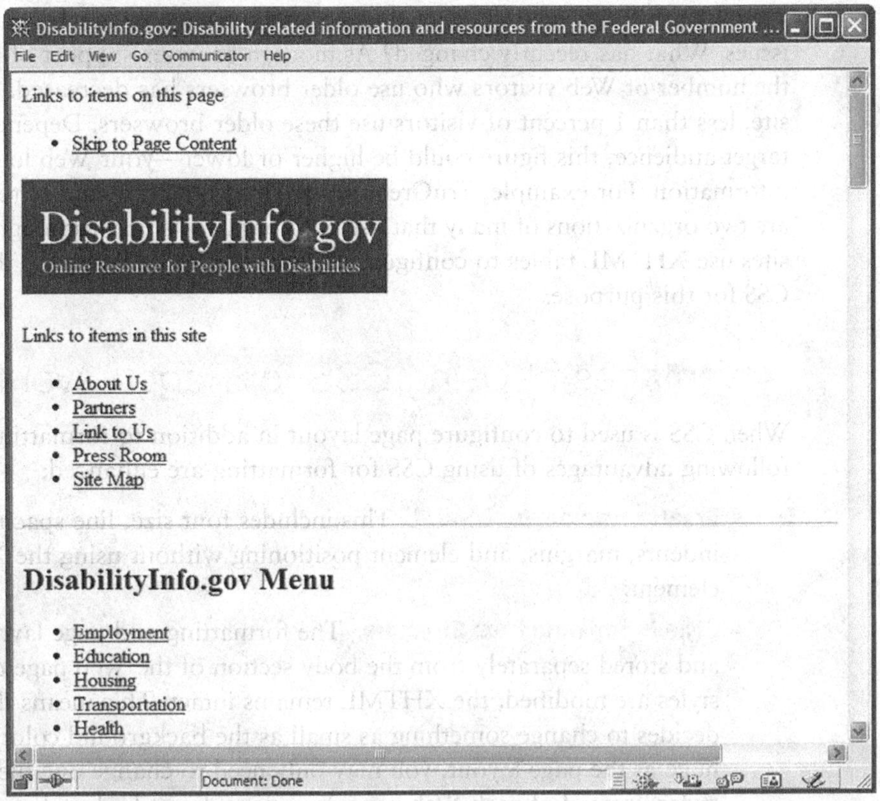

Figure 2 The DisabilityInfo.gov home page displayed in Netscape 4.79, an outdated browser

it is coded in the Web page. Because the site configures most of its graphics as background images within the external CSS style sheet, these graphics are unavailable to the older browser. The visitor experience is not exactly compelling when using an out-of-date browser. However, the site can still be navigated and information can be obtained.

Figure 3 shows the same page displayed using the Firefox LynxView extension to simulate a text browser. The text content is displayed in the order it is coded in the Web page. Notice how even with the newer CSS page layout techniques utilized, the page is usable when rendered in a text browser.

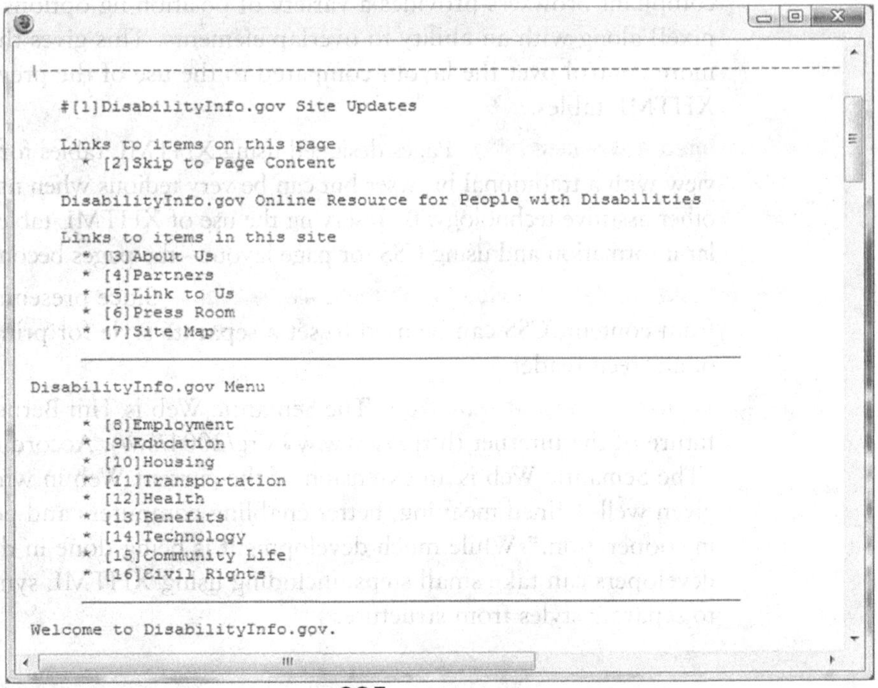

Figure 3 A text browser simulation of DisabilityInfo.gov's home page

Web developers have long delayed using CSS for page layout because of these rendering issues. What has recently changed? As modern browser support of CSS has increased, the number of Web visitors who use older browsers has decreased. For a typical Web site, less than 1 percent of visitors use these older browsers. Depending on your site's target audience, this figure could be higher or lower—your Web logs will provide this information. For example, TruGreen (http://trugreen.com) and wired (http://wired.com) are two organizations of many that use CSS for page layout. Although some existing Web sites use XHTML tables to configure page layout, most Web sites developed today use CSS for this purpose.

Advantages of Using CSS for Page Layout

When CSS is used to configure page layout in addition to formatting text and color, the following advantages of using CSS for formatting are enhanced:

- **Greater Typography Control.** This includes font size, line spacing, letter spacing, indents, margins, and element positioning without using the XHTML table element.
- **Style Is Separate from Structure.** The formatting and page layout can be configured and stored separately from the body section of the Web page document. When the styles are modified, the XHTML remains intact. This means that if your client decides to change something as small as the background color or as potentially huge as the page layout, you may only need to change one file that contains the styles, instead of each Web page document. For a look at how very powerful this can be, visit http://www.csszengarden.com and be amazed at how different pages with the same content and XHTML code (but different CSS) can look!
- **Potentially Smaller Documents.** Since both the formatting and page layout are separate from the document, the actual .html documents should be smaller.
- **Easier Site Maintenance.** Again, if the styles or page layout need to be changed it may be possible to complete the modifications by changing a single file only—the style sheet.
- **Increased Page Layout Control.** CSS used in conjunction with modern standards-compliant browsers provides a variety of positioning options (even down to the pixel) along with an ability to overlap elements. This gives the Web developer more control over the layout compared to the use of the previously popular XHTML tables.
- **Increased Accessibility.** Pages designed using XHTML tables for layout are easy to view with a traditional browser but can be very tedious when using a screen reader or other assistive technology. By reserving the use of XHTML tables for organizing tabular information and using CSS for page layout—the pages become more accessible.
- **Ability to Define Styles for Multiple Media Types.** Since presentation is separated from content, CSS can be used to set a separate style for printing, or possible use of a screen reader.
- **Support of the Semantic Web.** The Semantic Web is Tim Berners-Lee's vision of the future of the Internet (http://www.w3.org/2001/sw/). According to Berners-Lee, "The Semantic Web is an extension of the current Web in which information is given well-defined meaning, better enabling computers and people to work in cooperation." While much development is being done in this area, Web developers can take small steps, including using XHTML syntax and using CSS to separate styles from structure.

Disadvantages of Using CSS for Page Layout

If you review the screenshots of a site that uses CSS for page layout (Figures 1 and 2) you'll see a very obvious disadvantage. Visitors using older browsers will not experience your Web site in the same way as visitors using modern browsers. If you are using tables for page layout, this is not an issue. Why then are developers beginning to code mainstream Web sites using CSS for page layout? With good support of CSS by modern browsers and the increasing use of modern browsers, the advantages of using CSS to configure page layout usually outweigh the disadvantages. Of course, the target audience of a Web site should be a deciding factor. For example, if your target audience for an intranet site is a company that for some reason has standardized on Netscape 4.7 for the desktop, none of the advantages would be realized and it would be better to design the site using tables for page layout. The projected (and eventually actual) target audience should be considered when deciding on a page layout technique.

Even with the increased CSS support of modern browsers, there are still differences and bugs in their implementation of the W3C Recommendations. This is a disadvantage for Web developers, since coding and testing time is increased. Leading developers have created Web sites that document and discuss these issues (see http://www.quirksmode.org and http://www.positioniseverything.net). The CSS techniques in this chapter have been tested with Internet Explorer 8, Opera 9.64, Firefox 3, Google Chrome 2.0, Safari for Windows 3.2.3, and Safari for Mac 3.2.1.

Another potential disadvantage is the fact that experienced Web developers who are adept at coding pages using XHTML tables for layout will see productivity drop temporarily as they learn about CSS techniques and properties. Using CSS positioning is different from configuring pages with XHTML tables. Time and practice are needed when learning something new.

At this point you've seen some examples of using CSS for page layout and are aware of the issues related to using this technology. The next section discusses the **CSS Box Model**—a crucial building block of CSS positioning.

FAQ

Should XHTML tables never be used?

Many commercial Web sites still use XHTML tables for page layout. This is for a very good reason—tables are widely supported by browsers. As a Web developer you will most likely work on sites that use XHTML layout tables. However, a growing trend is to configure pages using CSS (sometimes called table-less layout). This does not mean that tables are bad, ineffective, or that they are never coded on Web sites that use CSS for page layout. Even Web sites with so-called "table-less" layouts may include tables to present information in a tabular manner or facilitate design of a small portion of the page.

2 The Box Model

Each element in a document is considered to be a rectangular box. As shown in Figure 4, this box consists of a content area surrounded by padding, a border, and margins. This is known as the Box Model.

Figure 4
The CSS box model

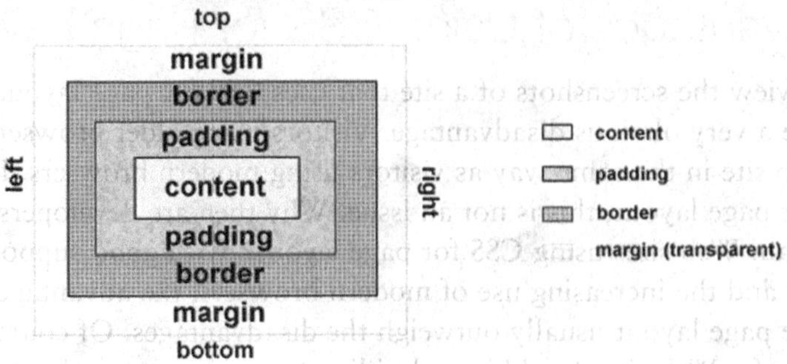

- The **content** area can consist of a combination of text and Web page elements such as images, paragraphs, headings, lists, and so on. The **visible width** of the element on a Web page is the total of the content width, the padding width, and the border width.
- The **padding** area is between the content and the border. The default padding value is zero. When configuring the background of an element, the background is applied to both the padding and the content areas.
- The **border** area is between the padding and the margin. The default border has a value of 0 and does not display. You have already worked with borders in Hands-On Practice.
- The **margin** determines the empty space between the element and any adjacent elements. The margin is always transparent. The solid line in Figure 4 that contains the margin area does not display on a Web page. Keep in mind that browsers often have default margin values set for the Web page document and for certain elements such as paragraphs, headings, forms, and so on. Use the `margin` property to override the default browser values.

Figures 5 and 6 display `<div>` elements containing text content. Let's take a closer look. Figure 5 shows a screenshot of two `<div>` elements placed one after another on a Web page. In Figure 6 the boxes are nested inside each other. In both cases, the browser used **normal flow** (the default) and displayed the elements in the order that

Figure 5
Two `<div>` elements displaying the box model

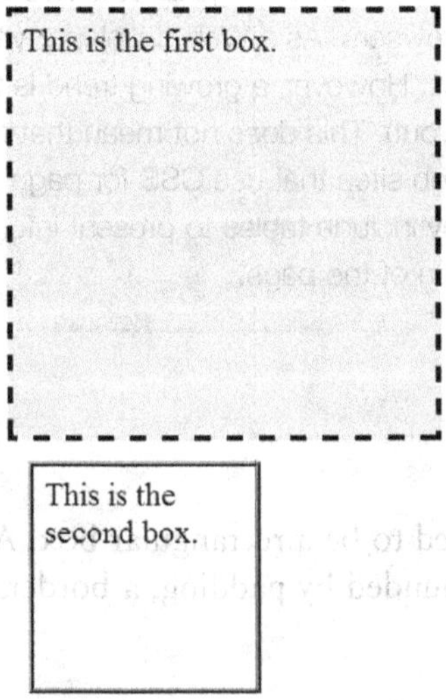

Figure 6
Nested elements showing the box model

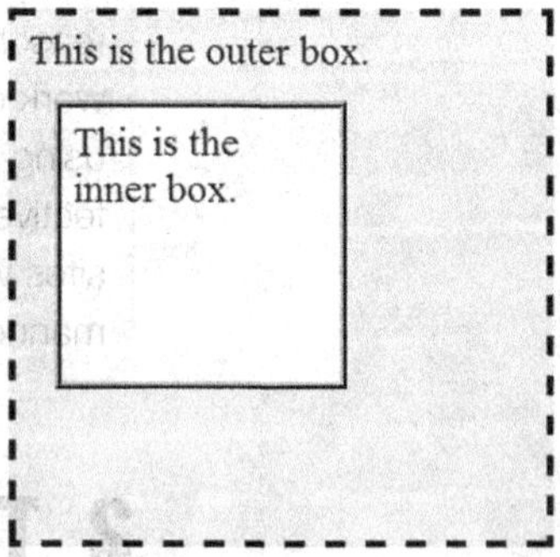

they appeared in the source code. You'll practice using Web pages that the browser renders using normal flow in the next Hands-On Practice. Then, later in the chapter, you'll experiment with positioning to configure the flow, or placement, of elements on a Web page.

HANDS-ON PRACTICE 1

You will explore the box model in this Hands-On Practice as you create the Web pages shown in Figure 5 and Figure 6.

Practice with Normal Flow

Launch a text editor and open the Chapter6/starter1.html file from the student files. Save the file with the name box1.html. This page is displayed in Figure 5. Edit the body of the Web page and add the following code to configure two `<div>` elements:

```
<div class="div1">
This is the first box.
</div>
<div class="div2">
This is the second box.
</div>
```

Now let's add the CSS to configure the "boxes." Add a new style rule for a class named `div1` to configure a light blue background, dashed border, width of 200, height of 200, and 5 pixels of padding. The code follows:

```
.div1 {  width: 200px;
         height: 200px;
         background-color: #D1ECFF;
         border: dashed;
         padding: 5px;
}
```

Create a style rule for a class named `div2` to configure a width and height of 100, white background color, ridged border, 10 pixel margin, and 5 pixels of padding. The code follows:

```
.div2 {  width: 100px;
         height: 100px;
         background-color: #ffffff;
         border: ridge;
         padding: 5px;
         margin: 10px;
}
```

Save the file. Launch a browser and test your page. It should look similar to the one shown in Figure 5. The student files contain a sample solution at chapter6/box1.html.

Practice with Normal Flow and Nested Elements

Launch a text editor and open the box1.html file from the student files. Save the file with the name box2.html. This page is displayed in Figure 6.

Edit the code. You will not modify the CSS but you will edit the XHTML. Delete the content from the body section of the Web page. Add the following code to configure two <div> elements—one nested inside the other.

```
<div class="div1">
This is the outer box.
  <div class="div2">
  This is the inner box.
  </div>
</div>
```

Save the file. Launch a browser and test your page. It should look similar to the one shown in Figure 6. Notice how the browser renders the nested <div> elements—this is an example of normal flow. The student files contain a sample solution at Chapter6/box2.html.

The examples in the Hands-On Practice happened to use two <divs>. However, the box model applies to XHTML elements in general—not just to <divs>. You will get more practice using the box model in this chapter. Notice that since the CSS did not use any configurations for positioning, normal flow was used and the second box is nested within the first box because it is coded inside the first <div> in the XHTML. Next, we will take a look at some properties that affect positioning: `position`, `float`, `display`, and `z-index`.

3 CSS Positioning Properties

You've seen how normal flow causes the browser to render the elements in the order that they appear in the XHTML source code. When using CSS for page layout there are times where you will want to specify the location of an element on the page—either the absolute pixel location, the location relative to where the element would normally display, or floating on the page. There are even times when you will want to modify the way an element displays or cause an element to appear partially or completely over another element. The CSS properties used to accomplish these tasks are discussed next.

Relative and Absolute Positioning

Use **relative positioning** to change the location of an element slightly, relative to where it would otherwise appear in normal flow. Use the `position:relative` property along with either a left, right, and/or top property. The **`left` property** configures the position of the element in relation to the left side of the containing element. The **`right` property** sets the position of the element in relation to the right side of the containing element. The **`top` property** indicates the position of the element in relation to the top of the document area in the containing element. The **`bottom` property** configures the position of the element in relation to the bottom of the containing element.

Figure 7 shows a Web page (see the student files, Chapter6/relative.html) that uses relative positioning and the `left` property to configure the placement of a `<div>` (assigned to the `id mycontent`) to the left of the normal flow. In this case, the containing element is the body of the Web page.

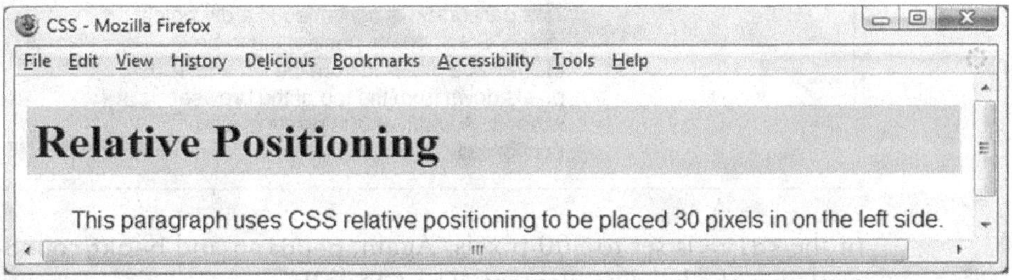

Figure 7
The paragraph is configured using relative positioning

The result is that the content of the `<div>`—the paragraph—is rendered 30 pixels in from the left where it would normally be placed at the browser's left margin. W3C Recommendations call for positioning to be applied to any element and Internet Explorer follows this recommendation. However, cross-browser support of positioning is more reliable when the `<div>` element is used for positioning. Notice also how the `padding` and `background-color` properties configure the heading element. The CSS follows:

```
#myContent { position: relative;
             left: 30px;
             font-family: Arial,sans-serif;
}
h1 { background-color: #cccccc;
     padding: 5px;
     color: #000000;
}
```

The XHTML source code follows:

```
<h1>Relative Positioning</h1>
<div id="myContent">
  <p>This paragraph uses CSS relative positioning to be placed 30
pixels in on the left side.</p>
</div>
```

Use **absolute positioning** to specify the location of an element precisely in a browser window. The `position:absolute` property along with either a `left`, `right`, and/or `top` property is needed to configure the placement.

Figure 8 shows a screenshot of a Web page that uses absolute positioning to configure a `<div>` (see the student files, Chapter6/absolute.html).

The `<div>` is assigned to the `content id` which is positioned 200 pixels in from the left margin and 100 pixels down from the top of the browser window. The result is that the paragraph contained within the `<div>` is rendered 200 pixels in from the left side and 100 pixels down from the top of the document area in the browser window. The width

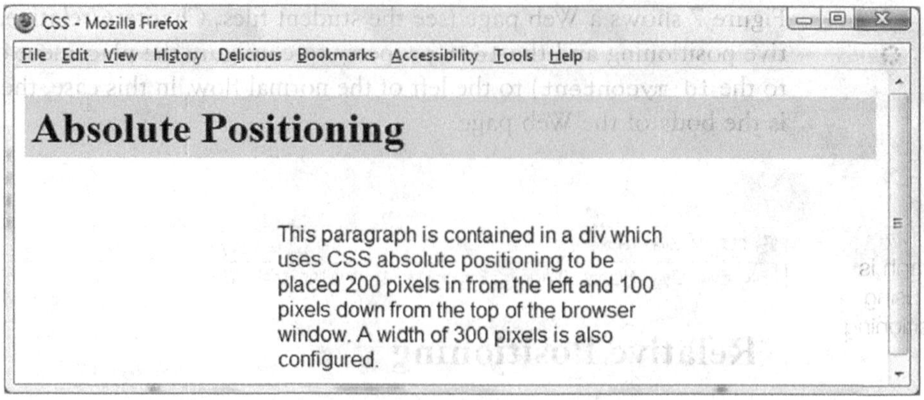

Figure 8 The paragraph is configured using absolute positioning

of the <div> is set to 300 pixels. Again, `padding` and `background-color` are used to configure the heading element. The CSS follows:

```
#content { position: absolute;
           left: 200px;
           top: 100px;
           font-family: Arial,sans-serif;
           width: 300px;
}
h1 { background-color: #cccccc;
     padding: 5px;
     color: #000000;
}
```

The XHTML source code follows:

```
<h1>Absolute Positioning</h1>
<div id="content">
<p>This paragraph is contained in a div which uses CSS absolute
positioning to be placed 200 pixels in from the left and 100 pixels
down from the top of the browser window. A width of 300 pixels is
also configured.</p>
</div>
```

When working with absolute positioning it is important to be aware that elements not absolutely positioned will be rendered following normal flow by the browser. Elements that are absolutely positioned are rendered outside of normal flow. You'll explore this behavior in the next Hands-On Practice.

HANDS-ON PRACTICE 2

Figure 9 shows screenshots of two Web pages with similar XHTML content. The Web page in the upper screenshot does not have any CSS applied. The Web page in the lower screenshot uses CSS to configure text, color, and the absolute position of a paragraph element. Launch a text editor and open the Chapter6/starter2.html found in the student files. When a browser renders the page it will use normal flow and display the XHTML elements in the same order as they are coded: <h1>, <div>, <p>, and <ul>. Launch a browser and display the page to verify.

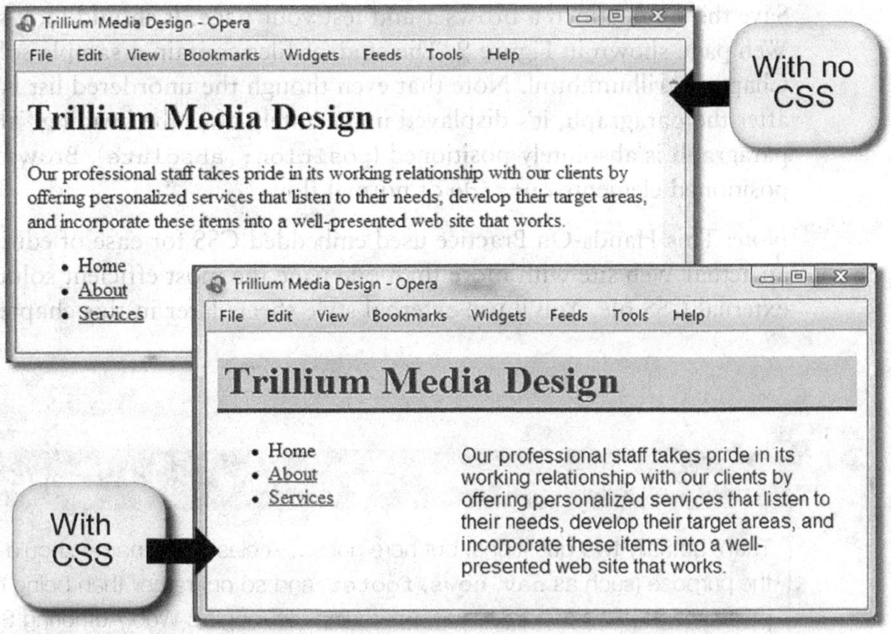

Figure 9 The lower Web page uses CSS absolute positioning

Let's add the CSS to make this page more "stylish" and look like the lower screenshot in Figure 9. Save the file with the name trillium.html. With trillium.html open in a text editor, modify the code as follows:

1. This page uses embedded styles. Code opening and closing `<style>` tags in the header section.

```
<style type="text/css">
</style>
```

2. Create style rules for the `h1` selector. Configure a background color (`#B0C4DE`), text color (`#000080`), a 3 pixel solid bottom border in the color `#000080`, and 5 pixels of padding on the bottom and left sides.

```
h1 { border-bottom: 3px solid #000080;
     color: #000080;
     background-color: #B0C4DE;
     padding: 0 0 5px 5px;
}
```

Note: The padding can be set for each side individually using the `padding-top`, `padding-right`, `padding-bottom`, and `padding-left` properties. You can use shorthand notation to set all four values in one `padding` property. The order of the numeric values determines which box side is configured (top, right, bottom, left).

3. Create style rules for a class named `content`. Configure the position to be absolute, 200 pixels from the left, 75 pixels from the top, a width of 300 pixels, and Arial or sans serif font typeface.

```
.content { position: absolute;
           left: 200px;
           top: 75px;
           font-family: Arial,sans-serif;
           width: 300px;
}
```

4. Assign the paragraph to the `content` class. Add `class="content"` to the opening paragraph tag in the body of the Web page.

Save the file. Launch a browser and test your page. It should look similar to the lower Web page shown in Figure 9. The student files contain a sample solution at Chapter6/trillium.html. Note that even though the unordered list is coded in the page after the paragraph, it's displayed immediately after the heading. This is because the paragraph is absolutely positioned (`position: absolute`). Browsers render absolutely positioned elements *outside* of normal flow.

Note: This Hands-On Practice used embedded CSS for ease of editing. However, for an actual Web site with more than one page the most efficient solution is to use an external CSS file. You'll use external style sheets later in this chapter.

FAQ

What's a good name for a class or id and how do I decide which to use?

That's actually two questions, but here goes... A class or id name should be descriptive of the purpose (such as `nav`, `news`, `footer`, and so on) rather than being descriptive of the presentation (such as `redText`). According to Google's Web Authoring Statistics Study, http://code.google.com/webstats, the 10 most commonly used class names are **`footer`**, **`menu`**, **`title`**, **`small`**, **`text`**, **`content`**, **`header`**, **`nav`**, **`copyright`**, and **`button`**.
If the style can be used on more than one element on a page, configure the style as a class. Use the . (dot) notation in the style sheet. Use the class attribute in the XHTML.

If the style is specific to only one element or if the element will be manipulated using DHTML, configure the style as an id. Use the # notation in the style sheet. Use the id attribute in the XHTML.

The `float` Property

Elements that seem to float on the right or left side of either the browser window or another element are often configured using the **`float` property**. The browser renders these elements using normal flow, and then shifts them as far as possible within their container (usually either the browser window or a `<div>`) to either the right or left. Use CSS to specify a width for a floated element unless the element already has an implicit width—such as an `img` element. Other content will flow around the float. Only block-level elements (such as `divs`, `paragraphs`, and `images`) can be configured to float. When floating an image, the `margin` property is useful to configure empty space between the image and text on the page. Figure 10 shows a Web page (see the student files, Chapter6/float.html) with an image that has been configured with `float:right`.

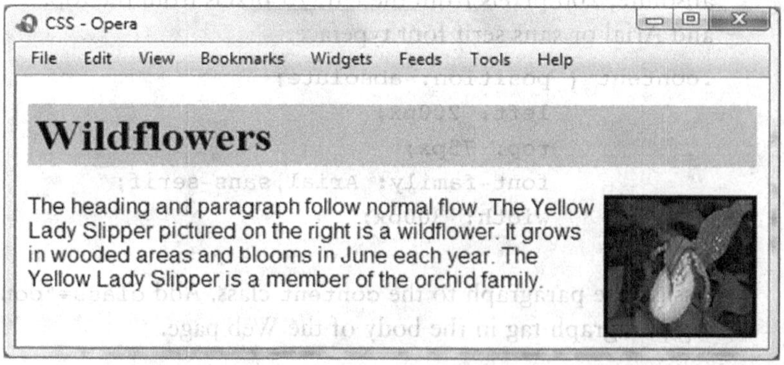

Figure 10 The image is configured with `float:right`

View Figure 10 and notice how the image stays on the right side of the browser viewport. An `id` called `yls` was created that applies the `float`, `margin`, and `border` properties. The attribute `id="yls"` was placed on the image tag. The CSS follows:

```
h1 { background-color: #A8C682;
     padding: 5px;
     color: #000000;
}
p { font-family:Arial,sans-serif;
}
#yls { float: right;
       margin: 0 0 5px 5px;
       border: solid;
}
```

The XHTML source code follows:

```
<h1>Wildflowers</h1>
<img id="yls" src="yls.jpg" alt="Yellow Lady Slipper" height="100"
width="100" />
<p>The heading and paragraph follow normal flow. The Yellow Lady
Slipper pictured on the right is a wildflower. It grows in wooded
areas and blooms in June each year. The Yellow Lady Slipper is a
member of the orchid family.</p>
```

HANDS-ON PRACTICE 3

In this Hands-On Practice you'll practice using the CSS `float` property as you configure the Web page shown in Figure 11.

Figure 11 The CSS `float` property left-aligns the image

Create a folder named ch6float. Copy the starter3.html and yls.jpg files from the Chapter6 folder in the student files into your ch6float folder. Launch a text editor and open the starter3.html file. Notice the order of the images and paragraphs. Notice that there is no CSS configuration for floating the images. Display starter3.html in a browser. The browser renders the page using normal flow and displays the XHTML elements in the order they are coded.

Let's add CSS to float the image and look more similar to Figure 11. Save the file with the name floatyls.html. With floatyls.html open in a text editor, modify the code as follows:

1. Add a style rule for a class name `float` that configures `float`, `margin`, and `border` properties.

   ```
   .float { float:left;
            margin-right:10px;
            border:ridge;
   }
   ```

2. Assign the image element to the class named float (use `class="float"`).

Save the file. Launch a browser and test your page. It should look similar to the Web page shown in Figure 11. The student files contain a sample solution at Chapter6/floatyls.html.

Take a moment to examine your file in a browser (see Figure 11) and consider how the browser rendered the page. The `<div>` is configured with a light background color to demonstrate how floated elements are rendered outside of normal flow. Observe that the image and the first paragraph are contained within the `<div>`. The `<h2>` follows the `div`. If all the elements were rendered using normal flow, the area with the light background color would contain both the child elements of the `<div>`: the image and the first paragraph. Additionally, the `<h2>` would be placed on its own line under the `<div>`. However, because the image is floated it is *outside* of normal flow—that's why the light background color only appears behind the first paragraph and why the `<h2>` text begins immediately after the first paragraph and appears next to the floated image. In the following sections you'll explore properties that can "clear" this `float` and improve the display.

The `clear` Property

The **`clear` property** is often used to terminate, or "clear", a float. You can set the value of the `clear` property to `left`, `right`, or `both`—depending on the type of float you need to clear. In our example, we need to clear the left float. Review Figure 11 and the code sample in the student files at Chapter6/floatyls.html. Notice that although the `<div>` contains both an image and the first paragraph, the light background color of the `<div>` only displays behind the screen area occupied by the first paragraph—it stops a bit earlier than expected. Clearing the float will help take care of this display issue. A common technique to clear a float within a container element is to add a line break element configured with the clear property. See the example in the student files at Chapter6/floatylsclear1.html. Observe that a CSS class is configured to clear the left float:

```
.clearleft { clear: left; }
```

Also, a line break tag assigned to the `clearleft` class is coded before the closing `</div>` tag. The code for the `<div>` is shown below:

```
<div>
  <img class="float" src="yls.jpg" alt="Yellow Lady Slipper"
height="100" width="100" />
  <p>The Yellow Lady Slipper grows in wooded areas and blooms in June
each year. The flower is a member of the orchid family.</p>
  <br class="clearleft" />
</div>
```

Figure 12 displays a screen shot of this page. Review Figure 12 and note two changes: the light background color of the <div> extends farther down the page and the <h2> text begins on its own line under the image.

Figure 12 The `clear` property is applied to a line break tag

If you are not concerned about the light background color display, another option is to omit the line break tag and, instead, apply the `clearleft` class to the <h2> tag. This does not change the display of the light background color, but it does force the <h2> text to begin on its own line, as shown in Figure 13 (see the student files at Chapter6/floatylsclear2.html).

Figure 13 The `clear` property is applied to a <h2> tag

The `overflow` Property

The **`overflow` property** can also be used to clear a float, although its intended purpose is to configure how content should display if it is too large for the area allocated. The default value of the `overflow` property is `visible`—the content is displayed, and if it's too large, the content will "overflow" outside the area allocated to it. Other values for the `overflow` property include `hidden` (the content is clipped to fit the room allocated), `auto` (the content fills the area and, if needed, scroll bars are displayed to allow access to the remaining content), and `scroll` (the content is rendered in the area allocated to it and scroll bars are displayed). When using `overflow`, to ensure cross-browser compatibility you also must configure a `height` or `width` for the selector. We'll use the `auto` value for our purpose of clearing the left-floated image. Review Figure 11 and the code sample in the student files at Chapter6/floatyls.html. Observe the `<div>` which contains the floated image and first paragraph on the page. Notice that although the `<div>` contains both an image and the first paragraph, the light background color of the `<div>` does not extend as far as expected; it is only visible in the area occupied by the first paragraph. You can use the `overflow` property assigned to the container element to resolve this display issue and clear the float. In this case we'll apply the `overflow` and `width` properties to the `div` selector. The CSS to configure the `div` in this manner is shown below:

```
div { background-color:#F3F1BF;
      overflow:auto;
      width:100%;
}
```

This CSS is all that is needed to be added to the code to clear the float and cause the Web page to display similar to Figure 14 (found in student files hapter6/floatylsoverflow.html).

Figure 14 The `overflow` property is applied to the `div` selector

Note that Figure 12 and Figure 14 are very similar. Keep in mind that you could configure additional CSS properties (such as `margin` or `padding`) to further modify the browser display.

You may be wondering about which CSS property (`clear` or `overflow`) is the best to use when you need to clear a float. The `clear` property is widely used and you should become familiar with its use. However, when it is likely that the floated content will take up more vertical space on the Web page than its companion content and the container element is configured with a background color and/or border, apply the `overflow` property to the container element (for example, a `<div>`). This will clear the float, avoid adding an extra line break tag, and ensure that the container element expands to enclose the entire floated element. Floating elements is a key technique in designing multicolumn page layouts with CSS.

The `display` Property

Some XHTML elements, such as the paragraph and heading elements, are block elements. A division (`<div>`) is also a block element. The browser renders these elements with 100 percent of the available width and displays a line break above and below—forming a "block." Other elements, such as anchor tags and span tags, are rendered directly inline—with no line break before or after them. These are called inline elements.

The **`display` property** configures if and how an element is displayed. An element configured with `display:none` will not be displayed. This is sometimes used when configuring styles to print a Web page. An element configured with `display:block` will be rendered as a block element (even if it is actually an inline element, such as an anchor tag).

The `z-index` Property

The **`z-index` property** is used to modify the stacking order of elements on a Web page. When using only XHTML there is no easy way to "stack" elements other than configuring backgrounds for pages or tables. The `z-index` property provides flexibility in the display of elements. The default `z-index` value is `"0"`. Elements with higher `z-index` values will appear stacked on top of elements with lower `z-index` values rendered on the same position of the page. Figure 15 is configured using absolute positioning and `z-index` properties.

Figure 15
This page uses absolute positioning and `z-index` properties

Notice how the three flower photos and the logo are arranged. It would be difficult to recreate this just using XHTML. This type of page design may be appropriate for the splash page of a Web site. You will recreate this Web page when you complete the next Hands-On Practice. The term splash page originates from client-server applications that display an introductory (or splash) screen while the program loads. Splash pages, sometimes called splash screens, can set the tone or introduce a Web site.

You have been introduced to the `position`, `float`, `clear`, `overflow`, `display`, and `z-index` properties. For your reference, Table 1 contains a list of CSS properties often used with formatting and page layout.

Table 1 CSS properties used with formatting and page layout

Property	Description	Commonly Used Values
`background-color`	Background color on an element	Any valid color
`background-image`	Background image on an element	`url(imagename.gif)` or `url(imagename.jpg)`
`background-position`	Position of the background image	Two percentage values or numeric pixel values. The first value configures the horizontal position and the second configures the vertical position starting from the upper-left corner of the container's box. Text values can also be used: `left`, `top`, `center`, `bottom`, `right`.
`background-repeat`	Controls how the background image will repeat	Text values `repeat` (default), `repeat-y` (vertical repeat), `repeat-x` (horizontal repeat), `no-repeat` (no repeat)
`border`	Shorthand notation to configure the `border-width`, `border-style`, and `border-color` of an element	The values for `border-width`, `border-style`, and `border-color` separated by spaces. For example: `border:1px solid #000000;`
`border-color`	Color of the border around an element	Any valid color
`border-style`	Type of border around an element	Text values `double`, `groove`, `inset`, `none` (the default), `outset`, `ridge`, `solid`, `dashed`, `dotted`, `hidden`
`border-width`	Width of a border around an element	A numeric pixel value (such as `1px`), percentage value, or the text values `thin`, `medium`, `thick`
`bottom`	Distance up from the bottom (of the containing element) to display an element	A numeric value (`px` or `em`) or percentage
`clear`	Specifies the display of an element in relation to floating elements	Text values `left`, `right`, `both`, `none` (default)
`color`	Text color	Any valid color
`display`	Controls how and if the element will display	Text values `none`, `block`, `inline`, `list-item`. Display set to `"none"` causes the element not to display.
`float`	Configures the horizontal placement (left of right) of an element within in a parent element	`right` or `left`
`font-family`	Name of a font or font family	Any valid font or a font family such as `serif`, `sans-serif`, `fantasy`, `monospace`, or `cursive`
`font-size`	Size of the text font	This varies; `pt` (standard font point sizes), `px` (pixels), the unit `em` (which corresponds to the width of the capital M of the current font), or percentages; the text values `xx-small`, `small`, `medium`, `large`, `x-large`, and `xx-large` are also valid

Table 1 CSS properties used with formatting and page layout (*continued*)

Property	Description	Commonly Used Values
`font-style`	Style of the font	**`normal`** (default), **`italic`**, **`oblique`**
`font-weight`	Boldness or weight of the font	This varies: the text values **`normal`**, **`bold`**, **`bolder`**, and **`lighter`** can be used; the numeric values **`100`**, **`200`**, **`300`**, **`400`**, **`500`**, **`600`**, **`700`**, **`800`**, and **`900`** can be used
`height`	Height of an element	A numeric value (**`px`** or **`em`**), numeric percentage, or **`auto`** (default)
`left`	Distance in from the left (of the containing element) to display an element	A numeric pixel value or percentage
`line-height`	Spacing allowed for the line of text	It is most common to use a percentage for this value. For example, a value of **`200%`** is double space.
`list-style-image`	Image used to replace "bullets" in an XHTML list	**`url(imagename.gif)`** or **`url(imagename.jpg)`**
`list-style-type`	Indicates the type of list item marker	Text values **`none`**, **`disc`**, **`circle`**, **`square`**, **`decimal`**, **`lower-roman`**, **`upper-roman`**, **`lower-alpha`**, **`upper-alpha`**
`margin`	Shorthand notation to configure the margin surrounding an element	A numeric value (**`px`** or **`em`**) or percentage; for example: **`body {margin: 10px;}`** will set page margins in the document to 10 pixels. If you set a value to 0 pixels, omit the **`px`**. Four numeric values (**`px`** or **`em`**) can be specified. The values configure the margins in the following order (**`margin-top`**, **`margin-right`**, **`margin-bottom`**, **`margin-left`**).
`margin-bottom`	Size of an element's bottom margin	A numeric value (**`px`** or **`em`**) or percentage
`margin-left`	Size of an element's left margin	A numeric value (**`px`** or **`em`**) or percentage
`margin-right`	Size of an element's right margin	A numeric value (**`px`** or **`em`**) or percentage
`margin-top`	Size of an element's top margin	A numeric value (**`px`** or **`em`**) or percentage
`min-width`	The minimum width of an element	A numeric value (**`px`** or **`em`**) or percentage
`overflow`	Controls the display of a block-level element if the element exceeds its set height or width	Text values **`visible`** (default), **`hidden`**, **`auto`**, **`scroll`**
`padding`	Shorthand notation to configure the amount of padding—the blank space between the element and its border	Two numeric values (**`px`** or **`em`**) or percentages. The first value configures the top and bottom padding, the second value configures the left and right padding: **`padding: 20px 10px;`** Four numeric values (**`px`** or **`em`**) or percentages. The values configure the padding in the following order: **`padding-top`**, **`padding-right`**, **`padding-bottom`**, **`padding-left`**.
`padding-bottom`	Blank space between an element and its bottom border	A numeric value (**`px`** or **`em`**) or percentage

continued

Table 1 CSS properties used with formatting and page layout (*continued*)

Property	Description	Commonly Used Values
`padding-left`	Blank space between an element and its left border	A numeric value (**px** or **em**) or percentage
`padding-right`	Blank space between an element and its right border	A numeric value (**px** or **em**) or percentage
`padding-top`	Blank space between an element and its top border	A numeric value (**px** or **em**) or percentage
`position`	Configures the positioning of an element	The value **relative** will position the element in relation to the normal flow. The value **absolute** will position the element at the exact pixel location.
`right`	Distance in from the right (of the containing element) to display an element	A numeric pixel value or percentage
`scrollbar-arrow-color`	Color of the arrow on the scroll bar (IE only)	Any valid color
`scrollbar-face-color`	Color of the sliding scroll bar (IE only)	Any valid color
`scrollbar-track-color`	Color of the track the scroll bar slides in (IE only)	Any valid color
`text-align`	The alignment of text	Text values **center**, **justify**, **left**, **right**
`text-decoration`	Determines whether text is underlined; this style is most often applied to hyperlinks	The text value **none** will cause a hyperlink not to be underlined in a browser thatnormally processes in this manner. The text value **underline** will configure hyperlink to be underlined.
`text-indent`	Indents first line of a block element	A numeric value (**em** or **px**), percentage
`text-transform`	Modifies appearance of text	Text values **none** (default), **capitalize**, **uppercase**, **lowercase**
`top`	Disance down from the top (of the containing element) to display an element	A numeric pixel value or percentage
`vertical-align`	Modifies the alignment of an inline element	Text values **middle**, **bottom**, **text-bottom**, **text-top**, **top**, **super**, **sub**, or a percentage value
`visibility`	Controls whether an element displays and takes up space on a Web page	Text values **visible**, **hidden**, **inherit**
`width`	Width of an element	A numeric value (**px** or **em**), percentage
`z-index`	The stack order of an element on a Web page; a higher value will display in front of elements with lower values	A numeric value; the default value is 0. May be negative although this can cause problems in Netscape.

HANDS-ON PRACTICE 4

Of course, the best way to learn new coding technologies is to practice them. In this Hands-On Practice you will configure two files: an external style sheet (wildflower.css), and a splash page similar to the one shown in Figure 15. You will use CSS to format and position the page elements.

Getting Started

Locate the yls.jpg, pls.jpg, showy.jpg, and trillium.jpg files in the Chapter 6 folder in the student files. Create a new folder called wildflowers. Copy the files to the wildflowers folder.

Part 1—Code the Splash Page

Review Figure 15 and notice the page elements: three images (yls.jpg, pls.jpg, and trillium.jpg), a logo, and a link. Figure 16 shows a wireframe of these elements arranged on the page.

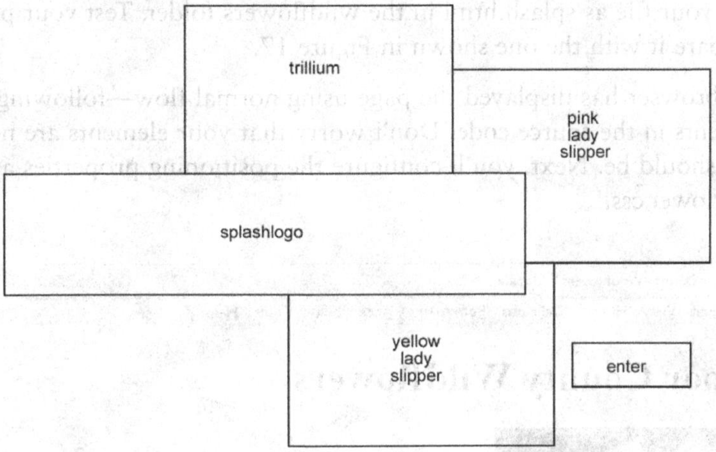

Figure 16 A sketch of the splash page elements

In this part of the Hands-On Practice you will code each page element using XHTML and wrap it in a `<div>` that is assigned to an `id`. Then, in Part 2 you will code CSS to configure a number of properties including the absolute position, border, font-family, and so on. As you code the splash page, splash.html, you will place the elements on the page and assign `id` values. In essence, you are configuring a set of boxes (using the box model). Launch Notepad and type in the following XHTML:

```
<!DOCTYPE html PUBLIC "-//W3C//DTD XHTML 1.0 Transitional//EN"
   "http://www.w3.org/TR/xhtml1/DTD/xhtml1-transitional.dtd">
<html xmlns="http://www.w3.org/1999/xhtml" lang="en" xml:lang="en">
<head>
  <title>Door County Wildflowers</title>
  <meta http-equiv="Content-Type" content="text/html; charset=utf-8" />
```

```
  <link rel="stylesheet" href="wildflower.css" type="text/css" />
</head>
<body>
<div id="splashlogo">
  <h1>Door County Wildflowers</h1>
</div>
<div id="trillium">
  <img src="trillium.jpg" alt="Trillium" width="200" height="150" />
</div>
<div id="yls">
  <img src="yls.jpg" alt="Yellow Lady Slipper" width="200"
height="150" />
</div>
<div id="pls">
  <img src="pls.jpg" alt="Pink Lady Slipper" width="200" height="150" />
</div>
<div id="enter">
  <a href="page1.html">Enter</a>
</div>
</body>
</html>
```

Save your file as splash.html in the wildflowers folder. Test your page in a browser and compare it with the one shown in Figure 17.

The browser has displayed the page using normal flow—following the order of the elements in the source code. Don't worry that your elements are not positioned as they should be. Next, you'll configure the positioning properties as you create the wildflower.css.

Figure 17 The splash page before the styles are coded

Part 2—Code the External Style Sheet

Let's take a moment to consider what type of positioning is needed for the splash page: the splash screen logo, the three images, and the link. Refer to the wireframe sketch in Figure 16 and to the screenshot shown in Figure 15. Type the CSS in your wildflower.css file as the styles are discussed as follows:

- **Splash Screen Logo Area.** This should be configured with the `id` value of `splashlogo`. This `id` will use absolute positioning, appear 210 pixels from the top and 80 pixels from the left of the browser viewport, use the background color of `#e8b9e8`, use a text color of black, display in Times New Roman or serif font with center-aligned text, have about 5 pixels of padding on the top and bottom sides, and have 20 pixels of padding on the left and right sides. There should be a 2 pixel solid border. This element will overlap the images so it must have a higher `z-index` value than the three images. The CSS follows:

```
#splashlogo { background-color: #e8b9e8;
              padding: 5px 20px;
              color: #000000;
              font-family: "Times New Roman", serif;
              position: absolute;
              text-align: center;
              z-index: 4;
              top: 210px;
              left: 80px;
              border: 2px solid #000000;
}
```

- **Trillium Image Area**

```
#trillium { position: absolute;
            z-index: 3;
            left: 220px;
            top: 80px;
}
```

- **Pink Lady Slipper Image Area**

```
#pls { position: absolute;
       z-index: 2;
       left: 420px;
       top: 130px;
}
```

- **Yellow Lady Slipper Image Area**

```
#yls { position: absolute;
       z-index: 3;
       left: 300px;
       top: 270px;
}
```

- **Hyperlink Area**

```
#enter { position: absolute;
         left: 520px;
         top: 350px;
         font-family: Verdana,sans-serif;
}
```

Save the wildflower.css file in the wildflowers folder.

FAQ

How do I know exactly what values to use for absolute positioning?

Lots of testing! When hand-coding a page that uses absolute positioning there is a lot of trial and error. It is helpful to sketch the page or create a prototype using a graphics application. Be patient—make your best guess, test, and repeat until the configuration is complete. The good news is that Web authoring tools such as Adobe Dreamweaver provide a visual editor that greatly streamlines this process.

Part 3—Test the Splash Page

Now that your styles are coded, test the splash.html page again. Your page should be similar to the screenshot shown in Figure 15. If there are differences, verify the `id` values in your XHTML and check the syntax of your CSS. You may find the W3C CSS validator at http://jigsaw.w3.org/css-validator helpful when verifying CSS syntax. The student files contain a copy of wildflower.css and splash.html in the Chapter6 folder.

CHECKPOINT 1

1. State three reasons to use CSS for page layout on a commercial site being developed today.
2. Describe the difference between relative and absolute positioning.
3. Describe the purpose of the `z-index` CSS property.

4 Exploring CSS Page Layout

You've just configured a Web page using CSS to position elements. You'll continue to explore using CSS for page layout as you create another page for the Door County Wildflowers site. As discussed earlier in this chapter, the CSS `float` property causes the browser to display XHTML elements outside of the normal flow. Elements configured with the `float` property appear to float on the right or left side of either the browser window or another XHTML element such as a paragraph. For best results, elements that float should have an intrinsic width (such as an image element) or have their width configured. In the next Hands-On Practice you'll gain more practice using floats.

HANDS-ON PRACTICE 5

In the previous Hands-On Practice you created the splash page for the Door County Wildflowers Web site. In this Hands-On Practice you'll add to this site—create a new content page (page1.html) and modify the wildflower.css external CSS file to configure page1.html to display similar to the one shown in Figure 18 (shown also in the color insert section).

Figure 18
The image is floating on the page

Go to the end of the chapter for a full color version of this figure

Getting Started

Locate the wildflowers folder you created in the previous Hands-On Practice.

Part 1—Code the Content Page

Review Figure 18 and notice the page elements: the logo, navigation area, floating right image, page content, and page footer. Figure 19 shows a wireframe sketch of these elements on the page.

Figure 19
Note how the elements are arranged on the page

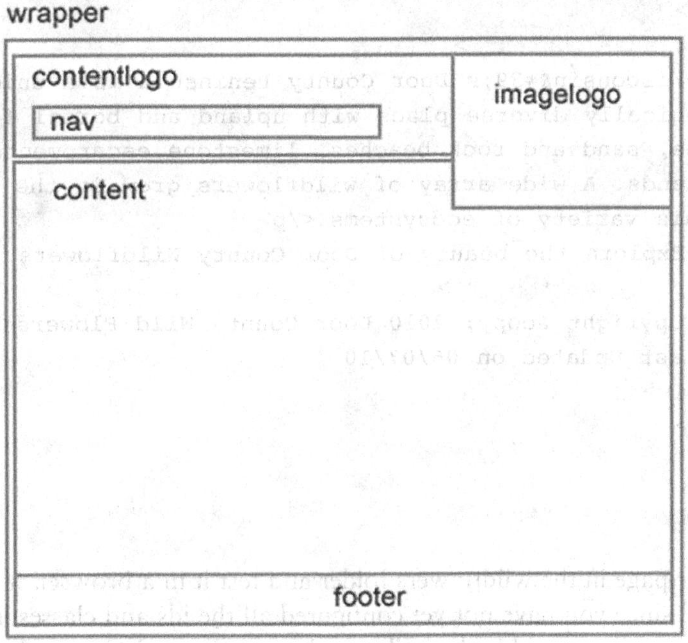

In this part of the Hands-On Practice, you will code each element in an XHTML document. These will be coded to use `ids` and `classes` that correspond to CSS, which configures a number of properties including the `margin`, `padding`, `border`, `font-family`, and so on. As you code the content page, page1.html, you will place the elements on the page and assign `id` and `class` values. You are applying the box model—the page layout is a combination of adjacent and nested boxes. Launch Notepad and type in the following XHTML:

```
<!DOCTYPE html PUBLIC "-//W3C//DTD XHTML 1.0 Transitional//EN"
  "http://www.w3.org/TR/xhtml1/DTD/xhtml1-transitional.dtd">
<html xmlns="http://www.w3.org/1999/xhtml" lang="en" xml:lang="en">
<head>
  <title>Door County Wildflowers</title>
  <meta http-equiv="Content-Type" content="text/html; charset=utf-8" />
  <link rel="stylesheet" href="wildflower.css" type="text/css" />
</head>
<body>
<div id="wrapper">
  <img id="imagelogo" src="pls.jpg" alt="Pink Lady Slipper"
  width="200" height="150" />
  <div id="contentlogo">
    <h1>Door County Wildflowers</h1>
    <div class="nav">
        <a href="home.html">Home</a>
        <a href="spring.html">Spring</a>
        <a href="summer.html">Summer</a>
        <a href="fall.html">Fall</a>
        <a href="winter.html">Winter</a>
    </div>
  </div>
  <div class="content">
    <p>Wisconsin&#39;s Door County Peninsula is a unique,
  ecologically diverse place with upland and boreal forest, bogs,
  swamps, sand and rock beaches, limestone escarpments, and
  farmlands. A wide array of wildflowers grow in the county because
  of this variety of ecosystems.</p>
    <p>Explore the beauty of Door County Wildflowers....</p>
    <div class="footer">
      Copyright &copy; 2010 Door County Wild Flowers<br />
      Last Updated on 06/07/10
    </div>
  </div>
</div>
</body>
</html>
```

Save your page in the wildflowers folder and test it in a browser. It will not look like Figure 18 since you have not yet configured all the ids and classes in the external style sheet. Your page should look similar to the one shown in Figure 20.

Figure 20 The page before CSS for positioning is configured

Part 2—Add Styles to the External Style Sheet

Open your wildflower.css file with Notepad and prepare to add additional styles to configure the page1.html page. Let's take a moment to consider what type of positioning is needed for the page shown in Figure 18, the page1.html page. Locate the following areas on the sketch in Figure 19: wrapper, logo area, logo image, navigation links, content, and footer. Type the CSS in your wildflower.css file as the styles are discussed as follows:

- **Wrapper.** Configure a container, or wrapper, area to contain page and configure a width of 700 pixels:

```
#wrapper { width: 700px;
}
```

- **Logo Area.** This should be configured with the `id` value of `contentlogo`. Configure this `id` so that the `background-color` is `#e8b9e8`, the text color is black, the `font-size` is larger, the minimum width is 500 pixels, and the padding is 10 pixels. The CSS to configure this follows:

```
#contentlogo { background-color: #e8b9e8;
               font-size: larger;
               min-width: 500px;
               padding: 10px;
               color: #000000;
}
```

- **Logo Image.** Notice how this image floats at the right edge of the browser window. Configure the id `imagelogo` with a right float. We have most often set the margin to be the same for all sides of an element's box. The margins can be set for each side individually using the `margin-top`, `margin-right`, `margin-bottom`, and `margin-left` properties. A short-hand version of this is to set all four values in one `margin` property. The order of the numeric values determines which box side is configured (top, right, bottom, left). In this page layout the margin at the top and right of the `imagelogo` should be set to 0; the bottom and left margins should be set to 5 pixels. Configure a solid border. The CSS follows:

```
#imagelogo { float: right;
             margin: 0 0 5px 5px;
             border: solid;

}
```

- **Navigation Links.** You could configure a class and apply that class to each anchor tag in the navigation area of your Web page. However, there is a more elegant method—use a **descendant selector**—which provides a way to reduce the number of classes and ids in your coding. In this case we will eliminate the redundant assignment of each navigation anchor tag to the same class. Using descendant selectors allows you to select elements that are descendants of (or contained within) another element. The container specified can be an html selector, a class, or an id. You specify the descendent selector with the following: container element, class or id name, a blank space, and the descendent element(s). For example, to configure styles for the anchor tags within the class named nav, the descendant selector is coded as `".nav a"`. Configure this to use 5 pixels padding, a background color of `#e8b9e8`, text color of dark blue (`#000066`), no underline (`text-decoration: none`), and Verdana, Arial or other sans-serif font. The CSS follows:

```
.nav a { padding: 5px;
         background-color: #e8b9e8;
         color: #000066;
         text-decoration: none;
         font-family: Verdana, Arial, sans-serif;
}
```

- **Overall Content.** Configure the content class to use Verdana, Arial, or sans-serif font and have a margin of 10 pixels.

```
.content { font-family: Verdana,Arial,sans-serif;
           margin: 10px;
}
```

- **Page Footer.** Configure a class called footer with `xx-small` font that is centered as follows:

```
.footer { font-size: xx-small;
          text-align: center;
}
```

Save the wildflower.css file in the wildflowers folder.

Part 3—Test the Content Page

Now that your styles are coded, test the page1.html page again. Your display should be similar to the screenshot shown in Figure 18. If there are differences, verify the `id` and `class` values in your XHTML. Also check the syntax of your CSS. You may find the W3C CSS validator at http://jigsaw.w3.org/css-validator helpful when verifying CSS syntax. The student files contain a copy of splash.html, page1.html, and wildflower.css in the Chapter6/wildflowers folder.

5 Two-Column Page Layout

A common design for a Web page is a two-column layout with left-column navigation and right-column logo and content. Figure 21 shows a page designed in this format using CSS.

Figure 21
A two-column page configured using CSS

Go to the end of the chapter for a full color version of this figure

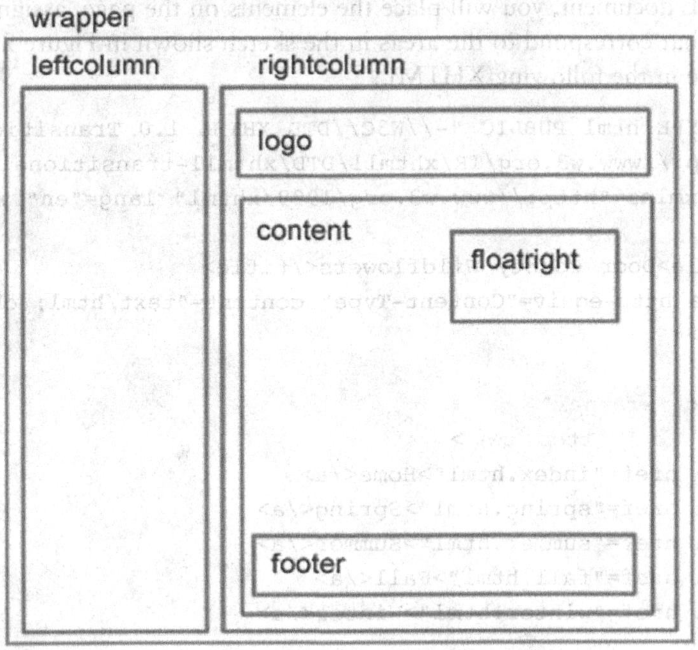

Figure 22
The two-column page layout

The page contains a number of elements, as shown in Figure 21. Compare the wireframe sketch in Figure 22 with the page displayed in Figure 21 (shown also in the color insert section).

The page is designed with a number of boxes that correspond to the following page areas: wrapper, left column, right column, logo, content, right-floating image, and footer. Each of these areas will correspond to a `class` or `id` configured using CSS. The key to this layout is that the left column is coded to float to the left using `float:left`. With the left column navigation area floating to the left, the browser renders the other content down the page using normal flow. In the next Hands-On Practice you will code the XHTML and CSS to create the page shown in Figure 21.

HANDS-ON PRACTICE 6

In this Hands-On Practice you will develop your first two-column Web page using CSS. As you create the Web page and CSS, keep in mind that using this technique is like creating a series of nested boxes. Refer to the Web page screenshot shown in Figure 21 and the page layout sketch in Figure 22 as you complete this Hands-On Practice.

Getting Started

Locate the showy.jpg file in the Chapter6 folder in the student files. Create a new folder called wildflowers2. Copy the file to the folder.

Part 1—Code the XHTML

Review Figures 21 and 22. Notice the following page elements: wrapper, left column, right column, logo, content, right-floating image, and footer. Each of these areas will be coded to use an `id` or `class` that corresponds to CSS, which configures a number of properties including the `padding`, `border`, `font-family`, and so on. As you code the XHTML document, you will place the elements on the page, assigning `id` and `class` values that correspond to the areas in the sketch shown in Figure 22. Launch Notepad and type in the following XHTML:

```
<!DOCTYPE html PUBLIC "-//W3C//DTD XHTML 1.0 Transitional//EN"
  "http://www.w3.org/TR/xhtml1/DTD/xhtml1-transitional.dtd">
<html xmlns="http://www.w3.org/1999/xhtml" lang="en" xml:lang="en" >
<head>
  <title>Door County Wildflowers</title>
  <meta http-equiv="Content-Type" content="text/html; charset=utf-8" />
</head>
<body>
<div id="wrapper">
  <div id="leftcolumn">
    <a href="index.html">Home</a>
    <a href="spring.html">Spring</a>
    <a href="summer.html">Summer</a>
    <a href="fall.html">Fall</a>
    <a href="winter.html">Winter</a>
  </div>
  <div id="rightcolumn">
    <div id="logo">
      <h1>Door County Wildflowers</h1>
    </div>
  <div class="content">
      <img src="showy.jpg" width="200" height="150" id="floatright"
        alt="Showy Lady Slippers" />
      <p>Wisconsin&#39;s Door County Peninsula is a unique,
ecologically diverse place with upland and boreal forest, bogs,
swamps, sand and rock beaches, limestone escarpments, and farmlands.
</p>
```

```
        <p>A wide array of wildflowers grow in the county because of
this variety of ecosystems.</p>
        <h2>Explore the beauty <br />of Door County Wildflowers.</h2>
      </div>
      <div id="footer">
        Copyright &copy; 2010 Door County Wild Flowers<br />
        Last Updated on 06/07/10
      </div>
    </div>
</div>
</body>
</html>
```

Save your page as twocolumn.html in your wildflowers2 folder. Test the page in a browser. Your display will not look like the one shown in Figure 21 because you have not yet configured the CSS. Your page should look similar to the page shown in Figure 23.

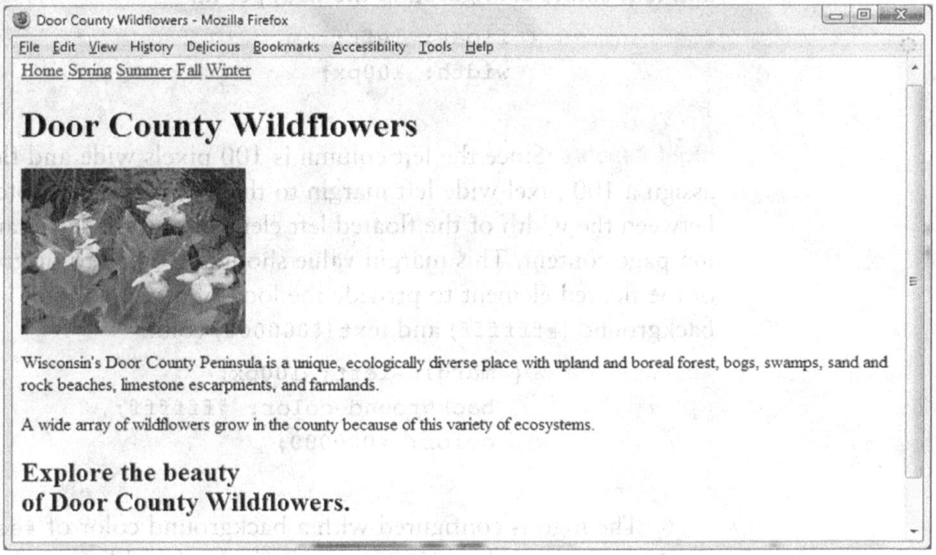

Figure 23 The two-column page before CSS is applied

Part 2—Configure the CSS

For ease of editing, in this Hands-On Practice you will code the CSS as embedded styles in the header section of the Web page. However, if you were creating an entire Web site you would most likely use an external style sheet as you did in the previous Hands-On Practice.

Launch Notepad and open twocolumn.html. Let's take a moment to consider what type of layout is needed for the page shown in Figure 21: wrapper, left column with navigation, right column, logo, content, right-floating image, and footer. Locate these areas on the sketch shown in Figure 22. Notice that the same font is used throughout the page and the page begins right at the browser margin. Launch Notepad and open your twocolumn.html file. In the header section of your Web page document, add a tag to begin the embedded styles: `<style type="text/css">`.

Now let's consider the CSS configuration. Type the CSS in your document as it is discussed as follows:

- **Body Tag.** This should be configured with the default fonts of Verdana, Arial, or any sans-serif font. The page margin should be set to 0 pixels.

```
body { font-family: Verdana,Arial,sans-serif;
       margin: 0;
}
```

- **Wrapper.** Configure a container, or wrapper, area to contain the two columns and configure default background color (`#e8b9e8`), text color (`#000066`), width (`100%`), and minimum width (`800px`).

```
#wrapper { background-color: #e8b9e8;
           color: #000066;
           width: 100%;
           min-width: 800px;
}
```

- **Left Column.** The key to this two-column page layout is that the left 100 pixel wide column is designed to float to the left. The left column uses the background and text colors configured in the wrapper id.

```
#leftcolumn { float: left;
              width: 100px;
}
```

- **Right Column.** Since the left column is 100 pixels wide and floats on the left side, assign a 100 pixel wide left margin to the right column. Note the correspondence between the width of the floated left element and the left margin of the companion page content. This margin value should be equal to or greater than the width of the floated element to provide the look of a two-column layout. Configure a background (`#ffffff`) and text (`#000000`) color.

```
#rightcolumn { margin-left: 100px;
               background-color: #ffffff;
               color: #000000;
}
```

- **Logo.** The logo is configured with a background color of `#eeeeee`, text color of `#cc66cc`, an extra large font size, 10 pixels of padding, and a solid black border that is 1 pixel wide.

```
#logo { background-color: #eeeeee;
        color: #cc66cc;
        font-size: x-large;
        border-bottom: 1px solid #000000;
        padding: 10px;
}
```

- **Content.** The content area will be easier to read if there is additional empty space on the top, right, and left sides. This can be configured using the `padding` property. Typically, you have set the same `padding` value for all four sides of the element's box. The padding set for the logo is an example of this. Padding can be set for each side individually using the `padding-top`, `padding-right`, padding-bottom, and padding-left properties. A short-hand version of this is to set all four values in one padding property. The order of the numeric values determines which box side is configured (top, right, bottom, left). In this page layout the padding at the top, right, and left sides of the content should be set to 20 pixels.

```
.content { padding: 20px 20px 0 20px;
}
```

- **Image Floating at the Right.** Configure the image with a 10 pixel margin and float:right.

```
#floatright { margin: 10px;
              float: right;
}
```

- **Footer.** Configure the page footer with very small text that is centered. A clear:right is needed to clear the float of the image. Configure 20 pixels of padding on the bottom of the footer.

```
#footer { font-size: xx-small;
          text-align: center;
          clear: right;
          padding-bottom: 20px;
}
```

- **Navigation Area.** You will use a descendent selector (#leftcolumn a) to indicate the styles for anchor tags within the leftcolumn id. Configure these navigation links with no underlines (text-decoration:none), a 15 pixel margin, and to use display:block, which will allow each anchor tag to act as a block element and be displayed on a separate line.

```
#leftcolumn a { text-decoration: none;
                margin: 15px;
                display: block;
}
```

Type the closing XHTML style tag as follows.

```
</style>
```

Save the twocolumn.html file in the wildflowers2 folder.

Part 3—Test the Page

Now that your styles are coded, test the twocolumn.html page again. Your page should be similar to the screenshot shown in Figure 21. If there are differences, verify the id and class values in your XHTML and check the syntax of your CSS. You may find the W3C CSS validator at http://jigsaw.w3.org/css-validator helpful when verifying CSS syntax. The student files contain a copy of twocolumn.html in the Chapter6/wildflowers2 folder.

This is just one of many ways that a two-column page layout can be coded. The best way to learn is to experiment by changing some of the properties and noting the result. It is a very good idea to test your pages in more than one browser. The pages in this chapter were tested using Internet Explorer 8, Opera 9, Safari for Windows and Mac, Google Chrome, and Firefox 3.

FAQ

How do I create a custom-color scroll bar?

It can be fun to color-coordinate the scroll bar with your Web site! Keep in mind that not all your Web visitors will see your handiwork. While this effect is supported by Internet Explorer, it is not supported by all browsers. To configure a scroll bar with colors that you choose, add the following styles to the body tag: `scrollbar-face-color`, `scrollbar-arrow-color`, `scrollbar-track-color`. For example:

```
body { scrollbar-face-color: #cc66cc;
       scrollbar-arrow-color: #006600;
       scrollbar-track-color: #cccccc;
}
```

Note: Your CSS will not pass W3C validation tests if you use these Internet Explorer only properties.

6 CSS Debugging Tips

Using CSS for page layout requires some patience. It takes a while to get used to it. One of the biggest issues is that even modern browsers implement CSS in slightly different ways. Testing is crucial. Don't make it your goal that the pages must look exactly the same on every browser. Expect your pages to look slightly different on various browsers. Design so they look best on the most commonly used browser (currently Internet Explorer) and display acceptably well on other browsers. There are Web pages devoted to CSS bugs and browser support of CSS. The following are a few that you will find helpful:

- http://web.archive.org//20040202153928/http://devedge.netscape.com/library/xref/2003/css-support/css1/mastergrid.html

  The original "Master List" created by Eric Meyer
- http://www.westciv.com/style_master/academy/browser_support/index.html

  A comprehensive browser compatibility list
- http://www.positioniseverything.net

  John and Holly Bergevin's site focuses on CSS bugs in modern browsers—it contains some great sample CSS page layouts
- http://www.quirksmode.org

  Peter-Paul Koch's site is dedicated to studying and defeating browser incompatibilities related to CSS and JavaScript
- http://reference.sitepoint.com/css

  Sitepoint's CSS Reference

CSS Debugging Techniques

Debugging CSS can be frustrating. The following are helpful techniques to use:

- **Manually Check Syntax Errors.** Sometimes a CSS style does not apply due to a syntax error. Carefully check your code. Many times the error is in the line above the style that is not correctly applied.

- **Programmatically Check Syntax Errors.** As mentioned earlier, you can use the W3C's CSS Validator at http://jigsaw.w3.org/css-validator to verify your syntax.
- **Configure Temporary Background Colors.** Sometimes your code is valid but the browser window is not configured the way you would expect. If you temporarily assign distinctive background colors such as red or yellow and test again, it should be easier to see where the "boxes" are ending up.
- **Configure Temporary Borders.** Similar to the temporary background colors, you could temporarily configure an element with a 3 pixel red solid border—this will really jump out at you and help you recognize the issue sooner.
- **Use Comments to Find the Unexpected Cascade.** Styles and XHTML attributes configured farther down the page can override earlier styles. If your styles are misbehaving, try commenting out (see below) some styles and test with a smaller group of statements. Then add the styles back in one by one to see where or when the breakdown occurs. Work patiently and test the entire style sheet in this manner.

Note that Comment Areas Are Ignored by Browsers. A style sheet comment begins with /* and ends with */. Comments can span multiple lines. A code snippet with CSS comments follows:

```
/* Set Page Margins to Zero */
body { margin: 0
}
/* temporarily commented out during testing
.nav { text-decoration: none;
}
*/
```

The first comment is used to document the style sheet and describe the style applied to the body tag. The second comment spans multiple lines. It begins on the line above the nav class and ends on the line below the nav class. This causes the browser to skip the nav class when applying the style sheet. This technique can be useful in testing when you are experimenting with a number of properties.

7 CSS Page Layout Resources

This chapter introduces you to using CSS for page layout configuration and should get you started in your exploration of this technology. It may help you to know that you are not alone in your quest to learn CSS. There are many resources with documentation, tutorials, and support for this technology. The page layout techniques discussed in this textbook are just an introduction to using this technology. There are many Web sites that offer additional insight and techniques for configuring page layout with CSS. The following are a few that you may find useful:

- http://glish.com/css

  Large collection of CSS page layouts and links to tutorials
- http://www.websitetips.com/css/index.shtml

  Comprehensive list of tutorials and CSS-related sites
- http://www.meyerweb.com/eric/css

  The site of Eric Meyer, a leading-edge Web developer

- http://www.w3.org/Style/CSS/learning
  W3C's list of CSS resources
- http://www.bluerobot.com/web/layouts
  A "reservoir" of CSS page layouts
- http://www.blooberry.com/indexdot/css
  CSS syntax reference list
- http://www.w3.org/TR/1998/REC-CSS2–19980512
  W3C CSS Level 2 Recommendation
- http://www.w3.org/TR/REC-CSS1–961217.html
  W3C CSS Level 1 Recommendation

CHECKPOINT 2

1. The two-column layouts you created in the previous Hands-On Practice did not use absolute positioning. Open the twocolumn.html page in a browser. Resize the browser window. Describe what happens. What type of page design layout (ice, jello, or liquid) is being used?
2. Describe one CSS debugging tip that you have found helpful.
3. Describe how to choose whether to configure an XHTML tag, create a class, or create an id when working with CSS.

CHAPTER SUMMARY

This chapter introduced Cascading Style Sheet rules associated with page layout. Techniques for positioning and floating elements and configuring two-column page layouts were demonstrated. This topic is very deep and you have much to explore. Visit the resources in the chapter to continue learning about this technology.

Visit the Web site http://www.webdevfoundations.net for examples, the links listed in this chapter, and updated information.

Key Terms

absolute positioning
border
`clear` property
content
CSS Box Model
CSS-P
descendent selector
`display` property
`float` property
`left` property
margin
normal flow
overflow property
padding
position property
relative positioning
`right` property
`top` property
visible width
`z-index` property

Review Questions

Multiple Choice

1. Which of the following is used to change the location of an element slightly in relation to where it would otherwise appear on the page?

a. relative positioning
b. the `float` property
c. absolute positioning
d. this cannot be done with CSS

2. Which of the following, from outermost to innermost, are components of the box model?

a. margin, border, padding, content
b. content, padding, border, margin
c. content, margin, padding, border
d. margin, padding, border, content

3. Which of the following is the default value of the `border` and `padding` properties for an element?

a. 1 pixel
b. 0 pixels
c. 3 pixels
d. 10 pixels

4. Which of the following configures a class called nav to float to the left?

a. `.nav { left: float; }`
b. `.nav { float: left; }`
c. `.nav { float-left: 200px; }`
d. none of the above

5. Which of the following is the rendering flow used by a browser by default?

a. XHTML flow
b. normal display
c. browser flow
d. normal flow

6. Which of the following is an example of using a descendent selector to configure the anchor tags within the `.nav` class?

a. `nav. a`
b. `a nav.`
c. `.nav a`
d. this cannot be done with CSS

7. Which of the following will configure padding that is 15 pixels on the top, 0 pixels on the left and right, and 5 pixels on the bottom?

a. `margin: 0px 5px 0px 15px;`

b. `margin: top-15, left-0, right-0, bottom-5;`

c. `padding: 15px 0 5px 0;`

d. `padding: 0 0 15px 5px;`

8. Which of the following is used along with the `left`, `right` and/or `top` property to configure the position of an element precisely?

a. `position: relative`

b. `position: absolute`

c. `position: float`

d. none of the above

9. Which of the following will configure a class called news to stack on top of other elements that have a `z-index` of 5?

a. `.news { z-index: high; }`

b. `.news { z-index: 4; }`

c. `.news { z-index: 6; }`

d. none of the above

10. Which of the following will insert a comment in CSS?

a. `// comment //`

b. `/* comment */`

c. `/- comment -/`

d. `<* comment *>`

Fill in the Blank

11. Configure a style with a(n) ____________ if the style will only apply to one element on a page.

12. If an element is configured with `float:right`, the other content on the page will appear to its ____________.

13. The ____________ is always transparent.

14. Use the `position:relative` property along with the ____________, ____________, and/or ____________ property to configure the position of an element in relation to the normal flow.

15. Configure a style with a____________ if the style could apply to more than one element on a page.

Apply Your Knowledge

1. Predict the Result. Draw and write a brief description of the Web page that will be created with the following XHTML code:

```
<html>
<head>
  <title>CircleSoft Web Design</title>
  <style type="text/css">
  h1 { border-bottom: 1px groove #333333;
       color: #006600;
       background-color: #cccccc
  }
  #content { position: absolute;
             left: 200px;
             top: 75px;
             font-family: Arial,sans-serif;
             width: 300px;
  }
  .nav a { font-weight: bold;
  }
  </style>
</head>
```

```
<body>
  <h1>CircleSoft Web Design</h1>
  <div id="content">
    <p>Our professional staff takes pride in its working
relationship with our clients by offering personalized services
that listen to their needs, develop their target areas, and
incorporate these items into a well-presented Web site that
works.</p>
  </div>
  <ul class="nav">
    <li>Home</li>
    <li><a href="about.html">About</a></li>
    <li><a href="services.html">Services</a></li>
  </ul>
  </div>
</body>
</html>
```

2. **Fill in the Missing Code.** This Web page should be configured as a two-column page layout with a right column 150 pixels wide. The right column should have a 1 pixel border. The padding in the left column content area needs to allow for the room that will be used by the right column. Some CSS properties and values, indicated by "_", are missing. Fill in the missing code.

```
<!DOCTYPE html PUBLIC "-//W3C//DTD XHTML 1.0 Transitional//EN"
  "http://www.w3.org/TR/xhtml1/DTD/xhtml1-transitional.dtd">
<html xmlns="http://www.w3.org/1999/xhtml" lang="en" xml:lang="en" >
<head>
<title>Trillium Media Design</title>
<meta http-equiv="Content-Type" content="text/html; charset=utf-8" />
<style type="text/css">
body { margin: 0;
       font-family: Verdana, Arial, sans-serif;
}
#rightcolumn { "_":"_";
               width: "_";
               background-color: #cccccc;
               height: 400px;
               border: "_";
}
#rightcolumn {
}
#logo { background-color: #cccccc;
        color: #663333;
        font-size: x-large;
        border-bottom: 1px solid #333333;
}
.content { padding: "_";
}
```

```
.footer { font-size: xx-small;
          text-align: center;
          clear: "_";
}
div#"_" a { color: #000066;
            text-decoration: none;
            padding: 3px;
            margin: 15px;
            display: "_";
}
</style>
</head>
<body>
<div id="rightcolumn">
  <a href="index.html">Home</a>
  <a href="products.html">Products</a>
  <a href="services.html">Services</a>
  <a href="about.html">About</a>
</div>
<div id="leftcolumn">
  <div id="logo">
    <h1>Trillium Media Design</h1>
  </div>
  <div class="content">
    <p>Our professional staff takes pride in its working
relationship with our clients by offering personalized services
that listen to their needs, develop their target  areas, and
incorporate these items into a well-presented Web site that
works.</p>
  </div>
  <div class="footer">
    Copyright &copy; 2010 Trillium Media Design<br />
    Last Updated on 06/08/10
  </div>
</div>
</body>
</html>
```

3. **Find the Error.** When this page is displayed using Internet Explorer 7, the heading information obscures the paragraph text. Correct the errors and describe the process you followed.

```
<!DOCTYPE html PUBLIC "-//W3C//DTD XHTML 1.0 Transitional//EN"
"http://www.w3.org/TR/xhtml1/DTD/xhtml1-transitional.dtd" >
<html xmlns="http://www.w3.org/1999/xhtml" lang="en" xml:lang="en" >
<head>
<title>CSS Float</title>
<meta http-equiv="Content-Type" content="text/html; charset=utf-8" />
<style type="text/css">
```

```
h1 { background-color: #eeeeee;
     padding: 5px;
     color: #666633;
     position: absolute;
     left: 200px;
     top: 20px;
}
p {  font-family: Arial,sans-serif;
     position;
     absolute;
     left: 100px;
     top: 100px;
}
#yls { float:right;
       margin: 0 0 5px 5px;
       border: solid;
}
</style>
</head>
<body>
<img id="yls" src="yls.jpg" alt="Yellow Lady Slipper" height="100"
  width="100" />
<h1>Floating an Image</h1>
<p> The Yellow Lady Slipper pictured on the right is a wildflower.
It grows in wooded areas and blooms in June each year. The Yellow
Lady Slipper is a member of the orchid family.</p>
</body>
</html>
```

Hands-On Exercises

1. Write the CSS for a class with the following attributes: a light blue background color, Arial or sans-serif font, dark blue text color, 10 pixels of padding, and a narrow dashed border in a dark blue color.
2. Write the CSS for an id with the following attributes: float to the left of the page, light beige background, Verdana or sans-serif large font, and 20 pixels of padding.
3. Write the CSS to configure a class that will produce a headline with a dotted line underneath it. Choose a color that you like for the text and dotted line.
4. Write the CSS for an id that will be absolutely positioned on a page 20 pixels from the top and 40 pixels from the right. This area should have a light gray background and a solid border.
5. Write the CSS for a class that is relatively positioned. This class should appear 15 pixels in from the left. Configure the class to have a light green background.
6. **Extending Hands-On Practice 6.** Design a two-column page layout with the navigation on the right side. Use the twocolumn.html file from Hands-On Practice 6 as a starting point. This file is in the Chapter6/wildflowers2folder in the student files.

Code an external style sheet file called rightcolumn.css and a Web page called rightcolumn.html. The Web page should have two columns. The right column will be the navigation column and the left column will be the content column. Hand in printouts of rightcolumn.css, the rightcolumn.html source code (print in Notepad), and the browser display of your rightcolumn.html to your instructor.

7. **Extending Hands-On Practice 6.** Design a two-column page layout with a logo area across the top. Review the Hands-On Practice 6 twocolumn.html file for some examples. These files are in the Chapter6/wildflowers2 folder in the student files. Code an external style sheet file called mydesign.css and a Web page called mydesign.html. The Web page should have two columns and a logo area across the top. Hand in printouts of mydesign.css, the mydesign.html source code (print in Notepad), and the browser display of your mydesign.html to your instructor.

8. **Extending Hands-On Practice 6.** In Hands-On Practice 6 you created two files for a version of the Door County Wildflowers Web site. The files are available in the Chapter6/wildflowers2 folder in the student files. You will create two additional content pages for the Door County Wildflowers site, called spring.html and summer.html, in this exercise. Be sure that all CSS is placed in an external style sheet, called mywildflower.css. (Modify pre-existing pages to use this style sheet.) Here is some content to include on the new pages:

   Spring Page (spring.html):

   - Use the trillium.jpg image (see the Chapter 6 folder in the student files).
   - Trillium facts: 8–18 inches tall, perennial, native plant, grows in rich moist deciduous woodlands, white flowers turn pink with age, fruit is a single red berry, protected flower species.

   Summer Page (summer.html):

   - Use the yls.jpg image (see the Chapter 6 folder in the student files).
   - Yellow Lady's Slipper facts: 4–24 inches tall, perennial, native plant, grows in wet shaded deciduous woods, swamps, and bogs, an orchid, official flower of Door County.

   Hand in printouts of mywildflower.css, spring.html source code (print in Notepad), summer.html source code, the browser display of spring.html, and the browser display of summer.html to your instructor.

9. **Extending Hands-On Practice 6.** Modify the twocolumn.html page you created in Hands-On Practice 6. This file is in the Chapter6/wildflowers2 folder in the student files. A Web page using jello design has content in the center of the Web page with blank margins on either side. You can code this using CSS by configuring the margin property of the body tag to use percentages for the left and right. For example:

   ```
   body {margin: 0 10%;}
   ```

   Hand in printouts of the source code (print in Notepad) and browser display for the Web page to your instructor.

10. Design a splash page called moviesplash.html about your favorite movie. Use absolute positioning and `z-index` to create an interesting display. First sketch the areas for images, text, and link to the first page on the site. Search the Web for photos of the movie. Next, locate images from the movie. When you code your

page use embedded CSS unless your instructor directs you otherwise. Hand in printouts of the moviesplash.html source code (print in Notepad), and the browser display of moviesplash.html to your instructor.

Focus on Ethics

(*Note*: It is unethical to steal an image from another Web site. Some Web sites have a link to their copyright policy. Most Web sites will give permission for you to use an image in a school assignment. If there is no available policy, e-mail the site's contact person and request permission to use the photo. If you are unable to obtain permission, you may substitute clip art or an image from a free site.)

Web Research

This chapter introduced using CSS to configure Web page layout. Use the resources listed in the text as a starting point. You can also use a search engine to search for CSS resources.

Create a Web page that provides a list of at least five CSS resources on the Web. For each CSS resource provide the URL, Web site name, and a brief description. Your Web page should use absolute positioning. Print both the source code (from Notepad) and the browser view of your Web page.

Focus on Web Design

There is still much for you to learn about CSS. A great place to learn about Web technology is on the Web itself. Use a search engine to search for CSS page layout tutorials. Choose a tutorial that is easy to read. Select a section that discusses a CSS technique that was not covered in this chapter. Create a Web page that uses this new technique. Consider how the suggested page layout follows (or does not follow) principles of design such as contrast, repetition, alignment, and proximity. The Web page should provide the URL of your tutorial, the name of the Web site, a description of the new technique you discovered, and a discussion of how the technique follows (or does not follow) principles of design. Print the external style sheet (if you used one), the Web page source code (from Notepad), and the browser view of your Web page.

WEB SITE CASE STUDY: Implementing CSS Two-Column Page Layout

This chapter implements CSS two-column page layout in the following Web sites.

JavaJam Coffee House

See the Chapter "XHTML Basics" for an introduction to the JavaJam Coffee House case. Figure 26 in that chapter shows a site map for the JavaJam Web site. The pages were created in earlier chapters. In this case study you will implement a new two-column CSS page layout for JavaJam. You will modify the external style sheet and the

Home, Menu, and Music pages. Unless your instructor directs you otherwise, use the Chapter 4 JavaJam Web site as a starting point for this case study.

Figure 24 displays a wireframe for the two-column page layout with a page container, logo, left column, right column, floating, and footer areas.

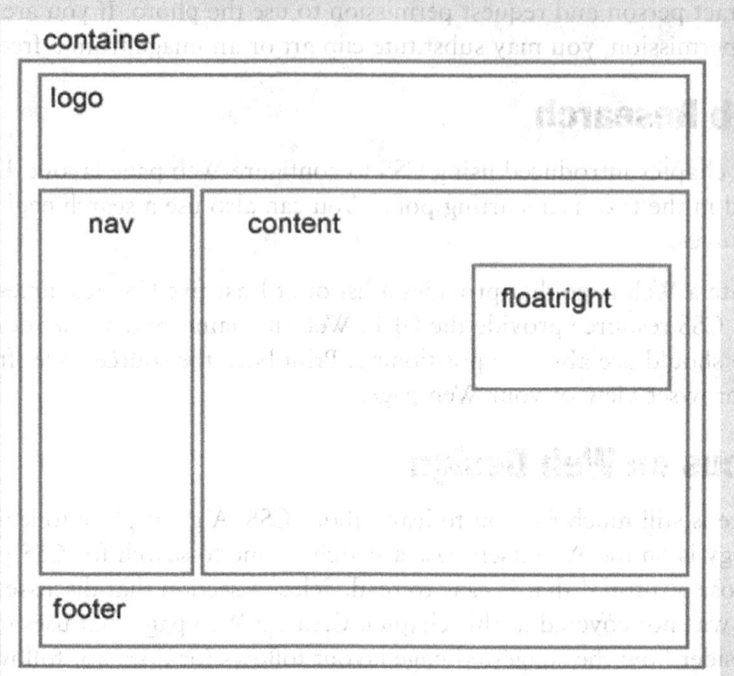

Figure 24
JavaJam two-column page layout

Hands-On Practice Case

1. **Create a Folder.** Create a folder called javajamcss. Copy all the files from your Chapter 4 javajam folder into the javajamcss folder. You will modify the javajam.css file and each Web page file (index.html, menu.html, and music.html) to implement the two-column page layout shown in Figure 24. See the new JavaJam Home page, as shown in Figure 25 (shown also in the color insert section).
2. **Configure the CSS.** Open javajam.css in Notepad. Edit the style rules as follows:
   - Add the following style declarations to the `container` id: background color (`#e8d882`), text color (`#000000`), and a 2 pixel black double border (`border: 2px double #000000`).
   - Configure the logo area. Create a new id named `logo` with a background (`#ccaa66`) and text (`#000000`) color, center alignment (`text-align: center`), no margin (`margin: 0;`), and a bottom border that is 2 pixels, double, and black (`border-bottom: 2px double #000000`).
   - Configure the left column navigation area. Add the following style rules to the nav id to configure an area that floats to the left, is 100 pixels wide, and has 10 pixels of padding on the top side.

Figure 25 The new JavaJam two-column index.html

Go to the end of the chapter for a full color version of this figure

- Configure the navigation hyperlinks. Use a descendant selector to add a new style rule for the anchor tags div within the nav id. Configure this selector to have no underlines on hyperlinks, a 15 pixel margin, have centered text, and be displayed as a block element (with line breaks above and below) by the browser.

```
#nav a { text-decoration: none;
         margin: 15px;
         text-align: center;
         display: block;
}
```

- Configure the right column content area with style rules for the content id to configure an area with a 150 pixel left margin, background (`#f1e8b0`) and text (`#000000`) color, 10 pixels of top and bottom padding, 20 pixels of left and right padding, and overflow set to auto to clear floating elements within the content area.

```
#content { margin-left: 150px;
           background-color: #f1e8b0;
           color: #000000;
           padding: 10px 20px;
           overflow: auto;
}
```

- Configure an area that floats to the right. Notice how the winding road graphic shown in Figure 25 floats on the right side—this is configured with the `floatright` class. Images are more compelling when separated from other elements (such as text) by empty space. Add 20 pixels of padding to the left side of this area.

```
.floatright { padding-left: 20px;
              float: right;
}
```

- Modify the `footer` id to display a 2 pixel double black top border (`border-top: 2px double #000000`). Also configure 20 pixels of `padding-top` and `padding-bottom` in the `footer` id.

Save the javajam.css file.

3. **Modify the index.html File.** Add `<div>` elements and modify the code as follows:
   - Configure the logo area. Assign the `<h1>` to the id logo.
   - Configure the left column navigation area. The navigation links are the only content in the left column. Remove other code, including any ` ` characters that may be present.
   - The right column content area should already be contained within the `div` assigned to the `content` id.
   - Configure the area that floats to the right. Modify the winding road image element. Remove the `align="right"` attribute and add `class="floatright"` to the winding road image element.

   Save the index.html file. It should look similar to the Web page shown in Figure 25. Remember that validating your XHTML and CSS can help you find syntax errors. Test and correct this page before you continue.

4. **Modify the menu.html and music.html Files.** Modify the code in these Web page files in a similar manner as you did in Step 3. Save and test your pages in a browser. As you test your pages, use the CSS and XHTML validators to help you find syntax errors.

5. **Bonus Style: `text-transform`.** Figure 26 shows an alternate design for the music.html page. Notice how the `<h2>` elements are styled differently—with all uppercase text (using a new property, `text-transform`) different background and text colors, font size, bottom border, and margin. Open javajam.css in a text editor and replace the `h2` selector style rules with the following:

```
h2 { text-transform: uppercase;
     background-color: #ffffcc;
     color: #663300;
     font-size: 1.2em;
     border-bottom: 1px solid #000000;
     margin-right: 20px;
}
```

   Save the javajam.css file. Test your pages in a browser. Your music.html page should look similar to the one shown in Figure 26. The other pages do not use `<h2>` elements and should appear as they did at the end of Step 4.

In this case study you changed the page layout of the JavaJam Web site pages. Notice that with just a few changes in the CSS and XHTML code, you configured a two-column page layout.

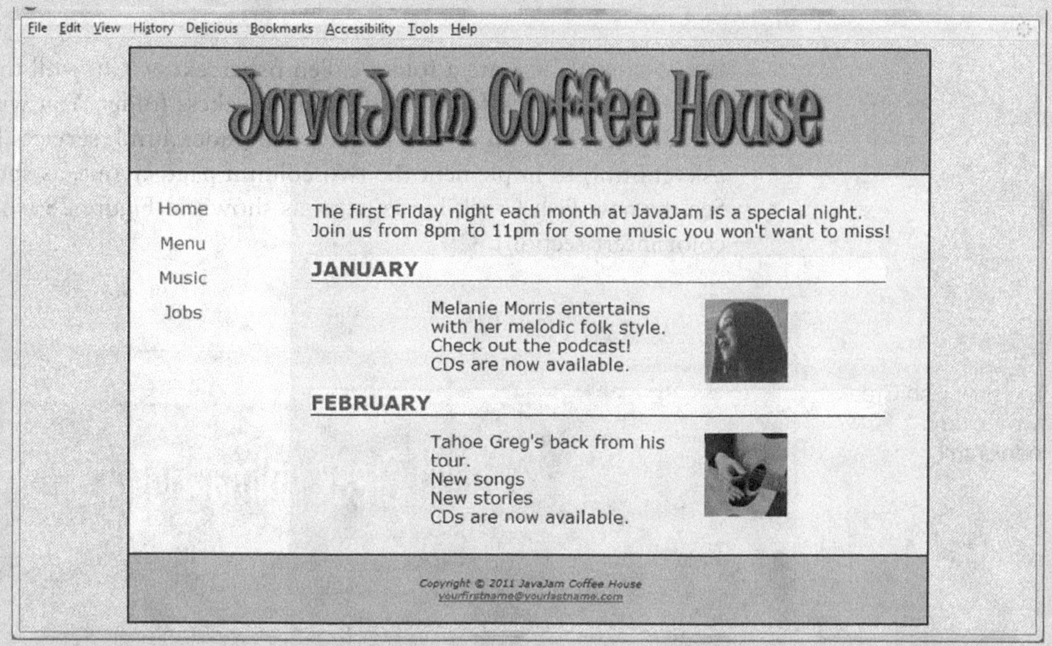

Figure 26
New style rules for the h2 selectors

Fish Creek Animal Hospital

See the Chapter "XHTML Basics" for an introduction to the Fish Creek Animal Hospital Case Study. Figure 30 in that chapter shows a site map for the Fish Creek Web site. The pages were created in earlier chapters. In this case study you will implement a new two-column CSS page layout. You will modify the external style sheet and the Home, Services, and Ask the Vet pages. Unless your instructor directs you otherwise, use the Chapter 4 Fish Creek Web site as a starting point for this case study.

Figure 27 displays a wireframe for the two-column page layout with a page container, logo, left column, right column, and footer areas.

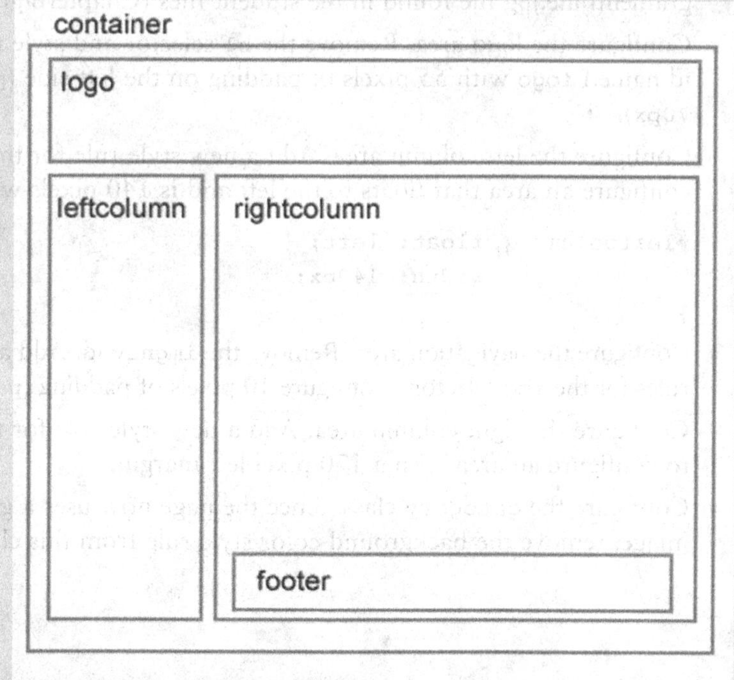

Figure 27
Fish Creek two-column page layout

Hands-On Practice Case

1. **Create a Folder.** Create a folder called fishcreekcss. Copy all the files from your Chapter 4 fishcreek folder into the fishcreekcss folder. You will modify the fishcreek.css file and each Web page file (index.html, services.html, and askvet.html) to implement the two-column page layout, as shown in Figure 27. See the new Fish Creek home page, as shown in Figure 28 (shown also in the color insert section).

Figure 28
The new Fish Creek two-column index.html

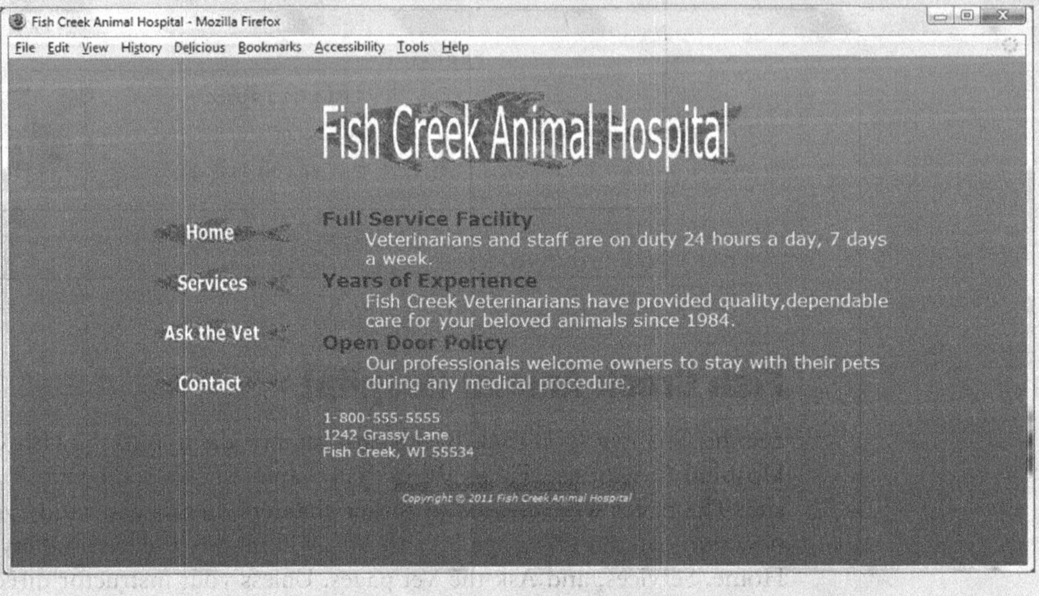

Go to the end of the chapter for a full color version of this figure

2. **Configure the CSS.** Open fishcreek.css in Notepad. Edit the style rules as follows:
   - Configure a subtle background image for the body selector. Use the gradientblue.jpg file found in the student files (Chapter6/gradientblue.jpg).
   - Configure the logo area. Remove the `h1` selector and style rules. Create a new id named `logo` with 55 pixels of padding on the left side (`padding-left: 70px`).
   - Configure the left column area. Add a new style rule for the `leftcolumn` id to configure an area that floats to the left and is 140 pixels wide.

```
#leftcolumn { float: left;
              width: 140px;
}
```

   - Configure the navigation area. Remove the `imgnav` id. Add a property to the style rules for the `img` selector—configure 10 pixels of padding (`padding: 10px`).
   - Configure the right column area. Add a new style rule for the `rightcolumn` id to configure an area with a 170 pixel left margin.
   - Configure the `category` class. Since the page now uses a gradient background image, remove the background-color style rule from this class.

- Configure the footer area. Configure the `footer` id to display centered text (`text-align: center;`). Remove the nav id.

Save the fishcreek.css file.

3. **Modify the index.html File.** Add `<div>` elements and modify the code as follows:
   - Configure the logo area. Assign the `<h1>` to the id `logo`.
   - Configure the left column. The navigation image links are the only content in the left column. Change `<div id="imgnav">` to `<div id="leftcolumn">`. Remove other code, including any ` ` characters that may be present.
   - Configure the right column. This area contains the definition list and the paragraph with the contact information. Code a `<div>` that surrounds this area. Assign the `<div>` to the id `rightcolumn`.
   - Configure the page footer area. You need to adjust the starting location of the `footer` id. Locate `<div id="footer">` in the code and remove it. Next, change `<div id="nav">` to `<div id="footer">`. The area assigned to the `footer` id now includes the text navigation, copyright information, and e-mail link. Replace the closing `div` tag between the text navigation and the copyright information with a line break tag.

   Save the index.html file. It should look similar to the Web page shown in Figure 28. Remember that validating your XHTML and CSS can help you find syntax errors. Test and correct this page before you continue.

4. **Modify the services.html and askvet.html Files.** Modify these Web page files in a similar manner as you did in Step 3. Save and test your pages in a browser. As you test your pages, use the CSS and XHTML validators to help you find syntax errors.

In this case study you changed the page layout of the Fish Creek Web site pages. Notice that with just a few changes in the CSS and XHTML code, you configured a two-column page layout.

Pasha the Painter

See the Chapter "XHTML Basics" for an introduction to the Pasha the Painter Case Study. Figure 34 in that chapter shows a site map for the Pasha the Painter Web site. The pages were created in earlier chapters. In this case study you will implement a new two column CSS page layout for Pasha the Painter. You will modify the external style sheet and of the Home, Services, and Testimonials pages. Unless your instructor directs you otherwise, use the Chapter 4 Pasha the Painter Web site as a starting point for this case study.

Figure 29 displays a wireframe for the two-column page layout with a page container, logo, left column, right column, and footer areas.

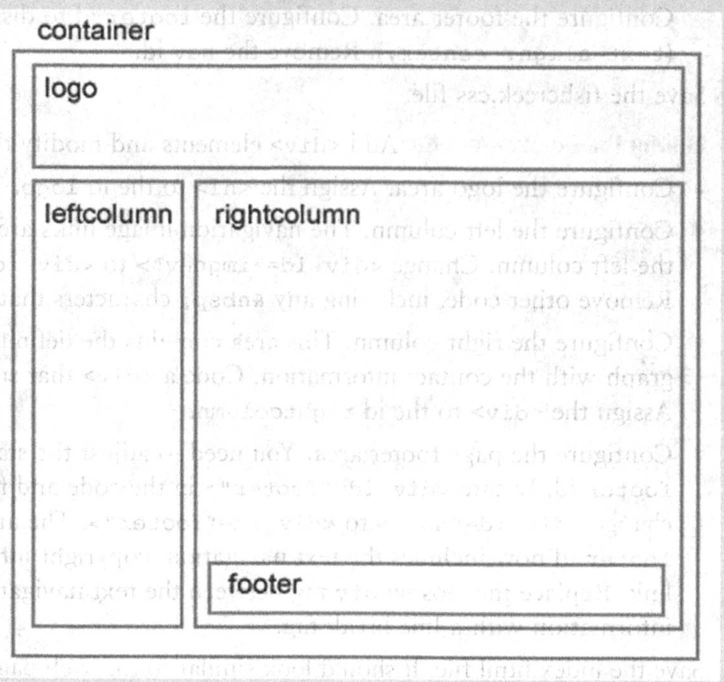

Figure 29
Pasha the Painter two-column page layout

Hands-On Practice Case

1. **Create a Folder.** Create a folder called paintercss. Copy all the files from your Chapter 4 folder into the paintercss folder. You will modify the painter.css file and each Web page file (index.html, services.html, and testimonials.html) to implement the two-column page layout shown in Figure 29. See the new Pasha the Painter home page, as shown in Figure 30 (shown also in the color insert section).

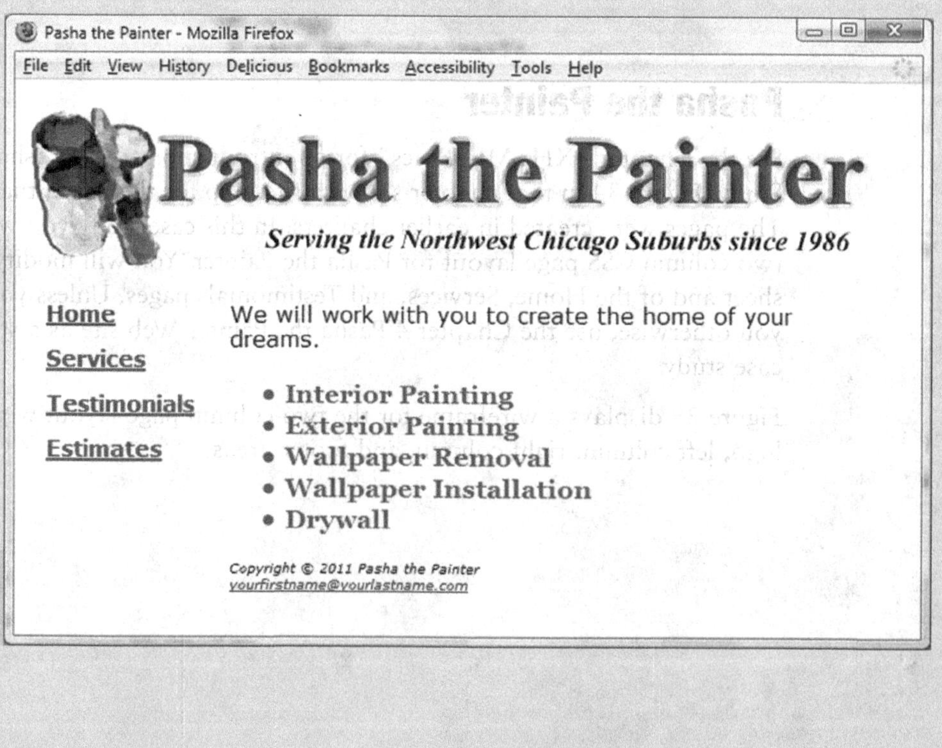

Figure 30
The new Pasha the Painter two-column index.html

Go to the end of the chapter for a full color version of this figure

2. **Configure the CSS.** Open painter.css in Notepad. Edit the style rules as follows:
   - Configure the left column area. Add a new style rule for the `leftcolumn` id to configure an area that floats to the left and is 150 pixels wide.

```
#leftcolumn { float: left;
              width: 150px;
}
```

   - Configure the navigation area. Remove the nav id. Add a descendent selector style rule for the `navigation` class to configure the anchor tags within the `leftcolumn` id as follows: with bold font, a 15 pixel margin on the right, bottom, and left sides, and displayed as a block element (with line breaks above and below) by the browser.

```
#leftcolumn a { font-weight: bold;
                margin: 0 15px 15px 15px;
                display: block;
}
```

   - Configure the right column area. Add a new style rule for the `rightcolumn` id to configure an area with a 150 pixel left margin and a 10 pixel top margin (`margin: 10px 0 0 150px`).
   - Configure an area that floats to the right. Add a new style rule for the `floatright` class.

```
.floatright { float: right;
              padding: 5px;
}
```

   Save the painter.css file.

3. **Modify the index.html File.** Add `<div>` elements and modify the code as follows:
   - Configure the logo area. Assign the `<h1>` to the id `logo`.
   - Configure the left column. The navigation links are the only content in the left column. Change `<div id="nav">` to `<div id="leftcolumn">`. Remove other code, including any ` ` characters that may be present.
   - Configure the right column. This area contains the content (paragraph and unordered list elements) and the footer section. Code a `<div>` that surrounds this area. Assign the `<div>` to the `rightcolumn` id.

   Save the index.html file. It should look similar to the Web page shown in Figure 30. Remember that validating your XHTML and CSS can help you find syntax errors. Test and correct this page before you continue.

4. **Modify the services.html and testimonials.html Files.** Modify these Web page files in a similar manner as you did in Step 3. Configure the room images on the testimonials.html page—on the opening image tag for each room photo, remove the `align="left"` attribute and add `class="floatright"`.

5. **Save and Test Your Pages in a Browser.** As you test your pages, use the CSS and XHTML validators to help you find syntax errors.

6. **Bonus Style.** Figure 31 shows an alternate design for the testimonials.html page. Notice how the `<h2>` elements are styled differently—it is set to float and is configured with a *negative* top margin. This allows the dark green box to stand out better on the page. The paragraph elements in this area are each assigned to a new class named `.desc` that configures a top border of the same color green and

Figure 31
New style rules for the `h2` selector

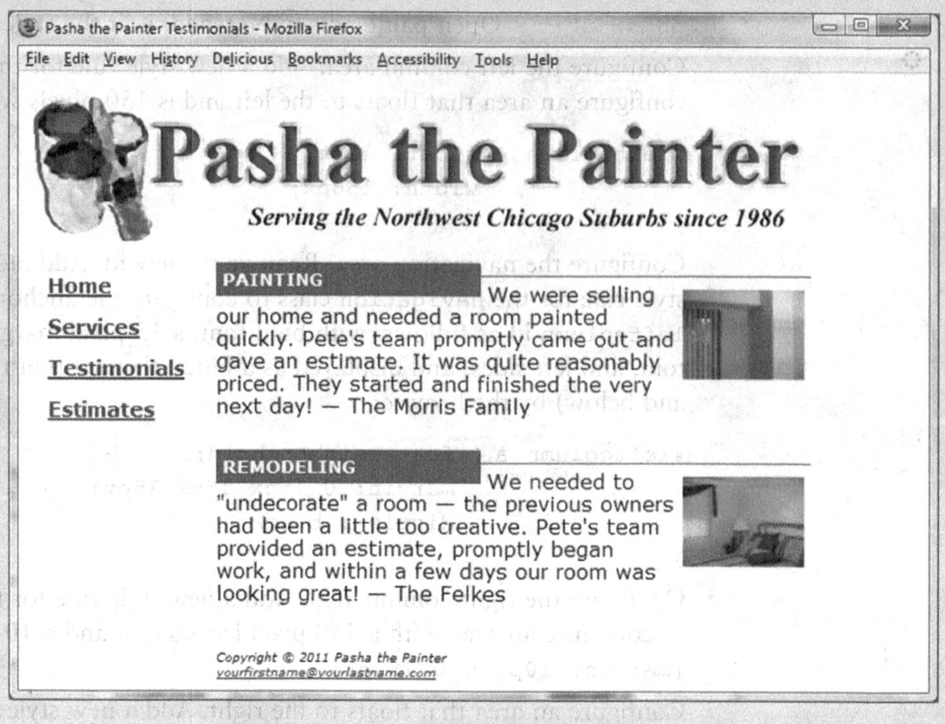

extra padding. Open painter.css in a text editor and update the style rules with the following:

```
h2  { margin: -10px 5px 5px 0px;
      padding: 5px;
      font-family: Verdana, sans-serif;
      font-size: .90em;
      float: left;
      width: 200px;
      background-color: #336600;
      color: #ffffff;
      text-transform: uppercase;
}
.desc { padding: 5px 0 20px 0;
        border-top: 1px solid #336600;
}
```

Save the painter.css file. Modify the testimonials.html page by assigning the paragraphs to the `desc` class. Save your file. Test your pages in a browser. Your testimonials.html page should be similar to the one shown in Figure 31. The other pages should display as they did at the end of Step 4. Consider modifying the unordered list on the Services page (services.html) to use <h2> and <p> elements (assigned to the `desc` class) instead—the result will be a more cohesive design for your Web site.

In this case study you changed the page layout of the Pasha the Painter Web site pages. Notice that with just a few changes in the CSS and XHTML code, you configured a two-column page layout.

Prime Properties

See the Chapter "XHTML Basics" for an introduction to the Prime Properties Case Study. Figure 38 in that chapter shows a site map for the Prime Properties Web site. The pages were created in earlier chapters. In this case study you will implement a new two-column CSS page layout for Prime Properties. You will modify the external style sheet and the Home, Listings, and Financing pages. Unless your instructor directs you otherwise, use the Chapter 4 Prime Properties Web site as a starting point for this case study.

Figure 32 displays a wireframe for the two-column page layout with a page wrapper, logo, left column, right column, and footer areas.

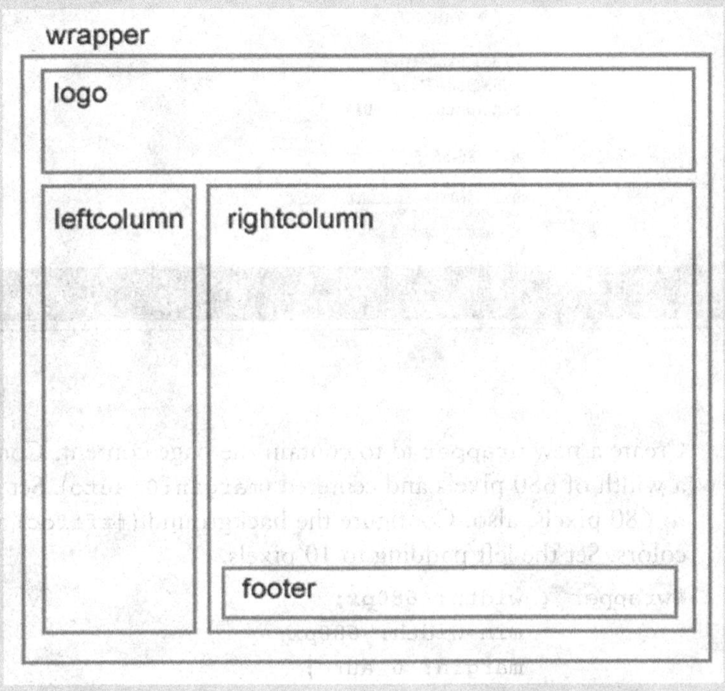

Figure 32 Prime Properties two-column page layout

Hands-On Practice Case

1. **Create a Folder.** Create a folder called primecss. Copy all the files from your Chapter 4 prime folder into the primecss folder. You will modify the prime.css file and each Web page file (index.html, listings.html, and financing.html) to implement the two-column page layout shown in Figure 32. See the new Prime Properties Home page, as shown in Figure 33 (shown also in the color insert section).
2. **Configure the CSS.** Open prime.css in Notepad. Edit the style rules as follows:
   - Configure the page background. Modify the style rules for the `body` selector. Set the `background-color` property to `#003366`. Configure the background image to be the primevertical.png image from the student files (see Chapter6/primevertical.png).

Figure 33
The new Prime Properties two-column index.html

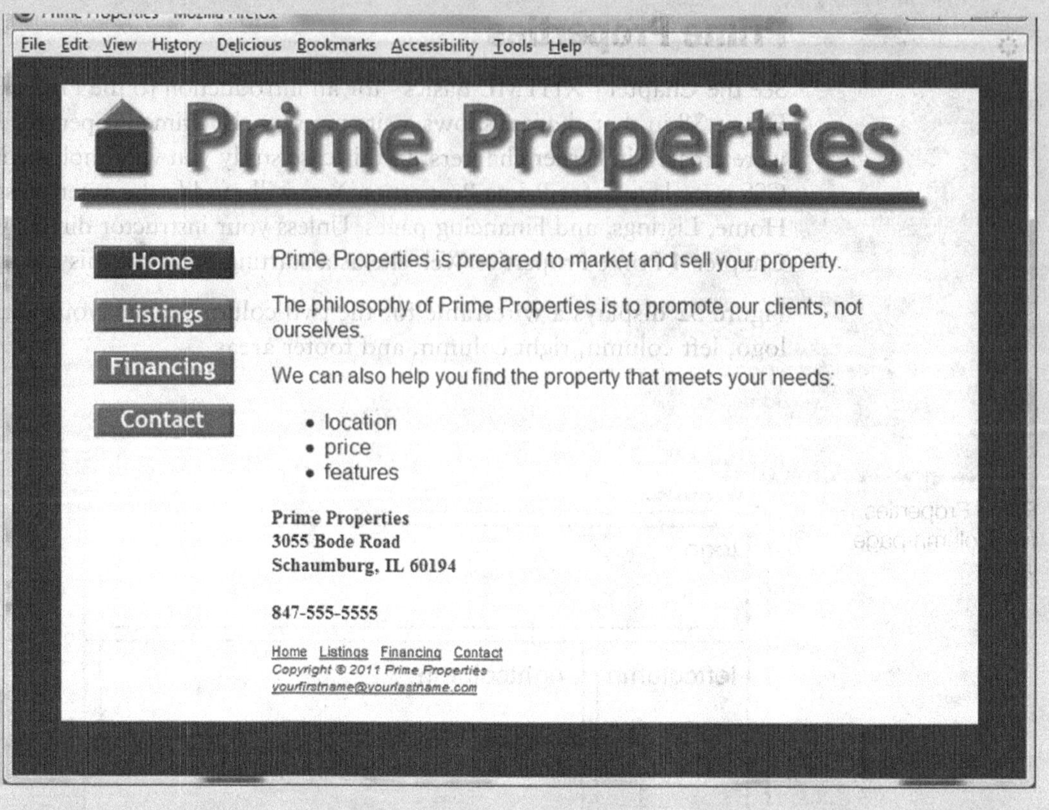

Go to the end of the chapter for a full color version of this figure

- Create a new `wrapper` id to contain the page content. Configure the area with a width of 680 pixels and centered (`margin:0 auto`). Set the minimum width to 680 pixels, also. Configure the background (`#ffffcc`) and text (`#003300`) colors. Set the left padding to 10 pixels.

```
#wrapper { width: 680px;
           min-width: 680px;
           margin: 0 auto;
           background-color: #ffffcc;
           color: #003300;
           padding-left: 10px;
}
```

- Configure the left column area. Add a new style rule for the `leftcolumn` id to configure an area that floats to the left and is 150 pixels wide.

```
#leftcolumn { float: left;
              width: 150px;
}
```

- Configure the navigation area. Configure a descendent selector style rule to configure the anchor tags within the leftcolumn id as follows: block element with a 15 pixel right, bottom, and left margin.

```
#leftcolumn a { display: block;
                margin: 0 15px 15px 15px;
}
```

- Configure the right column area. Add a new style rule for the `rightcolumn` id to configure an area with a 150 pixel left margin and 20 pixels of right and bottom padding (`padding: 0 20px 20px 0`).
- Configure the images on the listings.html page to float to the left. Add a new float:left style rule to the property class.

Save the prime.css file.

3. **Modify the index.html File.** Add `<div>` elements and modify the code as indicated below.
   - Configure the logo area. Assign the `<h1>` to the id `logo`.
   - Configure the left column. The navigation image links are the only content in the left column. Assign the `<div>` that contains the image links to the `leftcolumn` id, `<div id="leftcolumn">`. Remove other code, including any ` ` characters that may be present.
   - Configure the right column. This area contains the content (paragraphs, unordered list, and text navigation links) and the footer section. Code a `<div>` that surrounds this area. Assign the `<div>` to the `rightcolumn` id.

   Save the index.html file. It should look similar to the Web page shown in Figure 33. Remember that validating your XHTML and CSS can help you find syntax errors. Test and correct this page before you continue.
4. **Modify the listings.html and financing.html Files.** Modify these Web page files in a similar manner as you did in Step 3. Configure the property images on the listings.html page—on the opening image tag for each property photo, remove the `align="left"` attribute. Save and test your pages in a browser. As you test your pages, use the CSS and XHTML validators to help you find syntax errors.
5. **Bonus Style.** Figure 34 shows an alternate design for the financing.html page. Notice the image near the center of the content with the text "Mortgage FAQs."

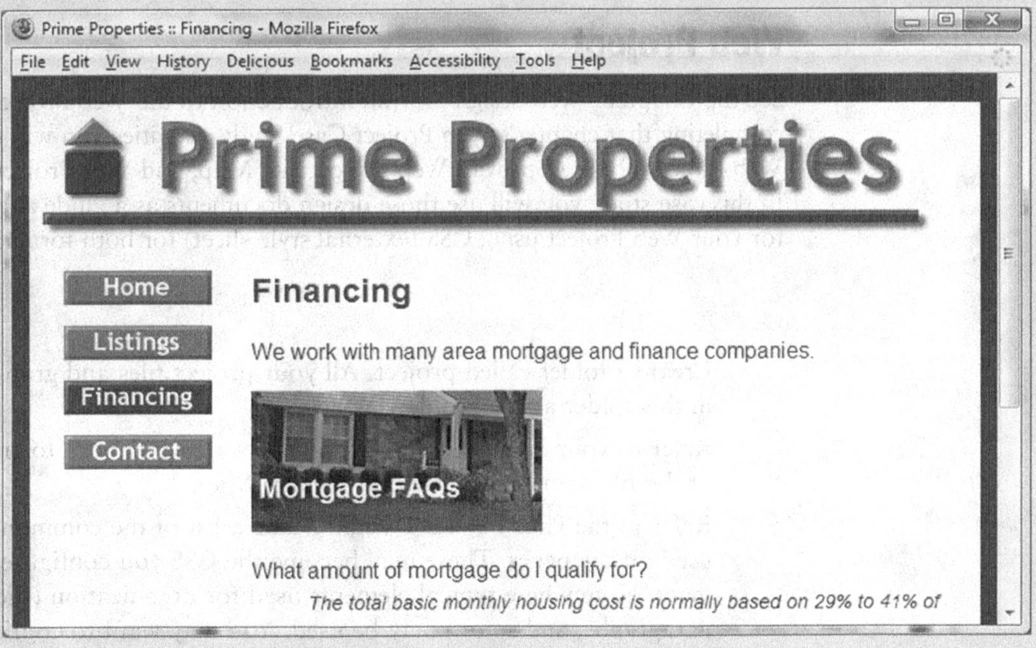

Figure 34
New style rules for the Mortgage FAQs heading

This was configured with CSS using an interesting technique. The XHTML is straightforward:

```
<h3 class="home">Mortgage FAQs</h3>.
```

CSS creates the effect. Styles are declared for the home class with the following properties: a background image that does not repeat and is positioned very carefully, a width of 200 pixels, light text, and generous padding.

```
.home { background-image: url(schaumburg.jpg);
        background-position: -100px -260px;
        background-repeat: no-repeat;
        color: #ffffcc;
        padding: 60px 5px 20px 5px;
        width: 200px;
}
```

Notice that the `background-position` property is used with carefully chosen values. As indicated in Table 1, the `background-position` property can use two numeric pixel values—horizontal and vertical. The *negative numbers* cause the background image to shift 100 pixels to the left and 260 pixels down from the top. The effect is somewhat abstract and ends up displaying just part of the image. In this case, it is a part of a house to tie in with the home financing theme. Padding is set quite high to allow room for the image to display around the text. The text color is light in order to contrast well with the image.

Save the prime.css file. Modify the financing.html page as indicated above—add `class="home"` to the `<h3>` element. Save the financing.html file. Test your pages in a browser. Your financing.html page should look similar to the one shown in Figure 34. The other pages should display as they did at the end of Step 4.

In this case study you changed the page layout of the Prime Properties Web site pages. Notice that with just a few changes in the CSS and XHTML code, you configured a two-column page layout.

Web Project

See the Chapter "Web design" for an introduction to the Web Project case. Upon completing that chapter's Web Project Case Study activities you will have completed a Web Project Topic Approval, Web Project Site Map, and Web Project Page Layout Design. In this case study you will use those design documents as a guide as you develop the pages for your Web Project using CSS (external style sheet) for both formatting and page layout.

Hands-On Practice Case

1. Create a folder called project. All your project files and graphics will be organized in this folder and subfolders as needed.
2. Refer to your Site Map to view the pages that you need to create. Jot down a list of the file names. Add these to the Site Map.
3. Refer to the Page Layout Design. Make a list of the common fonts and colors used on the pages. These may become the CSS you configure for the body element. Note where typical elements used for organization (such as headings, lists, paragraphs, and so on) may be used. You may want to configure CSS for these elements. Identify various page areas such as logo, navigation, footer, and so on—

and list any special configurations needed for these areas. These will be configured as classes in your CSS. Create an external style sheet, called project.css, which contains these configurations.

4. Using your design documents as a guide, code a representative page for your site. Use CSS to format text, color, and layout. Be sure to apply classes and ids where appropriate. Associate the Web page to the external style sheet.

   Save and test the page. Modify both the Web page and the project.css file as needed. Test and modify until you have achieved the look you want.

5. Using the completed page as a template wherever possible, code the rest of the pages on your site. Test and modify them as needed.

6. Experiment with modifying the project.css file. Change the page background color, the font family, and so on. Test your pages in a browser. Notice how a change in a single file can affect multiple files when external style sheets are used.

Answers

Checkpoint 1

1. Answers will vary. They could include the following: ease of site maintenance, separation of style from structure, increased accessibility, support of the Semantic Web, smaller documents, increased page layout control, support of multiple media types, and greater typography control.
2. Relative positioning allows you to alter the position of an element in relation to where it would otherwise be displayed using normal flow. Absolute positioning allows you to specify by pixels the exact location of an element in a Web page.
3. The `z-index` property provides flexibility in the display of elements. When using XHTML only there is no easy way to "stack" elements other than configuring backgrounds for pages or tables. The `z-index` property configures the stacking order of elements on a Web page. The default `z-index` value is `0`. Elements with higher `z-index` values will appear stacked on top of elements with lower `z-index` values rendered on the same position of the page.

Checkpoint 2

1. The page layout is liquid. Attributes of liquid page design include the following: pages take up 100 percent of the browser window—there is no blank margin on the left or right side of the page. The middle area expands and contracts when the page is resized. The content flows to fill whatever size window is used to display it.
2. Answers will vary. Some of the suggestions listed in the debugging section may be used.
3. Configure the XHTML tag as a selector if the style is expected to be applied every time that tag is used. Configure an id if the style is for a specific element that is expected to occur only once on a page. Configure a class if the style is expected to be applied to a variety of different XHTML elements.

Review Questions

1. a
2. a
3. b
4. b
5. d
6. c
7. c
8. b
9. c
10. b
11. id
12. left
13. margin
14. left, right, top
15. class

More on Links, Lists, and Layout

Chapter Objectives

In this chapter, you will learn how to ...

- Code relative hyperlinks to Web pages in folders within a Web site
- Configure a hyperlink to a named fragment internal to a Web page
- Add interactivity to Web pages with CSS pseudo-classes
- Configure a navigation layout list with CSS
- Configure three-column page layouts using CSS
- Configure CSS for screen, print, and mobile device display
- Utilize the "cascade" in CSS

Once you've had some experience coding XHTML and CSS, you're ready to explore a variety of techniques in this chapter including XHTML relative hyperlinks and named fragment hyperlinks, CSS pseudo-classes, navigation list layout, three-column page layout, styling for print, styling for mobile Web browsers, and an overview of the "cascade" in CSS.

From Chapter 7 of *Web Development and Design Foundations with XHTML*, Fifth Edition. Terry Felke-Morris.

1 Another Look at XHTML Hyperlinks

Hyperlinks make the Web a "web" of interconnected information. In this section you'll revisit the topic of hyperlinks and explore coding relative links, using the target attribute to open Web pages in a new browser window, and coding hyperlinks that are internal to a Web page.

More on Relative Linking

A relative link is used to link to Web pages within your site. You code relative links to display Web pages within the same folder. There are times when you need to link to files in other folders on your Web site. Let's consider the example of a Web site for a dog groomer that highlights services and products. The Web developer for this site created separate folders called services and products in order to organize the site. See the folder and file listing shown in Figure 1.

- groomer
  - index.html
  - contact.html
  - images
  - products
    - collars.html
    - shampoo.html
  - services
    - bathing.html
    - daycare.html

Figure 1
The dog groomer site contains the images, products, and services folders

Relative Link Examples

- To review, when linking to a file in the same folder or directory, the value of the `href` is the name of the file. For example, to link to the contact.html page from the home page (index.html), code the anchor element as follows:

```
<a href="contact.html">Contact</a>
```

- When linking to a folder located within the current directory, use both the folder name and the file name in the relative link. For example, to link to the collars.html page in the products folder from the home page (index.html), code the anchor element as follows:

```
<a href="products/collars.html">Collars</a>
```

- In Figure 1 the collars.html page is located in a subfolder of the groomer folder. The home page for the site, index.html is located in the groomer folder. When linking to a file that is up one directory level from the current page use `"../"` notation. To link to the home page for the site from the collars.html page, code the anchor element as follows:

```
<a href="../index.html">Home</a>
```

- When linking to a file that is in a folder on the same level as the current folder, the `href` value will use the `"../"` notation to indicate moving up one level and then down to the chosen folder. For example, to link to the bathing.html page in the services folder from the collars.html page in the products folder, code the anchor element as follows:

  ```
  <a href="../services/bathing.html">Dog Bathing</a>
  ```

Don't worry if the use of `"../"` notation and linking to files in different folders seems new and different. In most of the exercises in this book you will code either absolute links to other Web sites or relative links to files in the same folder.

Opening a Link in a New Browser Window

The **`target` attribute** can be used on the anchor to open a link in a new browser window. For example,

```
<a href="http://yahoo.com" target="_blank">Yahoo!</a>
```

will open Yahoo!'s home page in a new window. Why not create a test page and try it? The `target` attribute with the value `"_blank"` configures the Web page to open in a new browser window.

By now you should be comfortable with hyperlinks. You may have noticed that these links display the top of the Web page. Sometimes it is helpful to link to an exact position on a Web page instead of to the top of the page. Internal links are used for this function.

Linking to Fragment Identifiers

There are times when you need to provide the capability to link to a specific portion of a Web page. You can accomplish this by coding a hyperlink to a **fragment identifier** (sometimes called a named fragment or fragment id) which is simply an XHTML element assigned to an id. Lists of frequently asked questions (FAQs) often use this technique. Other applications of fragment identifiers include hyperlinks that skip to the content of a page or skip back to the top of the page.

There are two components to your coding when using fragment identifiers:

1. The tag that identifies the **named fragment** of a Web page. The tag must be assigned to an id. For example, `<div id="content">`.
2. The anchor tag that links to the named fragment on a Web page.

Focus on Accessibility

To see how these two components are used, consider that to provide for accessibility, Web pages may have a fragment identifier to indicate the beginning of the actual page content. When the visitor clicks on the "skip to content" hyperlink, the browser links to the fragment identifier and shifts focus to the content area of the page. This "skip to content" or "skip navigation" link provides a way for screen reader users to skip repetitive navigation links (see Figure 2). This is accomplished in two steps as follows:

1. **Establish Target.** Create the "skip to content" fragment identifier by configuring a `<div>` that contains the page content with an id, for example:

   ```
   <div id="content">
   ```

2. **Reference Target.** At the point of the page where you want to place a hyperlink to the content, type an anchor element. Use the `href` attribute and place a `#`

Figure 2 The "skip to content" link in action

(sometimes called a hash mark) before the name of the fragment identifier. The XHTML for a hyperlink to the named fragment "content" is

```
<a href="#content">Skip to Page Content>
```

The hash mark indicates that the browser should search for an id on the same page. If you forget to type the hash mark, the browser will not look on the same Web page; it will look for an external file. A named fragment does not have to be at the beginning of page content; it can be just about anywhere that would be useful to your Web visitors.

Legacy Alert. Fragment identifiers are not part of HTML 4, but you may find references to named anchors. Named anchors used the now-deprecated name attribute to identify or name the fragment. For example, `<a name="content" id="content"></a>`.

HANDS-ON PRACTICE 1

You will work with fragment identifiers in this Hands-On Practice. Locate the Chapter7/starter1.html file in the student files. Figure 3 shows a partial screenshot of this Web page.

Launch Notepad and open the starter1.html file. Save the file as favorites.html. Examine the source code and notice that the top portion of the page contains an unordered list with categories of interest (such as Hobbies, XHTML, CSS, and Professional Organizations) that correspond to the text displayed in the <h2> elements below. After each <h2> element is a definition list of topics and URLs related to that category. It might be helpful to Web page visitors if they can click a category item and immediately jump to the page area that has information related to that item. This could be a useful application of linking to fragment identifiers!

Figure 3
You will add hyperlinks to fragment identifiers

Modify the page as follows:

1. Code a named fragment for each `<h2>` element in the definition list. For example:

```
<h2 id="hobbies">Hobbies</h2>
```

2. Add hyperlinks to the items in the unordered list so that each entry will link to its corresponding `<h2>`.
3. Add a named fragment near the top of the page.
4. Near the bottom of the favorites.html page add a hyperlink to the top of the page.

Save the file and test it. Compare your work with the sample found in the student files (Chapter7/favorites.html).

There may be times when you need to link to a named fragment on another Web page. To accomplish this, place a `"#"` followed by the fragment identifier id value after the file name in the anchor tag. So, to link to the "Professional Groups" (given that it is a named fragment called "prof") from any other page on the same Web site, you could use the following XHTML:

```
<a href="favorites.html#prof">Professional Organizations</a>
```

FAQ

Why don't some of my hyperlinks to name fragments work?

A Web browser cannot display less than the height of the browser window. If there is not enough space left on the bottom of the page below the named reference, it cannot be displayed at the top of the page. Try adding some blank lines (use the `<br />` tag) to the lower portion of the Web page. Save your work and test your hyperlinks again.

2 CSS Pseudo-Classes and Links

Have you ever visited a Web site and found that the text hyperlinks changed color when you moved the mouse pointer over them? Often, this is accomplished using a special technique in CSS called a pseudo-class. The four pseudo-classes that can be applied to the anchor tag are shown in Table 1. The **link pseudo-class** configures the appearance of the hyperlink before it is clicked. The **visited pseudo-class** configures the appearance of the hyperlink after it is clicked. The **focus pseudo-class** configures the appearance of the hyperlink when it has keyboard focus—for example, by pressing the Tab key. This is helpful for users with a physical disability because it can inform them when they have reached a specific hyperlink when using the keyboard. The **hover pseudo-class** configures the hyperlink as the mouse is held or "hovered" over it. The **active pseudo-class** configures the appearance of the hyperlink while it is being clicked.

Focus on Accessibility

Notice the order in which the pseudo-classes are listed in Table 1. Anchor element pseudo-classes must be coded in this order (although it's okay to omit one or more of those listed). If you code the pseudo-classes in a different order, the styles will not be reliably applied. It's common practice to configure the focus and active pseudo-classes with the same styles.

Table 1 Commonly used CSS pseudo-classes

Pseudo-class	When Applied
link	Default state for a hyperlink that has not been clicked (visited)
visited	Default state for a visited hyperlink
focus	Triggered when the link has focus (for example, by pressing the Tab key on the keyboard)
hover	Triggered when the mouse moves over the hyperlink
active	Triggered when the hyperlink is actually clicked

The syntax of pseudo-classes uses a colon (:) to apply the **pseudo-class** to the anchor selector. The following code sample will configure text hyperlinks to be red initially. The sample also uses the hover pseudo-class, `a:hover`, to configure the links to change their appearance when the visitor places the mouse pointer over them so that the underline disappears and the color changes.

```
<style type="text/css">
a:link {  color: #ff0000;
}
a:hover {  text-decoration: none;
           color: #000066;
}
</style>
```

Figure 4 shows part of a Web page that uses a similar technique. Note the position of the mouse pointer over the Print This Page hyperlink—the text color has changed and has no underline.

While some Web design experts, such as Jakob Nielsen, recommend that Web developers not change the default look of text links, this technique is often used. Most modern browsers support CSS pseudo-classes. However, some visitors using mobile devices may not have easy access to mouse-like controls, for some tips on coding CSS for mobile visitors.

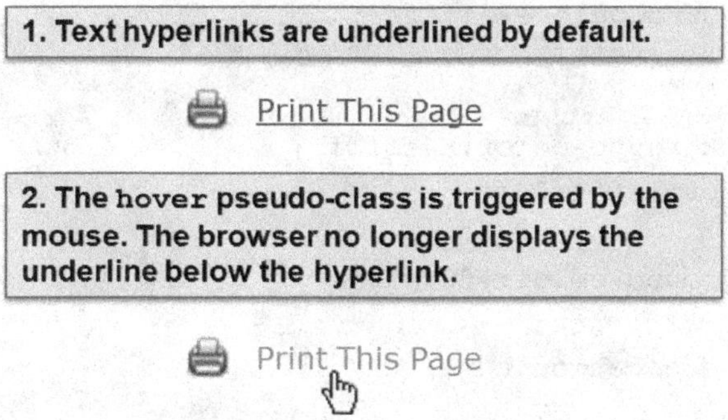

Figure 4 Using the hover pseudo-class

HANDS-ON PRACTICE 2

You will use pseudo-classes to create interactive hyperlinks in this Hands-On Practice as you create a series of pages that contain hyperlinks styled in different ways.

Part 1

The first page contains text links that you will configure to use CSS pseudo-classes. A sample is shown in Figure 5. When the mouse hovers over a link, it will change color and the underline will disappear. You will code embedded CSS to configure the link, visited, focus, hover, and active pseudo-classes for the `anchor` selector.

Figure 5 The hyperlink's underline disappears when the mouse hovers

Launch Notepad and type the following XHTML:

```
<!DOCTYPE html PUBLIC "-//W3C//DTD XHTML 1.0 Transitional//EN"
  "http://www.w3.org/TR/xhtml1/DTD/xhtml1-transitional.dtd">
<html xmlns="http://www.w3.org/1999/xhtml" lang="en" xml:lang="en">
<head>
<title>CSS Pseudo-class Example 1</title>
<meta http-equiv="Content-Type" content="text/html; charset=utf-8"/>
<style type="text/css">
body {   margin: 0 auto;
         width: 400px;
         text-align: center;
}
```

```
a:link { background-color: #ffffff;
         color: #ff0000;
}
a:visited { background-color: #ffffff;
            color: #00ff00;
}
a:focus { background-color:#000000;
          color: #cccccc;
          text-decoration:none;
}
a:hover { background-color: #ffffff;
          color: #000066;
          text-decoration: none;
}
a:active { background-color: #ffffff;
           color: #cccccc;
           text-decoration:none;
}
</style>
</head>
<body>
<div>
  <h1>Navigation Links</h1>
  <p><a href="http://yahoo.com">Yahoo!</a>
  <a href="http://google.com">Google</a></p>
</div>
</body>
</html>
```

Save your file as link1.html. Test your page in a browser and compare it with Figure 5. The student files contain a sample solution at Chapter7/link1.html. The browser applies the CSS pseudo-class rules to every link on the page. Experiment with hovering over the hyperlinks or using your keyboard to tab to the links. Press the Enter key to use the keyboard to activate a hyperlink. In this example, the CSS was coded using embedded styles, but an external style sheet also could have been used.

Part 2

Now you will create a page that uses CSS and pseudo-classes to configure navigation links that look like buttons. These can be used in place of image links to save on the bandwidth used by graphics. See the sample in Figure 6. When the mouse hovers over a navigation button, the text color and border change.

Figure 6 The hyperlink's appearance changes when the mouse hovers

You will use the border and padding CSS properties to configure the buttons. Let's review these properties. The `border` property configures the width (`border-width`), style (`border-style`), and color (`border-color`) of the border around an element. The `padding` property configures the amount of padding—the blank space between the element and its border.

Launch Notepad and type the following XHTML:

```
<!DOCTYPE html PUBLIC "-//W3C//DTD XHTML 1.0 Transitional//EN"
  "http://www.w3.org/TR/xhtml1/DTD/xhtml1-transitional.dtd">
<html xmlns="http://www.w3.org/1999/xhtml" lang="en" xml:lang="en">
<head>
<title>CSS Pseudo-class Example 2</title>
<meta http-equiv="Content-Type" content="text/html; charset=utf-8" />
<style type="text/css">
body {   margin: 0 auto;
         width: 550px;
         text-align: center;
}
#button a { border: 2px inset #CCCCCC;
            padding: 3px 15px;
            color: #FFFFFF;
            background-color: #000066;
            font-family: Arial, Helvetica, sans-serif;
            font-size: 1.2em;
            font-weight: bold;
            text-align: center;
            text-decoration: none;
  }
#button a:link { color: #FFFFFF;
}
#button a:visited { color: #CCCCCC;
}
#button a:focus { background-color:#000000;
                  color: #DDA0DD;
                  border:2px outset #000000;

}
#button a:hover { color: #66CCFF;
                  border:2px outset #cccccc;
}
#button a:active { color: #DDA0DD;
                   border:2px outset #000000;

}
</style>
</head>
```

```
<body>
<h1>CSS Buttons!</h1>
<div id="button">
  <a href="index.html">Home</a>
  <a href="products.html">Products</a>
  <a href="services.html">Services</a>
  <a href="contact.html">Contact</a>
  <a href="about.html">About</a>
</div>
</body>
</html>
```

Save your file as link2.html. Test your page in a browser and compare it with Figure 6. The student files contain a sample solution at Chapter7/link2.html. The `div` that contains the navigation buttons was assigned to the id button. The anchor tags within the button id were configured to have a button look with the `border`, `background-color`, and `padding` attributes. Then, CSS rules using an `anchor` selector with the `button` id and `link`, `visited`, focus, `hover`, and `active` pseudo-classes were configured.

Part 3

It is often the case that the design of the Web page requires the main navigation links to look different from the links within the content of the pages. You have already created a page, link2.html, with specially configured navigation links. You used the id called `button` to configure these links. In this part of the Hands-On Practice, you will add a line of text containing a hyperlink to the page to verify that the hyperlink retains the default browser appearance and behavior. Figure 7 shows a sample page.

Figure 7
The link to Yahoo! retains the default hyperlink properties

Launch Notepad and open your link2.html file. Save the file as link3.html. Modify the title to be "CSS Pseudo-class Example 3" and add the following paragraph under the navigation links:

```
<p>Visit <a href="http://yahoo.com">Yahoo!</a>.</p>
```

Save your file, test your page in a browser, and compare it with the one shown in Figure 7. The student files contain a sample solution at Chapter7/link3.html. Because the new link is not part of the defined id `button`, it retains the default hyperlink characteristics. If you needed yet another set of characteristics for links in another section of the page such as the footer, you could define a new id or class with a unique name and configure pseudo-classes, as was done in Part 2 of this Hands-On Practice.

As you can see, pseudo-classes—along with careful configuration of ids or classes, can be a powerful tool for a Web developer.

3 CSS Navigation Layout Using Lists

One of the advantages of using CSS for page layout involves the use of semantically correct code. Writing semantically correct code means using the markup tag that most accurately reflects the purpose of the content. Using the various levels of heading tags for content headings and subheadings, or placing paragraphs of text within paragraph tags (rather than using line breaks) are examples of writing semantically correct code. This type of coding is a step in the direction to support the Semantic Web. Leading Web developers such as Eric Meyer, Mark Newhouse, Jeffrey Zeldman, and others have promoted the idea of using unordered lists to configure navigation menus. After all—a navigation menu is a list of hyperlinks—semantically speaking it's a much better fit than coding hyperlinks in separate paragraphs or using the `display:block` property on anchor tags. Configuring navigation with a list also helps provide for accessibility. Screen reader applications offer easy keyboard access and verbal cues for information organized in lists, such as the number of items in the list.

Focus on Accessibility

WWW

Figure 8 shows the top portion of a revised twocolumn.html. In this version the CSS declaration for the `navBar` class was changed (`display:block` and `margin:15px` were removed), the left column was widened a bit, and the navigation links were coded in an unordered list. An XHTML code snippet follows:

```
<div id="leftcolumn">
<ul>
  <li><a href="index.html">Home</a></li>
  <li><a href="spring.html">Spring</a></li>
  <li><a href="summer.html">Summer</a></li>
  <li><a href="fall.html">Fall</a></li>
  <li><a href="winter.html">Winter</a></li>
</ul>
</div>
```

Figure 8
An unordered list to configure the navigation menu

Perhaps you would prefer that the bullets in the unordered list were not displayed. Use the **`list-style-type`** **property** to configure the list-item markers (bullets). The property `list-style-type:none` prevents the browser from displaying the bullets. See Appendix C for more list-style-type values.

Figure 9 shows the effect of configuring `list-style-type:none` for the new unordered list in the left column. The CSS is below:

```
#leftcolumn ul { list-style-type:none; }
```

Figure 9
An unordered list with `list-style-type:none`

Figure 10
An unordered list with an image replacing the bullet

If you would like a custom image to replace the bullet, use the **`list-style-image`** **property**. In Figure 10 an image named arrow.gif was configured to replace the bullets using: `list-style-image:url(arrow.gif)`. View the twocolumn1.html file in the Chapter7 folder in the student files to examine the code.

You may be wondering how to apply this technique to a horizontal navigation menu. The answer is CSS! List items are block elements. They need to be configured as inline elements to display in a single line. The `display:inline` property is used to accomplish this. Figure 11 displays a new version of the page using this technique. The page looks about the same as the original when displayed in a browser even though the XHTML and CSS are configured to use a list.

Figure 11
Horizontal navigation using an unordered list configured with CSS

The XHTML code snippet is the same as the one used for the vertical navigation menus shown at the beginning of this section. For the horizontal list to display properly, you must add a CSS configuration for the `<li>` selector within the nav class as follows:

```
.nav li {  display: inline;
           list-style-type: none;
}
```

Focus on Accessibility

View the home0.html and wildflower0.css files in the Chapter7 folder in the student files to experiment with this technique. See Chapter7/skipnav.html for a version of this page that includes a transparent image configured as an internal link to the named fragment maincontent. This "skip navigation" method allows visitors using screen readers to easily skip repetitive navigation links.

4 Three-Column CSS Page Layout

Often a Web page layout will consist of a header across the top of the page with three columns below: navigation, content, and sidebar. If you are thinking about this layout as a series of boxes—you're thinking correctly for configuring pages using CSS! Figure 12 shows a wireframe sketch of this page layout design. Figure 13 shows a Web page configured using this design. You will create this page in the next Hands-On Practice.

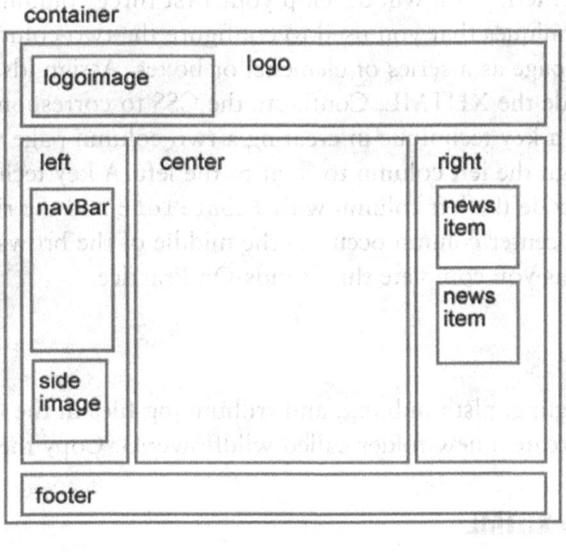

Figure 12
Sketch of three-column page layout

Figure 13
This three-column page layout is designed using CSS

Go to the end of the chapter for a full color version of this figure

HANDS-ON PRACTICE 3

In this Hands-On Practice you will develop your first three-column Web page using CSS. The same techniques that you used to configure the two-column page will apply here—think of the page as a series of elements or boxes. Assign ids or classes to the elements as you code the XHTML. Configure the CSS to correspond to the ids and classes. Recall that a key technique in creating a two-column page with left column navigation was to design the left column to float to the left. A key technique in our three-column page is to code the left column with `float:left` and the right column with `float:right`. The center column occupies the middle of the browser window. Refer to Figures 12 and 13 as you complete this Hands-On Practice.

Getting Started

Locate the showybg.jpg, plsthumb.jpg, and trillium.jpg files in the Chapter 7 folder in the student files. Create a new folder called wildflowers3. Copy the files to the folder.

Part 1—Code the XHTML

Review Figures 12 and 13. Notice the page elements: a logo area with both a logo and a background image that repeats; a left column with a navigation area and an image; a center column with paragraphs of text, a heading, and an image that floats to the right; a right column with two news items; and a footer. These will all be coded to use ids and classes corresponding to CSS, which configures a number of properties including the `float`, `margin`, `border`, `font-family`, and so on. The navigation menu links will be configured using an unordered list. As you code the XHTML document, you will place the elements on the page and assign `id` and `class` values that correspond to the areas in the sketch in Figure 12. Launch Notepad and type in the following XHTML:

```
<!DOCTYPE html PUBLIC "-//W3C//DTD XHTML 1.0 Transitional//EN"
  "http://www.w3.org/TR/xhtml1/DTD/xhtml1-transitional.dtd">
<html xmlns="http://www.w3.org/1999/xhtml" lang="en" xml:lang="en">
<head>
<title>Door County Wildflowers</title>
<meta http-equiv="Content-Type" content="text/html; charset=utf-8"/>
</head>
<body>
<div id="container">
  <div id="logo">
    <h1>Door County Wildflowers</h1>
  </div>
  <div id="left">
    <ul class="navBar">
     <li><a href="index.html">Home</a></li>
     <li><a href="spring.html">Spring</a></li>
     <li><a href="summer.html">Summer</a></li>
     <li><a href="fall.html">Fall</a></li>
     <li><a href="winter.html">Winter</a></li>
    </ul>
    <img class="sideimages" src="plsthumb.jpg" width="100"
    height="100" alt="Showy Pink Lady Slipper" />
  </div>
  <div id="right">
    <h4>The Ridges</h4>
    <p class="newsitem">The Ridges Nature Sanctuary offers wild
    orchid hikes during the summer months. For more info, visit
    <a href="http://www.ridgesanctuary.org">The Ridges</a>.</p>
    <h4>Newport State Park</h4>
    <p class="newsitem">The Newport Wilderness Society sponsors free
    meadow hikes at 9am every Saturday. Stop by the park office to
    register.</p>
  </div>
  <div id="center">
    <p>Wisconsin&#39;s Door County Peninsula is a unique, ecologically
    diverse place with upland and boreal forest, bogs, swamps, sand
    and rock beaches, limestone escarpments, and farmlands.</p>
    <p>A wide array of wildflowers grow in the county because
    of this variety of ecosystems.</p>
    <img src="trillium.jpg" width="200" height="150" alt="Trillium"
    id="floatright" />
```

```
    <h3>Explore the beauty <br />of Door County Wildflowers....</h3>
    <p>With five state parks, tons of county parks, and private
    nature sanctuaries, Door County is teeming with natural areas
      for you to stalk your favorite wildflowers.</p>
  </div>
  <div id="footer">
    Copyright &copy; 2010 Door County Wild Flowers<br />
    Last Updated on 06/10/10
  </div>
</div>
</body>
</html>
```

Save your page as threecolumn.html in your wildflowers3 folder. Test the page in a browser. Your display will not look like Figure 13 since you have not yet configured the CSS. The top of your page should look similar to the page shown in Figure 14.

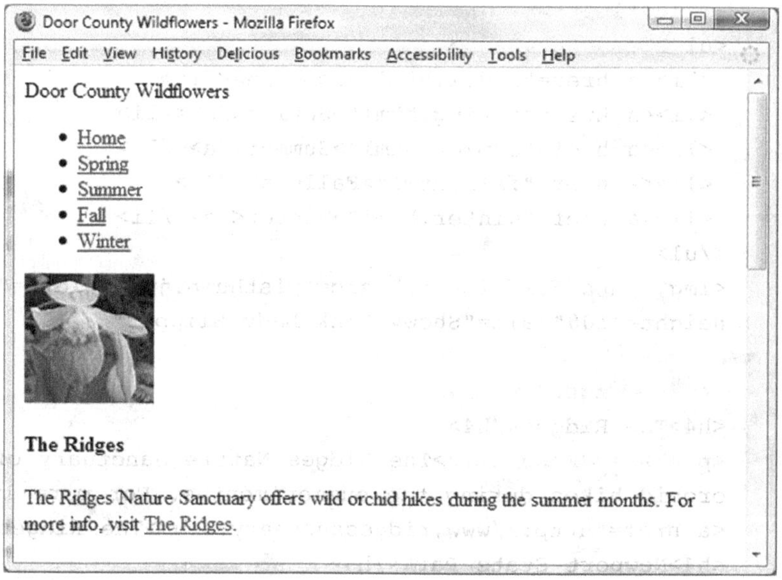

Figure 14 The three-column page before CSS is applied

Part 2—Code the Basic CSS

For ease of editing, in this Hands-On Practice you will code the CSS as embedded styles in the header section of the Web page. However, if you were creating an entire Web site you would most likely use an external style sheet.

Launch Notepad and open threecolumn.html. Let's take a moment to consider the main elements used on the page shown in Figure 13: logo, left column, right column, center column, and footer. The left column will contain a navigation area and a small image. The center column will contain paragraphs, a heading, and a right-floating image. The right column will contain a series of headings and news items. Locate these areas on the sketch in Figure 12. Notice also that the same font is used throughout the page and the page begins right at the browser margin. Launch Notepad and open your threecolumn .html file. In the header section of your Web page document, add a tag to begin the embedded styles:

```
<style type="text/css">
```

Now let's consider the CSS configuration. Type the CSS in your document as it is discussed as follows:

1. **Body Selector.** Set the margin to 0 pixels. Configure the background color to #ffffff.

```
body {   margin:0;
         background-color: #ffffff;
}
```

2. **Container.** Configure this area with background (#eeeeee) and text (#006600) colors, a minimum width of 700 pixels, and with font family of Verdana, Arial or sans-serif.

```
#container {   background-color: #eeeeee;
               color: #006600;
               min-width: 700px;
               font-family: Verdana, Arial, sans-serif;
}
```

3. **Logo.** Code this area so that the image showybg.jpg will repeat using `background-image:url(showybg.jpg)`. The text should be set to 2.5em font size and bold. The height of the logo area is 100 pixels—this corresponds to the height of the background image. Although it will most likely never display, configure the background color to #eeeeee. The text color should be #cc66cc. Set the left padding to 20 pixels. Configure a 2 pixel solid black border across the bottom of this area as follows:

```
#logo {   color: #cc66cc;
          background-color: #eeeeee;
          border-bottom: 2px solid #000000;
          height: 100px;
          background-image: url(showybg.jpg);
          padding-left: 20px;

}
```

4. **Left Column.** One of the keys to this three-column page layout is that the left column is designed to float to the left of the browser window. Configure a width of 150.

```
#left { float: left;
        width: 150px;
}
```

5. **Right Column.** One of the keys to this three-column page layout is that the right column is designed to float to the right of the browser window. Configure a width of 200 pixels.

```
#right {  float: right;
          width: 200px;
}
```

6. **Center.** The center column will take up all the room that is available after the left and right columns float. The content area has a special need for margins since the left and right columns are floating on either side. Set the left margin to 150 pixels, the right margin to 200 pixels, and the remaining side margins to 0. Configure

padding for this area, also. Set the background (`#ffffff`) and text (`#006600`) colors for this area.

```
#center { margin: 0 200px 0 150px;
          padding: 1px 10px 20px 10px;
          background-color: #ffffff;
          color: #006600;
}
```

7. **Footer.** Configure the page footer with very small text that is centered. Configure the background (`#ffffff`) and text (`#006600`) colors for this area. Set the top padding to 10 pixels. A `clear:both` is needed to clear the float of the right and left columns as follows:

```
#footer { font-size: .70em;
          text-align: center;
          color: #006600;
          background-color: #ffffff;
          padding-top: 10px;
          clear:both;
}
```

At this point you have configured the main elements of the three-column page layout. It's a good idea to save and do a quick test to make sure you are on the right track. Code the closing XHTML style tag: `</style>`.

Save the threecolumn.html file in the wildflowers3 folder. Test your page in a browser. It should look similar to the one shown in Figure 15. Note that there is still some detail work to do but you are well on your way!

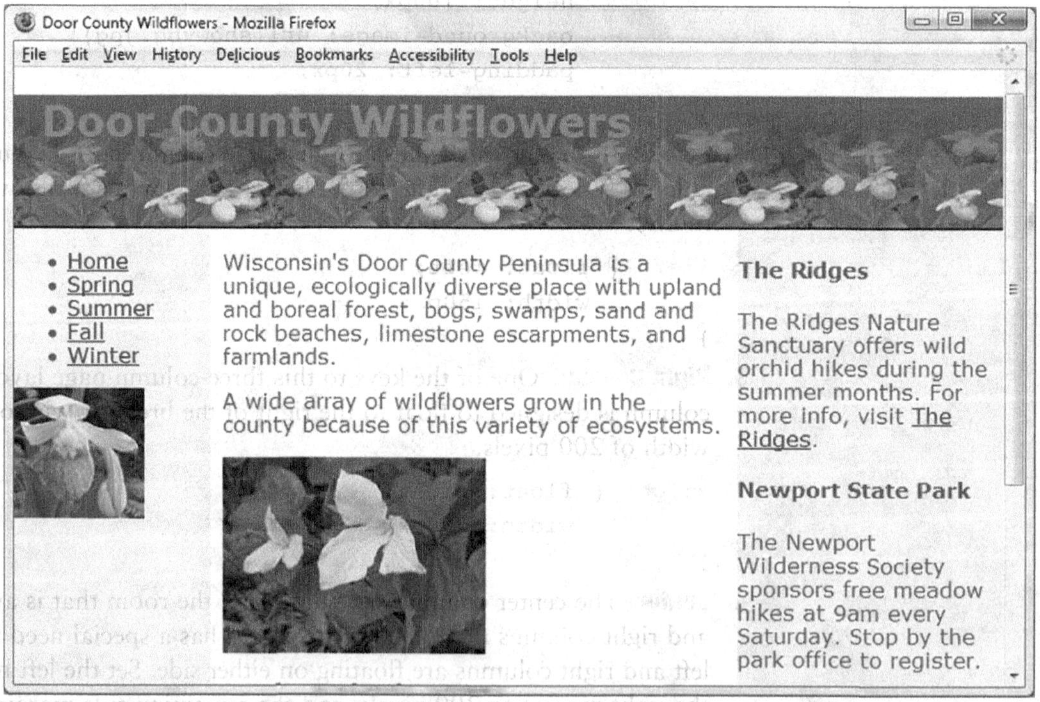

Figure 15 The CSS for the basic elements of the three-column layout is complete

Part 3—Continue Coding CSS

Now you are ready to continue with your styles. Open the threecolumn.html page in Notepad and position your cursor on a blank line above the closing style tag. First we will configure the components in the left column as follows:

1. **Logo Area.** Notice the extra space above the "Door County Wildflowers" text which is contained within `<h1>` element in the logo area. You can eliminate this extra space by setting a 0 top margin for the `h1` selector. Also configure the font-size to 3em for the `h1` selector.

```
h1 {  margin-top: 0;
      font-size: 3em;
}
```

2. **Navigation Menu.** Configure the unordered list to provide for a 20 pixel top margin and not to display any bullets.

```
.navBar {  margin-top: 20px;
           list-style-type: none;
}
```

Configure the navigation links to have no underline (`text-decoration:none`). Configure the font size to 1.2em. Pseudo-classes should be configured for link, visited, hover, active, and focus with different text colors as follows:

```
.navBar a {  text-decoration: none;

             font-size: 1.2em;
}
.navBar a:link {  color:#006600;
                  background-color: #eeeeee;}
.navBar a:visited {  color: #003300;
                     background-color: #eeeeee;}
.navBar a:focus {  color: #000000;
                   background-color: #ffffff;}
.navBar a:hover {  color: #cc66cc;
                   background-color: #eeeeee;}
.navBar a:active {  color: #000000;}
```

3. **Left Column Image (`sideimages`).** Configure this class with a margin of 30 pixels as follows:

```
.sideimages { margin: 30px;}
```

Next, we'll configure the contents of the center column. Styles for paragraphs, `heading elements`, and an image that floats to the right need to be constructed.

4. Configure the paragraph selector to use a margin of 20 pixels as follows:

```
p { margin: 20px; }
```

5. Configure the `h3` selector with the same text color as the logo and the same background color as the main body of the page as follows:

```
h3 {  color: #cc66cc;
      background-color: #ffffff;
}
```

6. **Image Floating at the Right.** Set the `floatright` id to use a 10 pixel margin and `float:right` as follows:

```
#floatright {  margin: 10px;
               float: right;
}
```

Now, we'll configure the styles for the contents of the right column. The announcements consist of a heading (contained within `<h4>` tags) and a paragraph (assigned to a class called `newsitem`).

7. Configure the heading to have a 1 pixel black solid bottom border, 2 pixels of padding at the bottom, a 10 pixel margin, the same text color as the logo, and the same background color as the right column:

```
h4 {  padding-bottom: 2px;
      border-bottom: 1px solid #000000;
      margin: 10px;
      color: #cc66cc;
      background-color: #eeeeee;
}
```

8. **News Items.** Configure a class called `newsitem` that uses a small font and has a 10 pixel margin as follows:

```
.newsitem {  font-size:.9em;
             margin: 10px;
}
```

Save the threecolumn.html file in the wildflowers3 folder.

Part 4—Test the Page

Now that your styles are coded, test the threecolumn.html page again. Your page should look similar to the screenshot shown in Figure 13. If there are differences, verify the `id` and `class` values in your XHTML. Also check the syntax of your CSS. You may find the W3C CSS validator at http://jigsaw.w3.org/css-validator helpful when verifying CSS syntax. The student files contain a copy of threecolumn.html in the Chapter7 folder.

FAQ

How do I create a custom-color scroll bar?

It can be fun to color-coordinate the scroll bar with your Web site! Keep in mind that not all your Web visitors will see your handiwork. While this effect is supported by Internet Explorer, it is not supported by all browsers. To configure a scroll bar with colors that you choose, add the following styles to the body tag: `scrollbar-face-color`, `scrollbar-arrow-color`, and `scrollbar-track-color`. For example:

```
body {  scrollbar-face-color:#cc66cc;
        scrollbar-arrow-color:#006600;
        scrollbar-track-color:#cccccc;
}
```

Note: Your CSS will not pass W3C validation tests if you use these Internet Explorer only properties.

CHECKPOINT 1

1. Describe a reason to organize the files in a Web site using folders and subfolders.
2. State a reason to use an unordered list to configure navigation links.
3. You are using CSS pseudo-classes on a Web page to configure the navigation links to look like buttons. You want the "regular" links in the Web page content to be configured as they normally would (not look like a button). Describe how you could configure the styles and XHTML to accomplish this.

5 CSS Styling for Print

Even though the advent of the "paperless society" has been talked about for decades, the fact is that many people still love paper and you can expect your Web pages to be printed. CSS offers you some control over what gets printed and how the printouts are configured.

This is easy to do using external style sheets. Create one external style sheet with the configurations for browser display and a second external style sheet with the special printing configurations. Associate both of the external style sheets to the Web page using two `<link>` elements. The `<link>` elements will utilize a new attribute, called `media` which is described in Table 2.

Table 2 The `media` attribute

Value	Purpose
screen	The default value; indicates the style sheet that configures typical browser viewport display on a color computer screen
print	Indicates the style sheet that configures the printed formatting
handheld	Indicates the style sheet that configures display on handheld mobile devices

Modern browsers will use the correct style sheet depending on whether they are rendering a screen display or preparing to print a document. Configure the link element for your browser display with `media="screen"`. Configure the link element for your printout with `media="print"`. An example of the XHTML follows:

```
<link rel="stylesheet" href="wildflower.css" type="text/css"
  media="screen" />
<link rel="stylesheet" href="wildflowerprint.css" type="text/css"
  media="print" />
```

Often `display:none` is used in the print style sheet to prevent banner ads, navigation, or other extraneous areas from appearing on the printout. Another common practice is to configure the font sizes on the print style sheet to use `pt` sizes—this will better control the text on the printout. You can also use styles to configure areas in the document, such as detailed contact info, that are only printed out and do not appear in the browser window. Figure 16 shows the print preview of the content page. Notice that the print preview includes the navigation area. Figure 17 displays an alternate version of the page that uses CSS to prevent the navigation area from printing. You will explore this technique in the next Hands-On Practice.

Figure 16
Print preview of the page displayed in Figure 6.18

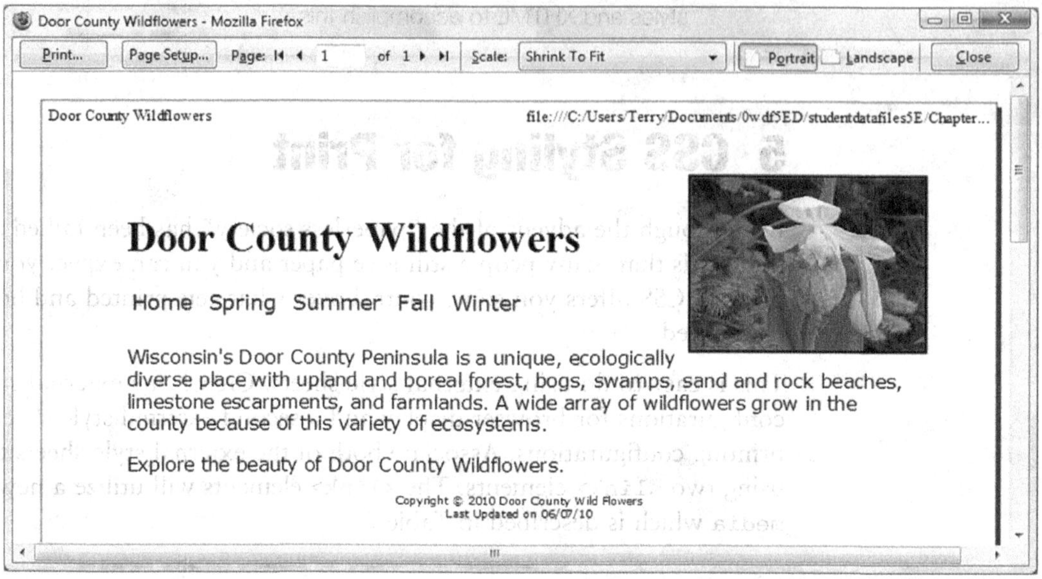

Figure 17
Print preview using CSS to remove the navigation from the printout

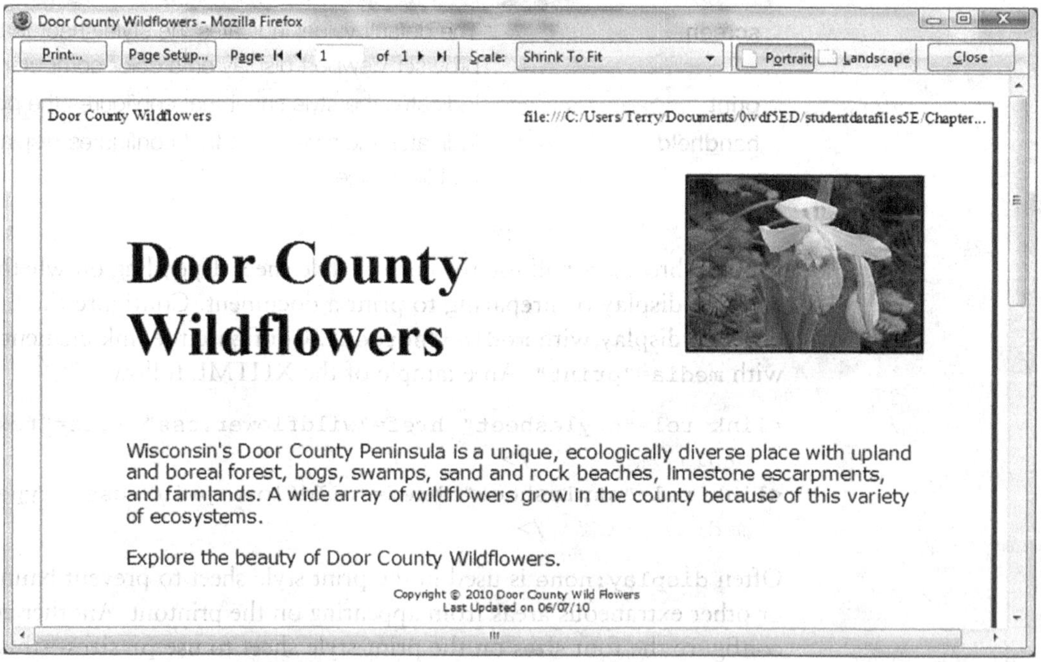

HANDS-ON PRACTICE 4

In this Hands-On Practice you will code special styles to use when printing a Web page. We will use the page1.html and wildflower.css files that you created in Hands-On Practice 5 as a starting point. Figure 18 shows the browser display of the page1.html.file. You will create a new version of the page1.html file and a new style sheet configured for printing. When printed, the logo will be configured using a 24 pt size and the navigation will not display.

Getting Started

Locate the pls.jpg, wildflower.css, and page1.html files in the student files, Chapter7 folder. Create a new folder called wildflowersPrint. Copy the files to the folder.

Part 1—Code the XHTML

Launch Notepad and open page1.html. This page is associated with an external style sheet called wildflower.css. The styles in wildflower.css should be used when the Web page is displayed on the screen. Add the **media attribute** with the value of `screen` to the link element for wildflower.css. Code a new link element to invoke an external style sheet called wildflowerprint.css for printing (`media="print"`). The XHTML follows:

```
<link rel="stylesheet" href="wildflower.css" type="text/css"
    media="screen" />
<link rel="stylesheet" href="wildflowerprint.css" type="text/css"
    media="print" />
```

Save the page1.html file in the wildflowersPrint folder.

Part 2—Code the New CSS

Launch Notepad and open wildflower.css. Since you want to keep most of the styles for printing, you will start by creating a new version of the external style sheet. Save wildflower.css with the name of wildflowerprint.css in the wildflowersPrint folder. You will modify three areas on this style sheet: the `contentlogo` id, the `content` class, and the nav class configuration.

1. Modify the `contentlogo` id so that the printer will use 24 point font size and has no background color. The CSS follows:
```
#contentlogo { color: #000000;
               font-size: 24pt;
               padding: 10px;
}
```
2. Modify the `content` class so that the printer will use 12 point font size. The CSS follows:
```
.content { font-family: Verdana,Arial,sans-serif;
           font-size: 12pt;
           margin: 10px;
```

3. Configure the nav class to not be printed with the page. Delete all styles associated with the nav class and replace them with the following CSS:

```
.nav { display: none;
}
```

Save your file in the wildflowersPrint folder.

Part 3—Test Your Work

Test your page1.html file in a browser. Select Print, Preview. Your display should look similar to the page shown in Figure 17. The logo and content font sizes have been configured. The navigation does not display. The student files contain a copy of page1.html and wildflowerprint.css in the Chapter7/wildflowersPrint folder.

FAQ

How can I control the page breaks when printing a Web page?

Use the CSS `page-break-before` or `page-break-after` properties to control hard copy page breaks. Well-supported values for these properties are `always` (the page break will always occur as designated), `avoid` (if possible, the page break will occur before or after, as designated), and `auto` (default). For example, to configure a page break before elements assigned to the class named `newpage`, configure the CSS as shown below:

```
.newpage { page-break-before: always; }
```

6 CSS Styling for the Mobile Web

Have you noticed how connected everyone seems to be these days? Access to the Web from cell phones, smartphones, and Internet tablets makes it possible to always be online. The research firm eMarketer.com predicts significant growth for mobile Web access, with a projected 134.3 million mobile Internet users by 2013. With this growth in mind, it's becoming more important to design Web pages that are accessible and usable for your mobile visitors. There are a few schools of thought on the best way to accomplish this, including developing a new mobile site with a .mobi TLD, creating a separate Web site hosted within your current domain targeted for mobile users, and using CSS to create a style sheet to configure your current Web site for display on mobile devices. We'll focus on the third approach with CSS in this section.

You can create a separate style sheet to configure the display on handheld devices, just as you configured a separate style sheet to control the printed format of a Web page. Associate the style sheet with your Web page using the media attribute (`media="handheld"`) on the `<link>` tag. An example is shown below:

```
<link href="mobile.css" rel="stylesheet" type="text/css"
media="handheld" />
```

Now that you know how to associate a handheld style sheet with a Web page, what's the best way to configure the page? Compare the regular browser display of the Disabilityinfo.gov site in Figure 18 with the handheld display in Figure 19—there's quite a difference!

Figure 18
The browser display of http://disabilityinfo.gov

Users of handheld devices experience a number of usability constraints. The list below describes these constraints and provides some recommended design, XHTML, and CSS techniques to overcome or compensate for limitations experienced by mobile Web users. However, a good starting point, whether you are designing for a standard browser or for a mobile device, is to code standards-based XHTML and CSS that passes W3C validation tests.

Figure 19
http://disabilityinfo.gov displayed with the dotMobi emulator (http://emulator.mtld.mobi/emulator.php)

- **Small screen size.** According to Opera Software, some currently common phone screen sizes include 128×160 pixels, 176×220 pixels, 240×320 pixels, 352×416 pixels, 640×320 pixels, and 640×480 pixels (large-screen phones). Even on one of the large phones, that's not a lot of pixels to work with! The workaround is to use a one-column design and avoid the use of floats, absolute positioning, tables, and frames. Descriptive page titles and heading tags will help to establish an effective mobile Web presence. Centered content and borders can work well for small screen display. Eliminate nonessential content with the CSS `display:none` property. For example:

```
#sidebar { display:none; }
```

- **Low bandwidth (slow connection speed).** Although the use of faster 3G networks is becoming more widespread, many mobile users experience slow connection speeds. Images usually take up quite a bit of bandwidth on a typical Web site. Techniques to improve mobile Web usability related to images include providing descriptive text for images, optimizing the file size of images, and avoiding using images for navigation. Consider replacing images with others configured for small-screen display. For example:

```
#imagelogo { background-image: url(smalllogo.gif); }
```

- **Font issues.** Mobile devices may have very limited font support. Configure font size using ems or percentages. Include generic font family names in your style sheet. For example:

```
p { font-family: Arial, sans-serif; }
```

- **Color issues.** Mobile devices may have very limited color support. Choose colors carefully to maximize contrast.
- **Awkward controls.** While smartphones with touch controls are becoming more popular, many mobile users will not have access to mouselike controls. Provide keyboard access to assist these users. Configure your XHTML using headings, navigation in ordered lists (some cell phones will provide numeric keypad access), Skip to Content hyperlinks, and Skip to Top hyperlinks to help your mobile visitors more conveniently navigate your site.
- **Flash support issues.** Many mobile devices do not support Adobe Flash multimedia.
- **Limited processor and memory.** Although mobile device processing speed and available memory are improving, they still cannot compare to the resources of a desktop computer. While this won't be an issue for the Web sites you create now, be mindful of this issue in the future as you continue to develop your skills and create Web applications.
- **Cost per kilobyte.** Depending on the service plan, some mobile Web visitors may be paying per kilobyte. Be aware of this and eliminate unnecessary images as described above.

Focus on Accessibility

As you reviewed the list above, you may have noticed that some of the techniques—such as writing descriptive alt text for images, choosing text and background colors with good contrast, and configuring Skip to Content hyperlinks—are the same as the recommended practices to provide for accessibility. In fact, there is quite an overlap in the design and coding techniques needed to create a Web site that is accessible for visitors with disabilities and those intended for mobile Web visitors. See http://www.w3.org/WAI/mobile/ for more information on this topic.

Once you've applied the design and coding techniques described above, it's important to test your Web site in mobile devices and/or emulators. Figure 20 shows a modified version of the Door County Wildflowers site displayed in the Opera browser's small screen view. Notice some differences with the regular browser display of this page in Figure 11—the logo image does not display, the navigation links are configured in a list, and there are additional navigation aids (Skip to Content and Back to Top hyperlinks). The effect of a

Figure 20 Opera's small screen view

new handheld style sheet and a few XHTML coding changes/additions to the navigation is a Web page that is more usable and accessible for mobile visitors.

As mobile devices evolve and mobile bandwidth improves, there are sure to be new developments in this area of Web design. If you are interested in exploring this topic further, you'll find the resources below helpful.

- http://dev.opera.com/articles/view/the-phone-factor-2/
- http://www.cameronmoll.com/archives/000577.html
- http://patterns.littlespringsdesign.com/index.php/Mobile_Style_Guides_Screen_Design,_Part_1
- http://patterns.littlespringsdesign.com/index.php/Mobile_Style_Guides_Screen_Design,_Part_2
- http://www.w3.org/TR/2008/REC-mobile-bp-20080729/

FAQ

Will every mobile device use my "handheld" style sheet?

Many mobile devices will apply the handheld style sheet when displaying your Web page. However, some mobile devices, such as the iPhone, iTouch, and Nokia Internet Tablet, run mini-browsers that render the style sheet configured for `media="screen"` and ignore the `media="handheld"` style sheet. You'll need to test your mobile device. For a quick check, visit http://htmldog.com/test/handheld.html to determine if your device applies a handheld style sheet.

7 The "Cascade"

Figure 21 shows the "cascade" (**rules of precedence**) that applies the styles in order from outermost (external styles) to innermost (actual XHTML coded on the page). This way site-wide styles can be configured but overridden when needed by more granular (or page-specific) styles.

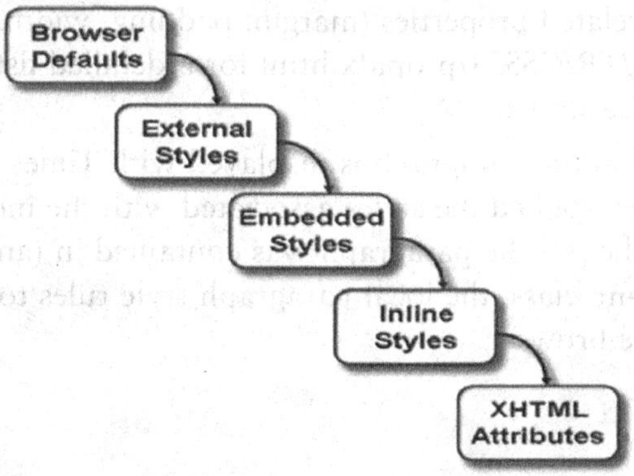

Figure 21 The "cascade" of Cascading Style Sheets

External styles can apply to multiple pages. If a Web page contains both a link to an external style sheet and embedded styles, the external styles will be applied first, and then the embedded styles will be applied. This allows a Web developer to override global external styles on selected pages.

If a Web page contains both embedded styles and inline styles, the embedded styles are applied first, and then the inline styles are applied. This allows a Web developer to override page-wide styles for particular XHTML tags or classes.

Any XHTML tag or attribute will override styles. For example, a `<strong>` tag will override corresponding font-related styles configured for an element. If no attribute or style is applied to an element, the browser default is applied. The appearance of the browser default may vary by browser and you might be disappointed with the result. Specify the properties of your text and Web page elements using CSS. Avoid depending on the browser default.

The overall CSS cascade was described above. In addition to this general cascade of CSS types, the style rules themselves follow rules of precedence. Style rules applied to more local elements (such as a paragraph) take precedence over those applied to more global elements (such as a `<div>` which contains the paragraph).

Let's look at an example of the cascade. The CSS and XHTML code is shown below. The CSS has two style rules: a rule creating a class named `content` which configures text using the Arial (or generic sans-serif) font family, and a rule configuring all paragraphs to use the Times New Roman (or generic serif) font family. The CSS follows:

```
.content { font-family:Arial, sans-serif; }
p { font-family: "Times New Roman", serif; }
```

The XHTML on the page contains a `<div>` with multiple elements, such as headings and paragraphs. Partial code follows:

```
<div class="content">
  <h1>Main Heading</h1>
  <p>This is a paragraph. Notice how the paragraph is contained in
  the div.</p>
  </div>
```

Here's how the browser would render the code:

1. The text contained in the heading is displayed with Arial font because it is part of the `<div>` assigned to the `content` class. It inherits the properties from its parent (`<div>`) class. This is an example of **inheritance**, in which certain CSS properties are passed down to elements nested within a container element, such as a `<div>` or `<body>` element. Text-related properties (font-family, color, etc.) are generally inherited but box-related properties (margin, padding, width, etc.) are not. See http://www.w3.org/TR/CSS21/propidx.html for a detailed list of CSS properties and their inheritance status.
2. The text contained in the paragraph is displayed with Times New Roman font because the browser applied the styles associated with the most local element (the paragraph). Even though the paragraph was contained in (and is considered a child of) the `content` class, the local paragraph style rules took precedence and were applied by the browser.

Don't worry if CSS and rules of precedence seem a bit overwhelming at this point. CSS definitely becomes easier with practice. You'll get a chance to practice with the "cascade" as you complete the next Hands-On Practice.

HANDS-ON PRACTICE 5

You will experiment with the "cascade" in this Hands-On Practice as you work with a Web page that uses external, embedded, and inline styles. Begin by creating an external style sheet called site.css that sets the `background-color` of the Web page to a shade of yellow (`#FFFFCC`) and the text color to black (`#000000`). The code follows:

```
body { background-color: #FFFFCC;
    color: #000000;
}
```

Next, create a Web page called mypage1.html that is associated with the file site.css and has an embedded style that sets the text color to blue. The file mypage1.html will contain two paragraphs of text. The XHTML used to code the first paragraph will not use any styles. The XHTML used to code the second paragraph will use inline styles to set the text color to red. The code for mypage1.html follows:

```
<!DOCTYPE html PUBLIC "-//W3C//DTD XHTML 1.0 Transitional//EN"
  "http://www.w3.org/TR/xhtml1/DTD/xhtml1-transitional.dtd">
<html xmlns="http://www.w3.org/1999/xhtml" lang="en" xml:lang="en">
<head>
<title>External Styles</title>
<meta http-equiv="Content-Type" content="text/html; charset=utf-8" />
  <link rel="stylesheet" href="site.css" type="text/css" />
  <style type="text/css">
  body { color: #0000FF;
  }
  </style>
</head>
<body>
<p>This paragraph applies the external and embedded styles &mdash;
note how the blue text color that is configured in the embedded
styles takes precedence over the black text color configured in the
external stylesheet.</p>
<p style="color:#FF0000">Inline styles configure this paragraph to
have red text and take precedence over the embedded and external
styles.</p>
</body>
</html>
```

Save both site.css and mypage1.html in the same folder. Display mypage1.html in a browser. Your page should look similar to the sample shown in Figure 22. The student files contain a sample solution at Chapter7/mypage1.html.

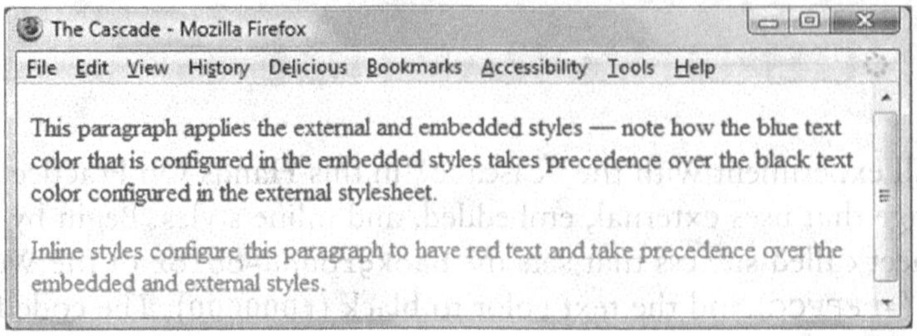

Figure 22 Mixing external, embedded, and inline styles

Take a moment to examine the mypage1.html Web page and compare it with its source code. The Web page picked up the yellow background from the external style sheet. The embedded style configured the text to be the color blue, which overrides the black text color in the external style sheet. The first paragraph in the Web page does not contain any inline styles, so it inherits the style rules in the external and embedded style sheets. The second paragraph contains an inline style of red text color—this setting overrides the corresponding external and embedded styles.

FAQ

Is there a quick way to apply the same styles to more than one XHTML tag or more than one class?

Yes, you can apply the same style rules to multiple selectors (such as XHTML elements, classes, or ids) by listing the selectors in front of the rule. The code sample below shows the `font-size` of `1em` being applied to both the paragraph and line item elements.

```
p, li { font-size: 1em; }
```

CHECKPOINT 2

1. State an advantage of using CSS to style for print.
2. Describe how to choose whether to configure an XHTML tag, create a class, or create an id when working with CSS.
3. List the following terms in the order that the properties and attributes are applied when using CSS.

   Inline styles
   External styles
   XHTML attributes
   Embedded styles

CHAPTER SUMMARY

This chapter explored a variety of Web development topics including XHTML relative hyperlinks, linking to fragment identifiers, CSS pseudo-classes, navigation list layout, three-column page layout, styling for print, styling for the mobile Web, and an overview of the "cascade" in Cascading Style Sheets.

Visit http://www.webdevfoundations.net for examples, the links listed in this chapter, and updated information.

Key Terms

active pseudo-class	inheritance	named fragment
the "cascade"	link pseudo-class	pseudo-class
focus pseudo-class	`list-style-type` property	rules of precedence
fragment identifier	`list-style-image` property	`target` attribute
hover pseudo-class	`media` attribute	visited pseudo-class

Review Questions

Multiple Choice

1. Which of the following attributes define a fragment identifier in a page?

a. `id`
b. `name`
c. `fragment`
d. `bookmark`

2. How would you link to the named fragment `#jobs` on the page employ.html from the home page of the site?

a. `<a href="employ.html#jobs">Employment Opportunities</a>`
b. `<a name="employ.html#jobs">Employment Opportunities</a>`
c. `<a link="employ.html#jobs">Employment Opportunities</a>`
d. none of the above

3. Which of the following causes an element not to display either in the browser window or on a printed page?

a. `display:block;`
b. `display: 0px;`
c. `display:none;`
d. this cannot be done with CSS

4. Which attribute below can be applied to an anchor tag to open a link in a new browser window?

a. window
b. target
c. rel
d. media

5. Which of the following is the attribute used to indicate whether the style sheet is for printing, screen display, or for mobile devices?

a. rel
b. type
c. media
d. content

6. Which of the following is true if a Web page contains both a link to an external style sheet and embedded styles?

a. embedded styles will be applied first, then the external styles will be applied
b. the inline styles will be used
c. external styles will be applied first, and then the embedded styles will be applied
d. Web page will not display

7. Which property and value is used to configure an unordered list item so that the bullet does not display?

a. `list-bullet:none;`
b. `list-style-type:none;`
c. `list-style-type:off;`
d. `list-marker:none;`

8. Which of the following pseudo-classes is triggered when the hyperlink has keyboard focus?

a. `hover`
b. `link`
c. `active`
d. `focus`

9. Which of the following properties configures an image to use as a bullet point in an unordered list?

a. `bullet-image`
b. `image-style`
c. `list-style-image`
d. `bullet-style-image`

10. Which of the following pseudo-classes is the default state for a hyperlink that has already been clicked?

a. `hover`
b. `link`
c. `onclick`
d. `visited`

Fill in the Blank

11. To indicate that an external style sheet is used to configure printing, code ____________ on the `<link>` element.

12. The ____________ is always transparent.

13. The ____________ pseudo-class can be used to modify the display of a hyperlink when a mouse passes over it.

14. ____________ is an attribute of the anchor element that can cause the new Web page to open in its own browser window.

15. The rules of ____________ describe how Cascading Style Sheet rules, XHTML attributes, and browser defaults are applied.

Apply Your Knowledge

1. Predict the Result. Draw and write a brief description of the Web page that will be created with the following XHTML code:

```
<!DOCTYPE html PUBLIC "-//W3C//DTD XHTML 1.0 Transitional//EN"
"http://www.w3.org/TR/xhtml1/DTD/xhtml1-transitional.dtd">
<html xmlns="http://www.w3.org/1999/xhtml" lang="en" xml:lang="en">
<head>
<title>Predict the Result</title>
<meta http-equiv="Content-Type" content="text/html; charset=utf-8" />
<style type="text/css">
body {  background-color: #000066;
        color: #CCCCCC;
        font-family: Arial,sans-serif;
}
h1 { background-color: #FFFFFF;
     color: #000066;
     padding: 20px;
}
.navBar li { list-style-type: none;
             display: inline;
             padding: 20px;
}
```

```
.navBar a { text-decoration: none;
            font-size: 1.2em;
}
.navBar a:link {color: #eeeeee; }
.navBar a:visited {color: #778899; }
.navBar a:hover {color: #3399CC; }
</style>
</head>
<body>
<h1>Trillium Media Design</h1>
<ul class="navBar">
  <li><a href="index.html">Home</a></li>
  <li><a href="about.html">About</a></li>
  <li><a href="services.htm">Services</a></li>
</ul>
<p>Our professional staff takes pride in its working relationship
with our clients by offering personalized services that listen to
their needs, develop their target areas, and incorporate these
items into a well presented web site that works.
</p>
</body>
</html>
```

2. **Fill in the Missing Code.** This Web page should be configured so that the left navigation column has a light pastel background color and floats on the left side of the browser window. Instead, the navigation displays with a white background color. CSS properties and values, indicated by "_" (underscore), are missing. Fill in the missing code to correct the error.

```
<!DOCTYPE html PUBLIC "-//W3C//DTD XHTML 1.0 Transitional//EN"
"http://www.w3.org/TR/xhtml1/DTD/xhtml1-transitional.dtd">
<html xmlns="http://www.w3.org/1999/xhtml" lang="en" xml:lang="en">
<head>
<title>Fill in the Missing</title>
<meta http-equiv="Content-Type" content="text/html; charset=utf-8" />
<style type="text/css">
body { background-color: #d5edb3;
       color: #000066;
       font-family: Verdana, Arial, sans-serif;
}
#leftcolumn { float: left;
              width: 120px;
}
#rightcolumn { "_": "_";
               background-color: #ffffff;
               color: #000000;
               padding: 20px;
}
</style>
</head>
```

```
<body>
<div id="leftcolumn">
  <ul>
    <li><a href="index.html">Home</a></li>
    <li><a href="spring.html">Spring</a></li>
    <li><a href="summer.html">Summer</a></li>
    <li><a href="fall.html">Fall</a></li>
    <li><a href="winter.html">Winter</a></li>
  </ul>
</div>
<div id="rightcolumn">
  <h1>Trillium Media Design</h1>
  <p>Our professional staff takes pride in its working relationship
  with our clients by offering personalized services that listen to
  their needs, develop their target areas, and incorporate these
  items into a well presented web site that works.
  </p>
</div>
</body>
</html>
```

3. **Find the Error.** The page below is intended for the navigation area to display on the right side of the browser window. What needs to be changed to make this happen?

```
<!DOCTYPE html PUBLIC "-//W3C//DTD XHTML 1.0 Transitional//EN"
"http://www.w3.org/TR/xhtml1/DTD/xhtml1-transitional.dtd">
<html xmlns="http://www.w3.org/1999/xhtml" lang="en" xml:lang="en">
<head>
<title>Find the Error</title>
<meta http-equiv="Content-Type" content="text/html; charset=utf-8" />
<style type="text/css">
body { background-color: #d5edb3;
       color: #000066;
       font-family: Verdana, Arial, sans-serif;
}
#rightcolumn { float: left;
               width: 120px;
}
#maincontent { padding: 20px 150px 20px 20px;
               background-color: #ffffff;
               color: #000000;
}
</style>
</head>
<body>
<div id="rightcolumn">
  <ul>
    <li><a href="index.html">Home</a></li>
    <li><a href="spring.html">Spring</a></li>
    <li><a href="summer.html">Summer</a></li>
```

```
      <li><a href="fall.html">Fall</a></li>
      <li><a href="winter.html">Winter</a></li>
    </ul>
  </div>
  <div id="maincontent">
    <h1>Trillium Media Design</h1>
    <p>Our professional staff takes pride in its working
    relationship with our clients by offering personalized services
    that listen to their needs, develop their target areas, and
    incorporate these items into a well presented web site that
    works.</p>
  </div>
  </body>
  </html>
```

Hands-On Exercises

1. Write the XHTML to create a fragment identifier at the beginning of a Web page designated by "top".
2. Write the XHTML to create a hyperlink to the named fragment designated by "top".
3. Write the XHTML to associate a Web page with an external style sheet named myprint.css to configure a printout.
4. Write the XHTML to associate a Web page with an external style sheet named mobile.css to configure display for handheld devices.
5. Write the CSS to configure an image file named myimage.gif as the "bullet" in an unordered list.
6. Write the CSS to configure an unordered list not to display a "bullet".
7. **Extending Hands-On Practice 3.** In Hands-On Practice 3 you created files for a version of the Door County Wildflowers Web site. These files are also available in the Chapter7 folder in the student files. In this exercise, you will create two additional content pages for the Door County Wildflowers site, called spring.html and summer.html. Be sure that all CSS is placed in an external style sheet, called mywildflower.css. (Modify pre-existing pages to use this style sheet). Rename threecolumn.html as appropriate. The following is some content to include on the new pages:

   Spring Page (spring.html):

   - Use the trillium.jpg image (see the Chapter7 folder in the student files).
   - Trillium facts: 8–18 inches tall, perennial, native plant, grows in rich moist deciduous woodlands, white flowers turn pink with age, fruit is a single red berry, protected flower species.

   Summer Page (summer.html):

   - Use the yls.jpg image (see the Chapter7 folder in the student files).
   - Yellow Lady's Slipper facts: 4–24 inches tall, perennial, native plant, grows in wet shaded deciduous woods, swamps, and bogs, an orchid, official flower of Door County.

Hand in printouts of mywildflower.css, spring.html source code (print in Notepad), summer.html source code, the browser display of spring.html, and the browser display of summer.html to your instructor.

8. **Configure Printing for Hands-On Practice 3.** Configure special printing for the threecolumn.html file created in Hands-On Practice 3. Use the threecolumn.html file from Hands-On Practice 3 as a starting point. This file is in the Chapter7 folder in the student files. Save a copy of this file as threecolumnprint.html. Modify the file so that it links to an external style sheet called threecolumn.css instead of using embedded styles. Save and test your page. Create a new style sheet, called myprint.css, which will prevent the navigation from displaying when the page is printed. Modify the threecolumnprint.html page to link to this file. Review the use of the `media` attribute on the link element. Save all files and test your page. Select File, Print Preview to test the print styles. Hand in printouts of myprint.css, threecolumn.css, threecolumnprint.html source code (print in Notepad), and the browser display of threecolumprint.html to your instructor.
9. **Modify the Design of Hands-On Practice 3.** Locate the threecolumn.html page you created in Hands-On Practice 3. This file is in the Chapter7 folder in the student files. A Web page using jello design has content in the center of the Web page with blank margins on either side. Configure the style rules for threecolumn.html to display the page in this manner. Hand in printouts of the source code (print in Notepad) and browser display for the Web page to your instructor.
10. **Practice Validating CSS.** Choose a CSS external style sheet file to validate—perhaps you have created one for your own Web site. Otherwise, use an external style sheet file that you worked with in this chapter. Use the W3C free CSS validator (http://jigsaw.w3.org/css-validator/). If your CSS does not immediately pass the validation test, modify it and test again. Repeat this process until the W3C validates your CSS code. Write a one or two paragraph summary about the validation process. Answer the following questions. Was it easy to use? Did anything surprise you? Did you encounter a number of errors or just a few? How easy was it to determine how to correct the CSS file? Would you recommend this to other students? Why or why not?

Web Research

You've been working a lot with navigation links in this chapter. There is one aspect that we did not discuss—configuring background images in navigation links using CSS, sometimes referred to as CSS Sprites. There are numerous tutorials on the Web that present this technique. Visit the following sites and choose a tutorial you find easy to read.

- http://www.cssplay.co.uk/menus/menu5teen.html
- http://www.from-the-couch.com/post.cfm/title/how-to-use-css-sprites
- http://www.alistapart.com/articles/sprites
- http://css-tricks.com/css-sprites
- http://www.smashingmagazine.com/2009/04/27/the-mystery-of-css-sprites-techniques-tools-and-tutorials
- http://www.shapeshed.com/journal/overlapping_tabbed_navigation_in_css

Choose and follow one of the tutorials listed above. Create a Web page that uses this new technique. The Web page should provide the URL of your tutorial, the name of the Web site, and a description of the new technique you discovered. Place your name in the e-mail address at the bottom of the Web page. Print the external style sheet (if you used one), the Web page source code (from Notepad), and the browser view of your Web page.

Focus On Web Design

Take a few moments and visit the CSS Zen Garden at http://www.csszengarden.com. Explore the site and note the widely different designs. What thought processes and decisions are needed as a person creates a new design for this site? Visit http://stopdesign.com/archive/2003/06/02/design-process.html, http://manisheriar.com/blog/anatomy-of-a-design-process, or http://www.bobbyvandersluis.com/articles/gardenparty.php for a behind-the-scenes look at how Web developers have approached this task. Reflect on their stories and suggestions. Write a one page (double-spaced) essay that describes ideas about the design process you'll be able to use as you begin to design Web sites for personal or professional use. Be sure to include the URL of the resources you used.

WEB SITE CASE STUDY: Navigation Links in a List

This chapter configures the main navigation in the following Web sites to utilize an unordered list.

JavaJam Coffee House

See the Chapter "XHTML Basics" for an introduction to the JavaJam Coffee House Case Study. Figure 26 in that chapter shows a site map for the JavaJam Web site. The pages were created in earlier chapters. You will use the existing Web site in the javajamcss folder (unless your instructor specifies otherwise) as a start and create a new version that configures the main navigation using an unordered list.

Hands-On Practice Case

1. Review Section 2 CSS Pseudo-classes and Links and Section 3 CSS Navigation Layout using Lists.
2. Modify the javajam.css file as needed to configure the main navigation links in an unordered list without "bullets". Also configure the main navigation links to change color when a mouse hovers over them.
3. Modify the index.html, menu.html, and music.html Web pages to display the main navigation links in an unordered list.
4. Launch a browser and test the pages in the javajamcss folder. Modify your java.css file as needed to configure your pages. Be sure to test in more than one browser.

Fish Creek Animal Hospital

See the Chapter "XHTML Basics" for an introduction to the Fish Creek Animal Hospital Case Study. Figure 30 in that chapter shows a site map for the Fish Creek Web site. The pages were created in earlier chapters. You will use the existing Web site in the fishcreekcss folder (unless your instructor specifies otherwise) as a start and create a new version that configures the main navigation and footer navigation using an unordered list.

Hands-On Practice Case

1. Review Section 3 CSS Navigation Layout using Lists.
2. Modify the fishcreek.css file as needed to configure the main navigation links and footer navigation links in an unordered list without "bullets". *Hint*: To eliminate the extra space on the left side of the fish navigation links, use CSS to configure the unordered list to have 0 margin and padding on the left side.
3. Configure the anchor selector's link, visited, and hover pseudo-classes to have light-colored text (for example, `#CCCCCC`, `#CCFFCC`, or `#FFFFFF`).
4. Modify the index.html, services.html, and askvet.html Web pages to display the main navigation links in an unordered list.
5. Modify the index.html, services.html, and askvet.html Web pages to display the footer navigation links in an unordered list.
6. Launch a browser and test the pages in the fishcreekcss folder. Modify your fishcreek.css file as needed to configure your pages. Be sure to test in more than one browser.

Pasha the Painter

See the Chapter "XHTML Basics" for an introduction to the Pasha the Painter Case Study. Figure 34 in that chapter shows a site map for the Pasha the Painter Web site. The pages were created in earlier chapters. You will use the existing Web site in the paintercss folder (unless your instructor specifies otherwise) as a start and create a new version that configures the main navigation using an unordered list.

Hands-On Practice Case

1. Review Section 2 CSS Pseudo-classes and Links and Section 3 CSS Navigation Layout using Lists.
2. Modify the painter.css file as needed to configure the main navigation links in an unordered list without "bullets". Also configure the main navigation links to change color when a mouse hovers over them. *Hint*: To eliminate the extra space on the left side of the main navigation links, use CSS to configure the unordered list to have 0 margin and padding on the left side.
3. Modify the index.html, services.html, and testimonials.html Web pages to display the main navigation links in an unordered list.
4. Launch a browser and test the pages in the paintercss folder. Modify your painter.css file as needed to configure your pages. Be sure to test in more than one browser.

Prime Properties

See the Chapter "XHTML Basics" for an introduction to the Prime Properties Case Study. Figure 38 in that chapter shows a site map for the Prime Properties Web site. The pages have already been created. You will use the existing Web site as in the primecss folder (unless your instructor specifies otherwise) as a start and create a new version that configures the main navigation and footer navigation using an unordered list.

Hands-On Practice Case

1. Review Section 2 CSS Pseudo-classes and Links and Section 3 CSS Navigation Layout using Lists.
2. Modify the prime.css file as needed to configure the main navigation links and footer navigation links in an unordered list without "bullets". Also remove the image buttons and, instead, configure CSS buttons with text that changes color when the mouse hovers over them. *Hint*: To eliminate the extra space on the left side of the main navigation links, use CSS to configure the unordered list to have 0 margin and padding on the left side.
3. Modify the index.html, financing.html, and listings.html Web pages to display the main navigation links in an unordered list.
4. Modify the index.html, financing.html, and listings.html Web pages to display the footer navigation links in an unordered list.
5. Launch a browser and test the pages in the primecss folder. Modify your prime.css file as needed to configure your pages. Be sure to test in more than one browser.

Web Project

See the Chapters "Web Design" and "Page Layout with CSS" for an introduction to the Web Project case. You will modify the main navigation and footer navigation to use an unordered list. If appropriate, also add interactivity to the main navigation area with CSS pseudo-classes.

Hands-On Practice Case

1. Review Section 2 CSS Pseudo-Classes and Links and Section 3 CSS Navigation Layout Using Lists.
2. Modify your project's external CSS file and Web page files as needed to configure the main navigation and footer navigation in an unordered list.
3. Optional: Modify your project's external style sheet to configure CSS link and hover pseudo-classes for your main navigation hyperlinks.
4. Launch a browser and test the Web pages. Modify your files as needed to configure your pages. Be sure to test in more than one browser.

Answers

Checkpoint 1

1. Organizing a Web site into folders can help increase productivity by organizing the files into file type (such as images or media), file function (Web page or script), and/or Web site section (products, services, and so on). Using folders and subfolders can be helpful when a project team (see Chapter 10) is developing a large Web site.
2. Since a navigation menu is a list of links, it is semantically correct to configure the menu using an unordered list. This technique is popular among Web developers.
3. There are a number of approaches to handle this. One approach is to create a special class and configure the pseudo-classes for use with that class. Apply this class to the navigation links. This will allow the "regular" anchor tags to use the default configuration and the navigation anchor tags (using the class) to use the special configuration. In the following example, the class intended for the navigation links is called nav.

```
.nav { border: 1px solid #cccccc;
       padding: 3px 15px;
       width: 100px;
       color: #FFFFFF;
       background-color: #006600;
       font-family: Arial, Helvetica, sans-serif;
       font-size: 110%;
       font-weight: bold;
       text-align: center;
       text-decoration: none;
}
a.nav:link     { color : #FFFFFF; }
a.nav:visited  { color : #CCCCCC; }
a.nav:hover    { color : #66CC33; }
```

   The XHTML for a navigation link is as follows:

```
<a class="nav" href="services.html">Services</a>
```

Checkpoint 2

1. The Web developer has the best of both worlds—the ability to configure both print and screen media.
2. Configure the XHTML selector if the style is expected to be applied every time that element is used. Configure an id if the style is for a specific element that is expected to occur only once on a page. Configure a class if the style is expected to be applied to a variety of different XHTML elements.
3. This follows the "cascade": external styles, embedded styles, inline styles, XHTML attributes.

Review Questions

1. a
2. a
3. c
4. b
5. c
6. c
7. b
8. d
9. c
10. d
11. `media="print"`
12. margin
13. hover
14. target
15. precedence

Tables

Chapter Objectives

In this chapter, you will learn how to ...

- Create a table on a Web page
- Apply attributes to format tables, table rows, and table cells
- Format an entire Web page within a table
- Use nested tables
- Use CSS to configure an XHTML table

Tables can be used to organize Web page content. They can also be used to provide structure and format the layout of an entire Web page. In this chapter, you will become familiar with coding XHTML tables to both organize information and format page layout. You'll configure tables using both XHTML and CSS.

From Chapter 8 of *Web Development and Design Foundations with XHTML*, Fifth Edition. Terry Felke-Morris.

1 Using Tables on Web Pages

Tables are commonly used on Web pages in two ways:

- To organize information
- To format the layout of an entire Web page

Although it is increasingly common to use CSS to configure page layout, some well-known sites, such as http://www.yankeecandle.com, http://www.league.org, and http://www.craigslist.org use the older method of XHTML tables for this function.

Overview of an XHTML Table

An XHTML table is composed of rows and columns, like a spreadsheet. Each individual table **cell** is at the intersection of a specific row and column. Each table begins with a **`<table>`** tag and ends with a `</table>` tag. There are a number of optional attributes for the `<table>` element, such as `border`, `width`, `summary`, `cellspacing`, and `cellpadding`. Each table row begins with a **`<tr>`** tag and ends with a `</tr>` tag. Each cell (table data) begins with a **`<td>`** tag and ends with a `</td>` tag. Table cells can contain text and graphics. In fact, table cells usually contain other XHTML tags such as paragraphs, headings, and tables. Be very careful to use opening and closing tags when working with tables. If you omit or misplace a tag the results are unpredictable and your page may not display at all. Figure 1 shows a sample table with three rows, four columns, and a border.

Figure 1 Table with three rows, four columns, and a border

Name	Birthday	Phone	E-mail
Jack	5/13	857-555-5555	jack04521@gmail.com
Sparky	11/28	303-555-5555	sparky@iname.com

The following is the sample XHTML code for the table shown in Figure 1:

```
<table border="1">
  <tr>
    <td>Name</td>
    <td>Birthday</td>
    <td>Phone</td>
    <td>E-mail</td>
  </tr>
  <tr>
    <td>Jack</td>
    <td>5/13</td>
    <td>857-555-5555</td>
    <td>jack04521@gmail.com</td>
  </tr>
  <tr>
    <td>Sparky</td>
    <td>11/28</td>
    <td>303-555-5555</td>
    <td>sparky@iname.com</td>
  </tr>
</table>
```

Notice how the table is described row by row. Also, each row is described cell by cell. This attention to detail is crucial to the successful use of tables.

What if you don't want a border on your table? The **`border` attribute** is optional. The table shown in Figure 1 uses a border with its width set to `1`. If you omit the `border` attribute, the table displays with no visible border. Figure 2 shows the same table with the `border` attribute omitted.

Figure 2
Table with no visible border

Name	Birthday	Phone	E-mail
Jack	5/13	857-555-5555	jack04521@gmail.com
Sparky	11/28	303-555-5555	sparky@iname.com

XHTML Table Headings

The **`<th>`**, or table heading, element can be used to distinguish column headings from table content. Figure 3 shows a table that uses the `<th>` element.

Figure 3
Using `<th>` tags on a table

Name	Birthday	Phone	E-mail
Jack	5/13	857-555-5555	jack04521@gmail.com
Sparky	11/28	303-555-5555	sparky@iname.com

The XHTML for the table shown in Figure 3 is shown below. Notice that the first row uses `<th>` instead of `<td>` tags.

```
<table border="1">
  <tr>
    <th>Name</th>
    <th>Birthday</th>
    <th>Phone</th>
    <th>E-mail</th>
  </tr>
  <tr>
    <td>Jack</td>
    <td>5/13</td>
    <td>857-555-5555</td>
    <td>jack04521@gmail.com</td>
  </tr>
  <tr>
    <td>Sparky</td>
    <td>11/28</td>
    <td>303-555-5555</td>
    <td>sparky@iname.com</td>
  </tr>
</table>
```

XHTML Table Captions

The **`<caption>`** element is often used with a data table to describe its contents. The table shown in Figure 4 uses `<caption>` tags to set the caption to Birthday List.

Figure 4
The caption for this table is Birthday List

Birthday List

Name	Birthday	Phone	E-mail
Jack	5/13	857-555-5555	jack04521@gmail.com
Sparky	11/28	303-555-5555	sparky@iname.com

The XHTML for the table follows:

```
<table border="1">
<caption>Birthday List</caption>
  <tr>
    <th>Name</th>
    <th>Birthday</th>
    <th>Phone</th>
    <th>E-mail</th>
  </tr>
  <tr>
    <td>Jack</td>
    <td>5/13</td>
    <td>857-555-5555</td>
    <td>jack04521@gmail.com</td>
  </tr>
  <tr>
    <td>Sparky</td>
    <td>11/28</td>
    <td>303-555-5555</td>
    <td>sparky@iname.com</td>
  </tr>
</table>
```

Notice how the `<caption>` element was placed after the beginning `<table>` tag but before the first `<tr>` tag.

HANDS-ON PRACTICE 1

You will work with a new version of the Trillium Web site. Create a new folder called trilliumch8 and copy the files index.html, services.html, trillium.css, trilliumbanner.jpg, and trilliumbullet.gif files from the student files Chapter8/starters folder.

Launch a text editor and open the services.html page from your trilliumch8 folder. You will modify the services page to look similar to the display shown in Figure 5. Locate the `<h2>` element. Create a table under this element with four rows and two columns. Configure the first cell in each row as a table heading. Use Figure 5 as a guide and type text in the table cells. Save your page and test it in a browser. A solution is located in the student files Chapter8/8.1 folder.

Figure 5
Table added to services.html

XHTML Table Attributes

Common `<table>` element attributes include `align`, `border`, `bordercolor`, `width`, `cellspacing`, `cellpadding`, `bgcolor`, `summary`, and `title`. The default display of rows and cells in tables can also be modified using attributes. The most commonly used attributes with the `<td>` element to configure table cells are `bgcolor`, `valign`, `rowspan`, and `colspan`. Since XHTML table attributes are widely used on the Web, it's a good idea to become familiar with them. You'll discover how to configure most of these features using CSS later in this chapter. Let's take a closer look at attributes used with `<table>` elements.

FAQ

Why doesn't my table display?

While Internet Explorer will display a table even if you forget about a closing tag here or there, other browsers such as Firefox can be very picky. Be sure to use Firefox to test pages that contain tables. Internet Explorer will often ignore a missing or misspelled tag and display your table. However, when Firefox encounters missing or unmatched table tags, it sometimes will not display parts of your Web page or display only a portion of the table.

As you read about each `<table>` element attribute, experiment with the Birthday List table. The best way to learn to write XHTML is to practice it.

The `align` Attribute. This attribute specifies the alignment of the table with the values `right`, `center`, and `left`. The table shown in Figure 6 has the `align` attribute set to `center`.

Figure 6
Centered table with `width` set to 75%

Even though it is still often used, the W3C has deprecated the use of the `align` attribute with the `<table>` tag. Later in this chapter you'll use CSS to replace the functionality of most of the table attributes—including configuring the horizontal alignment, borders, width, padding, and background color of XHTML tables.

The `border` Attribute. This attribute specifies whether and what type of visible border the table will have. The value ranges from 0 to 100, with 0 indicating that no border will be visible. The values between 1 and 100 determine the thickness of the visible border, where 1 indicates a relatively thin border and 100 indicates a very thick border. The table shown in Figure 7 has a border set to `10`.

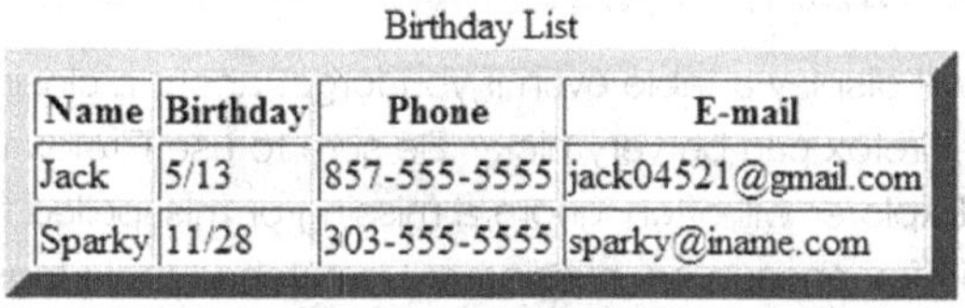

Birthday List

Name	Birthday	Phone	E-mail
Jack	5/13	857-555-5555	jack04521@gmail.com
Sparky	11/28	303-555-5555	sparky@iname.com

Figure 7
Table with a border set to `10`

The browser determines the border color and shading based on the page background color. If you want a specific color, also use the `bordercolor` attribute.

The `bordercolor` Attribute. This attribute specifies the color of the border. The values can be a color name or numeric value. See the color chart at http://webdevfoundations.net/color. The browser displays the border color as a solid color and does not shade the border when the `bordercolor` attribute is used. The bordercolor attribute is not part of the official W3C Recommendations but is included here because it is widely used and well supported by browsers. The table shown in Figure 8 has a border set to 5 and bordercolor set to a dark color.

Figure 8
Table with bordercolor set to a dark color

Birthday List

Name	Birthday	Phone	E-mail
Jack	5/13	857-555-5555	jack04521@gmail.com
Sparky	11/28	303-555-5555	sparky@iname.com

The width Attribute. This attribute specifies the width of the table in either pixels or in a percentage of the Web page. The table will stretch to fit the entire width of the page if 100% is used. If width is not specified, the browser determines the width of a particular table by calculating the width of the elements and text it contains. Use the width attribute when you want more control over your Web page. The table shown in Figure 6 is centered and has a width set to 75%. The XHTML code for the table tag is

```
<table border="1" align="center" width="75%">
```

FAQ

Which is better, specifying width by pixels or by percentage?

It depends. Keep in mind that visitors to your Web page will use monitors with different screen resolutions. If you need your table to have a fixed width that you specify, use pixels. If you'd like your table to be flexible and to resize with the browser window, use percentages. It's a good idea to test your Web pages using different screen resolutions.

The cellspacing Attribute. This attribute specifies the distance between the cells in pixels. If you omit the cellspacing attribute, the default value (usually around 2 pixels) is determined by the browser. The table shown in Figure 9 has cellspacing set to 10. The XHTML code for the <table> tag follows:

```
<table border="1" cellspacing="10">
```

Figure 9
Table with cellspacing set to 10

Birthday List

Name	Birthday	Phone	E-mail
Jack	5/13	857-555-5555	jack04521@gmail.com
Sparky	11/28	303-555-5555	sparky@iname.com

The cellpadding Attribute. This attribute specifies the distance in pixels between the cell contents and the edge of the cell. If you omit the cellpadding attribute, the default value is 1 pixel. An example with cellpadding set to 10 is shown in Figure 10. The XHTML code for the <table> tag follows:

```
<table border="1" cellpadding="10">
```

Figure 10
Table with `cellpadding` set to `10`

Birthday List

Name	Birthday	Phone	E-mail
Jack	5/13	857-555-5555	jack04521@gmail.com
Sparky	11/28	303-555-5555	sparky@iname.com

FAQ

Can I mix and match fixed widths and percentages?

Yes. The width attribute can be applied to table cells (`<td>` elements) as well as to the entire table (`<table>` element). If you are using a table to format an entire page, you might want a particular column used for navigation links to have a fixed width while the entire table uses a percentage width. As always, test your Web pages using different screen resolutions to make sure that you achieve your desired effect.

The `bgcolor` Attribute. This deprecated attribute specifies a background color for the table. The values can be a color name or numeric value. See the color chart at http://webdevfoundations.net/color. An example with a background color, no border, and `cellpadding` of 10 is shown in Figure 11. The XHTML code for the `<table>` tag follows:

```
<table border="0" bgcolor="#99CCFF" cellpadding="10">
```

Figure 11
Borderless table using `cellpadding` set to `10` along with a background color

Birthday List

Name	Birthday	Phone	E-mail
Jack	5/13	857-555-5555	jack04521@gmail.com
Sparky	11/28	303-555-5555	sparky@iname.com

Focus on Accessibility
WWW

The `summary` Attribute. This attribute specifies a summary of the table contents that can be accessed by a screen reader. The Web Accessibility Initiative (WAI) suggests using the `summary` attribute with tables containing data. For example:

```
<table border="0" width="75%" title="Birthday List"
 summary="This table contains a birthday list. Each row provides
 birthday and contact information for an individual. The columns
 contain name, birthday, phone, and e-mail address.">
```

Focus on Accessibility
WWW

The `title` Attribute. This attribute specifies a title of the table that can be accessed by a screen reader. The value of the `title` attribute is displayed by some browsers, such as Internet Explorer 5 (or later), when the mouse passes over the table area. The WAI prefers using the summary attribute or the caption element instead of the `title` attribute.

Applying Attributes to Rows and Cells

Many of the `<table>` element attributes discussed above can also be applied to `<tr>`, `<th>`, and `<td>` tags to customize the look of your table. In particular, the `bgcolor`, `align`, and `width` attributes are most often used. The following are commonly used attributes for <tr>, <th>, and <td> elements. Later in the chapter you'll use CSS to configure the background color, alignment, and width of these page areas.

The `align` Attribute. This attribute can be used to align the contents of a table row or table cell within a table. In Figure 12, the cells containing birthday information are configured to be centered by the `align` attribute on the <td> elements containing the birthday information.

Figure 12 Table with birthday information center-aligned

Birthday List

Name	Birthday	Phone	E-mail
Jack	5/13	857-555-5555	jack04521@gmail.com
Sparky	11/28	303-555-5555	sparky@iname.com

The XHTML code for the table follows:

```
<table border="1">
  <tr>
    <th>Name</th>
    <th>Birthday</th>
    <th>Phone</th>
    <th>E-mail</th>
  </tr>
  <tr>
    <td>Jack</td>
    <td align="center">5/13</td>
    <td>847-555-5555</td>
    <td>jack04521@gmail.com</td>
  </tr>
  <tr>
    <td>Sparky</td>
    <td align="center">11/28</td>
    <td>303-555-5555</td>
    <td>sparky@iname.com</td>
  </tr>
</table>
```

The `bgcolor` Attribute. This deprecated attribute can be used to apply a background color to a table row or cell. See Figure 13 for an example of applying a background color to alternating rows of a table using this attribute.

Figure 13 Table using a background color on alternate rows

Birthday List

Name	Birthday	Phone	E-mail
Jack	5/13	857-555-5555	jack04521@gmail.com
Sparky	11/28	303-555-5555	sparky@iname.com

The XHTML code for the table follows:

```
<table border="0" cellpadding="10" cellspacing="0">
  <tr bgcolor="#CCCCCC">
    <th>Name</th>
    <th>Birthday</th>
```

```
      <th>Phone</th>
      <th>E-mail</th>
    </tr>
    <tr>
      <td>Jack</td>
      <td>5/13</td>
      <td>857-555-5555</td>
      <td>jack04521@gmail.com</td>
    </tr>
    <tr bgcolor="#CCCCCC">
      <td>Sparky</td>
      <td>11/28</td>
      <td>303-555-5555</td>
      <td>sparky@iname.com</td>
    </tr>
</table>
```

FAQ

What if I want a more interesting table?

You can alter the gridlike look of a table by applying the `colspan` and `rowspan` attributes to `<td>` elements. As you get into more complex table configurations like these, be sure to sketch the table on paper before you start typing the XHTML code.

The `colspan` Attribute. This attribute specifies the number of columns that a cell will occupy. Figure 14 shows a row that spans two columns.

Figure 14
Table with a row that spans two columns

<table>
<tr><td colspan="2">This spans two column</td></tr>
<tr><td>Column 1</td><td>Column 2</td></tr>
</table>

The XHTML code for the table follows:

```
<table border="1">
  <tr>
    <td colspan="2">This spans two columns</td>
  </tr>
  <tr>
    <td>Column 1</td>
    <td>Column 2</td>
  </tr>
</table>
```

The `rowspan` Attribute. This attribute specifies the number of rows that a cell will occupy. An example of a column that spans two rows is shown in Figure 15.

Figure 15
Table with a column that spans two rows

<table>
<tr><td rowspan="2">This spans two rows</td><td>Row 1 Column 2</td></tr>
<tr><td>Row 2 Column 2</td></tr>
</table>

The XHTML code for the table follows:

```
<table border="1">
   <tr>
      <td rowspan="2">This spans two rows</td>
      <td>Row 1 Column 2</td>
   </tr>
   <tr>
      <td>Row 2 Column 2</td>
   </tr>
</table>
```

The `valign` Attribute. This attribute specifies the alignment of the text or image in the cell. The default vertical alignment is `middle`, shown in the `rowspan` example in Figure 15. Use the `valign` attribute when you need the contents of a cell to be vertically aligned at the top or bottom of a cell. Common values for the `valign` attribute are `top`, `middle`, and `bottom`. Figure 16 shows the `valign` attribute used to top align the contents of the first cell.

This spans two rows	Row 1 Column 2
	Row 2 Column 2

Figure 16
The first cell in this table uses the `valign` attribute

The XHTML code for the table follows:

```
<table border="1">
   <tr>
      <td rowspan="2" valign="top">This spans two rows</td>
      <td>Row 1 Column 2</td>
   </tr>
   <tr>
      <td>Row 2 Column 2</td>
   </tr>
</table>
```

HANDS-ON PRACTICE 2

You will continue to work with the Trillium Web site. Launch Notepad or another text editor and open the services.html page from your trilliumch8 folder. Center the table on the page with the `align="center"` attribute. Configure the width of the table to `75%`. Set the `cellpadding` to `5` and the `cellspacing` to `0`. See Figure 17 for an example.

Be sure to use the summary attribute to help provide for accessibility. Save your page and test it in a browser. Compare your work to the sample in the student files (Chapter8/8.2).

Figure 17 Sample services.html

Accessibility and Tables

Focus on Accessibility

This chapter has introduced two recommended methods to increase the accessibility of tables:

- Use <th> elements to indicate column or row headings.
- Use the `summary` attribute on the table element to provide an overview of the table contents.

If you are coding a simple data (informational) table it is sufficient to code <th> tags to indicate row or column headers. However, for more complex tables the group recommends specifically associating the table cell values with their corresponding headers. This technique uses the `id` attribute (usually in a <th> element) to identify a specific header cell and the **headers attribute** in a <td> element. Figure 18 shows a table that has been configured in this manner.

Figure 18 This informational table was coded with techniques to improve accessibility

School Attended	Years	Subject	Degree Awarded
Schaumburg High School	2005-2009	College Prep	H.S. Diploma
Harper College	2009-2010	Internet & Web Development	Web Developer Certificate

The XHTML code for the table follows:

```
<table border="1" width="75%" summary="This table lists educational
background. Each row describes educational experience at a specific
school. Columns contain school attended, years, subject, and degree
awarded.">
```

```
      <tr>
        <th id="school">School Attended</th>
        <th id="years">Years</th>
        <th id="subject">Subject</th>
        <th id="degree">Degree Awarded</th>
      </tr>
      <tr>
        <td headers="school">Schaumburg High School</td>
        <td headers="years">2005 - 2009</td>
        <td headers="subject">College Prep</td>
        <td headers="degree">H.S. Diploma</td>
      </tr>
      <tr>
        <td headers="school">Harper College</td>
        <td headers="years">2009 - 2010</td>
        <td headers="subject">Internet &amp; Web Development</td>
        <td headers="degree">Web Developer Certificate</td>
      </tr>
    </table>
```

FAQ What about the scope attribute?

The scope attribute specifies the association of table cells and table row or column headers. It is used to indicate whether a table cell is a header for a column (scope="col") or row (scope="row"). An example of the code for the table in Figure 18 that uses this attribute is shown below.

```
<table border="1" width="75%" summary="This table lists educational
background. Each row describes educational experience at a specific
school. Columns contain school attended, years, subject, and degree
awarded.">
  <tr>
    <th scope="col">School Attended</th>
    <th scope="col">Years</th>
    <th scope="col">Subject</th>
    <th scope="col">Degree Awarded</th>
  </tr>
  <tr>
    <td>Schaumburg High School</td>
    <td>2005 - 2009</td>
    <td>College Prep</td>
    <td>H.S. Diploma</td>
  </tr>
  <tr>
    <td>Harper College</td>
    <td>2009 - 2010</td>
    <td>Internet &amp; Web Development</td>
    <td>Web Developer Certificate</td>
  </tr>
  </table>
```

As you reviewed the code sample above, you may have noticed that using the **scope** attribute to provide for accessibility requires less coding than implementing the **headers** and **id** attributes. However, due to inconsistent screen reader support of the **scope** attribute, the W3C's Web Accessibility Initiative (WAI) WCAG 2.0 recommendations for coding techniques encourage the use of **headers** and **id** attributes rather than the **scope** attribute.

XHTML Table Row Groups

There are lots of configuration options when coding tables. Table rows can be put together into three types of table row groups: table head (<thead>), table body (<tbody>), and table footer (<tfoot>). This can be useful when you need to configure the areas in the table in different ways, using either attributes or CSS (see Section 3). The <tbody> tag is required if you configure a <thead> or <tfoot> area, although you can omit either the table head or table footer if you like. The code sample below (see student files Chapter8/tables/tablesections.html) configures the table shown in Figure 18 using <thead> and <tbody> groups.

```
<table border="1" width="75%" summary="This table lists educational
background. Each row describes educational experience at a specific
school. Columns contain school attended, years, subject, and degree
awarded.">
<thead>
  <tr>
    <th>School Attended</th>
    <th>Years</th>
    <th>Subject</th>
    <th>Degree Awarded</th>
  </tr>
</thead>
<tbody>
  <tr>
    <td>Schaumburg High School</td>
    <td>2005 - 2009</td>
    <td>College Prep</td>
    <td>H.S. Diploma</td>
  </tr>
  <tr>
    <td>Harper College</td>
    <td>2009 - 2010</td>
    <td>Internet &amp; Web Development</td>
    <td>Web Developer Certificate</td>
  </tr>
</tbody>
</table>
```

When you use table row groups, the <thead> and <tfoot> sections must be coded *before* the <tbody> section to pass W3C XHTML validation. See Chapter8/tables/tfoot.html for an example.

CHECKPOINT 1

1. Describe two reasons to use tables on a Web page.
2. Describe the difference between the `cellpadding` and `cellspacing` table attributes.
3. Describe one coding technique that increases the accessibility of an XHTML table.

2 XHTML—Table Page Layout

You may be wondering about the title of this section because you've been configuring page layout using CSS. While CSS **page layout** configuration is a more modern and preferred method, some current Web sites are still designed with table-based page layouts. You'll explore this coding technique in this section. Let's take a look at some well-known sites that at the time this was written use tables to format their Web pages—http://www.yankeecandle.com, http://www.league.org, and http://www.craigslist.org. As you surf the Web and analyze these and other sites, look for a Web page layout that appeals to you. View the source code by selecting View, Source from the browser menu bar (for IE7+ select Page, View Source). Examine how the page was formatted. You will find that many of the pages use tables. It is important not to copy a page, but rather to get ideas from many sources and organize them in a fresh, new way that is all your own. When designing a new Web page, it's a good idea to sketch your ideas on paper first.

Figure 19 shows a sketch of a common format consisting of a horizontal banner and three columns. Notice that the middle cell in the second row is used for spacing purposes only—to separate the navigation area from the content area. Sample XHTML code for this type of table layout follows:

```
<table border="0" width="80%">
  <tr>
    <td colspan="3"><h1>This is the banner area</h1></td>
    </tr>
    <tr>
    <td width="20%" valign="top">Place Navigation here</td>
    <td width="10"> </td>
    <td>Page content goes here</td>
    </tr>
</table>
```

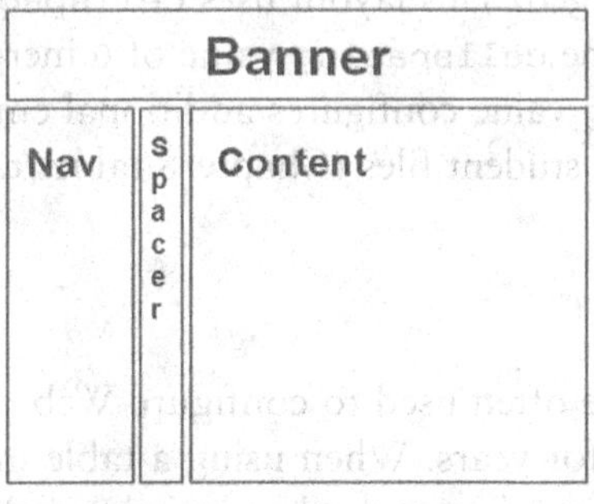

Figure 19
Using a table to format a Web page

A Web page using this type of table layout is shown in Figure 20 and can be found in the student files (Chapter8/tables/table1.html).

Figure 20
Page layout using a table

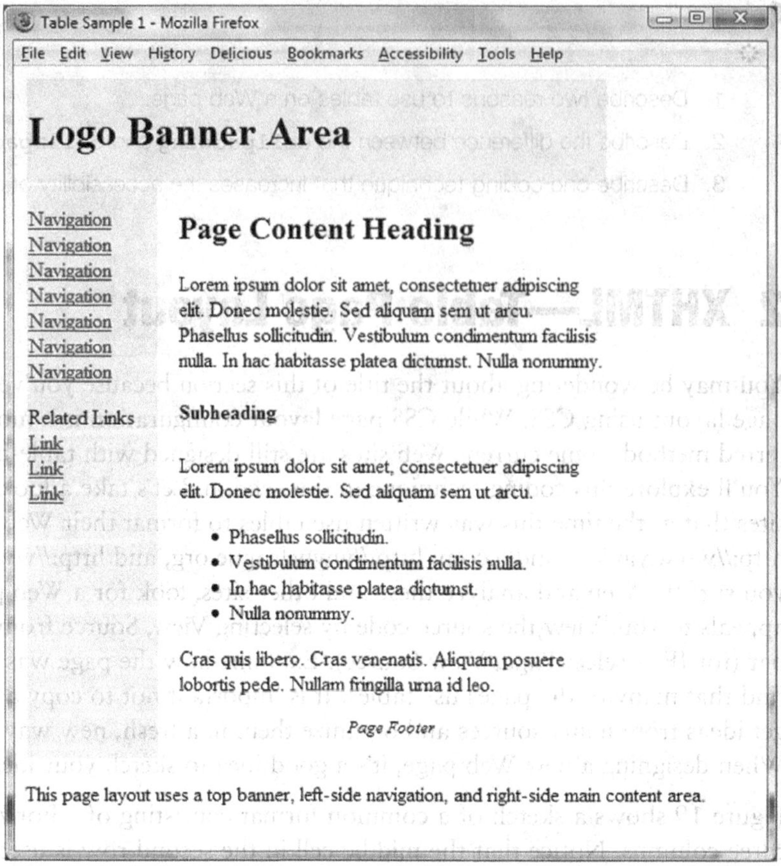

The ` ` character is coded in the table displayed by Figure 20 as a placeholder in the cell used for a spacer. Recall that ` ` is a special character that creates a non-breaking space.

The alignment of the table will be to the left by default. This can sometimes make the page look unbalanced when it is viewed with a monitor set to a higher resolution, such as 1280×1024. To prevent this display issue, use the `align` attribute (or CSS as described later in the chapter) to center the table. Assign the table a percentage width of the Web page. These techniques will cause all browsers of varying resolutions to display the table centered and extended across 80 percent of the Web page.

Figure 21 shows a similar Web page layout—only the `cellspacing` and `cellpadding` attributes on the table tag were changed. This layout uses `cellspacing` set to `0` and `cellpadding` set to `10`. Note how the `cellspacing` value of `0` merges the table cell backgrounds while the `cellpadding` value configures additional empty space around the text. Examine the source code in the student files (Chapter8/tables/table1a.html).

Accessibility and Layout Tables

Focus on Accessibility

WWW

You've become aware that tables are often used to configure Web page layouts on the Web. This technique has been used for years. When using a table in this manner it is important to understand that screen readers and other assistive technologies typically access a table in a *linear manner*—that is, they "read" the table row by row.

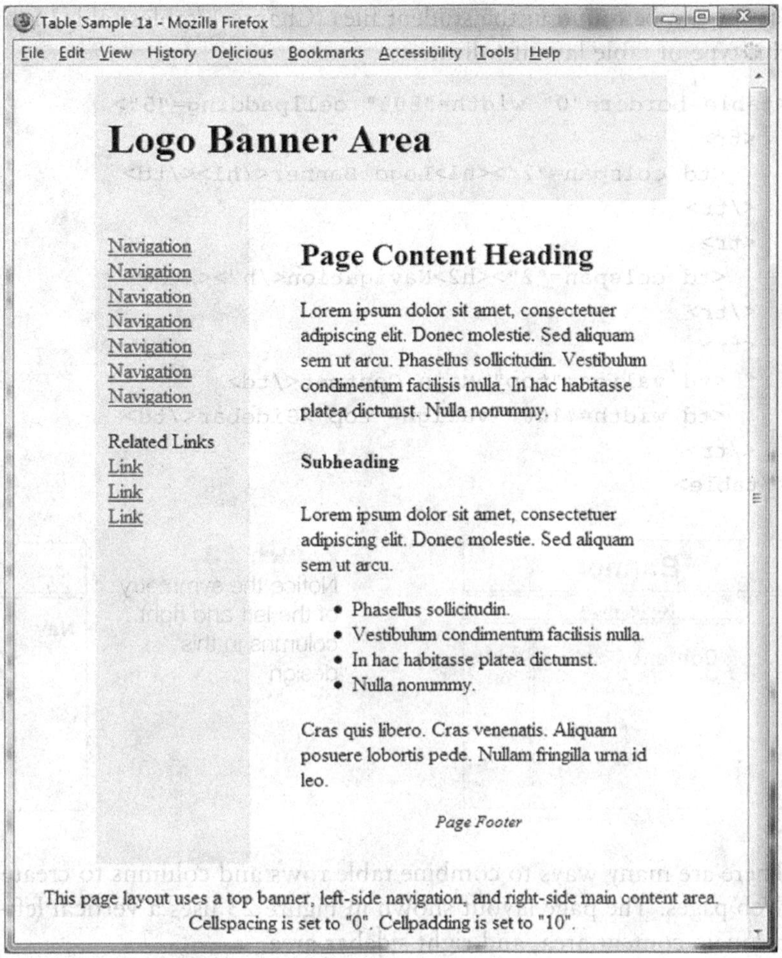

Figure 21 This table is centered and uses `cellspacing` set to 0

Review the table layout sketch shown in Figure 19. A screen reader would access the table row by row, from top to bottom. The order of the areas "read" would be: banner, navigation, spacer, and content. This would occur on each page configured in this manner. One major disadvantage of the layout shown in Figure 19 is that the navigation links would be "read" over and over as each page on the Web site is rendered.

As you explore other table layout designs in this chapter and create your own, keep in mind the way a screen reader would access the content. You may want to download a free screen reader and listen yourself! Try free trial versions of JAWS (http://www.freedomscientific.com/fs_downloads/jaws.asp) and Window-Eyes (http://www.gwmicro.com/Window-Eyes/Demo/).

More Sample Page Layout Tables

There are a variety of commonly used designs for page layout tables. This section contains examples of three commonly used page layouts to get you started using this technique.

The layout shown in Figure 22 shows banner, horizontal navigation, and two content columns. The narrower content column on the right (called a sidebar) is commonly used for advertisements or to showcase products and services offered. A page using this layout can be found in the student files (Chapter8/tables/table2.html). Sample code for this type of table layout follows:

```
<table border="0" width="80%" cellpadding="5">
  <tr>
    <td colspan="2"><h1>Logo Banner</h1></td>
  </tr>
  <tr>
    <td colspan="2"><h2>Navigation</h2></td>
  </tr>
  <tr>
    <td valign="top">Main Content</td>
    <td width="100" valign="top">Sidebar</td>
  </tr>
</table>
```

Figure 22
Horizontal navigation with right sidebar

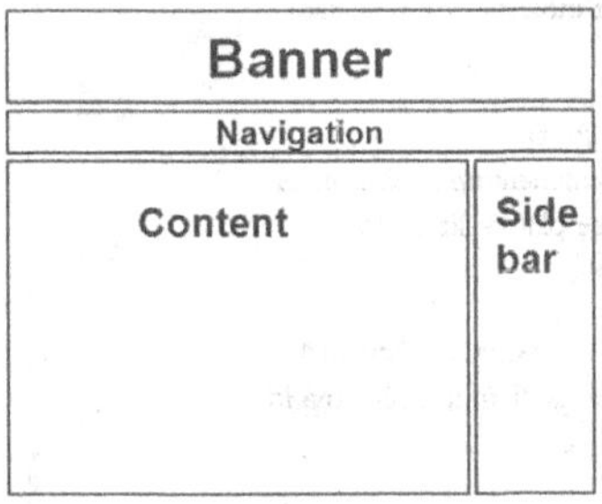

Figure 23
Notice the symmetry of the left and right columns in this design

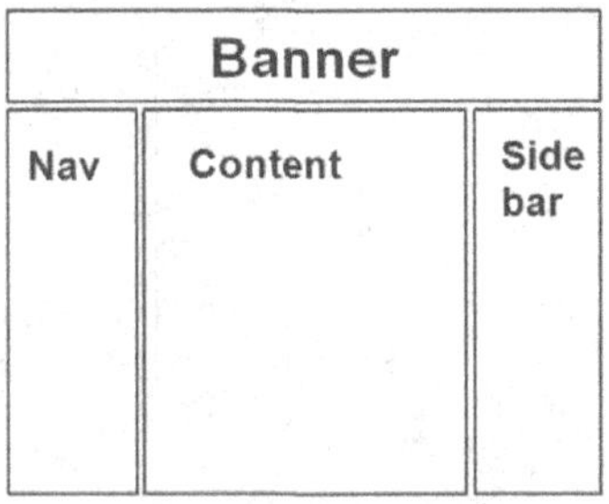

There are many ways to combine table rows and columns to create interesting, usable Web pages. The page layout shown in Figure 23 uses a vertical left-side navigation, center main content area, and right sidebar area.

The vertical navigation area allows room to display a wide variety of links and is more useful for a large site than the previous layout. A page using this layout can be found in the student files (Chapter8/tables/table3.html). Sample code follows:

```
<table border="0" width="80%" cellpadding="5">
  <tr>
    <td colspan="3"><h1>Logo Banner</h1></td>
  </tr>
  <tr>
    <td width="100" valign="top">Navigation</td>
    <td>Main Content</td>
    <td width="100" valign="top">Sidebar</td>
  </tr>
</table>
```

Flexible and Fixed Table Widths

The examples in the section above use a percentage table width of 80%. This creates a **flexible-width table** that the browser stretches to take up 80% of the browser window regardless of the screen resolution or window size. Review the table page layout examples in the student files (Chapter8/tables). In these examples, the columns used for navigation or sidebars are configured with a fixed width. The table cells used for the banner and main content are not configured with a width—this will cause the browser to stretch these cells to fill the available space. This provides a pleasing look on most browsers at most screen resolutions.

You do not have to use 80% for the percentage width. A table width set to 100% is used when you want the page to fill the entire browser window. See http://www.co.door.wi.gov for an example of a page configured in this manner.

You can also use a fixed value for a table width. This will provide a more consistent look across different browsers and platforms. Often the **fixed-width table** is centered on the page. The RedBox site, http://www.redbox.com, uses this technique with a width set to 746 pixels. The content is displayed in the center of the browser window with a balanced margin of dark red background on either side.

At this point you should have a basic understanding of the use of tables on Web pages. The best way to learn is to practice. Why not create a few experimental pages of your own?

HANDS-ON PRACTICE 3

Create a new folder called trilliumch8table and copy the contents of the Chapter4/4.5 folder found in the student files.You will create an alternate version of the home page that uses a table for the page layout. Launch Notepad or another text editor and open the index.html page from your trilliumch8table folder. Your page will look similar to the one shown in Figure 24.

Figure 24 The Trillium Home page before changes

In Notepad, you will modify this page so that it uses a table for layout. See Figure 19 for a layout sketch containing a top banner row that spans three columns and a second row with three columns: navigation area, spacer, and main content. The sample page is shown in Figure 25 (shown also in the color insert section).

Figure 25 New index.html using a table for layout

Go to the end of the chapter for a full color version of this figure

Compare it with the previous version of index.html page shown in Figure 24. The content is very similar but the pages look quite different! The table layout with vertical navigation creates visually separate areas. The page still uses the embedded style sheet.

The page content has been moved into a table. The XHTML code for the table follows:

```
<table border="0" width="80%">
  <tr>
    <td colspan="3"><h1>This is the banner area</h1></td>
  </tr>
  <tr>
    <td width="120" valign="top">Place Navigation here</td>
    <td width="10"> </td>
    <td>Page content goes here</td>
  </tr>
</table>
```

The layout of the new version of the home page is configured as follows:

- The table has `border`, `cellspacing`, and `cellpadding` set to `0`; and a width of `80%`.
- The background color on the table cell used for the banner area is set to `#d5edb3`.

- The background color on the table cell that contains the main navigation is set to `#5c743d`.
- The `summary` table attribute is set to the value `""` since the table configures the page layout.

Move the page contents into the table as indicated below:

- Replace `This is the banner area` with the logo image trilliumbanner.jpg.
- Replace `Place navigation here` with the `div` that contains the navigation images.
- Replace `Page content goes here` with the remaining code for the page. After making these modifications, save the newindex.html page and test it in a browser. Your page should look similar to the one shown in Figure 25. Compare your work to the sample in the student files (Chapter8/3/index.html).

Are you surprised at the way the content of the Web page was transformed just by using a table page layout and some color? While configuring page layout using CSS is a more modern and preferred method, some current Web sites are designed with table-based page layouts. Later on in the chapter you'll explore using CSS to configure properties of XHTML tables. In the next section, you'll get some practice coding nested tables.

Nested Tables

Recall that tables have two common uses on Web pages—to organize information and to format the page layout. Figure 26 shows a Web page that uses two tables—the school history table used in Figure 18 and the page layout table from Figure 19.

The technique used to nest a table within another is to place the interior table within a table cell (`<td>`) of the exterior table. Sample code for this type of table nesting follows. Examine the source code of the Web page shown in Figure 26 in the student files (Chapter8/tables/table4.html).

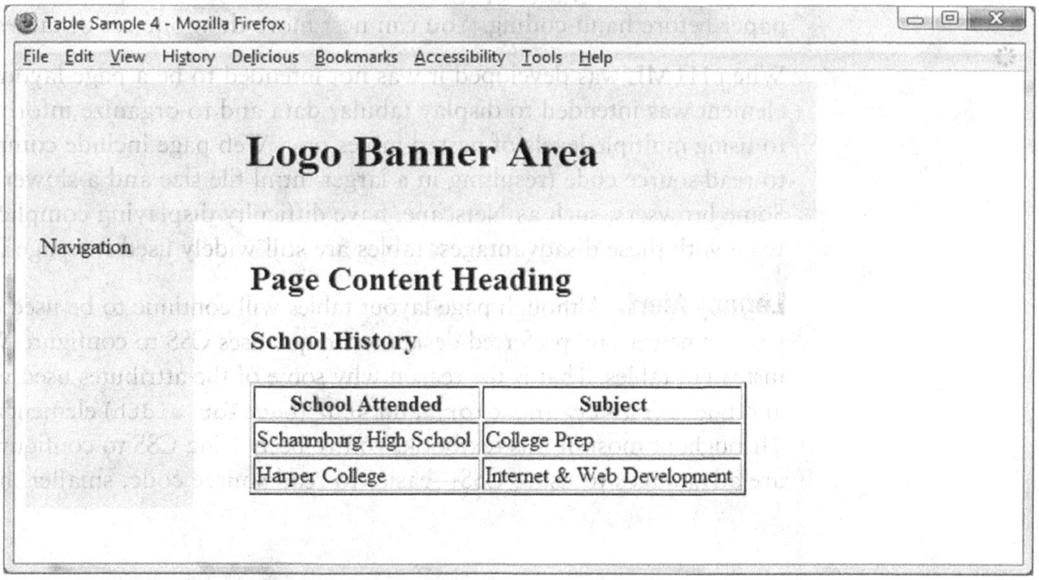

Figure 26
The school history table is nested inside the page layout table

```
<table width="80%" border="0" cellpadding="10" cellspacing="0">
  <tr bgcolor="#E6E6FA">
    <td colspan="3"><h1>Logo Banner Area</h1></td>
  </tr>
  <tr>
    <td width="100" valign="top" bgcolor="#E6E6FA">Navigation</td>
    <td width="10"> </td>
    <td valign="top"><h2>Page Content Heading</h2>
      <h3>School History</h3>
      <table width="90%" border="1" summary="This table lists
      educational background. Each row describes educational
      experience at a specific school. Columns contain school
      attended and subject.">
        <tr>
          <th>School Attended</th>
          <th>Subject</th>
        </tr>
        <tr>
          <td>Schaumburg High School</td>
          <td>College Prep</td>
        </tr>
        <tr>
          <td>Harper College</td>
          <td>Internet &amp; Web Development</td>
        </tr>
      </table>
    </td>
  </tr>
</table>
```

Use this technique when a Web page layout is configured with a table and you also want to use a table to further organize information on the page. Be careful to nest tables only when needed because **nested tables** can slow the browser display of Web pages. When designing a page with nested tables it is helpful to sketch your page on paper before hand-coding. You can nest more than one set of tables inside one another.

When HTML was developed it was not intended to be a page layout language—the table element was intended to display tabular data and to organize information. Disadvantages to using multiple levels of nested tables on a Web page include complicated and difficult to read source code (resulting in a larger .html file size and a slower browser display). Some browsers, such as Netscape, have difficulty displaying complicated nested tables. Even with these disadvantages, tables are still widely used for page layout.

Legacy Alert. Although page layout tables will continue to be used on the Web for many years, a newer and preferred design technique uses CSS to configure Web page layouts instead of tables. That is the reason why some of the attributes used with `<table>` (`align` and `bgcolor`), `<tr>` (`bgcolor`), and `<td>` (`bgcolor`, `width`) elements are deprecated. Throughout most of this textbook, you've been using CSS to configure page layout. There are advantages to using CSS—easier-to-read source code, smaller .html file sizes, and more efficient display by browsers that support this technology. Today's Web developers must be aware of both legacy page layout coding techniques (such as tables), and newer techniques such as CSS. In the next section you'll explore using CSS to configure properties associated with table elements.

CHECKPOINT 2

1. Describe a reason to use a percentage width for a table that configures a Web page layout. Provide an example of a page that uses this technique.
2. Describe a reason to use a fixed pixel width for a table that configures a Web page layout. Provide an example of a page that uses this technique.
3. True or False? Tables can be nested within other tables.

3 Using CSS to Style a Table

Earlier in this chapter you used XHTML attributes such as `align`, `width`, `cellpadding`, `cellspacing`, and `bgcolor` to configure the display of a table. In this section you'll explore using CSS to replace the functionality of these attributes. Table 1 lists corresponding CSS properties with XHTML attributes used to style tables.

Table 1 CSS properties used to style tables

XHTML Attribute	CSS Property

`align`	To align a table, configure the `width` and `margin` properties for the `table` selector.
	For example, to center a table:
	`table { width: 75%;`
	`         margin: auto; }`
	To align items within table cells:
	`text-align`

`width`	`width`
`height`	`height`
`cellpadding`	`padding`
`cellspacing`	To configure the table cells to share a common border and eliminate the default space between table cells configure the `border-collapse` property for the `table` selector. For example: `table { border-collapse: collapse; }`
`bgcolor`	`background-color`
`valign`	`vertical-align`
`border, bordercolor`	`border, border-style`
`none`	`background-image`

HANDS-ON PRACTICE 4

In this Hands-On Practice you will code CSS style rules to configure an informational table on a Web page. Create a new folder named trilliumtableCSS. Copy the following files from the Chapter8/starters folder to your trilliumtableCSS folder: myservices.html, trilliumbanner.jpg, and trilliumbullet.gif files. We'll use embedded styles for ease of editing and testing your page. Display the myservices.html file in a browser; the file should look similar to the one shown in Figure 17. Launch Notepad or another text editor and open the myservices.html file from your trilliumtableCSS folder. Locate the opening `<table>` tag as follows:

```
<table border="1" width="75%" align="center" cellpadding="5"
cellspacing="0" summary="A description of the Web site design,
interactive animation, e-commerce solution, and usability study
services provided by Trillium Media Design. Each row explains a
service with the name of the service in the first column and the
description of the service in the second column.">
```

Notice the attributes that configure the `border`, `width`, `alignment`, `cellpadding`, and `cellspacing` of the table. Delete these attributes from the `<table>` tag. You will code CSS to replace the functionality of these attributes.

1. Configure the `table` selector. Locate the embedded styles in the header section of the Web page. Add a style rule for the `table` selector in this area that configures the table to be centered, have a border, and a width of 75%.

   ```
   table { border: 1px solid #5c743d;
           width: 75%;
           margin: auto; }
   ```

   Save the file and display your page in a browser. The table area will look similar to the one shown in Figure 27. Notice that this configures a border surrounding the entire table but not surrounding each table cell.

Figure 27
The border outlines the table

Web Site Design	Whether your needs are large or small, Trillium can get your company on the Web!
Interactive Animation	Multimedia training and marketing animations are our specialty.
E-Commerce Solutions	Trillium offers quick and easy entry into the e-commerce marketplace.
Usability Studies	Trillium can assess the usability of your current site and suggest improvements.

2. Configure the `td` and `th` selectors. Add a style rule that configures a border and padding.

   ```
   td, th { border: 1px solid #5c743d;
            padding: 5px; }
   ```

   Save the file and display your page in a browser. The table area should look similar to the one shown in Figure 28. Each table cell is now outlined with a border.

Figure 28
CSS configures border and padding for each table cell

Web Site Design	Whether your needs are large or small, Trillium can get your company on the Web!
Interactive Animation	Multimedia training and marketing animations are our specialty.
E-Commerce Solutions	Trillium offers quick and easy entry into the e-commerce marketplace.
Usability Studies	Trillium can assess the usability of your current site and suggest improvements.

3. Notice the empty space between the table cells borders. The **`border-collapse` property** can be used to eliminate this space and "collapse" the table border. Add a style rule with the `border-collapse` property to the table selector as shown below.

```
table { border: 1px solid #5c743d;
        width: 75%;
        margin: auto;
        border-collapse: collapse;
}
```

Save the file and display your page in a browser. The table area should look similar to the one shown in Figure 29.

Figure 29
The CSS `border-collapse` property in action

Web Site Design	Whether your needs are large or small, Trillium can get your company on the Web!
Interactive Animation	Multimedia training and marketing animations are our specialty.
E-Commerce Solutions	Trillium offers quick and easy entry into the e-commerce marketplace.
Usability Studies	Trillium can assess the usability of your current site and suggest improvements.

4. Let's experiment with a slightly different design that uses background colors for the rows instead of cell borders. Modify the style rules, configuring the `td` and `th` selectors to have padding but without configuring a border.

```
td, th { padding:5px; }
```

Create a new class called `altrow` that sets a background color.

```
.altrow { background-color:#d5edb3; }
```

Modify the `<tr>` elements in the XHTML: assign the first and third `<tr>` elements to the `altrow` class.

Display your page in a browser. The table area should look similar to the one shown in Figure 30.

Figure 30
Rows are configured with alternating background colors

Web Site Design	Whether your needs are large or small, Trillium can get your company on the Web!
Interactive Animation	Multimedia training and marketing animations are our specialty.
E-Commerce Solutions	Trillium offers quick and easy entry into the e-commerce marketplace.
Usability Studies	Trillium can assess the usability of your current site and suggest improvements.

Notice how the background color of the alternate rows adds subtle interest to the Web page. Compare your work with the sample located in the student files (Chapter8/8.4/myservices .html). In this Hands-On Practice you configured the display of an XHTML table using CSS. You'll see this coding technique used increasingly in the future.

Recall from Section 1 that the `<thead>`, `<tbody>`, and `<tfoot>` tags designate groups of table rows. Figure 31 demonstrates the use of CSS to configure a table head, table body, and table footer with different styles.

Figure 31
CSS configures the `thead`, `tbody`, and `tfoot` selectors

Time Sheet

Day	Hours
Monday	4
Tuesday	3
Wednesday	5
Thursday	3
Friday	3
Total	**18**

The CSS styles a centered 200-pixel-wide table with a caption that is rendered in large, bold font; a table head section with a light gray (`#eaeaea`) background color; a table body section styled with slightly smaller text (`.90em`) using Arial or sans serif font; table body td selectors set to display with some left padding and a dashed bottom border; and a table footer section that has centered, bolded text and a light gray background color (`#eaeaea`). The CSS code is shown below.

```
table {  width: 200px;
         margin: auto;}
caption {  font-size: 2em;
           font-weight: bold;}
thead {  background-color: #eaeaea;}
tbody {  font-family: Arial, sans-serif;
         font-size:.90em;}
tbody td { border-bottom: 1px #000033 dashed;
           padding-left: 25px;}
tfoot {  background-color: #eaeaea;
         font-weight: bold;
         text-align: center;}
```

The XHTML code for the table follows.

```
<table summary="This table presents a time sheet. Rows contain days
of the week and the total hours. Columns contain days and hours.">
<caption>Time Sheet</caption>
<thead>
  <tr>
    <th id="day">Day</th>
    <th id="hours">Hours</th>
  </tr>
</thead>
<tfoot>
  <tr>
    <td headers="day">Total</td>
    <td headers="hours">18</td>
  </tr>
</tfoot>
<tbody>
    <tr>
      <td headers="day">Monday</td>
      <td headers="hours">4</td>
    </tr>
    <tr>
      <td headers="day">Tuesday</td>
      <td headers="hours">3</td>
    </tr>
    <tr>
      <td headers="day">Wednesday</td>
      <td headers="hours">5</td>
    </tr>
    <tr>
      <td headers="day">Thursday</td>
      <td headers="hours">3</td>
    </tr>
    <tr>
      <td headers="day">Friday</td>
      <td headers="hours">3</td>
    </tr>
  </tbody>
</table>
```

The example above demonstrates the power of CSS in styling documents. The <td> tags within each table row group selector (<thead>, <tbody>, and <tfoot>) inherited the font styles configured for their parent group selector. Notice how a descendent selector configures padding and border only for <td> tags that are contained within (actually, "children of") the <tbody> element. A file with the code shown above is located in the student files (Chapter8/tables/tfoot.html). Take a few moments to explore the Web page code and display the page in a browser.

FAQ

Is there a way to create a "table-like" page layout with CSS?

Yes; if you'd like to explore using CSS to style table-like layouts on Web pages, check out the CSS **`display`** property. The CSS **`display`** property configures if and how an element is displayed. You've already worked with **`display:none`**, **`display:block`**, and **`display:inline`**. Internet Explorer 8 was the last major browser to add support for the **`display:table`** property values. Rachel Andrew's article, *Everything You Know About CSS Is Wrong*, at http://www.digital-web.com/articles/everything_you_know_about_CSS_Is_wrong, encourages developers to embrace the **`display:table`** coding methods. Be aware that this technique is still quite limited. For example, there is no built-in mechanism to emulate the **`rowspan`** or **`colspan`** attribute in XHTML tables. However, this is in the works with the CSS3 draft recommendation at http://www.w3.org/Style/CSS/current-work, which includes new CSS specifications for working with multicolumn layouts and grid positioning.

CHAPTER SUMMARY

This chapter introduces both the XHTML techniques used to code tables to organize information and configure page layout and the CSS properties that configure the display of tables on Web pages. As you use these skills to design Web pages, keep in mind that while you'll see many examples of table page layout on the Web, configuring page layout with CSS is the preferred method.

Visit the Web site http://www.webdevfoundations.net for examples, the links listed in this chapter, and updated information.

Key Terms

<caption>
<table>
<tbody>
<td>
<tfoot>
<th>
<thead>
<tr>
align attribute
border attribute
border-collapse property
cell
cellpadding attribute
cellspacing attribute
colspan attribute
fixed-width table
flexible-width table
headers attribute
nested tables
rowspan attribute
scope attribute
summary attribute
title attribute
vertical-align property
valign attribute

Review Questions

Multiple Choice

1. Which XHTML attribute specifies the distance between the edges of each cell?
   a. cellpad
   b. cellpadding
   c. cellspacing
   d. cellborder

2. Which XHTML attribute specifies the distance between the cell text and the cell border?
   a. cellpad
   b. cellpadding
   c. cellspacing
   d. cellborder

3. Which XHTML tag pair is used to group rows in the footer of a table?
   a. <footer> </footer>
   b. <tr> </tr>
   c. <tfoot> </tfoot>
   d. none of the above

4. Which XHTML element uses a border attribute to display a table with a border?
   a. <td>
   b. <tr>
   c. <table>
   d. <tableborder>

5. Which XHTML tag pair is used to specify table headings?
   a. <td> </td>
   b. <th> </th>
   c. <head> </head>
   d. <tr> </tr>

6. Which XHTML attribute specifies the background color of a table?
   a. `background`
   b. `bgcolor`
   c. `background-color`
   d. `none of the above`
7. Which XHTML tag pair is used to begin and end a table row?
   a. `<td> </td>`
   b. `<tr> </tr>`
   c. `<table> </table>`
   d. none of the above
8. Which of the following are common uses of tables on Web pages?
   a. configuring the layout of an entire page
   b. organizing information
   c. forming hyperlinks
   d. both a and b
9. Which CSS property specifies the background color of a table?
   a. `background`
   b. `bgcolor`
   c. `background-color`
   d. none of the above

Fill in the Blank

10. The CSS ____________________ property can be used to configure the color and width of a table border.
11. The ____________________ attribute specifies the vertical alignment of the contents of a cell in a table.
12. A table with a width set to 600 pixels will look ____________________ on a monitor with resolution set to 640×480 than on a monitor with resolution set to 1024×768.
13. ____________________ is an attribute of the <table> element that provides accessibility.
14. ____________________ is a CSS property that can be used to configure the padding of table cells.

Short Answer

15. Explain why it is a good practice to use CSS to configure page layout instead of an XHTML table.

Apply Your Knowledge

1. **Predict the Result.** Draw and write a brief description of the Web page that will be created with the following XHTML code:

```
<!DOCTYPE html PUBLIC "-//W3C//DTD XHTML 1.0 Transitional//EN"
  "http://www.w3.org/TR/xhtml1/DTD/xhtml1-transitional.dtd">
<html xmlns="http://www.w3.org/1999/xhtml" lang="en" xml:lang="en">
<head>
<title>Predict the Result</title>
<meta http-equiv="Content-Type" content="text/html; charset=utf-8" />
</head>
<body>
  <table border="0" bgcolor="#cccccc" width="80%">
    <tr>
      <td bgcolor="#0000FF" colspan="3">
      <h1>Trillium Media Design</h1>
      </td>
    </tr>
```

```
            <tr>
               <td width="150">
                  <p>Home<br /><a href="about.html">About</a><br />
                  <a href="services.html">Services</a><br />
                  <a href="products.html">Products</a></p>
               </td>
               <td> 
               </td>
               <td>
                  <p>More than just another web development firm, Trillium
Media Design strives to celebrate creativity and the efficient
flow of information.</p>
                  <p> We aren&#39;t satisfied until every site we build is
the best in its class.</p>
               </td>
            </tr>
         </table>
</body>
</html>
```

2. **Fill in the Missing Code.** This Web page should have a table with a background color of #cccccc and a border. Some CSS properties and values, indicated by `"_"`, are missing. Fill in the missing code.

```
<!DOCTYPE html PUBLIC "-//W3C//DTD XHTML 1.0 Transitional//EN"
  "http://www.w3.org/TR/xhtml1/DTD/xhtml1-transitional.dtd">
<html xmlns="http://www.w3.org/1999/xhtml" lang="en" xml:lang="en">
<head>
<title>CircleSoft Web Design</title>
<meta http-equiv="Content-Type" content="text/html; charset=utf-8" />
<style type="text/css">
table { "_":"_";
        "_":"_";
}
</style>
</head>
<body>
<h1>CircleSoft Web Design</h1>
<table>
   <caption>Contact Information</caption>
   <tr>
      <th>Name</th>
      <th>Phone</th>
   </tr>
   <tr>
      <td>Mike Circle</td>
      <td>920-555-5555</td>
   </tr>
</table>
</body>
</html>
```

3. **Find the Error.** Why doesn't the table information display in the order it was coded?

```
<!DOCTYPE html PUBLIC "-//W3C//DTD XHTML 1.0 Transitional//EN"
  "http://www.w3.org/TR/xhtml1/DTD/xhtml1-transitional.dtd">
<html xmlns="http://www.w3.org/1999/xhtml" lang="en" xml:lang="en">
<head>
<title>CircleSoft Web Design</title>
<meta http-equiv="Content-Type" content="text/html; charset=utf-8" />
</head>
<body>
<h1>CircleSoft Web Design</h1>
<table>
  <caption>Contact Information</caption>
  <tr>
    <th>Name</th>
    <th>Phone</th>
  </tr>
  <tr>
    <tr>Mike Circle</td>
    <td>920-555-5555</td>
  </tr>
</table>
</body>
</html>
```

Hands-On Exercises

1. Write the XHTML for a two-column table that contains the names of your friends and their birthdays. The first row of the table should span two columns and contain the following heading: Birthday List. Include at least two people in your table.
2. Write the XHTML for a three-column table to describe the courses you are taking this semester. The columns should contain the course number, course name, and instructor name. The first row of the table should use `th` tags and contain descriptive headings for the columns. Use the table row grouping tags `<thead>` and `<tbody>` in your table.
3. Write the XHTML for table with three rows, two columns and no border. The cell in the first column of each row will contain one of the following terms: HTML, XML, and XHTML. The corresponding cell in the second column of each row will contain a definition of the term. Configure alternating rows to use the background color `#CCCCCC`.
4. Use CSS to configure a table that has a border around both the entire table and the table cells. Write the XHTML to create a table with three rows and two columns. The cell in the first column of each row will contain one of the following terms: HTML, XML, and XHTML. The corresponding cell in the second column of each row will contain a definition of the term.
5. Think of one of your favorite quotes by someone you admire. Write the XHTML code for a table to display the person's name in a table heading, their quote in a paragraph, and an absolute link to a Web site about them.

6. Modify the table you created in Hands-On Exercise 5 to be centered on the page, use a background color of #CCCC99, and display text in Arial or the browser default sans-serif font. Configure this table using CSS.

7. Create a Web page about your favorite movie that uses a two-column table containing details about the movie. Use CSS to style the table border and background color. Include the following in the table:

    - Title of the movie
    - Director or producer
    - Leading actor
    - Leading actress
    - Rating (R, PG-13, PG, G, NR)
    - A brief description of the movie
    - An absolute link to a review about the movie

    Place an e-mail link to yourself on the Web page. Save the page as movie8.html. Hand in printouts of the source code (print in Notepad) and the browser display of your page to your instructor.

8. Create a Web page that uses a table and describes two organizations that perform work related to Internet/Web standards and guidelines. Place the information in a table that comprises at least three columns and three rows. Include links to the Web site of each organization. Place an e-mail link to yourself on the Web page. Save the page as organization.html. Hand in printouts of both the source code (print in Notepad) and the browser display of your page to your instructor.

9. Create a Web page about your favorite music CD that uses a four-column table. The column headings should be as follows:

    - **Group:** Place the name of the group and the names of its principal members in this column.
    - **Tracks:** List the title of each music track or song.
    - **Year:** List the year the CD was recorded.
    - **Links:** Place at least two absolute links to sites about the group in this column.

    Include an e-mail link to yourself on the Web page. Save the page as band8.html. Hand in printouts of both the source code (print in Notepad) and the browser display of your page to your instructor.

10. Create a Web page about your favorite recipe. Organize the ingredients and directions in a single table. Use two columns for the ingredients. Use a row that spans two columns to contain the instructions for creating your culinary delight. Save the page as recipe8.html. Hand in printouts of both the source code (print in Notepad) and the browser display of your page to your instructor.

Web Research

Search the Web and find a Web page configured with one or more XHTML tables. Print the browser view of the page. Print out the source code of the Web page. (*Hint*: To print the source code, display the page using Internet Explorer, and select Page, View Source. Notepad will launch and display the page. Select File and Print.) On the printout, highlight or circle the tags related to tables. On a separate sheet of paper create some XHTML notes by listing the tags and attributes related to tables found on your sample page, along with a brief description of their purpose. Hand in the browser view of the page, source code printout, and your XHTML notes page to your instructor.

Focus on Web Design

Good artists view and analyze many paintings. Good writers read and evaluate many books. Similarly, good Web designers view and scrutinize many Web pages. Surf the Web and find two Web pages, one that is appealing to you and one that is unappealing to you. Print out each page. Create a Web page that answers the following questions for each of your examples:

a. What is the URL of the Web site?
b. Does this page use tables? If so, for what purpose—page layout, organization of information, or another reason?
c. Does this page use CSS? If so, for what purpose—page layout, text and color configuration, or another reason?
d. Is this page appealing or unappealing? List three reasons for your answer.
e. If this page is unappealing, what would you do to improve it?

Open your file in Notepad and print the source code for the page. Display your page in a browser and print the page. Hand in both printouts to your instructor.

WEB SITE CASE STUDY: Using Tables

This chapter incorporates an XHTML table in the following case study Web sites.

JavaJam Coffee House

See the Chapter "XHTML Basics" for an introduction to the JavaJam Coffee House Case Study. Figure 26 in that chapter shows a site map for JavaJam. The pages were created in earlier chapters. You will use the existing Web site in the javajamcss folder (unless your instructor specifies otherwise) for this case study. You will modify the menu page (menu.html) to display information in an XHTML table. You will use CSS to style the table. You have two tasks:

1. Add style rules to the javajam.css file that will configure the new table.
2. Modify the menu.html page to use a table to display information. Refer to Figure 32.

Figure 32
Menu page with table

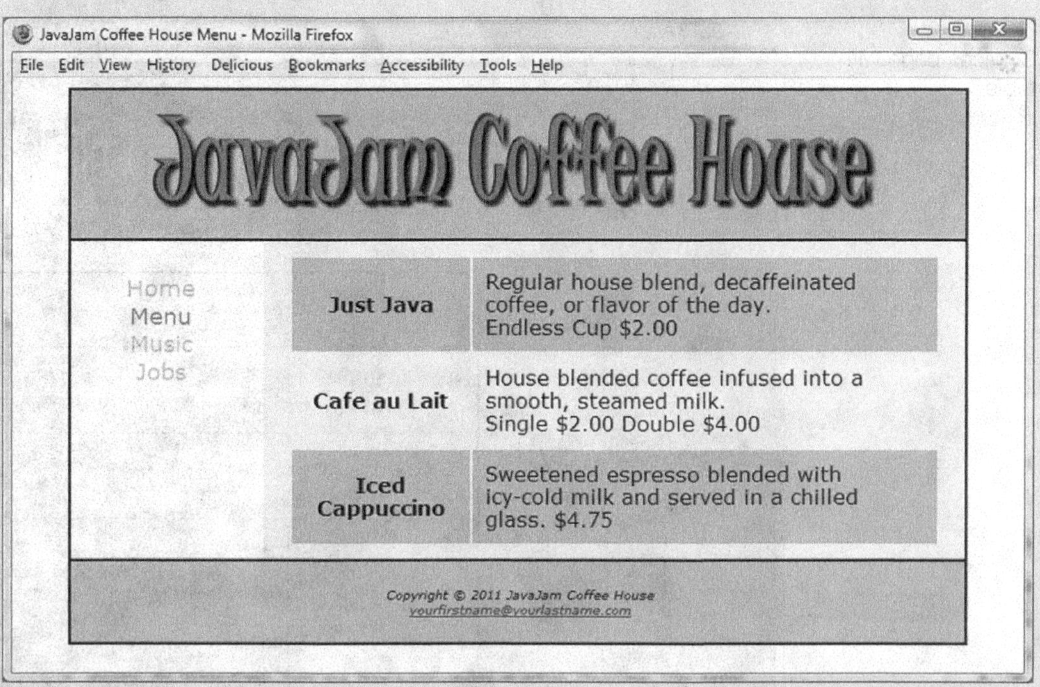

Hands-On Practice Case

1. **Configure the CSS.** Modify the external style sheet, javajam.css. Review Figure 32 and note the menu descriptions, which are coded in an XHTML table. Add style rules to the javajam.css external style sheet to configure a table that is centered, `td` and `th` selectors with 10 pixels of padding, and displays a background color of `#ccaa66` in alternate rows (use a class). Save the javajam.css file.
2. **Modify the Menu Page.** Edit the Menu file (menu.html) in Notepad. The menu descriptions are configured with a definition list. Replace the definition list with a table that has three rows and two columns. Use `<th>` and `<td>` elements where appropriate.

Save your page and test it in a browser. If the page does not display as you intended, review your work, validate the CSS, validate the XHTML, modify as needed, and test again.

Fish Creek Animal Hospital

See the Chapter "XHTML Basics" for an introduction to the Fish Creek Animal Hospital Case Study. Figure 30 in that chapter shows a site map for Fish Creek. The pages were created in earlier chapters. You will use the existing Web site in the fishcreekcss folder (unless your instructor specifies otherwise). You will modify the services page (services.html) to display information in an XHTML table. You will use CSS to style the table. You have two tasks:

1. Add style rules to the fishcreek.css file that will configure the new table.
2. Modify the Services page (services.html) to use a table to display information. Refer to Figure 33.

Figure 33
Services page with table

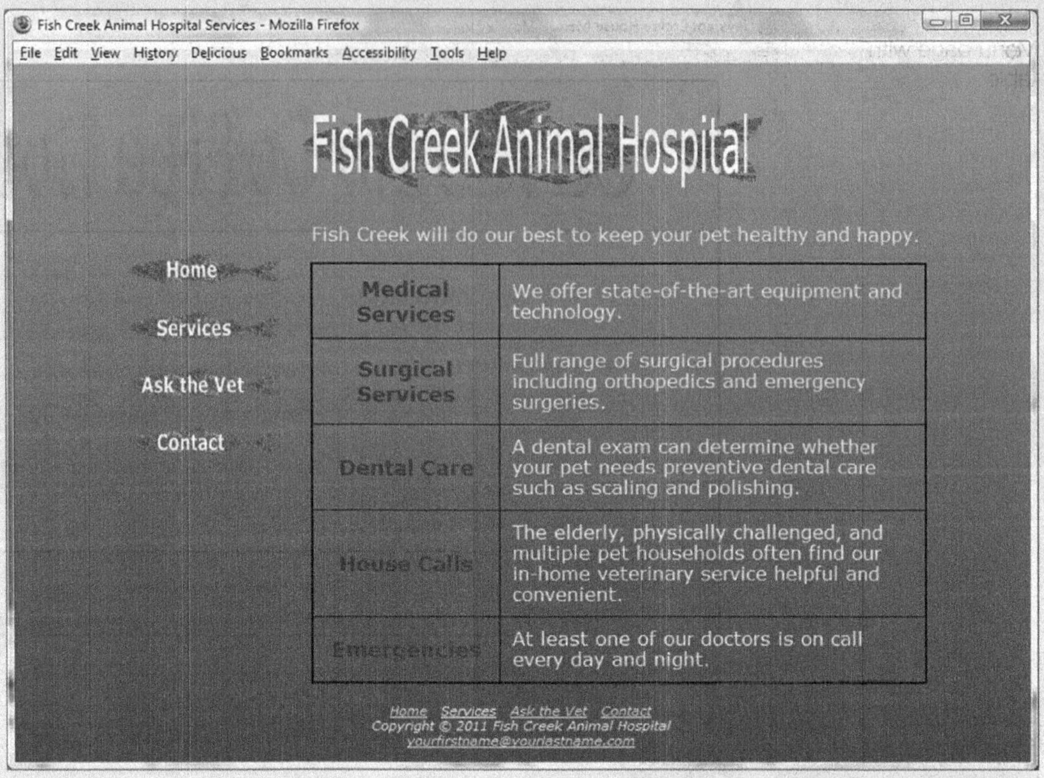

Hands-On Practice Case

1. **Configure the CSS.** Modify the external style sheet, fishcreek.css. Review Figure 33 and note the services descriptions, which are coded in an XHTML table. Add style rules to the fishcreek.css external style sheet as indicated:
   a. Configure a table that has a solid, dark blue, 2 pixel border.
   b. Configure the borders in the table to collapse.
   c. Configure `td` and `th` selectors with 10 pixels of padding and a solid, dark blue, 1 pixel border.

Save the fishcreek.css file.

2. **Modify the Services Page.** Edit the Services file (services.html) in Notepad. The services descriptions are configured with an unordered list. Replace the unordered list with a table that has five rows and two columns. Use `<th>` and `<td>` elements where appropriate. *Hint*: Assign the `<th>` element to the category class.

Save your page and test it in a browser.

If the page does not display as you intended, review your work, validate the CSS, validate the XHTML, modify as needed, and test again.

Pasha the Painter

See the Chapter "XHTML Basics" for an introduction to the Pasha the Painter Case Study. Figure 34 in that chapter shows a site map for Pasha the Painter. The pages were created in earlier chapters. You will use the existing Web site in the paintercss folder

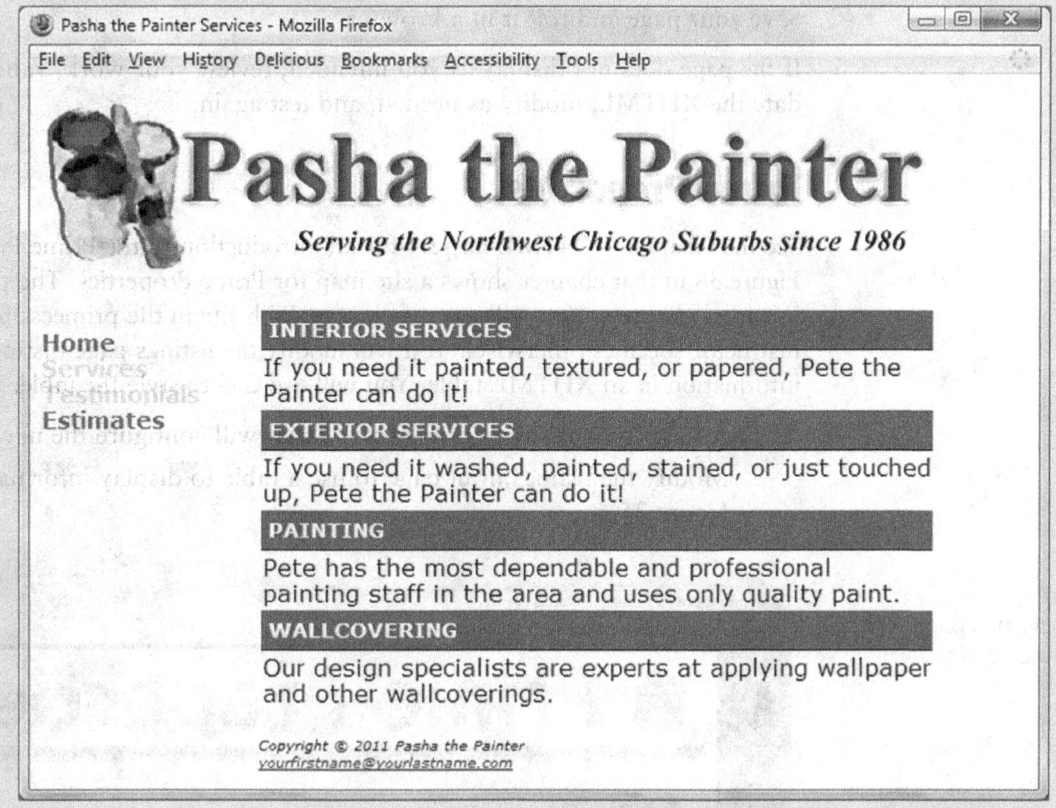

Figure 34 Services page with table

(unless your instructor specifies otherwise). You will modify the services page (services.html) to display information in an XHTML table. You will use CSS to style the table. You have two tasks:

1. Add style rules to the painter.css file that will configure the new table.
2. Modify the services.html file to use a table to display information. Refer to Figure 34.

Hands-On Practice Case

1. **Configure the CSS.** Modify the external style sheet, painter.css. Review Figure 34 and note the services descriptions, which are coded in an XHTML table. Add a style rule to the painter.css external style sheet that configures a class named `service`. The `service` class has a background color (`#336633`), text color (`#ffffff`), Verdana or sans-serif font typeface, bold font, font size of .90em, 5 pixels of padding, uppercase text (use text-transform), and a solid, black, 1 pixel bottom border. Save the painter.css file.
2. **Modify the Services Page.** Edit the services file (services.html) in Notepad. The names of the services are contained in `<h3>` elements. The descriptions of the services are contained within `<span>` tags assigned to the category class. You will modify the code to display the services information using a table that has eight rows and one column with each service name and each service description is in its own row. Each table row (`<tr>` tag pair) contains one `<td>` tag pair. As you code the table, remove the h3 tags and span tags. Assign the `<td>` elements that contain the service names to the service class.

Save your page and test it in a browser.

If the page does not display as you intended, review your work, validate the CSS, validate the XHTML, modify as needed, and test again.

Prime Properties

See the Chapter "XHTML Basics" for an introduction to the Prime Properties Case Study. Figure 38 in that chapter shows a site map for Prime Properties. The pages were created in earlier chapters. You will use the existing Web site in the primecss folder (unless your instructor specifies otherwise). You will modify the listings page (listings.html) to display information in an XHTML table. You will use CSS to style the table. You have two tasks:

1. Add style rules to the prime.css file that will configure the new table.
2. Modify the listings.html page to use a table to display information. Refer to Figure 35.

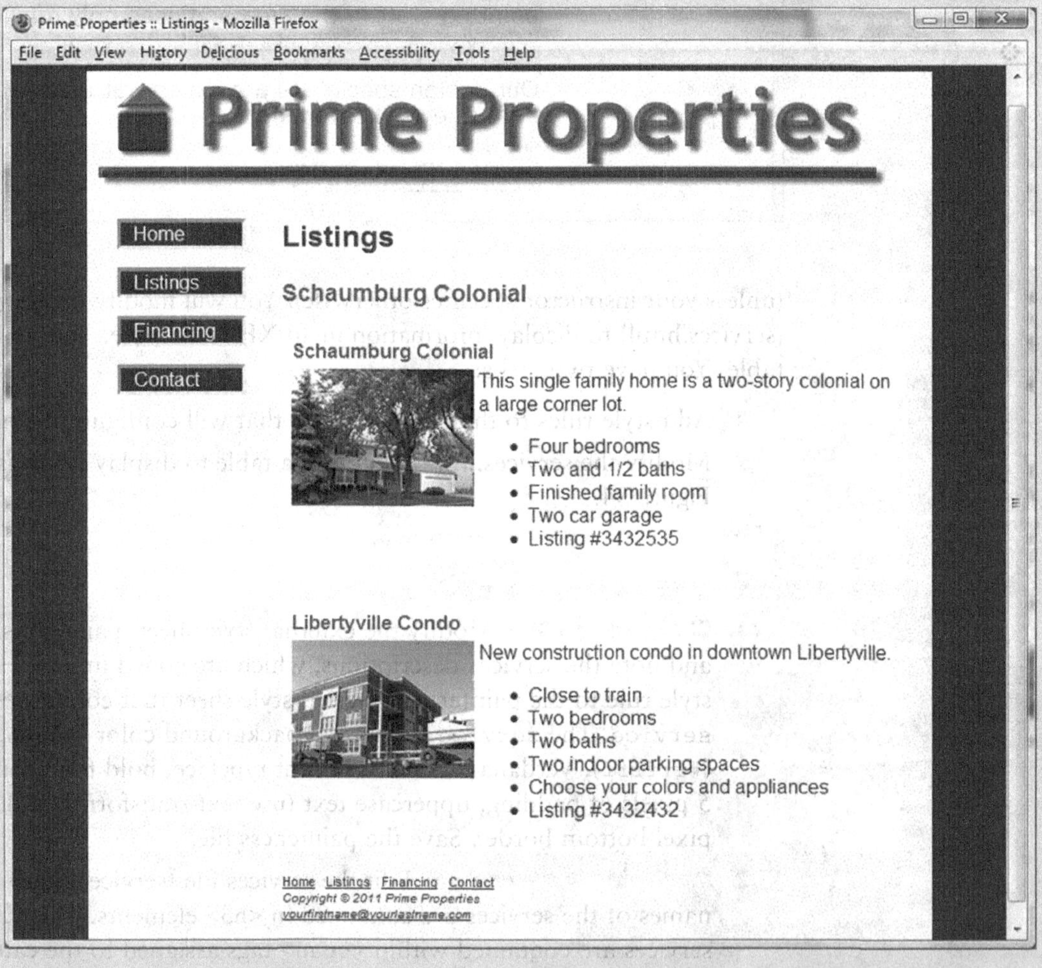

Figure 35
Listings page with tables

Hands-On Practice Case

1. **Configure the CSS.** Modify the external style sheet, prime.css. Review Figure 35 and note the property listing information, which is coded in two XHTML tables. Add style rules to the prime.css external style sheet to configure the following:
   a. A table with a background color (`#ffffff`) and 5 pixels of padding
   b. A `th` selector with left-aligned text in a green color (`#006600`)
   c. A `td` selector that is aligned vertically to the top
   Save the prime.css file.
2. **Modify the Listings Page.** Edit the Listings file (listings.html) in Notepad. The listings information currently uses the `<h4>`, image, paragraph and unordered lists elements. You will reconfigure this area with two tables—one for each real estate listing. Each table will have two rows. Refer to Figure 35. The first row in each table consists of one table cell that spans two columns—containing the real estate listing name. The second row in each table consists of two table cells. The first table cell in this row contains the image (remove the `floatleft` class from the image element). The second table cell contains the paragraph and unordered list.

Save your page and test it in a browser.

If the page does not display as you intended, review your work, validate the CSS, validate the XHTML, modify as needed, and test again.

Web Project

See the Chapters "Web Design" and "Page Layout with CSS" for an introduction to the Web Project case. You will modify the design of one of the pages to display information in an XHTML table. Use CSS to style the table.

Hands-On Practice Case

1. Choose one of your project Web pages to modify. Sketch a design of the table you plan to create. Decide on borders, background color, padding, alignments, and so on.
2. Modify your project's external CSS file (project.css) to configure the table (and table cells) as needed.
3. Update your chosen Web page and add the XHTML code for a table.

Save and test the page. Modify both the Web page and the project.css file as needed. Test and modify until you have achieved the look you want.

Answers

Checkpoint 1

1. Tables are often used to organize information and to format an entire Web page.
2. The `cellspacing` attribute configures the amount of empty space between the cells in a table. The `cellpadding` attribute configures the amount of empty space between the information contained within the cells and the edges of the cells.
3. There are a number of coding techniques that improve the accessibility of a table. These include the `summary` attribute, the `title` attribute, and configuring headers for columns or rows.

Checkpoint 2

1. Web site visitors use monitors with different resolutions. A Web page layout configured with a table using a percentage width is flexible. Examples will vary.
2. A Web page layout configured with a table using a fixed width will appear consistent when displayed on monitors with different resolutions. Often these pages are centered in the browser window. Examples will vary.
3. True. Tables can be nested within other tables. Nested tables are often used to organize information on a Web page document with a page layout configured by a table.

Review Questions

1. c
2. b
3. c
4. c
5. b
6. b
7. b
8. d
9. c
10. `border`
11. `valign`
12. larger
13. `summary` or `title`
14. `padding`
15. Although XHTML tables are still often used to configure page layout, CSS is a more modern and preferred method to configure page layout. Advantages of CSS include ease of maintenance and smaller Web page files (due to less XHTML code).

APPENDIX

XHTML Reference

XHTML uses the tags and attributes of HTML along with the syntax of XML. For the most part, you will use the same tags and attributes in HTML and XHTML; the major change is the syntax and additional restrictions in XHTML. This section provides an introduction to XML syntax and a detailed list of XHTML tags and attributes.

You will notice that a number of XHTML elements and attributes are deprecated, which means that they are currently supported but will be removed from the language in the future. Most of the deprecated elements relate to presentation features such as alignment text configuration. The W3C recommends using CSS to replace the functionality of the deprecated components. This section will be helpful as a reference as you design Web pages. It contains five major areas:

- XML Syntax
- General XHTML 1.0 Syntax Guidelines
- Basic Tags
- Header Section Tags
- Body Section Tags

1 XML Syntax

An XML document must be well formed. A well-formed document is a document that adheres to the syntax rules of the language. Here are the key syntax rules of XML:

- XML is case-sensitive.
- An XML document must contain one or more elements.
- All XML elements must have an opening tag and a closing tag. All tags are enclosed in angle brackets.

- All XML elements must be properly nested. Nesting is the use of one or more elements inside other elements. The most recently opened element must be the next one closed.
- All attribute values in XML must be contained in quotes.
- All XML documents must begin with a statement declaring it to be an XML document. The XML Declaration is shown below:

```
<?xml version="1.0" encoding="UTF-8"?>
```

While this technique is preferred by the W3C, the meta tag is more commonly used. The reason is that there are incompatibility and display issues when the XML declaration is used with some browsers (such as certain versions of Internet Explorer).

- All XML documents must have opening and closing tags that form the root element within which all other elements in the document are contained. The <html> and </html> tags serve this purpose for Web page documents.

2 General XHTML Syntax Guidelines

Since XHTML uses the syntax of XML, it must follow the XML syntax rules. The following guidelines specify examples of how this is accomplished when using XHTML:

1. All XHTML elements (the tags and their attributes) should be lowercase.
2. The <head> and <body> tags are required.
3. The <title> tag is the first tag in the header section.
4. All container tags must use their opening and closing tags.
5. All self-contained tags (sometimes called empty elements) must be properly closed. For example, use <hr /> instead of <hr>.
6. All attribute values should be contained in quotation marks.
7. All attributes should have values. For example, use

```
<input type="checkbox" checked="checked" name="IE" id="IE"
value="yes" />
```

instead of

```
<input type="checkbox" checked name="IE" value="yes" >.
```

8. Tags should not overlap, they should be properly nested. For example, use

```
<strong><em>This is important</em></strong>
```

instead of

```
<strong><em>This is important</strong></em>.
```

9. The following tag-specific nesting restrictions apply:
   - A <form> tag cannot contain another <form> tag.
   - An <a> tag cannot contain another <a> tag.
   - A <pre> tag cannot contain any of the following tags: <img />, <object>, <big>, <small>, <sub>, or <sup>.
10. Formatting should be configured with style sheets and the <font> tag should be avoided.
11. The name attribute is deprecated in XHTML 1.0 as applied to bookmarks and named fragment identifiers. This has the greatest effect on <a> and <map> tags.

XHTML uses the `id` attribute to configure bookmarks and named fragment identifiers.

12. The Web page document should declare the character encoding. The W3C recommends that the Web page code begin with an XML declaration as follows:

```
<?xml version="1.0" encoding="UTF-8"?>
```

However, in practice, some browsers (such as Internet Explorer 6) experience display issues when a Web page includes an XML declaration. So, the workaround (which still passes W3C XHTML validation) is to indicate the character encoding with a `meta` tag in the header section as shown below:

```
<meta http-equiv="Content-Type" content="text/html; charset=utf-8" />
```

13. If provided, the XML declaration should be followed with a Document Type Definition (DTD). Otherwise, the document should begin with a DTD. There are three DTDs: strict, transitional, and frameset. The strict DTD is not usually used by commercial Web sites because it requires the exclusive use of CSS and does not allow deprecated elements. Use the transitional DTD for most XHTML Web page documents. Use the `Frameset DTD` for Web page documents that describe a frameset. For more information see Table 1.

Table 1 XHTML document type definitions

DTD	Description
XHTML 1.0 Transitional	`<!DOCTYPE html PUBLIC "-//W3C//DTD XHTML 1.0 Transitional//EN" "http://www.w3.org/TR/xhtml1/DTD/xhtml1-transitional.dtd">` This is the least strict specification for XHTML 1.0. It allows the use of both CSS and traditional formatting instructions such as fonts. This DTD is used for most of the coding in this text.
XHTML 1.0 Strict	`<!DOCTYPE html PUBLIC "-//W3C//DTD XHTML 1.0 Strict//EN" "http://www.w3.org/TR/xhtml1/DTD/xhtml1- Strict.dtd">` Requires exclusive use of CSS. Does not allow any deprecated elements.
XHTML 1.0 Frameset	`<!DOCTYPE html PUBLIC "-//W3C//DTD XHTML 1.0 Frameset//EN" "http://www.w3.org/TR/xhtml1/DTD/xhtml1-frameset.dtd">` Required for pages using XHTML frames.

Note: In the Description column of this table, the number one (1) is set bold where it might otherwise be confused with the letter "el."

14. The root element (immediately after the DTD) must be an `<html>` tag that refers to the XML namespace and indicates the language, as shown in the following example:

```
<html xmlns="http://www.w3.org/1999/xhtml" lang="en" xml:lang="en">
```

3 Basic Tags

The XML Declaration

```
<?xml version="1.0" encoding="UTF-8"?>
```

This XML declaration indicates that the document is based on the XML 1.0 standard. It also indicates that the character encoding (the internal representation of letters, numbers, and symbols) used by this document is UTF-8, a form of Unicode. This XML declaration is recommended by the W3C to be the first line in a Web page document. However, in practice, this line is omitted and, instead, a `meta` tag that indicates character encoding is typically coded in the header section of the Web page.

The DOCTYPE (DTD) Tag

The DOCTYPE or DTD tag identifies the markup language used in a document. Three DTDs are valid in XHTML. They are listed in Table 1.

The <html> Tag

```
<html></html>
```

The `<html>` tag contains the code that describes the Web page document. The tag also describes the location of the documentation for the elements being used (called the XML namespace or `xmlns`). This additional information is added to the `<html>` tag in the form of an `xmlns` attribute. The `xmlns` attribute points to the URL of the XHTML namespace used in the document, the standard "http://www.w3.org/1999/xhtml." Optionally, you can add attributes to specify the language of the document (for example, English is "en," German is "de") to assist the interpreting of page content by search engines and screen readers. The lang and `xml:lang` attributes are used for this purpose. See http://www.loc.gov/standards/iso639-2/php/English_list.php for a list of language codes. The `<html>` tag is the first tag in a Web page after the DOCTYPE tag. For example:

```
<!DOCTYPE html PUBLIC "-//W3C//DTD XHTML 1.0 Transitional//EN"
  "http://www.w3.org/TR/xhtml1/DTD/xhtml1-transitional.dtd">
<html xmlns="http://www.w3.org/1999/xhtml" lang="en" xml:lang="en">
  ... the rest of your web page goes here ...
</html>
```

The <head> Tag

```
<head></head>
```

The `<head>` tag is required and encloses the header area of a Web page document. The main purpose of the header area is to describe the document. The header usually contains `<title>` and `meta` tags. It may also contain JavaScript code and CSS.

The <body> Tag

```
<body></body>
```

The `<body>` tag is required and contains the body area of a Web page document—the part of the document that is displayed in the browser window. It can contain many different types of XHTML tags along with text and JavaScript.

4 Header Section Tags

The <title> Tag

```
<title></title>
```

The `<title>` tag contains the title of the page, which displays in the browser's title bar. This tag must be the first tag in the header section.

The <meta /> Tag

```
<meta http-equiv="Content-Type" content="text/html; charset=utf-8" />
<meta name="keywords" content="a list of words that describe your site" />
<meta name="description" content="a brief description of your site" />
```

The self-contained `meta` tag has various purposes. The `Content-Type` `meta` tag declares the character encoding scheme used. Some `meta` tags such as keywords and description tags may be used by search engines.

The <link /> Tag

```
<link />
```

The self-contained `<link />` tag associates a Web page with an external style sheet. Table 2 shows `<link />` tag attributes and their values.

Table 2 `<link />` tag attributes

Attribute	Values	Usage
`href`	URL of the external stylesheet (.css file)	Identifies which style sheet is being used.
`rel`	`"stylesheet"`	Indicates the link is a style sheet.
`type`	`"text/css"`	Indicates the MIME type of the style sheet file.
`media`	`"print"`, `"screen"`, `"handheld"`, `"aural"`	Indicates the display medium (print, browser, mobile device, screen reader, and so on) intended for display.

The <base /> Tag

```
<base />
```

The self-contained `<base />` tag is most often used with pages displayed within a frameset. It sets a default target frame for the hyperlinks on the page. The attribute of target is set to the name of the window or frame in which all the hyperlinks should display.

The <script> Tag

```
<script></script>
```

This `<script>` tag configures a Web page to use client-side scripting. Table 3 shows `<script>` tag attributes and their values.

Table 3 `<script>` tag attributes

Attribute	Value	Usage
`language`	Usually `"javascript"`	Optional. Indicates the scripting language being used.
`src`	URL of the external script file, usually a .js file	Identifies the external file containing scripting commands. If this attribute is omitted, the script is contained between the `<script>` tags.
`type`	`"text/javascript"`	Indicates the MIME type of the JavaScript file.

An example follows:

```
<script type="text/javascript">
   ... JavaScript statements go here ...
</script>
```

When strict XML syntax is applied, any JavaScript statements should be surrounded by character data (CDATA) statements. This tells the XML parser to ignore the JavaScript statements as arbitrary character data and not to process them. The syntax is as follows:

```
<script type="text/javascript">
<![CDATA[
   ... JavaScript statements go here ...
]]>
</script>
```

Unfortunately, this generates a JavaScript error in many current browsers; therefore, it's not commonly used. This problem can be circumvented by accessing external JavaScript files, as shown here:

```
<script type="text/javascript" src="script.js">
</script>
```

In this case all the JavaScript statements are located in the external file called script.js and no CDATA statement is needed.

The <style> Tag

`<style></style>`

The `<style>` tag configures a Web page to use an embedded style sheet. The attribute of type is set to "text/css" and indicates the MIME type of the style sheet.

5 Body Section Tags

The <body> Tag

`<body></body>`

The <body> tag contains the body area of a Web page document. <body> tag attributes configure properties for the Web page. Table 4 shows <body> tag attributes and their values.

Table 4 <body> tag attributes

Attribute	Value	Usage
`alink`	A valid color; the W3C	Configures the color of the active hyperlinks recommends hexadecimal colors on the Web page. (Deprecated)
`background`	The name of an image file	Places a background image on the Web page. If the image is smaller than the page, it will be repeated, or tiled, on the browser window. (Deprecated)
`bgcolor`	A valid color; the W3C recommends hexadecimal colors	Configures the background color of the Web page. (Deprecated)
`bgproperties`	`"fixed"`	When combined with a background image, this property will fix the background image, simulating the effect of a watermark as the Web page visitor scrolls down the page. Only used by Internet Explorer.
`leftmargin`	Number of pixels	Configures the left margin of the Web page. Only used by Internet Explorer.
`link`	A valid color; the W3C recommends hexadecimal colors	Configures the color of the hyperlinks on the Web page. (Deprecated)
`marginheight`	Number of pixels	Configures the top margin of the Web page. Only used by Netscape.
`marginwidth`	Number of pixels	Configures the left margin of the Web page. Only used by Netscape.
`text`	A valid color; the W3C recommends hexadecimal colors	Configures the color of the text on the Web page. (Deprecated)
`topmargin`	Number of pixels	Configures the top margin of the Web page. Only used by Internet Explorer.
`vlink`	A valid color; the W3C recommends hexadecimal colors	Configures the color of the visited hyperlinks on the Web page. (Deprecated)

6 Core XHTML Attributes

The following attributes may be used to configure most XHTML elements. These attributes are valid in all elements except `base`, `head`, `html`, `meta`, `param`, `script`, `style`, and `title` elements.

The `class` Attribute

The `class` attribute is used to associate an XHTML element with a class that has been defined using CSS. The value should be a class name found in either the embedded or external CSS property rules utilized by the Web page.

The id Attribute

The id attribute uniquely identifies an element on a Web page. If is often used to associate an XHTML element with a unique id (unique to the particular page) that has been defined using CSS. The value should be an id name found in either the embedded or external CSS property rules utilized by the Web page.

The style Attribute

The style attribute configures inline style rules for an XHTML element. The value should be a valid CSS property rule.

The title Attribute

The title attribute configures a description of an XHTML element and its contents. This text may be accessed using a screen reader. Some browsers may display this text in a tooltip or in a summary list of elements (such as hyperlinks) found on a Web page.

7 Block-Level Elements

The <p> Tag

```
<p></p>
```

The <p> tag creates a paragraph of text. The browser displays the paragraph with a blank line before and after the paragraph. The align attribute specifies the horizontal placement of the paragraph. The values for the align attribute are "left" (default), "right", and "center". The align attribute is deprecated.

The Heading Tag

```
<h1></h1>
```

The heading tag contains headings and important points. The text contained between the heading tags is placed on its own line. There are six levels of heading tags: <h1> (the largest), <h2>, <h3>, <h4>, <h5>, and <h6> (the smallest).

The align attribute specifies the horizontal placement of the heading. The values for the align attribute are "left" (default), "right", and "center". The align attribute is deprecated.

The <blockquote> Tag

```
<blockquote></blockquote>
```

The <blockquote> tag indents text. The text contained between <blockquote> tags is indented from the left and right margins.

The <div> Tag

```
<div></div>
```

The <div> tag creates a separate division, or logical area, on a Web page. A line break occurs before and after the division.

The `align` attribute specifies the horizontal placement of the division. The values for the `align` attribute are `"left"` (default), `"right"`, and `"center"`. The `align` attribute is deprecated.

The <span> Tag

```
<span></span>
```

The <span> tag creates a separate logical area on a Web page without any line breaks before or after. It is often used to apply styles.

8 List Tags

The <dl> Tag

```
<dl></dl>
```

The <dl> tag creates a definition list. It is used with the <dt> and <dd> tags.

The <dt> Tag

```
<dt></dt>
```

The <dt> tag identifies a defined term in a definition list.

The <dd> Tag

```
<dd></dd>
```

The <dd> tag identifies a definition in a definition list.

The <ol> Tag

```
<ol></ol>
```

The <ol> tag creates an ordered, or numbered, list. It is used together with <li> tags. The deprecated `type` attribute on the <ol> tag configures the type of ordering. The deprecated `start` attribute configures the beginning value displayed in the list. Table 5 shows <ol> tag attributes and their values.

Table 5 <ol> tag attributes

Attribute	Value	Symbol
type	"1"	Numerals (the default)
	"A"	Uppercase letters
	"a"	Lowercase letters
	"I"	Roman numerals
	"i"	Lowercase Roman numerals
start	Numeric	Configures the beginning value displayed in the list

The <li> Tag

```
<li></li>
```

The <li> tag identifies a line item in ordered and unordered lists.

The <ul> Tag

```
<ul></ul>
```

The <ul> tag creates an unordered, or bulleted, list. It is used together with <li> tags. The deprecated `type` attribute on the <ul> tag configures the bullet displayed. Table 6 shows the <ul> tag attribute and its values.

Table 6 <ul> tag attribute

Attribute	Value
type	"disc" (default)
	"circle"
	"square"

9 Text-Level Elements

The <font> Tag

```
<font></font>
```

The <font> tag formats text. This tag is deprecated. Table 7 shows the <font> tag attributes and their values.

Table 7 <font> tag attributes

Attribute	Value	Usage
color	A valid color; the W3C recommends hexadecimal colors	Used to configure the color of the text. (Deprecated)
face	A valid font name such as "Arial" or "Times New Roman"	Configures the font type of the text. If the font specified is not installed, the text will display in the browser's default font. (Deprecated)
size	Absolute size: integers ranging from "1" to "7"; the default is "3"	Configures the size of the text. "1" is the smallest, "7" is the largest. (Deprecated)

Logical Style Tags

Logical style tags specify the logical use and format of the text. Table 8 shows logical style tags and examples of their use.

Table 8 Logical style tags

Element	Example	Usage
`<strong>`	**strong** text	Causes text to be emphasized or to stand out from surrounding text. Usually displays in bold.
`<em>`	*emphasized* text	Causes text to be emphasized in relation to other text on the page. Usually displayed in italic.
`<cite>`	*cite* text	Identifies a citation or reference.
`<code>`	`code` text	Identifies program code samples. Usually a fixed-space font.
`<dfn>`	*dfn* text	Identifies a definition of a word or term.
`<kbd>`	`kbd` text	Identifies user text to be typed. Usually a fixed-space font.
`<samp>`	*`samp`* text	Shows program sample output.
`<var>`	*var* text	Identifies and displays a variable or program output.

Physical Style Tags

Physical style tags configure the physical display of the text. Table 9 shows physical style tags and examples of their use.

Table 9 Physical style tags

Element	Example	Usage
`<b>`	**bold** text	Displays text in bold.
`<i>`	*emphasized* text	Displays text in italic.
`<big>`	big text	Displays text in larger than normal size.
`<small>`	small text	Displays text in smaller than normal size.
`<sub>`	subscript text	Displays in smaller text, below the baseline.
`<sup>`	superscript text	Displays text in smaller text, above the baseline.
`<strike>`	~~strikethrough~~ text	Displays text with a line through it. (Deprecated)
`<tt>`	`teletype` text	Displays text in teletype or fixed-space font.
`<u>`	underlined text	Displays text underlined; avoid using this because underlined text can be confused with hyperlinks. (Deprecated)

The
 Tag

```
<br />
```

The self-contained `<br />` tag creates a line break. The next XHTML element is displayed on a new line. The values for the deprecated `clear` attribute on the `<br />` tag are shown in Table 10.

Table 10 `clear` attribute values

`clear` Attribute Value	Result
`"left"`	The next element is displayed on a new line under any existing element blocking the left margin.
`"right"`	The next element is displayed on a new line after any existing element blocking the right margin.
`"all"`	The next element is displayed on a new line after any existing element blocking either the left or right margin.

The <hr /> Tag

```
<hr />
```

The self-contained `<hr />` tag creates a horizontal line on the Web page. Table 11 shows the `<hr>` tag attributes and their values.

Table 11 `<hr>` tag attributes

Attribute	Value	Usage

`align`	`"left"`
	`"center"` (default)
	`"right"`
		Aligns the horizontal line on the Web page. (Deprecated)

`color`	A valid color; the W3C recommends hexadecimal colors	Configures the color of the horizontal line. Not in W3C Recommendation; originally only used by Internet Explorer.
`noshade`	`"noshade"`	Prevents a shadow from being displayed under the line. (Deprecated)
`size`	Number of pixels	Configures the height of the line. (Deprecated)
`width`	Numeric percentage	Configures a line that takes up a percentage of the width of the browser window. `<hr width="50%" />` (Deprecated)
	Number of pixels	Configures a line that takes up an exact number of pixels in the browser window. `<hr width="60" />` (Deprecated)

The <a> Tag

```
<a></a>
```

The `<a>` tag, called the anchor tag, creates a hyperlink. The text or image contained between the `<a>` tags is displayed by the browser as a hyperlink, as in the following example:

```
<a href="http://mycompany.com">My Company</a>
```

This creates an absolute hyperlink to the URL specified, in this case mycompany.com.

```
<a href="mypage.html">My Page</a>
```

This creates a relative link to the named file, in this case mypage.html.

```
<a href="mypage.html" title="My Page">My Page</a>
```

This creates a relative link to the named file, in this case mypage.html. It will also display the text associated with the `title` attribute in a tooltip alongside the link when the visitor places the mouse pointer on the link.

```
<a href="mailto:me@me.com">Send e-mail to me@me.com</a>
```

This creates a link to an e-mail address. If a default mail program is configured for the browser, the mail program will launch and get ready to send a message with the e-mail address provided, in this case me@me.com.

```
<a href="#top">Back to Top</a>
```

This creates an internal link to a bookmark or named fragment on the same Web page, in this case to the named fragment called `top`.

```
<a id="top"></a>
```

This identifies a portion of a Web page as a bookmark or named fragment, in this case, the named fragment called `top`.

```
<a target="_parent" href="mypage.html">My Page</a>
```

This configures the window that the hyperlinked page will display in. The `target` attribute is most often used with frames. Table 12 lists <a> tag attributes and their values. Values for the `target` attribute are shown in Table 13.

Table 12 <a> tag attributes

Attribute	Value	Usage
`accesskey`	A character on the keyboard that appears in the hyperlink description	Configures a hot key to activate the link without using the mouse pointer.
`href`	A valid URL or Web page file name	Creates a link to the named page or named element.
`id`	Text name, alphanumeric, beginning with a letter, no spaces	Uniquely identifies the element. This value can be used by a corresponding hyperlink.
`name`	Text name, alphanumeric, beginning with a letter, no spaces	Identifies the element. This value is used by a corresponding <a> tag with an `href` attribute. This is deprecated in XHTML but is included for backward compatibility.
`tabindex`	Numeric	Changes the order of the links accessed by pressing the Tab key. Default order is the order the links are placed on the page.
`target`	See Table 13	Configures the window that displays the link. The default is the current window. See Table 13.
`title`	A brief text description	Configures a brief text description that will display in some browsers when a mouse pointer is placed over the link.

Table 13 `target` attribute values

`target` Attribute Value	Result
`"_top"`	Typically used to bust out of a frameset and display the hyperlinked page in the entire browser window.
`"_blank"`	Opens a new browser window to display the hyperlinked page.
`"_parent"`	Displays the hyperlinked page in the frame that contains the current frameset.
`"_self"`	Displays the hyperlinked page in the same window.
A valid frame name value configured in a frameset page	Displays the hyperlinked page in the named window.

10 Graphic Tags

The <img /> Tag

```
<img src="image.gif" />
```

The self-contained `<img />` tag, called the image tag, displays an image file. Table 14 shows `<img />` tag attributes and their values.

Table 14 `<img />` tag attributes

Attribute	Value	Usage
`align`	`"left"` (default), `"right"`, `"top"`, `"texttop"`, `"middle"`, `"absmiddle"`, `"bottom"`	Aligns the image relative to the text on the page. (Deprecated)
`alt`	A brief text description of the image	Provides accessibility to visitors unable to view the image.
`border`	Number of pixels for image border; `"0"` prevents the border from being displayed	Configures the border area on the image. (Deprecated)
`height`	Number of pixels	Configures the height of the image.
`hspace`	Number of pixels	Configures space to the left and right of the image. (Deprecated)
`id`	Text name, alphanumeric, beginning with a letter, no spaces	Identifies the image. The value must be unique and not used for other `id` values on the same XHTML document.
`longdesc`	URL of Web page with detailed description of the image	Used by some assistive technologies to provide accessibility to the information in the image.
`name`	Text name, alphanumeric, beginning with a letter, no spaces	Names the image so that it can be easily accessed by client-side scripting languages such as JavaScript. This attribute is deprecated in XHTML but is used to provide backward compatibility with browsers that support HTML.
`src`	Name of the image file (required)	Configures the image file to be displayed.
`title`	A brief text description	Configures a text description that will display when the visitor moves the mouse pointer over the image.

Table 14 `<img />` tag attributes (*continued*)

Attribute	Value	Usage
usemap	The text name of an image map	Corresponds to the name value on the associated <map> tag.
vspace	Number of pixels	Configures space above and below the image. (Deprecated)
width	Number of pixels	Configures the width of the image.

The <map> Tag

`<map></map>`

The <map> tag is a container tag that identifies the beginning and the end of an image map. The name attribute is used to associate the <map> tag with its corresponding <img /> tag. The <img /> tag is configured with the usemap attribute to indicate which map to use. Table 15 shows <map> tag attributes and their values.

Table 15 `<map>` tag attributes

Attribute	Value	Usage
id	Text name, alphanumeric, beginning with a letter, no spaces	Identifies the map. This value is used by the corresponding <img /> tag. The value must be unique and not used for other id values on the same XHTML document.
name	Text name, alphanumeric, beginning with a letter, no spaces	Identifies the map. This value is used by the corresponding <img /> tag. This is deprecated in XHTML but is included for backward compatibility.

The <area /> Tag

`<area />`

The self-contained <area /> tag configures a hyperlink on an image map. Table 16 shows <area /> tag attributes and their values.

Table 16 `<area />` tag attributes

Attribute	Value	Usage
alt	A brief text description of the portion of the image	Provides accessibility to visitors unable to view the image.
coords	Numeric pixels; see Table 17	Configures the coordinates of the clickable image area.
href	URL or Web page document name	Configures the Web page that will display when the area is clicked.
shape	"rect" indicates rectangle "circle" indicates circle "poly" indicates polygon	Configures the shape of the area.

Each shape has a different syntax used to list the coordinates (coords) of the hyperlink area. See Table 17.

Table 17 `<area />` tag shapes and `coords` attribute values

Shape	Coords	Meaning
`circle`	`"x,y,r"`	The coordinates at point (`x`, `y`) indicate the center of the circle. The value of `r` is the radius of the circle.
`poly`	`"x1, y1, x2, y2, x3, y3"`, and so on	The values of each (`x`, `y`) pair represent the coordinates of a corner point of the polygon.
`rect`	`"x1, y1, x2, y2"`	The coordinates at point (`x1`, `y1`) represent the upper-left corner of the rectangle. The coordinates at point (`x2`, `y2`) represent the lower-right corner of the rectangle.

11 Table Tags

The <table> Tag

`<table></table>`

The `<table>` tag creates a table. Table 18 shows `<table>` tag attributes and their values.

Table 18 `<table>` tag attributes

Attribute	Value	Usage
`align`	`"left"` (default), `"center"`, `"right"`	Specifies the horizontal alignment of the table. (Deprecated)
`bgcolor`	A valid color; the W3C recommends hexadecimal colors	Specifies the color of the background. This attribute can also be used with `<tr>`, `<td>`, and `<th>`. (Deprecated)
`border`	Number of pixels; `"0"` indicates no border	Specifies the size of the border around the cells.
`bordercolor`	A valid color; the W3C recommends hexadecimal colors	The color of the table border. Not part of the W3C Recommendation; originally only used by Internet Explorer.
`cellpadding`	Number of pixels	Specifies the amount of space between the cell's borders and its contents.
`cellspacing`	Number of pixels	Specifies the amount of space between cells.
`frame`	`"void"`, `"above"`, `"below"`, `"hsides"`, `"lhs"`, `"rhs"`, `"vsides"`, `"box"`, `"border"`	Specifies the parts of the outside border that should be visible.
`rules`	`"rows"` indicates the interior border displays between rows only `"groups"` indicates the interior border displays around groups only (see `<tbody>`, `<thead>`, and `<tfoot>`) `"all"` indicates the default border display	Configures the interior border in a table.
`summary`	A text description of the contents/organization/purpose of the table	Provides for accessibility. A visitor may obtain an overview of the table without reading it cell by cell. This attribute may be accessed by screen readers.

Table 18 `<table>` tag attributes (*continued*)

Attribute	Value	Usage
`title`	A text description of the table	This brief description may be displayed as a tooltip by some browsers. This attribute may be accessed by some screen readers.
`width`	Number of pixels or a percentage	Specifies the width of the table.

The <tr> Tag

`<tr></tr>`

The `<tr>` tag creates a table row. Table 19 shows `<tr>` tag attributes and their values.

Table 19 `<tr>` tag attributes

Attribute	Value	Usage
`align`	`"left"` (default), `"center"`, `"right"`	Specifies the horizontal alignment of the cells.
`bgcolor`	A valid color; the W3C recommends hexadecimal colors	Specifies the color of the background.
`valign`	`"top"`, `"middle"` (default), `"bottom"`	Specifies the vertical alignment of the cells.

The <td> Tag

`<td></td>`

The `<td>` tag creates a table cell. Table 20 shows `<td>` tag attributes and their values.

Table 20 `<td>` and `<th>` tag attributes

Attribute	Value	Usage
`align`	`"left"` (default), `"center"`, `"right"`	Specifies the horizontal alignment of the cell.
`bgcolor`	A valid color; the W3C recommends hexadecimal colors	Specifies the color of the background. (Deprecated)
`colspan`	Numeric	Specifies the number of columns spanned by a cell.
`headers`	The id value(s) of a column or row heading cell	Associates data cells with header cells. This attribute may be accessed by assistive technologies such as screen readers.
`height`	Number of pixels	Specifies the height of the cell. (Deprecated)
`nowrap`	`"nowrap"`	Forces the browser to display all the text in the cell on one line. (Deprecated)
`rowspan`	Numeric	Specifies the number of rows spanned by a cell.
`scope`	`"row"`, `"col"`	Specifies the scope of the table cell contents (`row` or `column`). This attribute may be accessed by screen readers but is not as well supported as the **`headers`** and **`id`** attributes.
`valign`	`"top"`, `"middle"` (default), `"bottom"`	Specifies the vertical alignment of the cell.
`width`	Number of pixels or a percentage	Specifies the width of the cell. (Deprecated)

The <th> Tag

```
<th></th>
```

The <th> tag creates a table header cell. Table header cells display text in bold font face and centered. Table 20 shows <th> tag attributes and their values.

The <caption> Tag

```
<caption></caption>
```

The <caption> tag creates a caption for the table. The valign attribute is used to place the caption above or below the table. The values for the valign attribute are "top" and "bottom". The deprecated align attribute specifies the placement of the caption. The values for the align attribute are "bottom", "center", "left", "right", and "top" (default).

12 Table Section Tags

The <thead> Tag

```
<thead></thead>
```

The <thead> tag defines a block of one or more table header rows.

The <tbody> Tag

```
<tbody></tbody>
```

The <tbody> tag divides a table into sections. It delineates one or more rows as a group. Use the rules attribute on the <table> tag to indicate the group visually.

The <tfoot> Tag

```
<tfoot></tfoot>
```

The <tfoot> tag defines a block of one or more table footer rows.

13 Frames Tags

The <frameset> Tag

```
<frameset></frameset>
```

The <frameset> tag configures a Web page that uses frames. The browser window is divided into multiple smaller windows so that multiple Web pages can be displayed and individually scrolled at the same time. Table 21 shows <frameset> tag attributes and their values. Examples of the rows and cols attributes are included.

Table 21 `<frameset>` tag attributes

Attribute	Value	Usage
`bordercolor`	A valid color; the W3C recommends hexadecimal colors	Specifies the color of the frame borders in the frameset. Default color is gray. Not part of the W3C Recommendation.
`cols`	Number of pixels, percentage, or `"*"` to indicate remaining window area	Reserves vertical areas (columns) of the browser window.
`frameborder`	`"0"` or `"1"` (default)	`"0"` indicates that no frame borders will be visible in the frameset. `"1"` indicates that frame borders will display in the frameset (default). Not part of the W3C Recommendation.
`framespacing`	Number of pixels	Specifies the width of the frame borders in the frameset. Not part of the W3C Recommendation.
`rows`	Number of pixels, percentage, or `"*"` to indicate remaining window area	Reserves horizontal areas (rows) of the browser window.
`title`	A brief text description	Provides a text description of the frameset that can be used by assistive technologies.

`rows` Attribute. The `rows` attribute specifies how the window will be divided vertically into rows of pixels (think of it as forming one row under another across the screen). The value can be a percentage of the browser window, a number of pixels, or the special asterisk value (*). The special asterisk value tells the browser to calculate the appropriate space for the window. A value is given for each frame row. There can be multiple frames. For example, to create a frameset with two horizontal frames—one using 25 percent of the window and the other using what is left of the window—the code is `<frameset rows="25%,*">`.

`cols` Attribute. The `cols` attribute specifies how the window will be divided horizontally into columns of pixels (think of it as forming one column next to another across the screen). The value can be a percentage of the browser window, a number of pixels, or the special asterisk value (*). The special asterisk value tells the browser to calculate the appropriate space for the window. A value is given for each frame column. There can be multiple frames. For example, to create a frameset with two vertical frames—one using 200 pixels of the window and the other using what is left of the window—the code is `<frameset cols="200,*">`.

The `<frame />` Tag

`<frame />`

The self-contained `<frame />` tag specifies a single frame or area of the window contained within a `frameset`. Table 22 shows `<frame />` tag attributes and their values.

The `<noframes>` Tag

`<noframes></noframes>`

The `<noframes>` tag configures what will display on browsers and other user agents that don't support frames.

Table 22 `<frame />` tag attributes

Attribute	Value	Usage
`bordercolor`	A valid color; the W3C recommends hexadecimal colors	Configures the color of the frame border. Not part of the W3C Recommendation.
`frameborder`	`"0"` or `"1"` (default)	`"0"` indicates that no frame borders will be visible for this frame. `"1"` indicates that frame borders will display for this frame (default).
`id`	Alphanumeric, no spaces; the value must be unique and not used for other `id` values on the same XHTML document	This attribute is optional. It provides a unique identifier for the frame.
`longdesc`	URL of Web page with detailed description of the frame	Provides a detailed text description of the frame. This may be accessed by assistive technologies.
`marginheight`	Number of pixels	Configures the top and bottom margins for the frame.
`marginwidth`	Number of pixels	Configures the width of the right and left margins for the frame.
`name`	Text name, beginning with a letter, no spaces	Names the frame, so that it may be targeted by other frames. This is deprecated in XHTML but is used to provide backward compatibility with browsers that support HTML.
`noresize`	`"noresize"`	Does not allow a Web page visitor to resize a frame by dragging the frame border with the mouse.
`scrolling`	`"yes"`, `"no"`, `"auto"` (default)	Configures whether the frame has a scroll bar. The default is `"auto"`, which configures the browser to add a scroll bar automatically when needed.
`src`	URL or file name	Configures what Web page will be displayed in the frame (required).
`title`	Text phrase that describes the frame	Configures the title of the frame. This can be accessed by screen readers and is recommended by the W3C to improve accessibility.

The <iframe> Tag

`<iframe></iframe>`

The `<iframe>` tag configures an inline frame. This is a special scrolling area that displays a different Web page document. This does not need to be associated with a `frameset` and can be placed on the body of any Web page. Some older browsers, such as Netscape 4, do not support inline frames. If the inline frame is not supported, place content that should be displayed between the opening and closing `<iframe>` tags. Table 23 shows `<iframe>` tag attributes and their values.

Table 23 <iframe> tag attributes

Attribute	Value	Usage
align	"left" (default), "right", "top", "middle", "bottom"	Specifies the horizontal alignment of the iframe. (Deprecated)
frameborder	"0" or "1" (default)	"0" indicates that no frame borders will be visible for this inline frame. "1" indicates that frame borders will display for this inline frame (default).
height	Number of pixels or percentage	Height of the inline frame
id	Alphanumeric, no spaces; the value must be unique and not used for other id values on the same XHTML document	This attribute provides a unique identifier for the inline frame.
longdesc	URL of Web page with detailed description of the contents of the inline frame	Provides a detailed text description of the frame. This may be accessed by assistive technologies
marginheight	Number of pixels	Configures the top and bottom margins of the inline frame.
marginwidth	Number of pixels	Configures the width of the right and left margins of an inline frame.
name	Text name, beginning with a letter, no spaces	Configures the name of the inline frame. This is required when using the target attribute to configure hyperlinks. This attribute is deprecated in XHTML but is used to provide backward compatibility with browsers that support HTML.
scrolling	"yes", "no", "auto" (default)	Determines whether scrollbars will appear if the document displayed is larger than the size of the inline frame.
src	Valid file name of a Web page document (required)	Configures the name of the file to be displayed in the inline frame.
title	Text phrase that describes the inline frame recommended by the W3C to improve	Configures the title of the inline frame. This can be accessed by screen readers and is accessibility.
width	Number of pixels or percentage	Configures the width of the inline frame.

14 Form Tags

The <form> Tag

`<form></form>`

The <form> tag configures a form that can accept information from a Web site visitor. The form information may be processed using a server-side script or executable program. Table 24 shows <form> tag attributes and their values.

Table 24 <form> tag attributes

Attribute	Value	Usage
action	File name or URL of the program or script that will handle the form data	Specifies the name of the server-side program or script that will handle the form data.
id	Alphanumeric, no spaces; the value must be unique and not used for other id values.	Provides a unique identifier for the form.
method	"post"	Preferred by the W3C. Sends the form data to the Web server as a part of the entity body of the HTTP response. Form data is not visible in the URL.
	"get" (default)	Sends the form data to the Web server as part of the URL.
enctype	"multipart/form-data"	Specifies that the form will accept a file as input (using an <input type="file" /> element).
name	Text name, beginning with a letter, no spaces	This attribute is optional. It names the form so that it can be easily accessed by client-side scripting languages such as JavaScript to edit and verify the form information before the server-side processing is invoked. This attribute is deprecated in XHTML but is used to provide backward compatibility with browsers that support HTML.
target	See Table 13	Specifies the window used to display the form response. The default is the current window. See Table 13.

15 Form Element Tags

The <input /> Tag

<input />

The stand-alone <input /> tag configures an input element for a form. The attributes and their values determine the type of input element displayed on the Web page. Table 25 shows <input /> tag attributes and their values.

Table 25 <input /> tag attributes

Attribute	Value	Usage
type	"text", "checkbox", "radio", -"hidden", "submit", "reset", "button", "image", "password", "file"	Configures a specific form element (required).
accesskey	A character on the keyboard	Configures a hot key that immediately places the cursor on the form element.
checked	"checked"	Used with type="checkbox" or type="radio". Indicates that the form element is selected.
disabled	"disabled"	Prevents the cursor from being placed in the form element.

Table 25 `<input />` tag attributes (*continued*)

Attribute	Value	Usage
`id`	Text name, beginning with a letter, no spaces	Provides a unique identifier for the form element that can be used to associate the element with a `<label>` tag or act as a named fragment identifier.
`maxlength`	Numeric	Configures the maximum number of characters allowed in a text input area.
`name`	Text name, beginning with a letter, no spaces	Names the form element. The name value is used by JavaScript, CGI, and other server-side processing.
`readonly`	readonly	Configures a textbox or password box as read only.
`size`	Numeric	Configures the width in characters of a text input area on screen.
`src`	File name of an image	Used with `type="image"`
`tabindex`	Numeric	Changes the order of the form element accessed by pressing the Tab key. Default order is the order the form elements are placed on the page.
`title`	A brief text description	Configures a brief text description that will display in some browsers when a mouse pointer is placed over the element.
`value`	Text or numeric characters	Provides the value given to a form element, which is passed to the form handler.

The `<textarea>` Tag

`<textarea></textarea>`

The `<textarea>` tag configures a multiline text input area on a form, sometimes called a scrolling text box. Text contained within the `<textarea>` tags will be initially displayed in the scrolling text box. Table 26 shows `<textarea>` tag attributes and their values.

Table 26 `<textarea>` tag attributes

Attribute	Value	Usage
`accesskey`	A character on the keyboard	Configures a hot key that immediately places the cursor on the form element.
`cols`	Numeric	Configures the number of columns in the text area.
`id`	Text name, beginning with a letter, no spaces	Provides a unique identifier for the form element that can be used to associate the element with a `<label>` tag or act as a named fragment identifier.
`disabled`	`"disabled"`	Prevents the cursor from being placed in the text area.
`name`	Text name, beginning with a letter, no spaces	Names the form element.
`readonly`	readonly	Configures a textarea as read only.
`rows`	Numeric	Configures the number of rows displayed on the screen in the text area.

(*continues*)

Table 26 `<textarea>` tag attributes (*continued*)

Attribute	Value	Usage
`tabindex`	Numeric	Changes the order of the form element accessed by pressing the Tab key. Default order is the order the form elements are placed on the page.
`title`	A brief text description	Configures a brief text description that will display in some browsers when a mouse pointer is placed over the element.

The <select> Tag

`<select></select>`

The `<select>` tag configures a select box to display a menu of items, sometimes called a list box or drop-down list box. The individual menu items are configured with `<option>` tags. Table 27 shows `<select>` tag attributes and their values.

Table 27 `<select>` tag attributes

Attribute	Value	Usage
`accesskey`	A character on the keyboard	Configures a hot key that immediately places the cursor on the form element.
`disabled`	`"disabled"`	Prevents the cursor from being placed in the select list.
`id`	Text name, beginning with a letter, no spaces	Provides a unique identifier for the form element that can be used to associate the element with a `<label>` tag or act as a named fragment identifier.
`multiple`	`"multiple"`	Allows multiple selections from the list.
`name`	Text name, beginning with a letter, no spaces	Names the form element.
`size`	Numeric	Provides the number of elements to be displayed. If size is configured, the select list is displayed as a scrolling list. If size is omitted, the select list is a drop-down list.
`tabindex`	Numeric	Changes the order of the form element accessed by pressing the Tab key. Default order is the order the form elements are placed on the page.
`title`	A brief text description	Configures a brief text description that will display in some browsers when a mouse pointer is placed over the element.

The <option> Tag

`<option></option>`

The `<option>` tag configures an item within a select element. The text contained between the `<option>` tags is displayed in the select box. Table 28 shows `<option>` tag attributes and their values.

Table 28 `<option>` tag attributes

Attribute	Value	Usage
`selected`	`"selected"`	Configures an option selected by default.
`value`	Text or numeric characters	A value given to a form element that is passed to the form handler if the item is selected.
`disabled`	disabled	Prevents this option from being selected.

The `<label>` Tag

`<label></label>`

The `<label>` tag configures a text label that is associated with a form element. Table 29 shows `<label>` tag attributes and their values.

Table 29 `<label>` tag attributes

Attribute	Value	Usage
`accesskey`	A character on the keyboard	Configures a hot key that immediately places the cursor on the form element.
`for`	Corresponds to the value of an `id` attribute on a form element	Associates a text label with a form element.
`title`	A brief text description	Configures a brief text description that will display in some browsers when a mouse is placed over the label.

The `<fieldset>` Tag

`<fieldset></fieldset>`

The `<fieldset>` tag configures a group of form elements. It is used together with the `<legend>` tag.

The `<legend>` Tag

`<legend></legend>`

The `<legend>` tag is only used within the `<fieldset>` tag. It configures a text description for the `<fieldset>` grouping. Table 30 shows `<legend>` tag attributes and their values.

Table 30 `<legend>` tag attributes

Attribute	Value	Usage
`accesskey`	A character on the key-board	Configures a hot key that immediately places the cursor on the first form element in the legend area.
`align`	`"top"`, `"bottom"`, `"left"`, `"right"`	Configures the alignment of the text legend. (Deprecated)
`title`	A brief text description	Configures a brief text description that will display in some browsers when a mouse pointer is placed over the text legend.

The <button> Tag

`<button></button>`

The <button> tag creates an area on the Web page that will act like a standard form button. It configures Web page content that is coded between the <button> and </button> tags as the form button. Table 31 shows <button> tag attributes and their values.

Table 31 <button> tag attributes

Attribute	Value	Usage
accesskey	A character on the keyboard	Configures a hot key that immediately places the cursor on the area.
id	Text name, beginning with a letter, no spaces	Provides a unique identifier for the form element that can be used to associate the element with a <label> tag or act as a named fragment identifier.
name	Text name, beginning with a letter, no spaces	Names the form element so that it can be easily accessed by client-side scripting languages (such as JavaScript) or by server-side processing. The name should be unique.
title	A brief text description	Configures a brief text description that will display in some browsers when a mouse pointer is placed over the area.
type	submit	Functions as a submit button.
	reset	Functions as a reset button.
	button	Functions as a button.
value	Text or numeric characters	A value given to a form element that is passed to the form handler.
disabled	disabled	Prevents the button from being clicked.

16 Miscellaneous Tags

The <abbr> Tag

`<abbr title="World Wide Web Consortium">W3C</abbr>`

The <abbr> tag provides a description for an abbreviation. Use the title attribute to specify the description.

The <acronym> Tag

`<acronym title="World Wide Web Consortium">W3C</acronym>`

The <acronym> tag provides a description for an abbreviation. Use the title attribute to specify the description.

The <address> Tag

`<address></address>`

The <address> tag contains an area with contact information (typically name and address) for a document.

The <applet> Tag

`<applet></applet>`

The <applet> tag is used to specify the beginning of a Java applet area in the body of a Web page. The closing tag, </applet>, specifies the ending of an applet area in the body of a Web page. Table 32 shows <applet> tag attributes and their values. The <applet> tag and its attributes are deprecated.

Table 32 <applet> tag attributes

Attribute	Value	Usage
alt	A text description of the applet.	Provides alternate content for visitors unable to access the applet.
code	The file name of a Java applet (.class extension); required	Configures the name of the applet file.
codebase	A folder name	Configures the name of the folder that contains the applet. This is needed if the applet is not in the same folder as the Web page.
height	Number of pixels	Configures the height of the applet area.
id	Alphanumeric, no spaces; the value must be unique and not used for other id values on the same XHTML document	Provides a unique identifier for the applet.
width	Number of pixels	Configures the width of the applet area.

The <param /> Tag

`<param />`

The <param> tag is used to pass values or parameters to an object or Java applet. This tag is always used with either an <applet> or <object> tag.

The <nobr> Tag

`<nobr></nobr>`

The <nobr> tag is not part of the W3C XHTML 1.0 specification. The tag is used to contain areas on a Web page, such as groups of images, which should remain on the same line regardless of the size of the browser window.

The <pre> Tag

`<pre></pre>`

The <pre> tag handles text in a special way. Any text contained between <pre> tags is considered to be preformatted text, such as computer program coding statements. Any line breaks or spacing will be preserved. This tag is rarely used.

The <object> Tag

`<object></object>`

The <object> tag can be used to place Java applets, audio, video, Flash, and other media on a Web page. It is a container tag and should be closed with an </object> tag. Table 33 shows <object> tag attributes and values that are used to display media files.

Table 33 `<object>` tag attributes

Attribute	Value	Usage
`classid`	Uniquely identifies the player software. For QuickTime, it must be set to `"clsid:02BF25D5-8C17-4B23-BC80-D3488ABDDC6B"`	Identifies an ActiveX control that must be installed on the visitor's PC. If the ActiveX control is not installed, the browser can automatically download and install it.
`codebase`	For QuickTime and Internet Explorer, this value must be http://www.apple.com/qtactivex/qtplugin.cab—the location of the most recent version of the QuickTime player.	Specifies a relative path for the location of the plug-in.
`data`	Valid file name, name of media file (required)	Provides the name of the file to be played.
`height`	Number of pixels	Specifies the height of media control console.
`type`	A valid MIME type such as `"audio/midi"`, `"audio/wav"`, and so on	Specifies the MIME type of the media file.
`width`	Number of pixels	Configures the width of media control console.

The <embed /> Tag

`<embed />`

The `<embed />` tag is not part of the W3C XHTML 1.0 specification but it is included here because it was often used in the past. The W3C recommends using the `<object>` tag instead. The `<embed />` tag can be used to place sound and other media in a Web page. It is a self-contained tag and does not have a corresponding closing tag. Table 34 shows `<embed />` tag attributes and their values.

Table 34 `<embed />` tag attributes

Attribute	Value	Usage
`align`	`"left"`, `"right"`, `"top"`, `"bottom"`	Optional; aligns the media control console.
`autostart`	`"true"`, `"false"`	Determines whether the media will play automatically when the page is loaded. If omitted, media may not automatically play.
`autoplay`	`"true"`, `"false"`	Optional. Used by some media players, including QuickTime. Determines if the media will play automatically when the page is loaded. If omitted, media may not automatically play.
`codebase`	For QuickTime and Internet Explorer, this value must be http://www.apple.com/qtactivex/qtplugin.cab—the location of the most recent version of the QuickTime player.	Specifies a relative path for the location of the plug-in.

Table 34 `<embed />` tag attributes *(continued)*

Attribute	Value	Usage
controller	"true", "false"	Optional. Indicates whether the media control console will display. Used with QuickTime.
controls	"console", "smallconsole", "playbutton", "pausebutton", "stopbutton", "volumelever"	Configures the appearance of the media control console.
height	Number of pixels	Configures the height of the media control console.
hidden	"true"	Hides the default media console.
loop	Numeric value or "true" for continuous play (may not be uniformly supported)	Repeats the media file.
pluginspage	URL	Optional. Location of download page for plug-in.
src	Valid file name, name of media file (required)	Provides the name of the file to be played.
type	A valid MIME type such as "audio/mpeg", "audio/wav", and so on	Optional; specifies the MIME type of the media file.
width	Number of pixels	Configures the width of media control console.

The <noembed> Tag

`<noembed></noembed>`

The <noembed> tag is not part of the W3C XHTML 1.0 specification but it is included here because it was often used in the past. The <noembed> tag is a container tag. It can appear after an <embed /> tag to provide alternate content that may be used by browsers or assistive technologies such as screen readers.

The Comment Tag

`<!-- your comment goes here -->`

The comment tag is special in that anything between the opening <!-- and the closing --> is considered to be a comment and is ignored by the browser. This tag can be used to document and describe XHTML.

APPENDIX

Special Characters

Special characters, or entity characters, such as the copyright symbol and the nonbreaking space, often appear on Web pages. Table 1 lists a selection of special characters in order of numeric codes. The most commonly used special characters are shown in bold. The W3C's list of special characters is found at http://www.w3.org/MarkUp/html-spec/html-spec_13.html.

Table 1 Special characters

Entity Name	Numeric Code	Descriptive Code	Character
Quotation mark	**"**	**"**	"
Ampersand	&	&	&
Apostrophe	**'**		'
Less than sign	**<**	**<**	<
Greater than sign	**>**	**>**	>
Nonbreaking space	** **	** **	**a blank space**
Inverted exclamation	¡	¡	¡
Cent sign	¢	¢	¢
Pound sterling sign	£	£	£
General currency sign	¤	¤	†
Yen sign	¥	¥	¥
Broken vertical bar	¦	¦	¦
Section sign	§	§	§
Umlaut	¨	¨	¨
Copyright symbol	**©**	**©**	©
Feminine ordinal	ª	ª	ª
Left angle quote	«	«	«
Not sign	¬	¬	¬
Soft hyphen			-
Registered trademark symbol	**®**	**®**	®
Macron	¯	¯	—
Degree sign	°	°	°
Plus or minus	±	±	±
Superscript two	²	²	^{2}
Superscript three	³	³	^{3}
Acute accent	´	´	´
Micro (Mu)	µ	µ	µ
Paragraph sign	¶	¶	¶
Middle dot	·	·	·
Cedilla	¸	¸	¸
Superscript one	¹	¹	^{1}
Masculine ordinal	º	º	º
Right angle quote	»	»	»
Fraction one-fourth	¼	¼	¼
Fraction one-half	½	½	½
Fraction three-fourths	¾	¾	¾
Inverted question mark	¿	¿	¿

Table 1 Special characters (*continued*)

Entity Name	Numeric Code	Descriptive Code	Character
Small e, grave accent	`è`	`è`	è
Small e, acute accent	`é`	`é`	é
En dash	`–`	`–`	–
Em dash	`—`	**`—`**	—
Vertical bar	`|`		|
Short, bold vertical bar	`❘`		❘

APPENDIX

CSS Property Reference

Cascading Style Sheet properties that are commonly used to format and configure page layouts are listed in this section. Unless otherwise noted, each property applies to all XHTML elements.

You should find the information in Table 1 and Table 2 useful as a quick reference to commonly used CSS properties and values. However, these tables do not contain all the CSS properties and values. The W3C CSS2 Recommendation (http://www.w3.org/TR/REC-CSS2/) includes a Property Index with a complete listing of all CSS properties at http://www.w3.org/TR/REC-CSS2/propidx.html.

Table 1 Cascading style sheet properties

Property		
`background-color`		
	Common Values:	Valid hexadecimal color value, RGB color value, or color name.
	Usage:	Configures the background color of an element.
	Example:	**`background-color:#cccccc;`**
`background-image`		
	Common Values:	URL keyword with valid image file name
	Usage:	Configures an image file as the background of an element.
	Example:	**`background-image:url(myimage.gif);`**
`background-position`		
	Common Values:	Two percentages, numeric pixel values, or position values (**`"left"`**, **`"top"`**, **`"center"`**, **`"bottom"`**, **`"right"`**)
	Usage:	Configures the position of the background image of an element.
	Example:	**`background-position:-100px -200px;`** The first value configures the horizontal position and the second configures the vertical position starting from the upper-left corner of the container's box. Use negative values for a more abstract or artistic background effect.
`background-repeat`		
	Common Values:	**`"repeat"`** (default), **`"repeat-y"`** (vertical repeat), **`"repeat-x"`** (horizontal repeat), **`"no-repeat"`** (no repeat)
	Usage:	Configures how the background image of an element will repeat (or be prevented from repeating).
	Example:	**`background-repeat:no-repeat;`**
`border`		
	Common Values:	The **`border-width`**, **`border-style`**, and **`border-color`** values separated by spaces.
	Usage:	Configures the border surrounding an element.
	Example:	**`border:1px solid #000000;`**
`border-bottom`		
	Common Values:	The **`border-width`**, **`border-style`**, and **`border-color`** values separated by spaces.
	Usage:	Configures the bottom border of an element.
	Example:	**`border-bottom:1px solid #000000;`**
`border-collapse`		
	Common Values:	**`"separate"`** (default), **`"collapse"`**
	Usage:	Configures the table and cell borders to collapse into a single border or display with separate borders.
	Example:	**`border-collapse:collapse;`**
`border-color`		
	Common Values:	Valid hexadecimal color value, RGB color value, or color name
	Usage:	Configures the color of an element's border.
	Example:	**`border-color:#333333;`**

Table 1 Cascading style sheet properties (*continued*)

Property	
border-left	
Common Values:	The **border-width**, **border-style**, and **border-color** values separated by spaces.
Usage:	Configures the left border of an element.
Example:	**border-left:1px solid #000000;**
border-right	
Common Values:	The **border-width**, **border-style**, and **border-color** values separated by spaces.
Usage:	Configures the right border of an element.
Example:	**border-right:1px solid #000000;**
border-style	
Common Values:	**"none"** (default), **"double"**, **"groove"**, **"inset"**, **"outset"**, **"ridge"**, **"solid"**, **"dashed"**, **"dotted"**, **"hidden"**
Usage:	Configures the type of border around an element.
Example:	**border-style:dotted;**
border-top	
Common Values:	The **border-width**, **border-style**, and **border-color** values separated by spaces.
Usage:	Configures the top border of an element.
Example:	**border-top:1px solid #000000;**
border-width	
Common Values:	A numeric value (such as **1px**) or values **"thin"**, **"medium"**, **"thick"**
Usage:	Configures the width of a border around an element.
Example:	**border-width:3px;**
bottom	
Common Values:	A numeric value (**px** or **em**) or percentage
Usage:	Configures the offset position from the bottom of the containing element
Example:	**bottom:20px;**
clear	
Common Values:	**"left"**, **"right"**, **"both"**, **"none"** (default)
Usage:	Specifies the display of an element in relation to floating elements.
color	
Common Values:	Valid hexadecimal color value, RGB color value, or color name
Usage:	Configures the foreground (text) color of an element.
Example:	**color:#0000ff;**
display	
Common Values:	**"none"**, **"block"**, **"inline"**, **"list-item"**, **"table"**, **"table-row"**, **"table-cell"**
Usage:	Controls how and if an element will display. Display set to **"none"** causes an element to not display.
Example:	**display:block;**

(*continues*)

Table 1 Cascading style sheet properties (*continued*)

`float`	
Common Values:	`"right"`, `"left"`
Usage:	Configures the horizontal placement (left or right) of an element in a parent element
Example:	`float:left;`
`font-family`	
Common Values:	Valid font name or a font family such as `"serif"`, `"sans-serif"`, `"fantasy"`, `"monospaced"`, or `"cursive"`
Usage:	Configures the type of font used to display an element.
Example:	`font-family:Arial, Verdana, sans-serif;`
`font-size`	
Common Values:	Numeric value (`pt`, `px`, or `em`), percentage, absolute size (`"xx-small"`, `"x-small"`, `"small"`, `"medium"` (default), `"large"`, `"x-large"`, `"xx-large"`), relative size (`"smaller"`, `"larger"`)
Usage:	Configures the size of the font used to display an element.
Example:	`font-size:smaller;`
`font-style`	
Common Values:	`"normal"` (default), `"italic"`, `"oblique"`
Usage:	Configures the style of the text.
Example:	`font-style:italic;`
`font-variant`	
Common Values:	`"normal"` (default), `"small-caps"`
Usage:	Configures the display as regular text or in small capital letters.
Example:	`font-variant:small-caps;`
`font-weight`	
Common Values:	Numeric value (`"100"`, `"200"`, `"300"`, `"400"`, `"500"`, `"600"`, `"700"`, `"800"`), relative value (`"normal"` (default), `"bold"`, `"bolder"`, `"lighter"`)
Usage:	Configures the boldness of the text.
Example:	`font-weight:400;`
`height`	
Common Values:	A numeric value (`px` or `em`), percentage, or `auto` (default)
Usage:	Configures the height of an element.
Example:	`height:300px;`
`left`	
Common Values:	A numeric value (`px` or `em`) or percentage
Usage:	Configures the distance in from the left (of the containing element) to display an element.
Example:	`left:100px;`
`line-height`	
Common Values:	Numeric value, percentage
Usage:	Configures the spacing allowed for a line of text. The value 200% configures double-spaced text.
Example:	`line-height:200%;`

Table 1 Cascading style sheet properties (*continued*)

Property	
`list-style-image`	
Common Values:	URL keyword with valid image file name
Usage:	Configures an image to replace "bullets" in an XHTML list.
Example:	`list-style-image:url(myimage.gif);`
`list-style-type`	
Common Values:	`"none"`, `"disc"`, `"circle"`, `"square"`, `"decimal"`, `"lower-roman"`, `"upper-roman"`, `"lower-alpha"`, `"upper-alpha"`
Usage:	Configures the type of "bullet" (list item marker) for an element in a list.
Example:	`list-style-type:circle;`
`margin`	
Common Values:	*Shorthand Notation:* A numeric value (`px` or `em`), percentage, or `"auto"` *Full Notation:* Four numeric values (`px` or `em`), percentage, or `"auto"`. The values configure the margins in the following order (`margin-top`, `margin-right`, `margin-bottom`, `margin-left`).
Usage:	Configures the margin surrounding an element.
Example:	*Shorthand Notation:* `body { margin: 0}` (sets the page margins in the document to zero) *Full Notation:* `margin:0px 10% 0px 10%;`
`margin-bottom`	
Common Values:	A numeric value (`px` or `em`) or percentage
Usage:	Configures the size of an element's bottom margin.
Example:	`margin-bottom:20px;`
`margin-left`	
Common Values:	A numeric value (`px` or `em`) or percentage
Usage:	Configures the size of an element's left margin.
Example:	`margin-left:100px;`
`margin-right`	
Common Values:	A numeric value (`px` or `em`) or percentage
Usage:	Configures the size of an element's right margin.
Example:	`margin-right:20px;`
`margin-top`	
Common Values:	A numeric value (`px` or `em`) or percentage
Usage:	Configures the size of an element's top margin.
Example:	`margin-top:5px;`

(*continues*)

Table 1 Cascading style sheet properties (*continued*)

Property	
max-width	
Common Values:	A numeric value (px or em), percentage, or **"none"** (default)
Usage:	Configures the maximum width of an element.
Example:	**max-width:700px;**
min-width	
Common Values:	A numeric value (**px** or **em**) or percentage
Usage:	Configures the minimum width of an element.
Example:	**min-width:400px;**
overflow	
Common Values:	**"visible"** (default), **"hidden"**, **"auto"**, **"scroll"**
Usage:	Controls the display of a block-level element if the element exceeds its set height or width.
Example:	**overflow:scroll;**
padding	
Usage:	Configures the amount of padding associated with an element.
Shorthand Notation Option 1:	
Common Values:	A numeric value (**px** or **em**) or percentage
Example:	**padding:20px;**
Shorthand Notation Option 2:	
Common Values:	Two numeric values (**px** or **em**) or percentages. The first value configures the top and bottom padding. The second value configures the left and right padding.
Example:	**padding:10px 15px;**
Full Notation:	
Common Values:	Four numeric values (**px** or **em**) or percentages. The values configure the padding in the following order (**padding-top**, **padding-right**, **padding-bottom**, **padding-left**).
Example:	**padding:10px 15px 10px 20px;**
padding-bottom	
Common Values:	A numeric value (**px** or **em**) or percentage
Usage:	Configures the blank space between an element and its bottom border.
Example:	**padding-bottom:10px;**
padding-left	
Common Values:	A numeric value (**px** or **em**) or percentage
Usage:	Configures the blank space between an element and its left border.
Example:	**padding-left:10px;**

Table 1 Cascading style sheet properties (*continued*)

Property	
`padding-right`	
Common Values:	A numeric value (`px` or `em`) or percentage
Usage:	Configures the blank space between an element and its right border.
Example:	`padding-right:10px;`
`padding-top`	
Common Values:	A numeric value (`px` or `em`) or percentage
Usage:	Configures the blank space between an element and its top border.
Example:	`padding-top:10px;`
`page-break-after`	
Common Values:	`"always"`, `"avoid"`, `"auto"` (default)
Usage:	Configures whether page breaks will occur after a specified selector when the document is printed.
Example:	`h2 { page-break-after: avoid; }`
`page-break-before`	
Common Values:	`"always"`, `"avoid"`, `"auto"` (default)
Usage:	Configures whether page breaks will occur before a specified selector when the document is printed.
Example:	`h2 { page-break-before: always; }`
`position`	
Common Values:	`"relative"`, `"absolute"`
Usage:	Configures the positioning of an element. Used in combination with `left`, `right`, and/or `top` properties.
Example:	`position:relative;`
`right`	
Common Values:	A numeric value (`px` or `em`) or percentage
Usage:	Configures the distance in from the right (of the containing element) to display an element.
Example:	`right:20px;`
`scrollbar-arrow-color`	
Common Values:	Valid hexadecimal color value, RGB color value, or color name
Usage:	Configures the color of the arrow on the scroll bar (Internet Explorer only).
Example:	`scrollbar-arrow-color:#ff0000;`
`scrollbar-face-color`	
Common Values:	Valid hexadecimal color value, RGB color value, or color name
Usage:	Configures the color of the sliding scroll bar (Internet Explorer only).
Example:	`scrollbar-face-color:#00ff00;`

(*continues*)

Table 1 Cascading style sheet properties (*continued*)

Property	
`scrollbar-track-color`	
Common Values:	Valid hexadecimal color value, RGB color value, or color name
Usage:	Configures the color of the track the scroll bar slides (Internet Explorer only).
Example:	`scrollbar-face-color:#000000;`
`text-align`	
Common Values:	`"center"`, `"justify"`, `"left"`, `"right"`
Usage:	Configures the alignment of text in an element. This applies to block-level elements.
Example:	`text-align:center;`
`text-indent`	
Common Values:	A numeric value (`em` or `px`) or percentage
Usage:	Configures the indent of the first line of a block element.
Example:	`text-indent:10px;`
`text-decoration`	
Common Values:	`"none"`, `"underline"`, `"overline"`, `"line-through"`, `"blink"`
Usage:	Determines whether text in an element is underlined. This style is most often applied to hyperlinks to remove the underline.
Example:	`text-decoration:none;`
`text-transform`	
Common Values:	`"none"`, `"capitalize"`, `"uppercase"`, `"lowercase"`
Usage:	Modifies the appearance of text in an element.
Example:	`text-transform:uppercase;`
`top`	
Common Values:	A numeric value (`em` or `px`) or percentage
Usage:	Configures the distance down from the top of the containing element to display an element.
Example:	`top:100px;`
`vertical-align`	
Common Values:	A numeric value (`em` or `px`), percentage, values (`"baseline"`, `"sub"`, `"super"`, `"top"`, `"text-top"`, `"middle"`, `"bottom"`, `"text-bottom"`)
Usage:	Configures the vertical alignment of an inline element.
Example:	`vertical-align:top;`
`visibility`	
Common Values:	`"visible"`, `"hidden"`, `"inherit"`
Usage:	Configures whether an element displays and takes up space on a Web page.
Example:	`visibility:hidden;`

Table 1 Cascading style sheet properties (*continued*)

Property	
`width`	
Common Values:	A numeric value (`px` or `em`), percentage, or auto (default)
Usage:	Configures the width of an element.
Example:	`width:60%;`
`z-index`	
Common Values:	A numeric value; the default value is 0
Usage:	The stack order of an element on a Web page. A higher value will display in front of elements with lower values.
Example:	`z-index:10;`

Table 2 Pseudo-classes Used with the Anchor Element

Pseudo-class	Usage
`link`	Default state for a hyperlink that has not been clicked (visited) Example: `a:link {color:#00FF00; }`
`visited`	Default state for a visited link Example: `a:visited {color:#003300; }`
`focus`	Triggered when the link has focus (for example, by pressing the Tab key on the keyboard) Example: `a:focus {color:#FFFF66; }`
`hover`	Triggered when the mouse moves over the hyperlink Example: `a:hover {color:#000000; }`
`active`	Triggered when the hyperlink is actually clicked (or the Enter key is pressed when the hyperlink has focus) Example: `a:active {color:#CCCCCC; }`

Index

Page references followed by "f" indicate illustrated figures or photographs; followed by "t" indicates a table.